U2

U2

A CONSPIRACY OF HOPE

Dave Bowler and Bryan Dray

SIDGWICK & JACKSON
LONDON

To Mom and Dad for all the hours spent reading to me many years ago and for love and help far beyond the call of duty.

For Denise with whom the best is yet to be.

Always
DAVID

To Trish, Emma and Rebecca for their constant love and help.

And to Mum, Dad, Gran, Joyce and Wal without whom none of this would have happened.

BRYAN

To the memory of Doctor Winston O'Boogie

First published 1993 by Sidgwick & Jackson

a division of Pan Macmillan Publishers Limited
Cavaye Place London SW10 9PG
and Basingstoke

Associated companies throughout the world

ISBN 0 283 06169 3

Copyright © Dave Bowler and Bryan Dray 1993

1 3 5 7 9 8 6 4 2

A CIP catalogue record for this book is available from the British Library

Typeset by Cambridge Composing (UK) Limited, Cambridge
Printed by Mackays of Chatham Plc

CONTENTS

It's no good being the biggest rock 'n' roll band in the world.
It's being the best.

Larry Mullen Junior

ACKNOWLEDGEMENTS

As ever, an enormous number of people have contributed to the eventual completion of this book. Principal among them is Dick Evans, who made time to speak to us over the Guinness on St Patrick's Day of all days and helped clear up some of the chronology of the earliest days of U2 as well as giving a flavour of the life and times of a Dublin garage band.

John Waters was very gracious in agreeing to the use of material from his excellent series *Wide Awake In Ireland*, broadcast on BBC Radio 4 earlier this year. Thanks must also go to Smita Patel for helping sort out the relevant permissions.

Greenpeace, and particularly John Sauven, were of great help in providing details on Sellafield and the case against Sellafield 2. Greenpeace and its activists are the real heroes of environmental action, not four Irish rock stars at a beach party, however useful they may be in winning publicity for the cause. Join Greenpeace at Canonbury Villas, London N1 2BR, England.

Much the same can be said of Amnesty International, whose work could never be praised highly enough. Our thanks go particularly to Richard Bunting. Join Amnesty International at 99–119 Roseberry Avenue, London EC1R 4RE, England; Private Bag 23, Broadway, NSW 2007, Australia; Sean McBride House, 8 Shaw Street, Dublin 2, Ireland.

To our American correspondent, Chuck Norton, grateful thanks for his enthusiasm, his U2 collection and for the uncovering of countless pieces of information.

Anyone wanting to know more about U2 should go immediately to *Hot Press*'s back pages, collected in two volumes as *The U2 File – A Hot Press History* and *U2 – Three Chords And The Truth*. Our gratitude to the *Hot Press* team for permission to reprint quotes from their august organ, as well as the use we made of them in our research, knows no bounds. Those interested in high-quality journalism on music, film and related topics could do far worse than invest in a subscription to *Hot Press*.

Press and radio have again proved invaluable in providing background information and interview material. A full list of sources can be found at the back of this book, but we would especially like to thank *Q*, the *NME*, *Sounds*, *Time Out*, *Melody Maker*, *Musician*, *Sky*, *Vox* and *Select* for their help, along with all the other writers whose work we plundered, particularly Robin Denselow and Faber and Faber for *When the Music's Over* and Brendan Kennelly and Bloodaxe Books for *The Book Of Judas*. The staff at the British Newspaper Library were also very helpful in our researches. Among others to whom we owe a debt are Omnibus Press for use of David Gans' *Talking Heads – The Band and their Music*; Granada TV for *World in Action*; Helicon for *The Hutchinson Encyclopedia*; William Heinemann Limited for Garry Wills' *Reagan's America*, and Tony Parker's *Red Hill, A Mining Community*; Mandarin for Bill Graham's *Another Time, Another Place*.

Once again, assorted music and comedy made the writing of this tome less painful than it might have been, among this number the *Drop The Dead Donkey* team, Jane's Addiction, Lush, the Hothouse Flowers and Elvis Costello. Had it not been for the timely intervention of Kitty Dean, the manuscript would have had to have been written on tablets of stone with a chisel and would have been even later in reaching our publisher. Final acknowledgements go to our families, who have become particularly adept at recognizing artistic temperament gone mad and are very quick to get out of the line of fire. Without them, none of this would have been possible.

We would also like to express our deepest thanks to all the staff at Principle Management in Dublin who have been unfailingly helpful throughout the preparation of this book. We would particularly like to thank Ashlyn Mehan for desperately needed assistance at the eleventh hour. Much the same can be said of Dave Carroll at Blue Mountain Music who gave us far more of his time than was wise!

11 O'Clock Tick Tock
'40'
A Celebration
Acrobat
A Day Without Me
Gloria
Hallelujah Here She Comes
I Threw A Brick Through A Window
I Will Follow
Like A Song
Love Is Blindness
Mysterious Ways
New Year's Day
One
Out Of Control
Red Light
Rejoice
Seconds
Shadows And Tall Trees
So Cruel
Spanish Eyes
Stranger In A Strange Land
Street Mission
Sunday Bloody Sunday
Surrender
Sweetest Thing
The Fool
The Ocean
Tomorrow
Twilight
Two Hearts Beat As One
With A Shout (Jerusalem)

Written by U2

A Room At The Heartbreak Hotel
A Sort Of Homecoming
Bad
Bullet The Blue Sky
Elvis Presley And America
Exit
God Part II
Hawkmoon 269
Heartland
Indian Summer Sky
In God's Country
Mothers Of The Disappeared
One Tree Hill
Red Hill Mining Town
Running To Stand Still
The Unforgettable Fire
Trip Through Your Wires
When Love Comes To Town
Wire

Words Bono, Music U2

She's A Mystery To Me

Written by Bono & The Edge

Luminous Times (Hold On To Love)

Written by U2 & Brian Eno

AUTHORS' NOTE

IN WHICH YET ANOTHER POMPOUS BLOWHARD PURPORTS TO POSSESS THE TRUE MEANING OF ROCK 'N' ROLL

This book has been put together on the back of a perceived link with one of the central themes of U2's work – that rock 'n' roll *matters*. It's written for all those people like ourselves who believe that the music is a vibrant part of pop culture, an art form, *our* art form, and that records like the Beatles' *White Album*, Lou Reed's *Magic & Loss*, the Band's *Music From Big Pink*, Elvis Presley's *Mystery Train* or Elvis Costello's *Shipbuilding* are works of art every bit as impressive, expressive, enjoyable, valid and important as any piece of literature, any painting or any classical symphony.

Music can heal, can break down barriers and borders, can educate. Bono may believe in sun tan lotion, in shampoo, in the ground beneath his feet and so do we, but we also believe in rock 'n' roll, even if we don't believe in rock 'n' roll stars. After what is now rapidly approaching two decades in the same band, he and the rest of U2 probably still believe in it too. Maybe it is all just a really good act, as the cynics suggest. Maybe after the show's over it's back to the hotel room to count the cash and the women. Maybe their image as true believers in rock 'n' roll and in what they do is all just a nice gimmick. Maybe.

'What's special about U2 is the music not the musicians' is Bono's view. It is a music that is by turns powerful, moving, contemporary, timeless, thought-provoking, occasionally absurd and, at times, playful. This book aims to look at some of the ideas and issues that they have brought to light and the ways in which they have confronted them. The title of this book, borrowed from Amnesty International, sums up the emotion that U2 at their best can inspire. This interpretation of the music and its genesis may be wildly different from U2's original viewpoint, but it is an honest representation of just what it means on this side of the stereo and it is to that music rather than the musicians that this volume, a musical appreciation rather than a biography, addresses itself. Some biographical detail is included but U2 are much more than a list of dates and record titles.

INTRODUCTION

The last handful of years have been a source of morbid fascination to those who, against all the available evidence and against all the odds, have maintained faith in the power of rock 'n' roll to play a central role in the development of popular culture and to take an active and important part in the debate which shapes the social, emotional and political attitudes of each successive crop of youth. Rock 'n' roll has lurched into mid-life crisis some forty years after its birth. Rock has again become the preserve of ponderous stadium bands, rejuvenated by the twin forces of Live Aid and its attendant legitimization of stadium rock and the marketing man's dream, the compact disc, which lead mortgaged thirty-somethings to return to music consumption, nostalgic for the freedom of their youth and its accompanying soundtrack. If you want an alternative to that, it seems to come out of Los Angeles with its preening, posturing glamm-metal bands who boast, even now, of their drinking, drugging, vomiting and womanizing. Pop music is probably in a worse state, devoid of any eccentricity or character, as faceless computer operators churn out a manifesto of blissed-out oblivion as the way the blank generation should meet the challenge of its times. In order to find artists who are still challenging, still touching the soul, you need to dig deeper and look further than at any time in the last thirty years, searching for diamonds in the dirt.

It's sometimes hard to believe that rock 'n' roll ever acted as a mouthpiece of protest, the focus for an ideology to change the world into one that was more peaceful, tolerant and thoughtful, or at the very least one which recognized that such a struggle was taking place. In retrospect, 'All You Need Is Love' seems almost laughably naïve – the Rutles, the Eric Idle-inspired Beatles spoof, was nearer the mark with 'All You Need Is Cash' – but it was an ideal worth espousing, and worth believing in. Your choice, 'All You Need Is Love' or 'E's are good'?

If the music could be enjoyed on a purely surface level, and it has to be stressed that this has to be its first objective, to many it was a badge of political or social belief, a rallying call behind which a counter-culture might grow, a fountain from which ideological

1

debate might spring, at the very least a declaration of individuality and of a refusal to step into the global corporate sausage machine. It was the soundtrack to a mood of positive change. Rock 'n' roll was, if anything, an attitude of mind – 'don't let the bastards grind you down' – one which has been eroded year by year and almost destroyed at the hands of greed and expediency, much to the relief of the higher echelons of society, unsettled by the prospect of a whole generation of non-conformists or, worse still, non-consumers to deal with.

That 'dream' has dissipated over the intervening years as 'me' has replaced 'us' as the core philosophy. The wellsprings of much of rock's greatest music, the UK and the USA, have changed, perhaps irrevocably, to colder, harsher nations, where greed and self-interest are the central teachings, the legacy of the fear and insecurity that ordinary people feel. The 'look after number one' philosophy has taken a stranglehold as the few successes are enabled, indeed encouraged, to ride roughshod over the unfortunate many. The politics of greed have proved irresistibly seductive to Thatcher's children, sufficiently enticing to quell any questioning of its central philosophy.

The question 'should rock 'n' roll have a bearing?' is one that is often asked. Should it just stick to providing ritual dance music and leave the serious issues to the philosophers and the politicians? Rock 'n' roll is a vital part of youth culture, indeed of twentieth-century culture per se. Lester Bangs saw it as democracy in action, an art form that anyone could have access to, while William S. Burroughs, a hugely influential and original figure in his own right and someone who knows a little about the production of alternative art forms, called it 'a sociological phenomenon of unprecedented scope and effect', noting that a book might eventually sell hundreds of thousands of copies while pop music immediately reached millions. It ill behoves it completely to overlook that opportunity to communicate, confront and confuse, that important responsibility (an odd phrase admittedly since in no small part rock feeds off its own stupidity and irresponsibility). Is it true though that in your dreams begin your responsibilities? If young people are the thinkers and leaders of tomorrow then it's important that another viewpoint is put to them rather than the simple media messages of greed is good, violence is fun and that every man for himself is the central lesson for life. Rock 'n' roll doesn't have to wave a flag, nail its colours to any political mast or support causes, though some of its most vital moments have come in that way, but it can challenge intellectually, spiritually and sexually. It can help form opinions or at least provide the balance to the arguments propounded by the vested interests. At the very least it can annoy, nag, pick holes. Rock 'n' roll that fails to challenge the listener is little more than cabaret, an accompaniment to chicken in a basket. Rock 'n' roll doesn't have to sell cola, computer games or jeans — to do so is to betray its spirit and cross over to the Establishment.

'Pure politics' has not been especially well served by rock 'n' roll over the years since many rock stars have often appeared confused or ill-informed, though paradoxically even this has been an important contribution inasmuch as general issues have been brought into the domain of popular culture. John Lennon, portrayed as the archetypal political rocker, was often at sea when making overt statements, so that a contemporary like Pete Townshend was 'embarrassed by him'. 'Bed Ins' and 'Happenings' may have grabbed newspaper coverage but often appalled those working conscientiously for peace or feminism, who felt that he and Yoko Ono trivialized and marginalized serious issues, enabling the powers-that-be to present them as a 'lunatic fringe'. Where Lennon did strike a chord regularly and successfully was as a humanitarian, not only with the sloganeering approach of 'Give Peace A Chance', but also with the way in which he stripped himself bare before his audience, exposing his weaknesses, his foibles, his problems. Songs like 'Help', 'Crippled Inside', 'Cold Turkey' and 'Mother' painted a compelling self-portrait of a man who, to the outside world, had everything he wanted, but had found that it wasn't what he wanted, that fame and fortune was a hollow trap into which he had stumbled, that it did not provide him with the security he craved nor the answers he needed. Lennon was neither the first nor the last to realize that rock 'n' roll is a medium that can be stretched to take on wider connotations than mere entertainment and there have been any number of thoughtful artists who have made important points about the human condition, 'politics' in the widest, non-partisan sense of the word.

If this can be a crucial component of great rock music, should it look in the direction of party political activity? Should we talk about the government? Nah, don't worry about the government. It may well be that rock stars telling their audience who to vote for is an unacceptable abuse of the power they sometimes hold over young, impressionable audiences, but nevertheless, taking a stance on issues on which they hold deep convictions is an important element of the original premise of rock 'n' roll; that is absolute freedom of expression. This music came into being at a point in time when musicians were being censored for their beliefs, at the height of the American Inquisition under Cardinal McCarthy. In its infancy, the pioneers of folk and blues music in America had to fight desperately hard for the freedom to make their music, sometimes even for the very liberty. In his excellent book *When The Music's Over*, Robin Denselow presents a detailed analysis of the origins of 'political pop' which is recommended reading for any students of the genre. Tellingly, he documents the McCarthy witch hunts in some depth, recalling the effect on powerful songwriters such as Pete Seeger, whose career in music had begun in earnest when he toured the USA with the great Woody Guthrie in the 1940s, and who was vilified and black-listed by New Deal America for his associations with the Communist Party, before closing with this observation: 'Rock 'n' roll would learn that it was born under a bad sign, born at a time when musicians had been censored for their politics. It would learn that there were traditions, both in the American music that had gone before and in the popular music in other parts of the world. Good times, romance and dance music are vital ingredients, but pop music can, and sometimes must, attempt far more.'

Evidently today's performers do have an obligation to carry on the work of performers like Guthrie and Seeger or the blues greats such as John Lee Hooker who operated under conditions every bit as harsh in the racially segregated southern states of America in the immediate post-War years, or Bob Marley, one of the most articulate and powerful voices that popular music has heard. That notwithstanding, it remains an artistic tightrope which few have walked with ease, those venturing beyond the moon in June and the sounds of the dancefloor often garnering critical rapture and commercial bankruptcy.

It is however patently obvious to those who care about their music that there is little that can compare with the adrenalin rush of a great rock 'n' roll riff welded seamlessly to a pungent lyrical attack. In recent times REM engineered the marriage as successfully as anyone on their *Document* album in 1987, a fierce indictment of the American way under Reagan. Songs such as 'Exhuming McCarthy' and 'Finest Worksong' left little doubt where the band stood in relation to their President. Peter Buck's plangent guitar work stood shoulder to shoulder with Michael Stipe's vociferous condemnation of his country's direction in some of the most exhilarating music of the 1980s. Four years later they were to produce an album of 'love songs' which gave them incredible world-wide success, yet *Out Of Time* as a considered statement on what can be described as 'the human condition' for want of a better cliché was no less essential a purchase than *Document* had been. Intelligence and originality of approach are the keys to great rock 'n' roll music of depth and value and 1992 has been a case in point. While Michael Jackson may have the most sincere of wishes to bring the world together in peace and harmony, his 'Heal The World' single was so astoundingly banal that all it inspired was a very real desire to knock some sense into its perpetrator, an obvious example that making a statement and strapping on a backbeat does not always a compelling social comment make. At the same time, there can have been few records more vital in any year than *Hypocrisy Is The Greatest Luxury*, the debut album by the Disposable Heroes of Hiphoprisy – intelligent lyrics, impressively delivered, a thought provoking critique of modern society. But who sold more records?

Ultimately, it is only worth exploring human relationships, social conditions or political freedom in a song if someone is listening. Preaching to the converted is a pointless, self-serving activity. An experimental spoon-playing band will have a relatively small core of fans whatever its message. Having a willingness and an ability to communicate is every bit as important as having a message and is perhaps the crucial ingredient in acquiring an audience. In that respect, U2 have achieved more than any other artist of the last decade, becoming probably the biggest band in the world by the time of their 1987 'Joshua Tree' tour.

Ever since their beginnings during the late 1970s punk and new wave explosion, U2 have resolutely ploughed their own furrow with a pointed disregard for the vagaries of musical fashion. The band was built around a spark of invention rather than on any sound musical foundation and lead singer Bono Vox has remarked that U2 were 'four people before we were four musicians', something which has been central to their work ever since. It was and is their closeness as people that drew and has kept them together and from which their burning desire to communicate with a new, original voice has grown. Seemingly bereft of any great masterplan, and therefore devoid of the cynicism engendered in the Machiavellian manipulator, they have followed their instincts and have, as a result, maintained a unique musical and lyrical vision as they have tackled the universal themes close to their hearts – adolescence, faith, doubt, oppression, failure, love, betrayal, fear, the relevance of rock 'n' roll, the destruction of human rights – as they have advocated a creed of understanding. Most importantly, the central theme of much of their work has been the asking of questions rather than the provision of answers.

When all the hype is over, U2 is made up of four ordinary men who happen to make extraordinary music. They are not deities, gods with all-encompassing solutions for the future of mankind. If the public perception of them as a band with all the answers comes via a cartoon of Bono preaching a sermon on the Mount, their most important and invigorating role during the brash dash for cash that was the 1980s was to remind us of our own mortality, our vulnerability and our own sense of dislocation through the personal confessions in their music. For a generation of people who were often baffled by events, they were willing to stand up for doubt, for confusion, for trying and failing.

The words 'I Still Haven't Found What I'm Looking For' coming from the world's number one band gave hope to others engaged in that search. Suddenly feeling confused was legitimized, you were no longer alone, their music became *our* music. There is no reason to expect that they can provide the answer to the ultimate question of life, the universe and everything, but where they have struck a chord is in their refusal to accept anything at face value or to lapse into the unquestioning apathy that pervades much of current thinking, not just in rock music but in political and philosophical debate. Like Lennon before them, they have been at their most potent on a humanitarian rather than party political level; perhaps the most political statements of all come in dealing with the human heart. It may not be possible for rock music to change the world, but it can *'change the world in me'*.

Over the decade and a half which U2 have spent together, they've undergone numerous twists and turns, re-inventions of their basic sound and approach, and the price of this restlessness has from time to time been failure every bit as extravagant as their ultimate success. They have at times appeared overwhelmed and confused by the contradictions inherent in their position but they've had the courage to step out of the spotlight, regroup and get back on their feet. In the past eighteen months they've returned from what was widely regarded as the self-serving, self-satisfied *Rattle and Hum* project, transforming themselves into a dark, brooding musical entity with a broader, blacker sense of humour, clothed in the trappings of glam rock, making those contradictions ever more apparent, accentuating the personal above the global in their songwriting. They may still be saying the same kinds of things they were saying on *War* ten years ago, but in finding different ways of saying them they have kept the audience and themselves interested. The common thread remains a degree of honesty and integrity that is rare, qualities which have made them one of the few truly dangerous bands around, an accolade that is bestowed on those who take artistic and commercial chances rather than those who spray audiences with bat's blood or who make a record using skeletons as percussion instruments. To be truly subversive requires subtle manipulation from within the belly of the beast. U2 have achieved that at times even if at others they've been on the receiving end.

The story of U2's growth is interesting in itself, far removed as it is from that of most rock bands. As the Irish writer John Waters has said, 'It's easy to mistake U2 for a normal rock band, albeit a hugely successful one, but they are much more than that. I believe that U2 are among Ireland's greatest modern artists.' What makes them special is that their development has often acted as a mirror to a changing world, the personal and political issues with which they've struggled offering outsiders an opportunity to reconsider their own stance. Bono has gone on record as saying that 'art is an attempt to identify yourself. Our revenge on, I suppose England, for the colonizing of both our geography and our consciousness was to abuse their language and reinvent it. You're trying to find your own voice against these very strong foreign voices.' U2 have had to reflect the world in which they live but have also posed questions of personal change in the same way some of the greatest artists in the music's history did some twenty, thirty or forty years ago, although their singular isolation as such a force has led to further misinterpretation – some of their press around the time of *The Joshua Tree* might have had them healing the sick and turning water into wine, but back on planet earth they're just a very good rock 'n' roll band. In a musical landscape increasingly devoid of ideas or ideology, they are one of the few bands capable of carrying the flame into the next century, where in a world of increasing political instability we might yet see the rebirth of a stimulating social and personal debate via popular culture. Artists are so often in the vanguard of the search for new land, new expression, new meaning, and rock 'n' roll as one of the most powerful mediums in popular culture has to take its place. U2 are on that cutting edge. In the following pages, their journey to date is chronicled and analysed in a musical and social context, their themes developed and the future considered.

chapter one

A SPARK IN THE DARK

In recent conversation, George Harrison has been at pains to stress that the Beatles were not merely a vehicle for the songs of Lennon and McCartney, but a real group. 'How many Beatles does it take to change a lightbulb?' goes the joke. Harrison's less than hilarious, but admittedly accurate answer is four. The same applies to U2. While some may see Bono as the guy who calls all the shots, writes all the songs, does all the interviews, cures lepers and for an encore brings peace to the world while three other blokes stand behind him, the truth is less clear cut. In the tradition of some of the greatest rock 'n' roll bands, U2 are a real group, made up of four vital components. If Guns N' Roses only really need Axl Rose and Slash in their line-up, if Simple Minds can operate with just Jim Kerr and Charlie Burchill as a songwriting nucleus, if the Smiths were Morrissey and Marr, that line of thinking cannot be applied to U2. Take away any member of the group and it's no longer U2, in terms of its sound, its principles or its operations. The light won't come on.

For a group that came to be regarded as a cornerstone of the new wave movement, attempting to eke out painful cover versions of Peter Frampton, Moody Blues and Bay City Rollers songs was a less than auspicious start, but these were the staples of early U2 rehearsals. The band came together in Dublin in the autumn of 1976 at the behest of Larry Mullen Junior, who had hopes of starting a group at his school, Mount Temple. Larry had been a fan of early 1970s acts such as the Sweet, Roxy Music and T. Rex and was already an accomplished drummer, having played in marching bands, and he it was who set the ball rolling with a note on the school notice board. Music teacher Robert Bradshaw recommended that another pupil, Dave Evans, get in touch as he had shown an interest in playing guitar. Dave had an old acoustic and also shared an electric guitar and amplifier with his brother Dick who went along for the ride. At Larry's invitation they were then joined by one of the school's lesser academic lights, Adam Clayton, a single-minded boy who had very definite ideas about what he did and did not want to do with his life. Playing bass in a rock 'n' roll band held a definite attraction. Paul Hewson also attended the first get-together which took place in the kitchen of Larry's parents' home in Artane. The quorum was completed by Ivan McCormick, owner of a Stratocaster copy, thus providing the Larry Mullen Band with an impressive four guitarists to go with the bass and drums. Also present at the initial meeting was Peter Martin, who had designs on being the group's manager since, despite having his own guitar and amp, he was unable to play. This new band churned out a cacophony before adjourning, intending to hold future rehearsals at school. Paul Hewson quickly established some kind of leadership of the group with his relentless energy, Peter realizing that his potential role had disappeared before him. Ivan wasn't slow to notice that he was out of his depth, generally finding himself trading his electric guitar for Dave's battered acoustic. Adam was left to ease him out of the band with the excuse that they had got a pub gig and he was too young to play, an early example of his easy way with a convenient line. This finally gave them some kind of shape with Adam and Larry as rhythm section, Dave and Dick playing guitar, leaving Paul to create for himself the role of lead singer. The group took the name Feedback and began their first tentative steps together.

For each of the boys who found a place in Feedback, it was a refuge of sorts from a world with which they were less than comfortable, Adam Clayton later saying that 'It wasn't sort of "let's form a band and let's write great songs", it was more to enjoy the whole experience of being a band of four people with one cause; a cause you could develop and become emotionally involved in. It was much more the whole experience.' Of them all, Adam was the most obvious potential rock 'n' roller having briefly been in a band at his previous school and having already established an enviable record of non-conformity by the age of sixteen. Born in Chinnor, Oxfordshire on 13 March 1960, he was five when his parents Brian, an RAF pilot, and Jo moved to Dublin to enable his father to take up an appointment with Aer Lingus, Adam having spent his early days in Tanganyika. The family of four – Adam had a sister, Sarah Jane – settled on the coast in Malahide, one of the more prosperous, Protestant areas of the city, with Adam briefly attending St Andrew's Church of Ireland school, as did Dave Evans. In 1968 he moved on to boarding school at Castle Park, to which he took an immediate dislike and where he was consequently academically unsuccessful. The school worked rigidly within the principles of a normal English public school, a system which the independently minded boy could not come to terms with. He was agreeable but less than diligent, though acts of rebellion were rare and generally amusing rather than violent. The most obvious comment to make on his upbringing was that it was reasonably normal, English and middle-class.

This continued when in 1973 he moved on to the co-educational boarding school, St Columba's College in Rathfarnham, where he again distinguished himself by some unorthodox behaviour. The disciplines of schoolwork were not something to which he could address himself, later commenting that 'I just wasn't prepared for the Establishment to write me off just because I didn't fit into their academic concept.' Having attended public school, the training ground for the future élite of English society, Adam had acquired the strength of purpose which such schools endeavour to instil in the putative captains of industry. He used that strength in a thoroughly different way, seizing on music as a possible avenue to follow. It was at St Columba's that he became involved in playing music. He'd had a cheap guitar for a short while, but a friend, John Lesley, invited him to join a group, on condition that he got a bass guitar. His mother met him in Dublin after school one day and was delighted to buy the instrument simply because she was relieved that he was finally taking an interest in extracurricular activities at the school. It was also a useful bargaining tool in requiring an improvement in school work. The improvement proved temporary, however, as Adam continued to transgress what he regarded as unreasonably petty school rules, which ultimately led his parents to decide that he would fare equally well at the nearest free school, Mount Temple, which he entered in 1976.

Mount Temple was very much out on its own in terms of the Irish educational system. It was the first comprehensive, non-denominational, co-educational school in the country, a bold statement in itself in a society that segregates people according to their faith. In a country so inextricably linked with religion, the very idea of education based not on religious doctrine but on the principle of education itself attracted massive attention in the national press, the more so since sectarian violence had broken out in Northern Ireland with British troops going in to keep the peace in 1969. Bloody Sunday, 30 January 1972, when thirteen people were murdered by the Security Forces in Londonderry, was a very recent memory. The question of religious freedom was as vexed a question as at any time in the country's recent history. Under such circumstances, it was highly appropriate that Paul Hewson should be part of Mount Temple's intake and should complete his schooling there, since he was the child of a mixed marriage, his father Bobby a Catholic, mother Iris a Church of Ireland Protestant. Born on 10 May 1960, Paul was raised in Ballymun with his brother Norman, seven years his senior.

Paul was brought up in the Protestant faith, going to church each Sunday with his mother while his father would go off to Mass. The image of a family's separation even when both parents were practising their belief in God is a very powerful one and themes of struggle, division, redemption and reconciliation have been recurrent in U2's music. The almost constitutional divisions between Catholic and Protestant were a source of real confusion to Paul and many other children growing up in similar circumstances. How could the simple, supposedly joyous act of worshipping God separate a boy from his friends or split a tightly knit family down the middle every Sunday? His confusion was reinforced at his primary school, Glasnevin National, where he was taught in the Protestant faith, which further removed him from the experience of his father. If this had little impact on the relationship between the two, it did make Paul more understanding of people with different ideas to his, but also more curious about other forms of belief. Being of a particular religion simply because you were born into it made little obvious sense to someone born into two distinct strains of faith.

In 1971, St Patrick's Secondary School welcomed Paul, though he was less than delighted to attend, having harboured hopes of following his brother into high school, an ambition that was thwarted by the cost which was too heavy a burden for his father's GPO salary. Paul looked at the school with the same disdain that Adam had lavished on Mount Temple. By the following summer, he and the school had seen enough of one another to realize that they were incompatible. Fortunately, Mount Temple was opening its doors for the 1972–3 academic year and Bobby was perfectly happy for his son to enrol there. He had seen plenty of petty bigotry in his time and was interested in the idea of a school run on educational rather than denominational lines, something suitable for a child of Paul's curiosity. He was happy to have the opportunity of a fresh academic start, for his problems at St Patrick's had been caused largely by feelings of disappointment and of being out of place rather than through any lack of intelligence. Perhaps more importantly for one who laid himself open to questions of spirituality, being educated at a school which took an all-embracing view of religion gave him a great opportunity to explore and question.

Paul's life changed irrevocably in September 1974 when his mother collapsed with a brain haemorrhage following her father's funeral. She died four days later. She had been his ally in arguments at home, a bridge between his restless energy and the working men of the house who wanted some peace and quiet when they returned home. She was also the person to whom he could express doubt and insecurity, something that was impossible in amongst the rough and tumble of school life, where such an attribute would be pounced on as a sign of weakness. Subsequently, he was only able to allow that part of himself to emerge in his dealings with school girlfriends Maeve O'Regan and later Alison Stewart, who Paul was eventually to marry on 21 August 1982. Amongst the lads at school, he was often the character around whom the others would congregate, a garrulous extrovert, a boy with plenty to say and something of a chameleon, later to be described by Dave Evans as 'a nice bunch of guys'.

Dave, like Adam, was born in England, in Barking, on 8 August 1961, but had moved to Malahide a year later. His parents were both Welsh, his father Garvin being an Elder of the Presbyterian Church, mother Gwenda a Baptist, another example of a familial religious divide. His brother Dick was a couple of years older and a sister, Jill, was born in Dublin soon after the move brought about by his father's engineering job with Plessey. Dave began school at St Andrew's and proved himself quick and intelligent, self-contained and amusing. Mount Temple was his next stop but the bigger institution was not to his liking; he was quiet and found it difficult to get to know new people in the rowdy big school environment. It was fortunate that he had interests beyond school life on which he could focus his agile mind. He began to master the rudiments of the guitar along with his brother and also took piano lessons, a fairly natural progression since he'd been surrounded by music since the earliest days of childhood, a by-product of a Welsh background in which choirs and choral singing played no small part.

Paul and Adam had already shown evidence that they did not fit into normal accepted patterns of behaviour for assorted reasons. On the surface, Dave was better equipped for the outside world, but that was largely a result of academic ability. On a personal level he was as much out on a limb as Paul and Adam and looking for something to which he could make a telling contribution. As the future was to prove, Dave was not just a boy of intelligence, but one capable of original thought, looking for a vehicle through which to express himself. When Larry's notice was brought to his attention, he was keen to become involved. Musically there was an obvious attraction; he was beginning to achieve a degree of accomplishment on his instrument and the opportunity of playing with like-minded people was very interesting as well as being great fun. There were added benefits too; by being part of a group, there was the chance to win social acceptance in the company of others, while taking on the position of guitarist in a rock band certainly bestowed kudos on an individual that could help ease a shy youngster's problems. Dick's involvement had pluses and minuses for Dave. He was a familiar face who was on a similar wavelength, but Dick was also a more accomplished player in spite of Dave having taken Spanish guitar lessons at school. His presence provided a chance for the younger brother to get one over on his elder, a familiar competitive filial instinct and an incentive that gave Dave all the encouragement he needed to develop quickly as a guitarist.

Larry Mullen was, as we've seen, the catalyst in putting the group together with his request for guitarists at school. Of the four, his background was the most conventional. Born in Artane, a Dublin suburb, to Catholic parents, Larry Senior and Maureen, on 31 October 1961, with a sister, Cecilia, who was four years older, he started school locally before moving to Scoil Colmcille in the city, *the* Irish school, which taught in the native tongue as a preparation for later life at university, where a knowledge of Irish was essential. Academically competent without being outstanding, he'd taken to the drums when he was nine, having already tried to master the piano, and soon began to take drum lessons with Joe Bonnie, one of the leading showband and session players in the country. He found himself a place in the Post Office Workers' Union Band by March 1975, a result of his dad's connections as a Civil Servant with the Department of Health and Environment, and he continued to learn and improve. Completing his studies in Dublin, he moved on to Mount Temple largely because it was close to home and offered a wider range of academic options than most other establishments. Like Dave, Larry was rather quiet and removed from the rest of school life at Mount Temple but his drumming gave him a sense of purpose; playing the drums was something he was naturally gifted at and which set him apart. He was a great fan of glam rock, the sound of the early 1970s, and soon discovered that he was able to play along to his favourite records without undue difficulty. The obvious move now was to start a band of his own, to create his own music rather than playing along passively to that of his heroes on *Top of the Pops*.

Having sorted out those who were and weren't able and willing to make a contribution to the group, Feedback now had a nucleus of five people. The personalities within were very competitive, which had positive repercussions musically but, more importantly, here was a collection of young people who were looking for a place in the world, a place to belong. They were all prone to the confusions that adolescence brings, but each had separate identity problems, each was an outsider of sorts. Adam had clearly given up on the rigid disciplines of the system, just as it had given up on him, and was looking for another way to make his name, Dick remembering that 'Adam didn't have any qualifications and he kind of had no choice but to create something for himself – he was never going to get a normal job and he never wanted one. He was very determined over the music – he had an uncle or something who was a millionaire and he fancied the idea and that whole self-made man thing.'

Adam also stood out by virtue of his resolutely English accent, a cultured tone that stood out all the more among the broad Dublin brogues at Mount Temple. While he might consider himself an Irishman having spent much of his life there, he was anything but a conventional Dubliner. Dave and Dick were similarly misplaced with a vague Welsh lilt betraying their origins as much as their surname did, marking them out from the crowd. Musically Dave was more assured and able to stamp his presence on the fledgling group by liberating Ivan McCormick's guitar, although personally he was far from one of the gang at school, going so far as to admit later that by virtue of his nationality and religion he felt almost freakish, a factor in his personal reticence.

If Dick, Dave and Adam were marked out in part by their British backgrounds, Paul had been shaped by the conflicting religions he found at home, by the devastating loss of his mother which had transformed his home life and by the conflicting characters and emotions to which he played host. The amateur psychiatrist would immediately point to the loss of a parent as a trauma responsible for an individual embarking on a never-ending quest for the love and recognition denied him at an early age, perhaps pointing to Lennon and McCartney, Hendrix or Madonna as other successful musicians who were driven to their calling by a similar tragedy. Comparable cod-psychology might inquire whether, freed of the need to please a member of an older generation, such individuals are more able to concentrate on gaining the approbation of their peers and are therefore able to cultivate a greater degree of contemporary relevance. These ideas may have some validity in general terms, but generalities are difficult to apply to individuals, especially individuals as disparate and strong-willed as those that made up Feedback. For any further explanation of Paul's view of psychiatrists/psychologists, 'Out of Control', U2's debut single, made it clear that boys and girls might go on to make children but *not like this one*: everyone is an individual. Paul had always had a burning need to communicate with others, to ask questions, to establish a bond with them. If his loss had an impact in any 'professional' rather than a deeply personal sense, it was to sharpen that need, not create it.

His curiosity had led him to prayer meetings and to inquiring about the beliefs of other people he met. A close friend, Derek Rowan, and his family were members of the Plymouth Brethren religious sect, which taught that God's communication with man came directly through the word of the Bible and that established churches and their leaders could only disrupt and pervert that communion. Paul was understandably taken with this idea, having seen his own family split on a weekly basis by religion; a higher spirituality seemed to be the key, not liturgical dogma. Over the course of their latter days at school, Paul and Derek came into contact with other like-minded spirits who felt out of place, unhappy with the prospect of the mundane nine-to-five job that was awaiting them after school, if they were lucky. Some of the individuals were outrageous in their dress and behaviour, inspired by rock stars like Bowie and Bolan, others just had a contempt for the system. Gradually a social group began to form, which met at Paul's house after school, non-conformists with bright ideas about a different life. They established themselves as Lypton Village and took new names; they'd had no choice in those given to them at birth so this was an opportunity to demonstrate that they were ready and able to take back control of themselves and their lives.

Lypton Village was an essential part of Paul's development as a boy, offering both a life outside society and intelligent, imaginative conversation. It also gave an inkling that maybe you could take on the world and win. Dick, never a member of the Village, recalled that 'a mythology grew up around it, people had little sayings that were intriguing. It was a bunch of friends, like a tribe, cut off from other people developing a way of looking at the world. At the time I thought I should write a book about it until I read "The Electric Kool Aid Acid Test", because that was what it felt like.' Ideas were the currency of Lypton Village and there was no shortage of them. Paul's views were sometimes different to those of his colleagues, who tended to more exhibitionist and, perhaps, elitist means of expression. As later events were to prove when a number of his colleagues in Lypton Village went on to form the Virgin Prunes, they were confrontational and exclusive to a degree, using the weapons of surrealism to comment on and attack ordinary values, whereas Paul's ambition was to connect, to reach and move people as an inclusionist, populist figure, thereby achieving a more subtle confrontation of an audience's beliefs. His membership of two organizations at once, Feedback and the Village, was a very clear sign that he wanted to be able to engage in a wide-ranging dialogue with others of similar, if not identical, views. To the outside world, Lypton Village's most important contribution to Paul Hewson was to name him Bonovox, the name of a hearing-aid shop on Dublin's O'Connell Street, something with which he wasn't entirely happy until he later realized that it made a reasonable Latin approximation of the term 'good voice'! To Paul/Bono it was a crucial part of his growth as an individual. He had found somewhere to belong, a place where his voice counted as much as anyone else's. Between them, Feedback and the Village formed very different but very important homes to different elements of his character.

Lypton Village became solid supporters of Feedback, without bestowing membership on any of the other members of the band, although Dave Evans was given an honorary name, The Edge, chosen by Bono after a hardware store that he would pass on his way into the city. The name was apparently chosen because it matched the shape of his head, although it was a very appropriate description of the original, angular way in which he approached the guitar. The Village regularly attended rehearsals and early concerts although there were very clear distinctions between their outlook on the world and that of the band.

Despite the fact that the group's initial success was to be built in no small part on a marked lack of 'cool' in performance and behaviour, especially on the part of Bono, there was great store laid on street credibility. Generally in rock 'n' roll, that translates as the band members being 'working-class heroes', but it would be true to say that these lads were anything but stereotypical working-class youths; indeed their backgrounds tended towards the middle class. They had each in various ways rejected the laddish rebellion which so permeated youth culture, because they were reasonably secure materially and because their school was not the kind of oppressive institution that inspires such rebellion. A multi-denominational establishment which actually provided a classroom for rehearsals was a veritable paradise in an Ireland where education was rigidly taught on religious lines. They were not the holier-than-thou boys of popular legend, but they did exploit their perceived security more intelligently than many. Adam, though a misfit in academic terms, did decide to take his music very seriously and worked hard to reach a level where he could make a career for himself that was far more interesting than those to be had by achieving examination passes. The Edge, Larry and Bono were attracted by music as the best means of expressing themselves, but they were equally intrigued by spirituality and by the exploration of avenues that have generally been as far removed from rock 'n' roll as it's possible to get. Dick was an aspiring guitarist who allegedly could play the guitar parts on Yes's 'Close To The Edge' backwards, having tired of playing them conventionally, although he actually denies the compliment!

As a rock group, Feedback was pretty incompetent on a musical level, Dick's version of events being that 'Bono was the only one who couldn't really do anything, but we were all very enthusiastic and learning at the same time. It started out in a pretty amateurish way before it began to evolve.' Their first live performance took place at a school talent contest, beginning their career with Peter Frampton's 'Show Me The Way', which was, according to Neil McCormick, brother of putative Feedback guitarist Ivan and later a journalist on Dublin's impressive *Hot Press* magazine, 'probably dreadful'. Nonetheless, he was overwhelmed by the experience since it was the first live electric music he'd heard. Bono was similarly moved and recalled it as one of the very best concerts they ever played, not musically, but emotionally, a comment which strikes at the very heart of the U2 ethos and captures the keystone of their later success. Emotional connection rather than musical excellence was at the very core of their performance. The chemistry which existed between the individuals in the band gave rise to 'a spark. There was the evidence of a little light in the corner and we started to work towards that.' Bono's simple explanation of U2's origins tells a great deal about what the band was about and what they were trying to achieve, as does the advice of eminent nineteenth-century writer Ralph Emerson to the scholars of Dartmouth College, a creed of self-reliance which the band have followed so closely it might have been passed on personally: 'Be content with a little light, so it be your own. Explore and explore. Be neither chided nor flattered out of your position.'

It's far too much of a cliché to say that Feedback/U2 was born out of some evangelical zeal to change the world. Not only is it a cliché, it's a lie. As Bono was later to admit when 'Desire' was released in 1988, 'you don't join a band to save the world but to save your own arse and get off the street,' although some of Bono's later pronouncements and behaviour do give the impression that somewhere deep inside he might just believe that a song can turn things around. Late 1970s Ireland was unlike mainland Britain in that it was experiencing a brief period of economic renaissance, but nevertheless the future for youngsters still consisted of the mundane nine to five, something for which Adam and Bono in particular had made clear their distaste. Being in a group was far more interesting. Even then, if being in a rock band was the modern day equivalent to running away from home to join the circus, there was no reason why you couldn't do new and interesting things with a form that was becoming stale. Feedback comprised five intelligent young men who were keen to do something original and who realized that somehow they had almost immediately stumbled upon a line-up of kindred spirits with a commitment to rock 'n' roll and to innovation.

The spark that they discovered on that debut appearance masked their very obvious musical deficiencies, though they were not blind to them and put in considerable hard work to achieve reasonable competence as quickly as possible. It was this inefficiency that set Feedback, who by their second concert were trading as the Hype, one of Bowie's early group monikers, and playing 'Nights In White Satin', on the road to an original sound. As they had seemingly no idea of how to approach other people's songs, they began to experiment with writing their own. Where so many bands had formed around a nucleus of one or two serious musicians who had spent hours locked in their bedrooms practising solos by their idols and as a consequence aping them, the Hype were almost incapable of following that road, as one cover version amply demonstrated. 'We did a gig in a disco at a church hall and we played Thin Lizzy's "Don't Believe A Word",' recalls Dick. 'It starts with the bass, then one guitar comes in, then the other, but no-one was in tune with anyone else so it sounded indescribable!' Had they been a little more experienced and instrumentally adept, early U2 albums might have sounded rather more like the Moody Blues or Peter Frampton and their story might have been radically different and considerably shorter! Their musical naïvety was central to their early development. They were starting with a sheet of paper which was virtually blank, a few reference points replacing the more typical comprehensive list of heroes to be emulated.

Other external factors conspired to shape the sound of the Hype. Their musical influences were made up of the average early teenage mix of the good, the bad and the ugly, those they would later proudly proclaim like the Beatles or the Stones and those who they would try to forget in much the same way as other survivors of that period attempt to draw a veil over loon pants, and the Bay City Rollers. Around the time that they were forming a group, the punk and new wave scene was beginning to take a grip. Despite contrary reports, Feedback was formed at around the same time as the Sex Pistols and the Clash, not later as a direct result. Punk rock did not really take a hold anywhere outside London until 1977, by which time the band was well off the ground. It also had a very different resonance in Ireland to that which it had in Britain.

Even at this distance it's hard to decipher just how much punk in the UK was to do with music, how much with social conditions and a prevailing attitude of 'no future' and how much with the marketing of new fashion accessories. The 'no future' aspect was particularly irrelevant to Ireland – as noted there was a brief period of economic optimism at the time – but more significantly, Ireland had never been the centre of an empire, a country that had dominions the world over. It had no nostalgia for a supposedly better time in the past when 'the map of the world was pink and a better place for it.' Ireland has for centuries been a country where wild dreams of prosperity had been just that, wild dreams. Domestic expectations were consequently on a smaller scale, hardened by years of sometimes bitter experience and without the demands for automatic employment which had become almost a birthright in post-War Britain, and should indeed be a basic human right in any civilized country.

If punk's supposed social conscience had little impact in Ireland, the idea of tearing down the existing musical order was something which did connect, but while punk seemed to offer little in its place, the Hype wanted to build something new. Conciliation and communication were their words, not mindless, thoughtless destruction. They had more in common with the American new wave and the bands coming out of New York like Talking Heads, Television and the Patti Smith Group, along with the doyen of an older New York wave, Lou Reed, mixed in. As the individuals in the Hype were getting older, they were developing a more sophisticated taste in music, replacing the records they had listened to with these new sounds from America. These were records without pretension or pomposity but minimal, direct statements that spoke to the audience in a way that Bono felt ELP and their ilk demonstrably did not. Talking Heads for instance rejected much of what American FM radio had to offer and produced a taut, tense, slimmed-down variant of funk that owed something to the collaborations between Fripp, Eno and Bowie in the mid 1970s, and leader David Byrne used this as a backdrop for his ironic observations of contemporary American society.

This was an artistic movement that was very close to the heart of The Edge in particular. Having initially been drawn to groups such as the Mahavishnu Orchestra and Yes he had quickly rejected them when he decided that he had no chance of being able to play that kind of music himself. He was intrigued by a minimalist sound, had already taken on board some of Fripp's and Eno's music and become a fan of Tom Verlaine's inventiveness as much as of his playing on Television's records. This kind of stripped-down style required less purely technical musical ability but did demand that the player be able to engender a greater element of 'feel' or emotion with his work and to weed out superfluous notes to arrive at a final definitive statement. It was the difference between pattern-bombing and an incisive attack on a specific target and that idea very definitely helped to shape the direction in which the Hype wanted to head. It became noticeable that their attempted cover versions had moved from the Moody Blues through David Bowie to the point where they began to play 'Mannequin' by the seminal Wire, although this was an unfolding process over the course of eighteen months. Their direction was to evolve over the course of gigs and rehearsals and see them moving away from what was initially almost a heavy rock sound characterized by loud guitar thrashing to the more controlled power that was to emerge on their early records.

In addition to coming to grips with their music, the Hype had to overcome another hurdle which did not apply to their UK counterparts – showbands provided additional enemies for Irish youth. Until pirate radio stations began to emerge in 1977 there was no popular music radio in Ireland and the music scene was dominated by showbands made up of accomplished musicians who played their versions of the hits of the day, trudging around a lucrative circuit of live venues earning a handy living while rendering themselves artistically comatose, 'electrified mutations of the post-War dance bands' as Bill Graham, a writer for *Hot Press* and a central figure in the U2 story, described them. Their popularity made it very difficult for up-and-coming groups to get gigs and gain live experience. They had a stranglehold on venues, campaigned against discos that played the real versions of the records they were copying and ruled the live music roost. Bono recalls that they had to beat the bar system because they wanted to hear other people's material while Dick adds, 'It was a struggle to get gigs. There was no rock establishment so if you wanted to get a gig as a rock band, you were treated as being a bit suspicious.' Larry and The Edge actually did a few sessions with a bar band, the Drifting Cowboys, in 1977 where they were made well aware of the money to be had on the country and western treadmill, but happily they and the rest of the group turned down the temptation to change styles.

These bands were every bit as fierce an enemy of the Hype as Pink Floyd was of the Sex Pistols, equally repugnant. Not only were they tame, sanitized versions of proper rock 'n' roll groups, upholding the Establishment's values, their power was forcing real Irish talent out of the country in order to make a living out of their music. Rock music remained largely an underground phenomenon in Ireland, not a form which the punters had become tired with but one which was still illicit and exciting, outside the normal boundaries much as it had been in the UK and the USA in the late 1950s. On visiting Ireland to interview Bono and see U2 in action in March 1980, *NME*'s Paul Morley vividly described the country's 'musical artificiality and stagnant stupidity (which) drably undermines the development of its youth'. For Irish rock 'n' roll groups the music was not a devalued currency but something which retained a degree of freshness, a mystique that it had lost elsewhere at the tail end of the 1960s, Bono admitting in that same Morley piece that 'this is an incredible area to be getting involved in. Popular music. Phew!' To those who were committed to the music, rock 'n' roll did still matter in Ireland, which explains in part why U2 stood out so clearly when they finally made it to the international stage among contemporaries to whom rock 'n' roll was just a cool pose and a passport to the promised land of sex and drugs.

'Ireland,' wrote John Waters for his BBC radio series *Wide Awake In Ireland*, 'is a country of vast energies and wild enthusiasms full of exhilarating possibilities if only it could shake free of its poor opinion of itself.' The Hype were not lacking in that confidence, themselves perhaps a product of the 'privilege' of living in Dublin rather than the remote rural outposts of the country. Dublin is, without doubt, a city of far greater significance to its country than London is to England or Edinburgh to Scotland. In those countries, there is life beyond the capital but to many, particularly the political élite in the city itself, Dublin is Ireland and Ireland is Dublin, the country's 'entire future is in the hands of a small clique' of Dublin's intelligentsia. They feel that there is a 'competence gap' between themselves and the rest of the country, that people of the outlying districts need to see a moral justification for any action that is taken and are unable to think in a rational fashion. Waters opined, 'Dublin despairs of the country's alleged lack of sophistication and at the same time there is a deep frustration on the ground about the failure of politics to adapt to reality ... because the system itself is immobilized by the narrowly focused liberal agenda of contraception, divorce and abortion.' U2 in their earliest incarnation were an intriguing mix of both these elements, Dublin cockiness that enabled them to ride the obstacles that were later to block their path along with an interest in that 'liberal agenda' and an accompanying shift in the cultural status quo, allied to a distrust of politics and politicians that was not too far removed from the sensibility of those in rural districts.

U2 also came to represent what became recognized in Ireland as a (peaceful) civil war between two generations, those from before the 1960s and those who came later. In his series, Waters talks of the neuroses of the 1960s generation, a group of people who are torn between an emotional attachment to a previous age in Ireland and their rational detachment from it which is translated into a desire to move on from the past. In part it's been characterized by a rejection of the twin churches of Ireland, be it for atheism or other spiritual movements and by the replacement of religious ceremonies with the need to 'sacramentalize' particular life events. U2 were prey to that, their music often being deeply personal – *Boy* was a rites of passage opus, *Achtung Baby* marked the struggle for love and the disintegration of relationships in the 1990s.

In a country that had relatively little heritage in the rock 'n' roll form and less access to live music, with few international bands venturing even to Dublin never mind elsewhere, there were fewer clichés to fall into, not so many examples to follow and more trends to set. The absence of any real rock tradition along with the group's inability to play other people's songs really did force them to dream the whole thing up from scratch with very few preconceptions to weigh them down. The absence of any real rock facilities gave them a bloody-mindedness that was to play no small part in their future, Bill Graham perceptively noting that 'this impoverishment may have given U2 their ambition, the sense that they had more to prove.' That may well have been true on the international stage, but first they had to make some kind of mark in Dublin.

Adam took the lead in gaining gigs, although when they did get the chance to play it was often in pubs which were unable to let in the friends of the band because they were under-age. To a degree, the Hype were lucky to be able to get any gigs at all, but Dublin had been lit up by the emergence of the Boomtown Rats led by Bob Geldof, Adam recalling that 'everyone was enthused by the Rats, so we just hassled the venues 'till they gave us a gig.' As the most voluble member of the troupe, talking an undeniably impressive game and casually tossing musical buzz words into conversations whenever possible, Adam was excellent company and easy to get on with. He also looked the part, an archetypal rock 'n' roller with the chequered school history, the 'rebel' that every band seemed to have, his rebellion being all the more remarkable for the company he kept.

Sadly, though his references were impeccable, his bass playing was initially less inspirational and it was fortunate that none of his colleagues had achieved virtuoso status. His ability to baffle the band with jargon protected him until eventually 'We discovered he wasn't even playing the right notes!' according to Bono. Maybe as a safety net, perhaps simply because he was best qualified, Adam carved out a niche for himself in a managerial capacity, Dick pointing out that 'Adam was really the most responsible for starting it all and providing the initial impetus until Bono began to take more charge with Edge in the middle. There were those obvious power struggles early on.' School wasn't taking up much of his time – after February 1978, it wasn't taking up any – and he gave himself whole-heartedly to the future of the band, perhaps realizing that this was his big opportunity to make a go of something. More than anyone, Adam had the fierce commitment to the group that was to be an integral part of their early survival and growth. He talked the others into believing in the band and what it could achieve, he talked the whole thing into existence. His ability to bluff his way through the first rehearsals was put to good use in attracting the right people to the group, a charm that won friends, gigs and fans. He had absorbed certain lessons with regard to setting up a group and getting gigs but, more importantly, he was quick to seek help and astute in deciding just who to contact.

Among these early converts to the cause was Steve Averill aka Steve Rapid, lead singer with the Radiators From Space, a man described by Bill Graham as 'a perfect adviser . . . he typified the aware, altruistic activists punk threw up everywhere.' Averill was later to become the designer of U2's record sleeves, where the use of black and white photography with bold red lettering became both an eye-catching 'advertisement' of the group and something which was a conceptual link with their oft-stated determination to use rock's 'primary colours' of drums, bass and guitar in a new way. It was therefore appropriate that the designer should, along with other advice, give them their new and final name. If the group had finally bowed to the inevitable demise of the name the Hype, which was admittedly awful, they had few ideas of what they could call themselves. Musically they were trying to do something different and original and they wanted a name that didn't carry any preconceptions with it, one that would make the uninitiated think 'what might they sound like' as opposed to names like the Clash, Led Zeppelin or the Sex Pistols, which made things obvious from the outset. Averill's suggestion of U2 came from the name of a US military aeroplane which was shot down in 1960 and caused a heightening in East–West tension leading to the increased defence spending of the 1960s and 1970s, while a U-2 mission in 1962 uncovered Soviet bases in Cuba, prompting the Cuban Missile Crisis. In the context of a band, the name U2 seemed rootless, ambiguous, inclusive in the sense of 'you too' and yet almost anonymous, a challenge to the music and musicians to give this name some meaning. Prophetically, the U-2 aeroplane flew higher and further than any of its predecessors.

chapter two

A GARAGE BAND FROM CAR PARK LAND

Having got the Hype off the ground, the remainder of 1977 was spent in trying to gain as much live experience as possible, whilst rehearsing and attempting to write new material, fitting in home-work as and when they could. Adam was to finish school in February 1978 while Bono, having been granted a place at University College in Dublin from September 1977, had that offer revoked when it was discovered that he had failed his examinations in Irish, a subject mandatory before taking up a place there. He returned to Mount Temple to continue studying, but now he only had time for the Hype and the music. Edge was soon to follow suit when, following his final exams in 1978, his parents allowed him a sabbatical year before enrolment at Technical College for the Autumn term in 1979.

The Hype's approach to live music was engagingly fresh if a little chaotic; the typical, indeed requisite cool pose that 'real' bands employed was thrown out of the window. Bono in particular would take to the stage and demand attention, even when the Hype were merely a support group with few friends in the audience. He would stalk the stage, insisting that people look at him and listen to his words, to the group's music. The group was essentially, and again this was a rarity, built around the drums as Larry was clearly the best musician, quite literally putting heart and soul into their performances. To this day, U2 concerts at their very best are cathartic, all-enveloping events and it was in these early days that that tradition was begun. Consistency, however, was something which was to elude them in these early shows and the band freely admit that they were able to give an extraordinary performance filled with power, with light and shade, and yet a couple of days later they could be a complete disaster, partly because Bono in particular was always keen to experiment and introduce new ele-ments to his performance as front-man and partly because their own music was, if powerful, also fragile. If any constituent part of a song failed to work on the night, the whole thing might collapse like a house of cards. With a group of musicians who were very definitely struggling to find their feet, this gave concerts a hint of danger, added spice which marked them out as a group to watch. The spark was always there even if the performance was more elusive.

If Bono's antics were the source of the band's initial attraction, the musicians behind him were gradually honing those primary colours into a raw, intriguing sound that owed little to anyone else and much to the spirit of adventure that fuelled the group. Naturally their initial efforts nodded in the direction of their predecessors with 'Cartoon World' bearing a passing resemblance to the Kinks' 'All Day & All Of The Night', while a punkish thrash characterized other songs largely as a result of their instrumental limitations, but there were definite signs of original minds at work. The five-piece that made up the Hype were soon to become the four-piece U2 however.

As the Hype had progressed and were able to play concerts more frequently, the level of commitment and determination to succeed was commensurately greater; having started out as a fun way to spend their time, music was now taking on a bigger role in their lives. Or at least it was for four of them, because Dick was the odd man out. 'They became very intense about it and I wasn't, it was almost a generation gap type of gulf between us. I just didn't fit in, the attitude more than anything. Edge for instance really wanted a career, although he didn't know what it was going to be, whereas I always thought of myself as going to college, getting a degree then doing something else. I was more interested in science. I never at any stage thought, "Yeah, I want to be in a band and that's all," whereas everyone else was starting to feel that way. It was getting more obvious and then it became an engineered thing to try and break it to me gently before Adam kicked me out basically! He kept dropping hints like "Oh you are going to college aren't you?" and I was saying, "Well, sort of!" It became more career-oriented than I wanted and so I left the group.' Dick's final appearance was at the Project Arts Centre when the first twenty minutes featured the five-piece as the Hype before Dick left the stage, leaving the other four as U2. Dick was later to return to music as a member of the Virgin Prunes, a band that had a very different attitude to their music.

The first major appearance as U2 was in Limerick on St Patrick's Day, March 1978, at the behest of Larry who had seen a newspaper advert for a talent contest sponsored by Harp Lager and *The Evening Press*, with £500 and a demo session with CBS up for grabs. Having played a show at the Project Arts Centre in Dublin the previous night, by the time they got off the train in Limerick, Bono's voice had gone missing and things were not looking too positive. All the same they got through the heats, where they performed before judges who included Billy Wall from RTE Radio, the national station, and Jackie Hayden of CBS Records, on hand to see just who would be making their way into the studio as winners.

Hayden later wrote that on first sight, only U2 and one other group, East Coast Angels, an older glam rock outfit, had anything to offer and agreed with Wall that one of the two would surely win the final held that evening before an audience. U2 themselves were anything but certain, impressed as they were by the professionalism and musical ability of the mainly showband competition, but they gave a good account of themselves, turning in one of their better performances, and succeeded in taking home the first prize, some welcome publicity and a record company fan. In addition, it helped to persuade Bill Graham of *Hot Press* to go and see the group. Graham had been one of the names on Adam's list of important contacts for some time and he'd been telephoning him regularly to persuade him to meet the band and see them live. As he was a journalist on Dublin's music newspaper, getting Graham on their side with the attendant coverage he could provide for them was essential. He met the group in early April and accompanied them to that first demo session held at Keystone Studios which promoted the first major U2 article in *Hot Press* number 23, 'Yep! It's U2.'

That session was a low-budget, low-key affair, overseen and produced by Hayden himself. He recognized their naïvety, their raw-edged sound and felt that recording their songs direct to tape was the most obvious method of trying to capture the power they had live. This was also a time-saving device to enable Hayden to record a number of songs to give CBS an idea of U2's whole range. The demos were less than impressive, Bono appearing as a sub-David Byrne style vocalist at times although The Edge was obviously beginning to develop as a musician, leaving behind some of the rock riffs and introducing the style for which he was to gain acclaim, and Larry, although he had a tendency to overplay, acquitted himself reasonably well in spite of being called away from the session by his father who wanted to make sure that he was up for school the following day. Ultimately the session was useful in familiarizing U2 with the recording studio, but did little else for them, the songs still in an embryonic state, showing promise yet to be fulfilled.

By now, with Steve Averill and Bill Graham as advisers and with some record company interest in the offing, a full-time manager began to look like an asset they couldn't do without. Adam had muddled through and done a good job but they needed someone with wider experience, more contacts and a knowledge of the ins and outs of the music industry. Graham felt that an old college friend of his, Paul McGuinness, might fit the bill.

McGuinness had had a nomadic childhood because his father was in the RAF. He was born in Hanover and had spent time in West Germany, the UK and Malta. His mother was from Ireland and his father had Irish ancestry and so, at the age of 10 in 1961, Paul went to a Jesuit boarding school, Clongowes, in Kildare, from where he progressed to Trinity College, Dublin, in 1968. Always interested in the arts, his first taste of the music world came when he promoted a concert by Donovan in Dublin, but it was in film that he got his first real experience of work, acting as assistant director on a number of commercials. Music returned though when he began to manage Irish folk-rockers Spud, who had risen to prominence on the back of the boom led by Horslips. They were initially successful but eventually, when decisions had to be made, the group opted to remain in Ireland and work the national circuit rather than take the risk of looking further afield. Realizing that he could go no further with them, Paul parted company. Nevertheless, this brief involvement had given him a taste for management and had also provided him with outline ideas for the future.

There are obvious parallels to be drawn between Adam and Paul: both had been moved around a lot during childhood, were both urbane, cosmopolitan, self-assured characters who had very clear ideas of what they wanted and were determined to work towards those goals. If Bono was the guy who wanted to communicate with the audience, Adam and Paul were those most aware that there was a whole world of audiences to be attracted and that Dublin and Ireland, while essential to the group's creative muse, were just a part of that world. In such a relatively small country, one with little access to pop music, numerous groups had previously built up a national following with relative ease but then found it hard to translate that to the international stage and were quickly dropped by record companies. By 1978 very few Irish talents had made any real impact even in the UK – Thin Lizzy, the Boomtown Rats, Van Morrison, Rory Gallagher – which is scandalous when one remembers the impressive contribution made by the Irish to other art forms throughout this century and unbelievable if one looks at just how much talent has come from the country since U2 emerged.

McGuinness was pressed by both Adam and Bill Graham to see U2 live but was unsure, particularly as he had little faith in punk rock, which he had heard was their main influence. He finally went to see U2 play a support slot at the Project Arts Centre on 25 May, though he had an ulterior motive in going since the headliners, the Gamblers, owed his sister money and he wanted to persuade them to pay her. After U2's set, he met the band and outlined his ideas about a group aiming for greater success and acceptance than that which Dublin could provide. Like Averill, who they had already asked to manage them, Graham and countless others before him, he found the group to be intelligent, curious, asking the right questions and giving the right answers. He was also impressed to learn that they were sufficiently mature to turn down a less than lucrative deal that CBS Ireland had already offered to them. While many groups would sign the first contract they saw, U2 had the sense to realize that they weren't yet drinking in the Last Chance Saloon but were a young, developing band with time on their side. Sensing that they were a group he could cultivate a successful relationship with, McGuinness agreed to manage them, advising them to play fewer gigs in order to make those they did play a real event and to give them more time to develop their songs and musicianship in the rehearsal room.

Being based in Dublin was sometimes frustrating for an up-and-coming rock band, but it did have its advantages in that a group was able to grow at its own pace without the glare of publicity that could be turned on a band in London by the weekly press before they were ready. As 1978 progressed, U2 were able to refine the basic constituents of their sound to a point where they had a very clear identity all their own. Adam remained interested in the machinery of the group and took a leading role in the image that they wanted to project on photos, gig posters, etc. Musically he was widening the range of his ability and was creating a bass style that worked well alongside Larry's drums. Larry had left school in 1978 and had got a job as a messenger to gain the security he was unsure U2 could provide. Larry's work was to cause problems with soundchecks for concerts, his drums being pieced into the sound as the final instrument rather than the basic grounding on which the rest of the musicians built. His absence from day-time photo sessions was overcome by recruiting Bono's school friend Derek Rowan, now operating as Guggi in the Virgin Prunes, as a stand-in but there was some disquiet in the ranks over his position. It wasn't until November of that year, when the death of Larry's mother in a car accident resolved the questions for him: the support he received from the group and from Bono in particular, who had suffered the same trauma a few years earlier, helped him through his loss and he responded by quitting his job and throwing himself into the group.

The Edge was the musical focal point of U2 thanks to his development of a minimal guitar style which was different and exciting and allowed him to leave the hard rock leanings of his earliest playing far behind as his influences widened – where a Bowie style riff had coloured 'Street Mission', 'Life On A Distant Planet' owed more to Blondie's 'Union City Blue' – and his own vision of the instrument came into play. The chiming melodic quality and the refreshing use of harmonics that distinguished U2's opening salvo when they finally got a world-wide recording deal was arrived at during work carried out in the shed of his parents' home. It was many miles from the nihilistic thrash of punk but still had that energy, power and anger. It could also be a calming sound, a frail, pastoral property that was a unique expression of doubt and frailty, a highly effective contrast to the swagger and bluster of their contemporaries.

Edge came to this sound partly through his own desire to be original and partly as a reaction to Adam's individual bass style, which was developing nicely. 'The Dream Is Over', for instance, was coloured by some impressive melodic runs. 'Adam is very extravagant . . . he wasn't interested in taking the bottom end of the sound spectrum at all . . . in order to give the group any sort of clarity, therefore, I had to stay away from the bottom end of the guitar.' As a consequence, he was left with just the higher notes to play with, which translated into that particularly distinctive ringing tone.

The Edge was undeniably adept at creating music that mirrored and complemented Bono's lyrical ideas with such sympathy that the two were seamless, a welcome change from the ungainly grafting of a lyric onto an inhospitable musical idea. As lyricist, Bono looked at the life he was leading and at the world around him and so Dublin clearly informed his words. Elementary imagery was and has remained an important part of his vocabulary and the setting of Dublin and its environs plays a large part in that, giving rise to lyrics that capture the power of the ocean, the grandeur of the natural world, the strength of storm, tide or fire to overcome man and his efforts. These themes have given a scale to the words that has matched the cinemascopic music they've so often produced. His early lyrics were also about the streets where he lived, adolescence, growing up, conflicting emotions. 'I write more about the things that *really* concern me, whereas I think a lot of writers write about things they'd *like* to concern them,' he told *Hot Press*. This sincerity did cut through to audiences, even if at times they were embarrassed by his earnest performance or were alienated by this hyperactive fool who so desperately wanted to reach them. In writing about those things that really mattered to him, Bono also had to confront the thorny topic, at least in rock 'n' roll terms, of his interest in spiritual matters, which continued to fascinate and confuse.

Ultimately, this spiritual questioning led members of Lypton Village to discover a charismatic Christian group in Dublin called Shalom. As time progressed, Bono, Larry and The Edge all found their way to the meetings, which they found gave them a degree of peace that they had not discovered in the teachings of the better-established religions in Ireland. Shalom is just one example of the way in which the existing churches have alienated people over the last century to the point where alternative methods of worship have taken on greater importance. The division of Protestant and Catholic was the most obvious manifestation of the failure of organized religion in Ireland but there were other factors such as the enforced discipline and dogma of a church school education that turned so many young people away from spiritual exploration.

In Ireland itself, Father Pat O'Brien, a writer, has said that 'There is a deep anger about the way the Church treats its people in general' and the Irish Catholic Church's doctrinaire stance on women, contraception, abortion, women in the Church, priests in the Church have alienated so many people. It has been said that in the twentieth century, the clergy in Ireland lost the faith of everyone – finding that it could not win the arguments that were ranged against it, it simply chose to close the conversation, thereby escalating the process of disenchantment.

Shalom was a Christian group that, initially at least, did return to the teachings of the Bible without the other regimens of organized religion and as such it dovetailed perfectly with the needs of the three members of U2, though Adam had little interest in the concept at the time, while Dick went along to one meeting before deciding, 'I just didn't like it. Everyone was interested in religious groups at school, but I was always suspicious of it. The impression I got was that although Shalom started out as a very light-hearted thing, it seemed to become more and more inward looking.' Shalom was later to prove intrusive, questioning the validity of being in a rock 'n' roll band, asking if there were not better uses for the talents of the three – working, for example, in deprived inner city areas – arguing on the crucial principle of the surrendering of the ego as an essential self-sacrifice, a pre-requisite of a life in God. This led to insoluble conflict that was to work itself into later music – very directly on *October* – and cause them to leave Shalom, but at first it was an atmosphere that suited them well and gave them strength in their personal attempts to make sense of adolescence and of the world outside.

Here again was early evidence of what was to be recognized as the very core of the U2 experience, the courage to express emotions that others would rather suppress allied to an ability to articulate those feelings. Again, where so many bands would strap on the rock 'n' roll pose of self-assurance and absolute confidence, U2 were peering through the doubt, almost celebrating it as a very real and natural human emotion. Confusions both sexual and spiritual were admitted and Bono was to address himself to them in an interview with *Hot Press*, saying, 'I have problems, things like girls, sex. But we're also dealing with spiritual questions, ones which few groups ever touch even if I know that teenagers do think about these matters.'

This became a mainstay of the songs through the two personas that Bono used in performance, an interesting contradiction in itself in that one so open, so keen to give himself, had to use characters to be able to do so. The first character was The Boy, around whom the first album was constructed, an ordinary youngster prey to the problems that so many have, while the other was The Fool, who apparently came from Shakespearean study but who might just as easily have been born from Iggy's *The Idiot*, a record which Dick remembers Edge being required to learn for possible future covers, since that was very obviously an influence on much of Bono's manic on-stage act, a performance in which he gave of himself to the audience, a self-sacrifice not far removed from the surrendering of the ego that Shalom was later to emphasize. The Fool was to disappear from the act relatively quickly, certainly before they reached the status of recording artists, but was an integral part of the concert experience in 1978–9, defining U2's wilful lack of cool. His theme song included the line '*I break all the rules*', which was an excellent summing-up of just what U2 were doing. It also presented an intriguing look at Bono's view of prevalent on-stage behaviour, '*a street jester*', '*a hero of society*', '*a hero pretends no pain*' and '*a cartoon in motion*'. Along with songs like 'Cartoon World', an absurdist Lypton Village comic-strip-style view of the mundanity of the nine-to-five existence, it introduced a more playful, humorous side to U2 that wasn't to be so overt again until Zoo TV in 1992. On the subject of Zoo TV, the influence of Lypton Village and the Virgin Prunes on that extravaganza is important, Dick Evans remarking, 'Zoo TV seems to be a more highbrow kind of thing. There was a point where the Prunes were trying to challenge and almost take the piss out of the audience and that's part of what U2 are doing now. We were just never together enough to get the technology sorted out! I detect a humour in U2 for the first time since the early days. Maybe Bono's just getting older and more relaxed, he's not afraid to laugh at himself.'

'The Fool' was one of three songs they chose to record in November at what was to all intents and purposes their first real demo session. This was produced by Barry Devlin of Horslips, whose opinion was respected by McGuinness and whom he trusted to give an informed reading of the band and its potential. 'Shadows And Tall Trees' was another of the three and the only one that made it onto *Boy*, the debut album of two years later. It showcased another element of U2, another piece of a very different jigsaw to that put together by other hopeful 'new wave' acts. This was a gentle, atmospheric, eloquent ballad of sorts, which put The Boy on the outside of society looking in, portraying the very real lack of self-esteem that is such a part of growing up for many, a pause for thought that was some distance removed from the breakneck pace deemed essential for rock 'n' roll in 1978.

The third piece was their customary set closer, 'Street Mission', which captured The Boy more accurately than the others with its talk of '*I love to watch myself grow*' and '*I need something*'. The juxtaposition of the physical changes and the personal growth of adolescence, a personal search for some kind of meaning, was particularly powerful and nicely enigmatic. Was the 'something' of which Bono sang a spiritual need or the need for a sexual partner that fuels so much juvenile rock 'n' roll? Did it echo 'Pictures of Lily' or was it a youngster's plea for 'Help!'? This ambiguity was an attractive part of U2, allowing an audience to select whichever meaning it wanted, whether it was accurate or not, and turn it towards their own lives, particularly useful in an age where youthful audiences were rejecting spirituality for hedonism. Providing a window to their own emotions has been a central and precious thread of U2's music from the very beginning.

'Street Mission' worked well lyrically, but musically it served to show where U2 had come from rather than where they were going, which may account for its departure from their repertoire. It contained a section of very typical early 1970s hard-rock guitar that was vaguely reminiscent of bands like Rush and Yes who were supposedly being swept away by the new wave and it ended on a note not far removed from Bowie's 'Suffragette City', elements diametrically opposed to their desire to break new ground.

One of the recurring themes in U2 songs at the time was 'the street' as the natural habitat of the boy with nothing to do. Street credibility was something that was important to the band but in a very different manner to the affected pose of so many rock 'n' rollers. The street was real to U2, the place where they lived and grew up, not a mythical oasis of self-possession where everyone behaved like an extra from *West Side Story*. They were gauche, naïve kids just like their audience and they played up to the fact to win approval, a startling idea at the time. 'I'm just throwing away a thing we call cool here and it deserves to be thrown away,' Bono told Dublin's National Stadium on a triumphant night a year later and this was very much the basis of their appeal to the ordinary kids in their ordinary clothes. Rock bands were supposed to be unapproachable, in command, on a plateau that those below couldn't reach. The only difference between U2 and *their* audience was that U2 were on the stage; take that and their electrical armour away and they were the same as everyone else. Their teenage Angst, their insecurity, their desperation found a mouthpiece in Bono, eager to please, so keen to capture every eye that he could fall over himself in the process and bring the fragile edifice of U2 crashing down with him. If this was a strength of the band, it could also be a weakness, in that they found it difficult to curb the inconsistency that had plagued them from the start and which was to cost them dear in terms of record company interest. Recognizing this, Bono, in the company of the Virgin Prunes' Gavin Friday, took a few casual lessons in stagecraft from Dublin actor and writer Mannix Flynn and Conal Kearney, a one time pupil of Marcel Marceau.

U2's commitment to their community was maintained in early 1979. In keeping with McGuinness' philosophy they had restricted their availability throughout 1978, playing fewer shows, though they did support big-name visitors such as the Stranglers, Advertising and the Greedy Bastards, an unlikely pick-up band that included Phil Lynott of Thin Lizzy and Steve Jones and Paul Cook of the Sex Pistols, as well as playing to their own audience at McGonagles and the Project Arts Centre. McGonagles created a barrier between them and their crowd as many fans couldn't get in because of its enforced '18s & Over' policy, which was due to the licensing laws. To defeat this problem a new venue was established in the spring of 1979 near the Gaiety Green market, where a disused indoor car park was transformed on Saturday afternoons into the home of youthful rock 'n' roll. More than any of the gigs they'd done before, the half dozen they played in the car park established them as a promising group with a very distinct audience all their own, playing songs such as 'Cartoon World', 'Speed of Life' and 'The Dream Is Over', which began a tradition of reinterpreting other people's song titles or lyrics that continued into 'Boy/Girl', a Gavin Friday composition, 'Gloria', 'Sunday Bloody Sunday' and 'God Part 2'. The car park became 'an atmosphere we created in' according to Bono. It became their home, the place they felt most at ease, Bono recalling that when U2 played in pubs the audiences would 'laugh at us' mostly out of embarrassment or incredulity at his desperation and the sincerity of these kids who were much younger than their audience. To actually enjoy a band so young might be bruising to the ego.

If some record companies had been frightened away by the wavering graph of their live performance, Jackie Hayden at CBS had kept an eye on proceedings and had persuaded their UK A&R operation to send over Nicky Graham to watch them on a couple of occasions, all of which culminated in Chas de Whalley, who had already been contacted by McGuinness, travelling to Dublin's Windmill Studios to produce another demo for the band. Three songs were chosen, 'Out of Control', 'Stories For Boys', a strong piece of power pop that in musical terms was a forerunner for later efforts such as '11 O'Clock Tick Tock', and 'Boy/Girl', a live favourite that had seen Bono introduce a routine requiring a cigarette to be passed to him by the crowd. He could take an illicit draw, 'a cameo supposed to dramatize all the secret cravings before the boy met manhood', as Bill Graham described it.

If Bono only wrote about the things that concerned him, 'Out Of Control' took that to the nth degree. The title was a nice paradox in that it set the innocent listener up for a traditional tale of abandoned excess while actually being an articulate confession of the helplessness of the human condition – there are two key 'decisions' in life, birth and death, over which the boy has no control. Going beyond that by implication, if there is no control over that does the individual have control over anything? Does free will exist or is it illusory? Them's heavy lyrics for a boy to write on his eighteenth birthday, but for good measure the psychologists' angle was explored, attacking the view that whatever a person does in later life is determined *'in his childhood'* – you have some free will until you're ten, by which time you become programmed for the rest of your life? A restless song of doubt and anger, of questions and of a search for answers, it effectively set U2's agenda.

The three songs had been played effectively with U2 at last sounding like a real band in the studio as they progressed musically and learned how to exploit one another's strengths and hide their weaknesses. Although the production was less than sparkling, it was workmanlike, leaving Jackie Hayden 'astounded . . . something was definitely happening.' He was to be more astounded when a few weeks later CBS UK decided to pass on U2, apparently because they felt they would be a long-term project rather than an instant cash cow, though admittedly matters were not helped by the inevitability of a poor U2 set whenever any of the CBS top brass were in attendance. Both Hayden and McGuinness failed to see the logic behind what was a grievous blow to the band; after all CBS had had a twelve-month relationship with U2 and were the only company that had expressed a strong interest in them.

Fighting back was the only solution which presented itself. Bono went to London with the demo tapes to present himself and the band to the record companies and, just as importantly, the London music press who were quite rightly identified as being crucial in helping the band win an audience in the UK. The influence of *Sounds, Melody Maker* and the *New Musical Express* could not be underestimated and Bono was happy to win general approval from them, with *Sounds'* Dave McCullough being particularly keen. Back home, after a series of meetings, U2 accepted a CBS recording deal for Ireland only, which gave them the rights to the Irish market on all U2 material for a five-year period whatever other record deals the group might secure elsewhere. The most obvious first step was to release a debut single. Tapes already existed of three songs produced at the expense of CBS and so there needed to be little discussion of just what songs were going to be used. Chas de Whalley's demos were slated for September release.

Although U2 and Paul McGuinness had never been keen on a purely Irish release, if for no other reason than that Irish records by Irish bands tended to be patronized, generally ending up in the bargain bins, the single release seemed a sustainable concept. McGuinness in particular had always regarded Ireland as an irrelevance in terms of its impact on their ultimate international acceptance but he was well aware that a hit in Ireland might make the London–based labels sit up and take notice. The plan which he arrived at in alliance with Hayden was to be the first real example of the strategic thinking and cunning that went on behind the marketing of U2. To gain maximum attention for the single it would carry three tracks instead of the more usual two, making it better value for money for the punters. The single would also be promoted by means of a front cover and interview with *Hot Press*, unknown for a band without a recording pedigree, but almost a matter of course for a magazine that was already a staunch supporter of the group. Another tactical coup involved the new national pop radio station RTE 2 and its most influential DJ Dave Fanning, who, as a pirate broadcaster, had played his part in ushering in this new era of radio.

Fanning was well aware and appreciative of U2, having been one of the many people approached by Adam in the days of the Hype for advice and assistance. He'd seen U2 on numerous occasions, even reviewing their performance at the Dark Space 24-hour event held at the Project that February for *Hot Press*. His producer, Ian Wilson, was contacted by McGuinness and agreed to invite the Edge and Bono on to one of Dave's shows to let them play the three songs in order to promote the upcoming release. To maintain the spirit of involvement which U2 had created with their fans, they were then polled by RTE 2 so that they could choose the A-side. Not only was it a nice and appreciated gesture to those who had helped U2 reach this stage, it was also a clever manipulation. If you've just chosen the A-side, you've got to buy the record haven't you? Additionally it ensured that it was the most popular side that got the radio play – and having played a part in its selection, RTE 2 had a degree of self-interest in promoting the record whenever possible to remind people of their role and so increase their own standing with this 'new' rock market – theoretically the most attractive song for less committed listeners and so more likely to attract their attention. The people's choice? 'Out of Control', which became the leading track on the 'U2-3' EP.

U2 not only wanted to involve their fans, they wanted to involve the staff at their record company, and so a special play-back of the single was arranged at Windmill Lane, where Bono, Larry, The Edge and Adam all met the entire CBS staff and indulged in some hectic pressing of the corporate flesh in a prime example of their interest in anyone and everyone who might have an impact on their career and of the meticulous attention to detail which Paul McGuinness had brought to their affairs. If all of this showed a precocious eye for promotion, the *coup de grâce* came with the actual formatting of the record. Unusually for the times, it came out on both 7 inch and 12 inch vinyl, each differently packaged to attract buyers to perhaps purchase two copies, a fairly routine ploy for almost every artist in the world nowadays but in 1979 a new and original departure. The 12 inch was strictly limited to 1000 copies, all of which were individually numbered by Jackie Hayden himself. Within three days of release it became the biggest-selling 12 inch ever in Ireland, giving it an initial push into the Irish charts which was then consolidated by the success of the 7 inch which, unlike its bigger brother, sported a picture sleeve designed by Steve Averill, making it equally attractive to devoted fans while others who just liked the song were happy to be able to get hold of the record in any format.

The first ever U2 release deserves to be treated as a special case. It was their first single and the stakes were high for failure in the small Irish market might have finally put off the London record companies for good. It must be remembered that in the context of record marketing in 1979 the idea of a 12 inch single for a non-dance act was as much an endearing novelty as a piece of marketing gimmickry, but the concept of multi-formatting has persisted through their career and has become an industry standard.

For a band that has been characterized and caricatured as idealistic, altruistic and concerned with giving value for money, this aggressive promotion is something of a contradiction. The record company's argument is that no one forces people to buy more than one version of a single, but with a band like U2 that has a very strong commitment from its fans they are at least keen to get every song released, if not in every format. When, for instance, 'Mysterious Ways' was released as a single in 1991, the CD and 12 inch carried mutually exclusive tracks, albeit largely unimpressive remixes of the song itself, which virtually guaranteed that long-term fans would buy two copies of the single, thus improving its chart potential. 1984's 'Pride' covered similar ground with a second (limited edition) 12 inch release that boasted a version of '11 O'Clock Tick Tock' that was unavailable elsewhere, giving the record a boost to sales in its later weeks after the initial burst of activity had subsided, again a tactic that has become commonplace with two-CD sets but which was relatively unknown at the time.

At the very least, it's a contradiction that has to be recognized as far as U2 are concerned, a band that would rather look foolish on stage than appear cynical, being themselves the subject of what might reasonably be termed cynical marketing techniques. The conundrum is particularly interesting in view of the oft-repeated slogan of having control of all their activities. Concert ticket prices have remained fairly reasonable when measured against other acts of their stature, the quality of their merchandise has been good, but when the record company becomes involved value for money has become increasingly questionable, as has been the case with virtually every other act in the world. This apparent conflict, one of the perils of success, has been something they have appeared uncomfortable with over the years, although they had recognized the need to make some concessions to the industry as early as the release of 'U2-3'. 'We want to get that . . . artistic freedom which derives from money and success and we'll work very hard to get there. And we're willing to compromise to a certain extent' was Bono's view on the occasion of that first *Hot Press* cover feature in October 1979. In wanting to achieve the widest possible audience for their music, music they believed in without reservation and which they felt could move people and make them think, they were forced to join that vicious circle which has resulted in the marketing we see today. To gain an audience requires heavy promotion, be it advertising, tour support, whatever. This incurs cost. For a record company to recoup their investment requires more promotional work in order to sell more records, a spiral that goes on and on until, hopefully, one day an artist wins a global audience and is in profit, selling records with minimal promotion because of an outstanding track record. Then some of their earnings are ploughed back into up-and-coming artists, which means that the major artists are required to sell yet more records to pay for this other investment. This requires more promotion and so it goes on. U2 are, in this regard, no different to any other act. Some of their singles have not represented great value for money and they have been as guilty as anyone of taking marketing ploys to the extreme. Where they are distinct from many of their contemporaries is in refusing to let market forces interfere with the music itself.

Such naked ambition from a rock 'n' roll band was unusual in Dublin, or indeed in the UK. While every band might secretly dream of filling Wembley Stadium and covering the bathroom wall with platinum discs, it was not the best way of promoting one's street credibility. As in so many areas, U2 chose to fly in the face of tradition. They dreamt of a big music with a big future, of having things to say and wanting people to hear them, and they were not afraid of saying so, an honesty which won admirers and detractors in equal measure, especially in a country where the attitude to success was ambivalent to say the least. Bono was ultimately to note that 'in Los Angeles they see the guy in the mansion on the hill and they say, "One day, I'm gonna live in that mansion." In Dublin they see the guy in the mansion on the hill and they say, "One day I'm gonna get that bastard!",' a bitter-sweet attitude that has helped them keep their feet on the ground. The punk purists in the city were dismayed by their ambition and their self-confidence, which at times came across as arrogance. It's a part of U2's story that they did not ride to success on a magic carpet of ever-increasing acceptance and goodwill. The single-minded determination which now so characterizes them was forged in the heat of indifference and opposition.

Opposition didn't only come from Dublin; the London record companies remained resolutely unconvinced about U2's potential. Admittedly, U2 were jinxed with certain companies, especially Chrysalis, who had only to show up to ensure an awful gig according to McGuinness, but others showed wilful stupidity. EMI, for instance, seemed very interested in signing them and came out to Dublin for what promised to be the last look before inking a contract, Tom Nolan from their A&R department having realized the potential on show on 'U2-3'. The higher echelons of the company attended a gig at the Baggot Inn but left early in order to catch the Specials, whom they'd earlier rejected, on the *Old Grey Whistle Test*! A&M, home of the Police, were also interested and spoke of giving U2 time to grow and develop, but again the top brass happened upon a show where nothing worked and that was that.

Stranger still was CBS' continuing lack of interest since their Irish arm had seen U2 on a good night, had proved that U2 could release a strong single and capture sales and yet still there was no commitment from the London office. Another recording session was organized, this time in London, with Chas de Whalley again producing. The session, in December, was scheduled for the day after a gig on their first touring visit to England, where they played a number of London venues, building on their growing popularity with the media. Paul Morley, reviewing a concert at the Moonlight Club in West Hampstead where they supported the Dolly Mixtures, noted in the *NME* the band's 'uncouth grace' and their 'obvious commercial potential', a truth which had previously eluded A&R departments throughout the capital. Again, it was anything but plain sailing, for the Hope & Anchor saw them entertain a crowd of nine, but there were benefits from the trip – they played as support act to Talking Heads, heroes of their own and perhaps *the* band to go and see. Consequently U2 were able to play before sizeable crowds and win some friends.

If that was a triumph, the very fact that they made it over to London at all was a greater achievement. Money to cover costs had been organized. It was to come from a seemingly lucrative publishing deal that Paul McGuinness had set up with Bryan Morrison Music. An advance was agreed but, days prior to them leaving for London, the publisher contacted McGuinness to change the conditions of the deal, take it or leave it. On principle he left it and the band set about raising money for the trip from parents and friends, another act that says a great deal about their self-reliance and their refusal to deal with people they couldn't rely on. With that crisis over, there was still time for a further disaster, with Edge and Adam involved in a road accident that left the guitarist with a badly injured hand.

These were traumas that just had to be overcome, however. U2 and McGuinness had already realized that their strength at present lay in live performance – when they got it right. The 'U2-3' EP had been well received in Ireland but it remained little more than a hopeful demo from a hopeful band to the London companies. The band recognized that their live shows were hopelessly erratic and that this was the root of their problems, with A&R people always seeming to attend the worst shows. Now, with a series of gigs right on their doorstep, including the prestigious Talking Heads supports, they gave themselves a real chance to prove their promise once and for all, with the knowledge that they had ten attempts to get it right.

It proved to be the turning point which they had hoped for. One of the record companies that came to see them on the back of their increasing press coverage was Island, in the person of its chief press officer Rob Partridge and head of A&R Bill Stewart. They were impressed with the young Dubliners and, if they were not actively looking for one, it was certainly true that Island's roster was short of a good rock 'n' roll band, which made U2 all the more attractive.

In retrospect, it was odd that Paul McGuinness hadn't concentrated his efforts on Island at an earlier stage. One of the few genuine independents with any muscle and one which had a very good relationship with the Warner company in America, it was the personification of the U2 principle of putting artistic ideals first, believing that the economic factors would inevitably fall into line as a result. What other label would have played host to two artists as esoteric or eccentric as Robert Fripp and Brian Eno, already established as inventive influences on The Edge in particular. Much has also been made of the Bob Marley connection. Here was a man interested in freedom and equality, a poet who was unafraid of talking about matters of spirituality and who determinedly ploughed his own musical furrow with dignity and integrity intact. Surely there would be an empathy between him and a group like U2 who were doing very different things musically but with similar guiding principles. His presence on the Island roster must have meant a lot to them. In actual fact it was just a happy coincidence that they were label mates. The members of U2, while aware of Marley, were less than well acquainted with his music – reggae was never the force in Ireland that it had been in the UK – and it was to be a number of years before the strength of character and the humanity that informed his music were to make an impression on them, whereupon he became a much quoted figure, 'Exodus' frequently finding its way into U2's live shows. That coincidence became a cruel irony when, in May 1981, Marley died of cancer. The torch that Bob Marley, one of the handful of truly great men in the history of popular music, had lit at Island was to be passed on to U2, a 'garage band from garage land', who signed a deal with them in March 1980.

chapter three

ISLAND

The London tour of December 1979 had rekindled the hope of some imminent record company activity but had also shown U2 the other side of the corporate box they were hoping to step into, gigs where the A&R men propped up the bar rather than jostled for position at the front of the stage and where the talk was of percentages, deals and money rather than music and ideas. That their music did strike a chord was brought home to them on returning to Ireland, though, where they scooped five awards in the annual *Hot Press* Readers' Poll.

February was to see the release of 'Another Day', their second CBS Ireland single. 'Another Day' itself was less impressive than the songs on 'U2-3' and betrayed its hurried recording although it did capture some of the pace and sound of their concerts and their hard rock leanings. 'Twilight' was its B-side, another song spoiled by the haste with which it was recorded. According to Bono it was quite literally recorded in just five minutes, and an unimpressive arrangement obscured the potency of a piece that was, when improved upon, central to their debut album. This time the single's promotion was in the hands of the group themselves, who went on tour across Ireland visiting places where any live rock 'n' roll was unheard of. After playing in Tullermeny's Garden of Eden club, Bono told Paul Morley that playing the showband haunts was 'a great challenge . . . They might never see another amplifier again. EVER!' Sometimes the challenge was met, at other times U2 were a stumbling noise alienating people who didn't know how to react to them or to any other rock group. Not just a promotional jaunt, it was also recognition that this might be their last chance to visit these outposts and introduce them to rock 'n' roll – if U2 were to get the deal they wanted, time would suddenly become a precious commodity taken up with the required touring schedule around the more traditional rock 'n' roll markets of the UK, Europe and the USA. Bono was even to admit that there was a very real possibility that U2 might have to move to London, at least temporarily, to further their career and to gain fresh inspiration for the songs they wanted to write in the future. With typical commitment and loyalty to their own country, U2 wanted to face the challenge of transforming this musical wilderness into a place energized and moved by the power of music while they still had time.

An equally stiff challenge faced the group at the end of their slog around the homeland – a headline gig at the National Stadium in Dublin with its capacity of 2000. Initially sceptical about the idea, McGuinness was convinced by the *Hot Press* awards that there was a following strong enough to sustain it and he agreed to the proposals put forward by Dave Kavanagh, their booking agent. Bono later claimed that many had attended to watch them fail, consequently filling the venue. If that was true, U2 were able to face them with absolute confidence. A show in Belfast early in the tour was attended by Bill Stewart's deputy at Island, Annie Roseberry. She saw the same level of potential that had inspired her boss and so U2 were at last on the brink of their deal. It was offered to them by Bill Stewart at the National Stadium, where Bono again recalls that 'we turned it down, the ultimate bluff and we finally got what we wanted.' As much as any incident, that refusal illustrates the self-possession and self-belief in the U2 camp. Had Island left the negotiations, there were few places left to go. Not only that, but expenses were outstripping income and they found themselves under heavy financial pressure. That they remained true to their principles, which centred around the freedom to make and, most importantly, release any record they chose, says a great deal.

The contract wasn't actually signed until they returned to London for their first concentrated assault on Britain in March 1980. An Irish showcase concert played before a crowd which included more executives from Island was a minor triumph. Paul Rambali in the *NME* summed up the U2 conundrum in saying they were 'committed and determined and eager to cut across. So eager they sometimes rush and stumble,' early failures that had put off countless record companies until Island had finally seen through to the 'genuine, unique contact'. On 23 March, U2 were officially Island recording artists, although, true to fashion, even the signing, at the Lyceum Theatre in London, was unconventional. 'We were penniless, really broke, so it was a feeling of great relief that we had the money to get home,' Bono recalled for Radio 1. 'Someone said that we actually had to sign the contract by the following morning . . . we needed to find a private place so where better than the ladies' toilet at the Lyceum!'

It would be naïve to suggest that Island Records was purely in the business of making records that had soul and spirit but no chance of selling. True, U2's honest emotional expression would strike a chord and hopefully assure sales and status, but the real truth at the root of Island's support was the fact that U2 were a top-drawer rock 'n' roll band. All the trappings and acclaim and essays on their importance that have gone with the territory since then have obscured the fact that, when it's all stripped away, U2 make records that people want to hear. It's an age-old trap that analysts fall into when looking back over a band's career; the music is overlooked in the scramble to examine the excess baggage. Quite simply, U2 eventually got a break and became successful because they were a great group making great music. Island Records saw that too. Once conversations were entered into, the deal was as good as signed. U2 were perfectly open about their ambitions, their demand for complete control of their work, their willingness to tour the world, recognizing that that was where the group's strengths lay, in their all-encompassing *desire*. Why was it important that U2 should succeed? 'Never before has there been an art form so versatile and it's being abused, it's being commercialized and it's being bent . . . we're standing against that, it's one-up for the positive side of the pop culture.'

Early on, when they spoke to the press of their destiny, Bono often said that they were meant to become one of the great groups. The sort of juvenile bluster that would normally be dismissed out of hand as self-mythologizing wishful thinking seemed to have some resonance when U2 expressed it, perhaps because they spoke of music more than they did of sales graphs. Even so, it was still a little alarming to read an interview with Bono where he proclaimed 'we're gonna break America like no British band has broken it in a long time.' Their music had no direct lineage save some rudimentary new wave leanings, but in terms of artistic achievement he was very clearly drawing parallels with the Beatles and the Rolling Stones. That was where U2 were heading. There could have been few words more encouraging to a prospective record company than that.

Since Island Records is synonymous with its founder Chris Blackwell, it's odd that U2 were signed without any involvement from him personally. That very fact sheds light on Island's 'corporate' ethos at the time – Blackwell's ideas and ideals were very much the lifeblood of the company but it was structured in such a way that people were allowed to look without interference for talent that met the exacting requirements that he had instilled in them. He had strong, intelligent, articulate staff searching for strong, intelligent, articulate artists, an impressive faith and belief in people on both sides of the company desks, another principle U2 responded to because it was one that they held equally dear.

Island Records were to emerge as the obvious company for U2, which proves that some of the others who passed on the band had remarkably little idea of what they were looking at. The Edge was to point to this shortsightedness as conclusive evidence of just how far at sea most companies were, that they were run as industries by businessmen who wouldn't recognize a great band if you hit them over the head with one. Certainly, the innately conservative nature of many companies did prejudice the chances of U2, as has continued to be the case over the last decade. So much record company activity is based on following fashion and getting there just in time to see it finish, in cloning themselves to death, in staging fatuous, unwanted revivals.

Once the deal was signed, work needed to be carried out in other directions. A debut Island Records single was set to be recorded over the Easter period at Windmill Lane with Martin Hannett at the controls. Hannett had become something of a celebrity himself in an era where producers were beginning to attract the same level of fame as the artists with whom they worked. Having worked with the Teardrop Explodes, his most famous association was with Joy Division, an equally idiosyncratic line-up, but one whose world-view was very different and who fitted into the prevailing despondent musical culture more snugly. At times U2 dealt with the dark side of the psyche, but somehow they succeeded in doing so optimistically rather than with weary 'end of the world' resignation. Securing Hannett's services was a tremendous achievement for the band and was an important stepping stone towards getting to grips with studio technology. Hannett was the first experienced and successful pro-ducer they had had a chance to work with and he taught them that harnessing and channelling their creative energies in the right direc-tion was essential within the studio environment, his main complaint being that their priority was speed rather than accuracy. Dick Evans, however, there as an observer, recalls that Hannett was quite difficult to work with.

By this stage, many of U2's ideas for *Boy*, their debut album, had been privately mapped out and they were keen that their first Island single should be separate from that, a track that existed for itself, one apart from the prospective LP. The song was '11 O'Clock Tick Tock', an exhilarating burst of energy that was their live opener, an exciting introduction to this new band that so many would be hearing for the first time. Adam and Larry had progressed in leaps and bounds as a rhythm unit, Larry's snare drum recorded at an almost deafeningly high volume for the time, and they held the song together as The Edge effectively dispensed with any rhythm playing but rather darted in and out of the song with some telling bursts of incendiary guitar work that matched the song's apocalyptic nature as a narrative of a civilization on the edge, at the eleventh hour, ready for collapse.

'11 O'Clock Tick Tock' was in part an explosive reaction to the manifestation of that breakdown in the London club scene they had just been exposed to, the 'all dressed up and nowhere to go' mentality that was the pervasive atmosphere around London's hippest venues and night clubs. So many people desperate to be seen in the right places, dedicated followers of fashion all hoping for something to hold onto, forming cliques to generate a sense of community that was only available to them within the ritual of club life, wanting a place to belong and yet all looking hopelessly in the wrong direction. The denigration of the rock concert, of rock 'n' roll and all that it represented to U2 into some backdrop for conversation and clothes was something to fight against. The cocktail set, for whom rock 'n' roll was just another fashion accessory and who were jaded by its very availability, were to prove a long-standing enemy, inspiring the naked aggression of much of the *War* album three years later.

Bono spelled out his first reaction to England's capital city in the *NME*: 'London is supposed to be permissive. London is supposed to be freedom! London is traps. London is boxes. London is chained in bondage, in fact. And if a band coming from thick Paddy land – and that is not true – comes along and tells these people what's up they might not be awfully pleased.' The home of musical fashion was rarely so comprehensively trashed and these were thoughts that again put numerous influential backs up in the home of the business, leaving many eager for the fall of these upstarts from 'the land of the little people'. Objectively, U2 proved that the truth can hurt – so much 'glamour', so much 'excitement', so much self-congratulation and so little substance. Little wonder that much of the best British music to emerge in the early 1980s came from the provinces, where there was a sharp realism generated by their less affluent, more neglected local economies.

There were contradictions inherent in that put-down, as Adam was especially keen to sample the delights of night-club life in Britain and was often to be found crawling back to his hotel room in the early hours of the following morning rather the worse for wear, often being the missing person if post-gig interviews were required. The resolution of his behaviour with that of the others was a thorny problem and one which led to some discord within the camp. Adam became isolated from the others on the road during the run-up to the making of the *October* album, although loyalty to each other meant that whatever problems there were were kept very firmly behind closed doors, between the band and Paul McGuinness, a staunch ally and sometime companion of Adam's. The crunch argument was that Adam was as committed to the band as anyone, his after-work socializing had no detrimental impact on the music or his performance and he was perfectly entitled to go his own way. For a group that wanted to talk rather than preach, it would be the ultimate hypocrisy to preach to another member of the band. Individuality, the selection of a different path, the introduction of a different agenda was, after all, one of the very things that U2 was all about.

Time was eventually to bridge any gap that might have existed between the four, partly as the others loosened up and partly as Adam was to tone down his extracurricular activities, telling *Hot Press*, 'I thought that I was kind of pushing it a bit . . . ultimately what happened was I became bored with it because it is a fairly trivial world and I got it out of my system,' later observing that the band's spirituality was equal to all following his self-proclaimed 'wilderness years'. Adam's change of pace must have been hastened by a particularly harrowing incident that took place in Dublin on the evening of 2–3 March 1984. Having failed to stop at a Garda checkpoint, Adam was pursued by a Garda on a motorcycle. When he finally stopped the car, he was inevitably questioned as to his failure to stop at the checkpoint, replying that he was a celebrity and couldn't be certain if it was actually the Garda who were trying to stop him, going on to say he hadn't time to stop and talk and that the Garda in question would do himself a lot of harm as he was well-known high up. Adam turned on his car's ignition and refused a request to switch it off. The Garda reached through the window to switch the engine off and Adam drove away dragging him behind the car for forty-five feet. The Garda continued his pursuit to Adam's home, where Adam remained uncooperative, assistance being required to take him to Rathmines Garda Station where a medical certificate proved that he was driving with excess alcohol. Having later apologized to the Garda in question and admitted to being 'distressed and embarrassed by the incident', Adam was fined £125 for that offence and a further £100 for dangerous driving and disqualified for two years. While a subsequent run-in with the law for the possession of cannabis was a little awkward and potentially damaging in terms of obtaining visas for countries such as Japan, it was still mild fare when compared with most rock 'n' roll activity, especially as he was released without a conviction on payment of £25,000 to the Women's Aid Refuge Centre. Adam has more recently confessed that it is the other members of U2 who are now likely to be out at night rather than himself!

In view of the involvement that The Edge, Larry and Bono had with the Christian movement, spirituality plays some part in '11 O'Clock Tick Tock' should the listener choose to look for it. If people were looking for hope in club life, maybe they were looking in the wrong place. They might think they knew what they wanted but '*it was the questions we had wrong*', a line that might equally apply to U2's constant quest for ideas and knowledge, an admission of doubts that were as strong as their faith, or simply a reminder to themselves not to sink into complacency now that they were recording artists. '11 O'Clock Tick Tock' also pointed to some degree of alarm over music's role, an alarm which was to grow in proportion to their own success, the concert ritual replacing the church ceremony, a building filled with people who weren't there because of the band, but out of pure habit and the desire to be seen, blindly accepting the religion of the electric guitar, any electric guitar, without asking why. Apathy and laziness were attitudes which U2 did not appreciate, which is why they tried so hard to involve *all* the members of the audience at any given gig. Even if the reaction was negative, at least it was a reaction.

Perhaps the song was too densely packed to cut through to the singles buying public who, in May 1980, did put an Irish artist at number one, but sadly it was Johnny Logan rather than U2. Hannett's production, while interesting in view of the markedly different sound they achieved on *Boy*, was ultimately a distraction, shifting the record into a similar sphere to that occupied by Joy

Division. The presence of Hannett guaranteed good reviews, the *NME* calling it 'a masterpiece', but there was a realization that the album might work better with another producer at the helm, a transition eased when Hannett was unavailable to record a second single with U2, pleading prior commitments with Joy Division.

The depth of the song and the sentiments it contains tend to obscure the fact that U2 were enjoying their first steps into the record business, that they had a lively sense of humour and were revelling in the contact they were having with their developing fan base, which grew with the release of the single in May 1980, was further swollen with the extensive British tour undertaken in its support, covering fifteen shows in a little over a fortnight, and which was consolidated later in the year by two further tours. Press comment was favourable bordering on the hysterical as with Paulo Hewitt's *Melody Maker* review of the gig at the Clarendon Hotel in London in July: 'The finest display of awe-inspiring rock that I've witnessed in a long time. It contained just about every emotion that rock has ever attempted to evoke, from anger to savagery, beauty and that indefinable essence where words become useless and you realize that you're in the presence of something so special, so precious that you want to hold it.' A little over the top perhaps, but it did capture U2's unique approach to gigs. Their years in Dublin had been spent wisely, learning their stagecraft away from the intense glare of London's music press.

More than that, they had learned and understood the basic principles of rock 'n' roll and valued them highly. Made hungry by their strictly limited access to live music, that which they did have retained the power and possibilities which British bands had lost sight of years ago through over-consumption. U2 were able to re-introduce the passion of performance that had been an integral part of live music years before and which hadn't been seen in ultra-cool London for many a long day and so they were able to touch people with their honesty just as they had in Dublin. Bono was later to say that, wherever you go, people may react differently at first but deep down 'they all sweat the same!' On the few occasions that they were unable to break through the cool reserve U2 foundered as Bono tried new and more desperate gambits to open up a crowd that lived for this moment of superiority. The band refused to surrender, falling on their faces but always ready to get back on their feet for the next audience who, if taken aback at first, perhaps openly shocked by such shameless populism, such self-abnegation, such naked need, were finally won over by the intensity of the music and Bono's glorious egoless egocentricity.

The front man's volatility and sensitivity was naturally the focal point of the live show, the most apparent point of contact between group and crowd, a position which can give rise to all kinds of personal problems. Bill Graham shrewdly observed that 'Christianity may have been a special shield for Bono . . . protected from those identity and ego problems that can upset those singers who find their fame has neither savour nor reason.' Put on the whole armour of God that ye may be able to stand against the wiles of the Devil? Surrender and the giving of oneself were recurrent themes both lyrically and in performance, a seemingly irreconcilable conflict in so many ways with the 'look at me' desperation that was part of the live presentation.

Bono's bag of personal contradictions was of course the key to his acceptance on stage. His own paradoxes, frailties, strengths and weaknesses made him into a very human character rather than the creature from another planet persona cultivated by Bowie, the outrageousness of Guggi and Gavin from the Virgin Prunes or the cool, controlled, calculating figure that was cut by Ian McCulloch of Echo & the Bunnymen. Bono was little different from the audience, volubly inarticulate, gracefully awkward, confidently unsure, a ragbag of neuroses that reminded people of their own vulnerability, a man with whom they could identify.

Having introduced themselves to British audiences, the time had come for U2 to record an album. With Martin Hannett discounted, the producer's chair needed a new incumbent. Avoiding committing themselves to another producer who might not work out, the band and Island agreed that the best course of action would be to record a second single to test out someone else with a view to making the album together, a decision seemingly borne out by the instrumental B-side, 'Things To Make and Do', which was very much a 'sound test'. Steve Lillywhite was selected, having already worked with Siouxsie & The Banshees and Penetration, a favourite band of Bono's. He came to the record fresh from producing one of the most sonically interesting records of the early 1980s, Peter Gabriel's third album, one which had challenged many of the preconceptions that existed around the recording studio. Lillywhite was regarded as an original mind who was very happy to experiment with new sounds and ideas but who was also strong enough to pull everyone together in the studio and to get the best out of them. More importantly after their not altogether successful beginnings with Martin Hannett, Steve Lillywhite was a producer who did not have his own instantly recognizable sound. He didn't push records into a particular corner that he liked but rather he was in the business of helping people make the records that they wanted, enabling them to achieve the sound they heard in their own heads. U2 knew what they wanted *Boy* to sound like. Their problem was with the technical side of operations. In making their second Island single, 'A Day Without Me', Steve Lillywhite proved that he was more than capable of dealing with that.

'A Day Without Me' was a close relative of 'Out of Control', another song that referred to the universal teenage obsession with death, in this case the effects of a suicide on those close to the victim, something which took on a bitter irony coming as it did in the aftermath of the suicide of Ian Curtis, lead singer with Joy Division, in May 1980. The song opened with Bono proclaiming, '*a landslide in my ego*', and proceeded to look at just how easily the world would carry on without him, again a teenage preoccupation with lack of self-worth as the song merely hinted at the minor distress his loss would cause. The sound of the music was the giant leap forward for which they had searched. The guitar called people in to listen with a fuller sound than the earlier records had used, a joyous clarion call backed by a rhythm section that was punchier and more direct. '11 O'Clock Tick Tock' had felt claustrophobic but 'A Day Without Me' was bigger music, a song for the cinema screen rather than the TV. U2's developing vision and understanding of the recording situation had found a natural sympathizer in Steve Lilly-white. All the ingredients were in place as they began work on *Boy*, their debut LP.

chapter four

INNOCENCE

Popular music has always been largely the preserve of the young, a music that generally takes a hold on its listeners in the early teens, and yet it is a form that has rarely covered that period of adolescence with any depth, sensitivity or understanding. There are great legions of 'boy meets girl, boy loses girl' heart-throb songs which appeal to a particular audience and there are songs about childhood memories but it is not often that the awkwardness and anxiety inherent in growing up is intelligently addressed. 'Mature' performers move on to other issues, be it their personal lives, world issues or just plain escapist entertainment, putting what can often be an embarrassing time firmly behind them, or if daring to tackle the subject, doing so in a condescending 'well, I got better' manner. The teeny-boppers meanwhile try to take their audiences away from the worries of acne, broken hearts and growing pains into a fantasy world of glamour and comic book photo-stories that are written 'especially for you'.

Boy was an album that repudiated that trend. Following the dictum 'to thine own self be true,' U2 wrote about what they knew and what concerned them. Having reached recording status at a relatively young age, adolescence was still a very vivid memory. Adam, the oldest of the four, was still only twenty years of age while Larry wouldn't celebrate his nineteenth birthday until just after the release of *Boy*. As a consequence the record was effectively a rites of passage saga dealing with growing up and the journey into the adult world, a thorny subject which could have led to mawkish melodramatics and introverted, nonsensical navel-gazing. Instead it was an exciting, original and thoroughly absorbing examination of a formative time when everything is a life or death issue and desperately real, a time before cynicism has chipped away at a sense of wonder, made by intelligent artists who could still recall the process without feeling awkward about it.

The very act of making a record about growing up, of personal development and change was one filled with potential disasters. It's a time in life regarded with suspicion by the older guard, seen as just a phase to be endured when the child becomes a royal pain in the neck to all and sundry, a period dismissed as filled with petty obsessions, unbalanced judgements, inflated egos and more emergent hormones than could be good for anyone. Against that patronizing attitude it might also be recalled that feelings of all shades are rarely as powerful or as vivid again as they are in adolescence – perhaps it's because they are being experienced for the first time or maybe the physical changes that take place lead to a heightened mental and emotional awareness. Whatever the case, the passions of youth are of an intensity not often equalled in adult life. If artists are involved in the task of translating human experiences into a form where others can empathize with them then there is never again such a rich and varied range of sensations to report upon as there is in childhood. This was a patent truism to U2 since it was all that they had hitherto experienced – 'the atrocious crime of being a young man . . . I shall neither attempt to palliate or deny'.

Innocence became the central phrase when talking about *Boy*, a sense of wonder and development that was quite markedly different from the gloom that most rock and pop music was celebrating at the time, through Joy Division, the Specials or Echo & the Bunnymen, while punk had mutated and left a legacy of bands like Discharge or the 'Oi!' antics of the Cockney Rejects. Those kinds of music were clearly reacting to the politics of the time. Some had taken punk nihilism to its inevitable conclusion and were both advocating and indulging in violence, others were attacking the government and yet more were reflecting the intense gloom that young people in Britain were feeling. If they had felt alienated and at a loss in 1976, the early 1980s was a far worse time to be a young person in Britain. Young people were marching out of schools, colleges and universities and straight into the same dole queue as their parents, thrown out of work by monetarist policies. As unemployment went through the roof, young people had rarely felt so vulnerable or alone – no hope, no prospects, no money, no chance of any freedom. Purely by chance, U2's record caught the mood of confusion, fear and lost innocence that engulfed many whose adolescence had been forcibly extended simply because they didn't have the opportunity to go out into the world. In that sense it was as powerfully political and devastatingly accurate a record as anything released in the UK that year. It would have been absurd for anyone to expect U2 to comment explicitly on the problems of Britain in 1980 since they were from Ireland, a land that had its own social and economic problems, and had only recently spent any time in this country. Where they made a connection was in singing about universal emotions, by writing about the person within rather than the outside world in which they live. Though cynicism was understandable at such a depressing time in Britain, it was not something to which they were party. They stood for 'an emotional positivism' as *Hot Press* described it, a celebration of the individual instead of a requiem for a lost generation, despite their occasionally melancholic tone. That wistful air of melancholy was something peculiar to their Irish upbringing as Fintan O'Toole, a correspondent for the *Irish Times* has remarked: 'Irish culture has been marked . . . by a Catholic fatalism which sees the world as being a veil of tears and which almost likes the idea. We're easy with the ideas of chaos and doom.' U2 worked within chaos and tried to react against that fatalistic air, but there were tones of resignation in some of their songs, a trait which has persisted.

Boy was a highly potent work, its ambiguity allowing people into its world, giving them the chance to draw whatever they wanted from this impressive sound, to make parallels with their own lives. The atmosphere of the record was established particularly power-fully by its sleeve, a simple black and white head-and-shoulders portrait of a young boy. The boy was Peter Rowan, brother of Guggi from the Virgin Prunes, a youngster who had already appeared on the 'U2-3' sleeve in Ireland. The imagery was perfectly clear: this kid was a representative of all this generation that was growing up, going through the same problems and wondering just what the world had got in store. His wide-eyed innocence was what the record was about, a time of mystery, uncertainty, development and explo-ration, a time before the world had tried to knock him into the shape it wanted. Above all, a time before cynicism. How sad and yet inevitable therefore that the cover courted controversy. It was alleged to have overtones or paedophilia or homosexuality and was adjudged sufficiently indecent for it to be replaced in America, an ironic allegory of the harsh cruelty that the outside world would later inflict on the boy. That a gesture of naïvety could be so misconstrued was as powerful a comment as any made in the music. A simple picture of a child was now out of bounds, it could not be taken at face value. Worse yet, went the line of criticism, U2 were deliberately exploiting the boy, who actually knew the band very well, in order to gain publicity and a following in gay clubs!

Dispensing with misanthropic objection, once past the cover all kinds of adolescent expression were housed in the record's grooves, such that any listener with an open mind could take something from it. The line of reasoning was in part described by 'Into The Heart', where the group argued that they could protect themselves from descent into similar misanthropy and the attendant egotistical mal-evolence by reminding themselves of a time when they were children, untouched by the dilemmas of adult life. Even though on 'The Ocean' they were to invoke Wilde's Dorian Gray as part of their refusal to grow old, 'Into The Heart' also recognized that the sanctuary of childlike comprehension was but a temporary respite, a place where they couldn't stay indefinitely.

That recognition played a leading role in the album's two pivotal pieces, 'Shadows And Tall Trees' and 'Twilight'. The title for 'Shadows And Tall Trees' was taken from William Golding's Nobel Prize-winning novel *Lord of the Flies* and looked at the sudden realization that the word is a dark, foreboding place. Bono's plaintive cry for the listener to find *'anything redeeming'* in him was a breathtaking encapsulation of that adolescent moment when the boy/man 'wept for the end of innocence, the darkness of man's heart' from which rises immediate self-loathing as he finds himself part of the machine. It's also interesting to note another example of the links between U2 and the Virgin Prunes. In performance the Virgin Prunes would sometimes employ a pig's head impaled on a stick, the central image of *Lord of the Flies*.

Bono had already spoken of the artistic association between U2 and the Virgin Prunes bearing similarities to the long-standing relationship between David Bowie and Iggy Pop, one rooted in the mainstream, the other in the extreme. Dick Evans, the link between the two groups, felt that some of the connections were accidental, but that some arose from a sense of rivalry. 'There was a lot of that between Gavin and Bono. I think in hindsight Gavin was really rebelling against Bono, maybe out of jealousy because U2 were bigger, although there was a brief stage when the Prunes were actually bigger than U2. Looking back, I think it was an attempt to do something that would be completely unacceptable to the other side until eventually it became the norm.' There were differences of approach too, as Dick recalls: 'U2 were always career oriented whereas the Prunes were more diffuse. Gavin just had the urge to express himself. The most intense gigs were the first few when he was working as a clerk, which he really hated, so the Prunes was real escapism rather than realism. It was great fun, you just started hammering away on the guitar and got lost. You'd have no idea where you were in a song while Gavin was trying to get rid of this frustration or anger. The Prunes started from a different place to U2 but there was some kind of mixing ideas because we were friends.'

'Twilight', which was again attacked as being suggestive of child abuse because of the line *'boy meets man in the shadow'* looked at the same feelings as 'Shadows And Tall Trees' but with greater emphasis on physical growth. It did not seem to occur to 'Worried of Hounslow' that the song actually dealt with the transition into adult life, the boy's changing reflection in the mirror, the fear of the adult responsibilities he's about to have foisted upon him. It was, in common with much of the rest of *Boy*, a song ripe with implication as to the boy's burgeoning sexuality and accompanying curiosity, but not in the way that those critics felt. 'Twilight' was a sensitive piece of personal journalism, a heartfelt evocation of confusing, conflicting thoughts. It conjured up memories of Bono's life on the street corner with the other members of Lypton Village – 'we mocked the adult world and agreed we'd never grow up because all we saw was silliness.' As he and the rest of the band aged physically, they wanted to avoid sinking into the mundanities of life – physical growth was now something to be afraid of rather than the joy it had been in 'Street Mission' – and had to remind themselves that there were other more important things, spiritual growth being one of them.

Boy was released without any fanfare as to the Christian beliefs held by Bono, Larry and The Edge, partly because the band didn't want to discuss their views outside the context of their music and partly because others felt that such a revelation might harm them and reduce their potential audience. Since the lyrics were never obviously connected solely with their faith, it was a subject left alone, only surfacing gradually in the aftermath of *Boy*. Bono had admitted to *Hot Press* that 'I don't want to talk to the world about it because we will face a situation where people will see us with a banner over our heads.' In spite of such refusals, that was ultimately to become one of the best known of the U2 cartoons.

Nevertheless, that search and the faith they had found informed a number of the songs. 'I Will Follow' in particular used very clear cut 'road to Damascus' imagery with '*I was lost, I am found*', the singer having been stuck on the outside of life until he found some reason for his existence, some faith, although again the listener could choose to apply the general idea of the lyric to the strength given by a personal relationship, some choosing to apply the lyric to Bono's bond with his mother. This was the sense of belonging that he felt and that he was perhaps pointing the fashionable set of '11 O'Clock Tick Tock' towards. Bono in particular has often said that he points an accusing finger at no one but himself, but there was certainly an impression around the time of *Boy* that he might be chastising the rest of us, overcome with some kind of evangelical zeal. 'The Ocean' adopted a tone of self-righteousness too, asserting that the lot of the world would improve if only '*they'd listen to what I said*' although that was an implication later denied by Bono, who regarded it as an accurate expression of teenage self-absorption and arrogance.

Lyrically, the songs were thought-provoking and at times intensely moving but they were not short in the musical department either. Larry held the group together very tightly as a unit with some solid drumming that gave Adam the freedom to work out the melodic bass parts to which he was best suited. They were inventive, only occasionally hesitant and the contrasts in their personalities, with Adam's extravagance tempered by Larry's down-to-earth style, provided a stable base from which The Edge could work. Though U2 were very definitely a real group of four people where each had an important role to fulfil, on record The Edge was the fulcrum of the band. Quite simply, he was a singer who didn't sing and so his guitar became his voice which captured atmospheres every bit as eloquently as – and at times even more so than – Bono's words. Some of the songs, like 'I Will Follow', which came out as a single to coincide with the album's release, or 'A Day Without Me', rode in on a surge of adrenalin, a glorious rush of sound that defied the listener to ignore them. 'An Cat Dubh' was introduced with wailing guitar, but there were gentler moments which almost delved into an ambient sound, such as 'The Ocean', which gave the illusion of an Eno production of Fleetwood Mac's 'Albatross', while he also occasionally employed a Byrdsian chime, but reference points were few and far between in a startlingly economic style.

The Edge was an adept exponent of aggressive, acidic guitar, which initially led to U2 being thrown in with the Bunnymen and the Teardrop Explodes as part of some spurious psychedelic guitar revival, but there was the very distinct impression that he was keen to rein that side of his playing in because it was too easy and because it edged U2 towards a clichéd hard-rock sound. A daring creativity was the cornerstone of his musical vision and the impressionistic style he often employed dovetailed neatly with Bono's similarly indirect approach to lyrics. The collaboration with Steve Lillywhite was thoroughly successful, not just in harnessing their talents but in the additional effects that were used. The adventurous touches of sound brought into 'I Will Follow' and 'The Ocean' were seemingly an extension of the experiments which he had been party to on Peter Gabriel's record. The vast sound that had been achieved on pieces like 'Intruder' from that album was also brought to bear on *Boy*, resulting in a huge elemental music that powerfully evoked a sense of awe although at times the whole thing did seem to strain a little too hard, the band too keen to take on epic proportions on almost every song.

There was a very clear definition to *Boy*, a sense of a band from the outside trying to put rock's house in order. If the music did not initially strike you as being Irish, ultimately it did betray their cultural roots, in the choice of language, both verbal and musical. Although there were no overtly traditional Irish musical influences or instrumentation to be discerned on the record, the impressionistic literacy of the songs and the inventive musical imagery, together with the inexhaustible passion of the truly committed, called to mind those Irish writers who had distinguished themselves down the centuries with their originality. This was the music of a country that had nurtured Joyce and Yeats, that had inspired the fractured narratives of Beckett although, perhaps more accurately, Irish writer John Waters deemed their frame of reference to be more widely Celtic than specifically Irish. More than just a vocabulary which was very distinctly their own, there was a clear mission to involve listeners, to embrace them and to communicate with them, the logical studio-based version of their live performances, but temperamentally something suited to their forebears and the traditions of Irish folk music. Like those singers and songwriters before them, U2 had a story to tell and an absolute passion with which to tell it, a desire which was their very life force. U2 were later to justify *Rattle and Hum* as a project which let them get to the roots of their music and to proclaim that they had no working knowledge of Irish music or its history. Academically that may have been the case but instinctively they were Irish musicians making Irish music. The tools and external influences of the late twentieth century were the only real difference. Take away the electricity and play the songs acoustically and at their heart lay stories that were not far removed from folk-song fare.

The critical reaction to *Boy* was expansive and favourable, with reviewers plugging into its optimism, its ebullience and its undeniable fresh-faced excitement with the world. Much was made of the frailty and vulnerability which was exposed in Bono's vocals, yet this was as much a function of his anxiety during recording as any deliberate affectation. Had Bono achieved the powerful self-possessed growl which now demands attention and which is occasionally accused of having a hollow grandeur or wallowing in bombast, the brickbats they now receive might have been directed at *Boy*. Some of the sentiments it contained were presented in self-assured, self-confident style and it remains perhaps their most egotistical album in many respects, deliberately so to the extent to which it intends to capture adolescent obsession. Even so, some of the 'look at me' sensibility from the stage show was prevalent in the music and if they had already come to realize that they couldn't change the world, there was little sign of that resignation here. This was the sound of a group that thought it could take on all comers, Bono saying, 'if people come along expecting the world from U2 then they're gonna get it. I'm not scared we won't be able to give it to them.' These were not the words of a man worried about the group's potential.

Boy was sensitive, passionate, innocent, evocative and atmospheric but it was also ambitious and not just in the artistic sense. It was an early snapshot of a band who had high hopes for their music and whose tone suggested an agenda different to that normally held by rock 'n' rollers. They seemed to be a group who knew exactly where they wanted to go, why and what they wanted to do when they got there. Bono spoke of the group at the time as 'a long-term project' and it was very clear that they were hoping to achieve much with their music. There was a greater sense of certainty and assurance about *Boy* than there was about *Rattle and Hum*, which was castigated for its pomposity and bluster but which was in fact, for all its faults, a record of naked doubt far more than one of achievement. With *Boy*, that doubt was less evident in the songs but far more obvious in Bono's exposed voice, which, along with the sparse playing, saved the record from press attack.

Boy was an excellent first blast from a band that obviously had many more shots in its locker and one which deserved the superlatives that were heaped upon it. The one nagging question that existed was 'What will they write about next?' Having written an album that had been built around adolescence, one which was almost a retrospective of the best of U2 to date, it was clear that the following album would have to be about other things. With the strength of youthful feeling behind them, would they be able to come up with similarly moving music on other matters within a year? The biggest hint that they would came from the penultimate track on *Boy*, an aggressive, deeply arresting piece called 'The Electric Co.', which was again translated onto record from personal experience with such effect that it was plain U2 were awake to the world around them and could themselves be sufficiently moved by external events to convert them into musical statements. 'The Electric Co.' was based upon the treatment meted out to a friend in a hospital after he had professed the belief that he was Jesus Christ. Admitted for psychiatric treatment, he was regularly subjected to bursts of ECT (electroconvulsive therapy), which consisted of passing an electric current through his brain to induce convulsions, a kind of shock treatment to rid the patient of his depression or delusions. Bono was to complain in *Hot Press* that 'the doctors can sometimes produce an effect but they don't know the cause. ECT, it's nothing more than witchcraft.' The friend did attempt to escape from the hospital, claiming sanctuary in its chapel before ultimately trying to take his own life with an electric saw.

That someone who was supposedly being returned to 'normality' by the use of electricity should choose to make an attempt on his own life using the same force is a hugely disturbing image and opens up a whole bag of questions on the propriety of using such extreme treatments and the negative effects they may have. Does the strength of current become such a driving force in the patient's life that it becomes all-enveloping, connecting with every emotion that remains? For an electric rock 'n' roll group, the idea that the energy source which made their shows and records possible could also be used in such seemingly barbaric circumstances was such a powerful contradiction that it demanded a response. On its own the lyric was vague, but when allied to The Edge's jagged guitar lines which conjured up the bursts of electricity, the song was a clear indictment of experimenting with people's lives. U2 nailed their colours firmly to the mast which opposed human experimentation, the reduction of people to the status of medical guinea pigs.

'The Electric Co.' was to become a major set piece in concert with Bono reacting as the patient, The Edge's guitar the shock of electricity. That concert treadmill began in earnest following the release of *Boy*, with U2 returning to the UK to reinforce the great strides they had made on their previous tours earlier in the year, having also made their first appearances in mainland Europe. Once more there was little doubt that, if U2 were becoming a more interesting act on record, live they were without peers. America was the next obvious port of call and they flew into the country for a brief visit in December with Bono's parting shot, 'they're gonna want us in the US.' Signs were already favourable with Warners impressed with initial encouraging reports from Island Records. Most crucial of all, Paul McGuinness had signed an agency deal with Frank Barsalona of Premier Talent, probably the most influential booking agent in America and one who could number among past and present clients Led Zeppelin, Jimi Hendrix, the Who and Bruce Springsteen. Barsalona had taken on U2 sight unseen purely on the recommendation of Chris Blackwell, who finally caught U2 live in London in the summer of 1980 and who had been suitably impressed. As long as U2 could deliver the goods, America was ready for them.

chapter five

AMERICA

Loss had surrounded the development of U2, whether it was in the deeply personal ones that Larry and Bono had suffered, or the deaths of fellow musicians with whom there was some empathy. Bob Marley their label-mate had been diagnosed as having cancer and would die the following year while Ian Curtis, with whom they had shared a producer, had already committed suicide. As U2 started their opening salvo on America soil, the biggest artistic loss took place on 8 December in New York City, three days before U2 were due to play the Mudd Club there. John Lennon was gunned down while signing an autograph for a crazed fan, who was arrested moments later by police who found him calmly reading J. D. Salinger's *The Catcher in the Rye* and who was later to testify that he was the Holden Caulfield, the novel's principal protagonist, of his generation. It was indeed ironic that Lennon, one of the men and musicians most admired by U2, was murdered by a man who allegedly committed the crime to increase the readership of a book that was regularly mentioned in the reviews for *Boy* as being similarly melancholic and stubborn in its refusal to face up to growing old and its rejection of 'phonies'.

From the historian's point of view, it was oddly appropriate that Lennon, a man whose songs shaped rock 'n' roll and whose brutal honesty and insight would illuminate the medium and inspire legions of future songwriters, should leave the scene just as a new group who also believed in honesty, in originality, in rock 'n' roll and in people were heading into town and that that group should ultimately accomplish artistic and commercial success along with a cultural acceptance that was comparable only with the Beatles. It makes a nice line and makes you wonder just exactly what the Hype were doing in Memphis on 16 August 1977, but actually it wasn't until 1988 with *Rattle and Hum* that U2 were alleged to have taken on the mantle of all rock's greatest figures. The scenes that greeted U2 in the USA couldn't have been further removed from those which met the Fab Four in 1964. U2mania had not broken out, although they were already building a solid fan base, particularly through college radio which was instrumental in boosting 'alternative' music that got little attention on more mainstream, commercially based channels.

It's instructive to recall that U2 were just one of a number of bands from Europe that were looking to take America by storm. Joy Division had obviously dropped out of the running with the death of Curtis but Echo & the Bunnymen were widely touted as the kind of band that could make great inroads and, indeed, their 'Rescue' single tended to be more popular, at least initially, with the radio audience than any of U2's material. The Teardrop Explodes were similar alternative radio staples and in subsequent years New Order, Depeche Mode and Siouxsie & The Banshees among many others were pushed forward as the next big thing from Europe. Of these, only U2 really made the breakthrough across the country and became stadium-fillers when, if anyone had seemed most likely to at the tail end of 1980, it was the Bunnymen.

There were a number of factors at work in the first instance when U2 made their initial impact on American audiences, a foundation on which they were to build in the following years when a great deal of their music was based on American experience and American song forms. Just as they had carefully planned their assault on the UK, just as they had specific strengths which would catch the UK market, so the US campaign was based on certain obvious advantages which U2 had over their contemporaries. U2 had already proved themselves to be a superb live band in Ireland, where they swept the board in the *Hot Press* poll, and in Europe, but there were many other good live bands that didn't make the transition. The all-important difference in American terms was attitude; the much hoped-for British invasion of the early 1980s failed to materialize simply because the bands concerned weren't hungry enough and felt that American audiences weren't worthy of their attentions. British bands who grew up to perform with reserved cool, emotions kept well in check, feigning or feeling no interest in their crowd – who knew enough of the requirements of British rock to reciprocate – didn't often take kindly to the more raucous behaviour of American crowds who were effusive, enthusiastic and obviously out for a good time. English bands and audiences were far more insular. A band could completely alienate its fans by spending time in the States, while for the artists themselves, the ultimate ambition seemed to be a headliner at Hammersmith Odeon, maybe eventually moving up to Wembley Arena, although even that was seen as a politically incorrect move. To go beyond Hammersmith was to join the cabaret circuit and ideally you should continue to play the Lyceum in London or Glasgow's Barrowlands.

Echo & the Bunnymen had produced an equally stunning debut album with *Crocodiles* and were to continue to make some of the most inspirational records of the 1980s until they lost the plot on 1987's *Echo & the Bunnymen*, above and beyond which they were a tremendously powerful and atmospheric live act, adept at creating very strong moods with their music. In Ian McCulloch they possessed an enigmatic front man ideal for European audiences, who loved his portrayal of a man slightly smudged by alcoholic indulgence, a Liverpudlian cocktail comprising two parts Jim Morrison to one Jacques Brel. His one-liners were always potent and he and the band could regularly hold home audiences spellbound. American crowds were less tolerant of these Bohemian leanings, were often unable to understand his Scouse drawl and were confounded by concerts that opened with taped Gregorian chants. That McCulloch never chose to endear himself to an audience scarcely helped. In Britain where his reputation was safe, he could survive bad-mouthing Manchester at its own Free Trade Hall, but the same sort of reaction to American clubs and people did not work. Echo & the Bunnymen remained resolutely European, although not in the affected and effete English style that has brought Morrissey such success, and were unable or unwilling to make the compromises that America would demand.

The Bunnymen had charged to success in Europe, helped in no small part by McCulloch's regularly outrageous press comments. 'Mac the Mouth' was easily quotable, describing U2 at one stage as music for plumbers and bricklayers, also commenting that although John Lennon had compared himself to Jesus Christ 'that wasn't quite the same as saying better' and this very definitely eased their path as newspapers queued up to give them maximum coverage. Bono was an equally entertaining interviewee, though rarely in the same manner, and press coverage was less important to a band that wanted to play live above all else – that was the only way they felt that people would be able to fully comprehend what U2 were all about. In America, the press played a far smaller part in breaking bands with national magazines like *Rolling Stone* giving space only to the biggest names, not struggling newcomers from across the water. Playing live was the best, possibly the only, way of creating your own audience and in that department, U2 were best suited to the challenge, while other British bands were more attentive to their home crowds. In 1984 for instance, the Bunnymen devoted a couple of months to the UK, playing multiple shows in small theatres, while U2, reflecting the worldwide stage on which they wanted to play, gave less than a dozen concerts there.

'U2 Live In America' came by way of a two-pronged attack. Having opened up with the brief pre-Christmas visit, they returned to the 'Land of the Free' in March 1981 after spending the first couple of months of the new year on the road in Europe, not leaving until June, whereupon they played a few more UK dates for good measure. The heavy workload that U2 took on was very firm evidence of their commitment to making their records a success, a rare piece of honesty that could, and to an extent did, blow their credibility. To the pundits, this was U2 falling over, ignoring their real fans at home (a bit rich since home was Dublin, not London) to go in search of dollars. While others sneered at their blatant desire to be big and successful, U2 viewed it as a challenge to them personally and to their music. The music was about reaching people, the sharing of common experience, the celebration of rock 'n' roll's liberating power, the sanctity of the individual. That truly joyous climax was not something that could be achieved if only 250 people were listening to your record. *If* rock 'n' roll could change anything, it could do so only by communicating to as wide a group of people as possible. It was also time that a group chose to stare down the old clichés of success, the Faustian pact and of sex & drugs & rock 'n' roll, clichés that had almost become absolute truisms in the 1970s. Punk might have attempted to scrawl a line in the sand that was to mark a new beginning, one which cut adrift all the old excesses, but it had then replaced them with its own failings, the sacred refusal to accept success. Surely groups could make it big without losing their ideals, without blanding out, without selling their souls to the record company, ideals could have a place in rock music and did not have to be pushed to one side as soon as they began to interfere. For U2 as four individuals, it was a challenge to win that success and then live with it, use it to break down borders within music, subvert the machinations of the record industry and, in the process, get some real songs onto the radio alongside the traditional diet of sanitized disco music.

If U2 were the ideal band to break on the basis of live work, a band that didn't need to be pushed on stage but one that jumped at every opportunity to play its music, they needed solid backing. Their crew had slowly been built, mainly from in and around Dublin, to a point where they were surrounded by trusted allies who could be relied on to do a thoroughly professional job, while their manager was intelligent and quick to learn. They were all young men more than capable to standing up to the physical strain that three months spent criss-crossing America in a van would place them under and sufficiently excited by the opportunities afforded to them to keep going, but the strain was reduced by having Premier Talent on their side, who made sure that U2 played the right venues at the right time in a sensible sequence based on a sane, logical itinerary. The knowledge that they were travelling according to a well-planned strategy certainly helped smooth out the wrinkles that could creep in during a long and arduous tour, a worry further diminished by the very fact that they relished the prospect of travelling, experiencing new places and people, learning from them, much as they had when they visited London for the first time and found it working its way into songs like '11 O'Clock Tick Tock'. 'To tour is to live as far as I'm concerned. I want to improve my education, my way of life,' Bono told Radio Forth in 1981.

U2 were faster than most to realize that American radio would only play them when it had to and that they would have to reach their constituency via the road. Americans had become particularly cynical with British bands heading over, playing for a few weeks, at most a month, before heading home. Bono was quick to make the distinction between U2 and the others, regularly telling audiences between numbers that U2 were an Irish band, that they were in the USA because they wanted to be, that they weren't forced to come by the record company and that they were there for three months to cover the country adequately and to meet the people. Where their contemporaries had been content with ringing the doorbell and running away, U2 were going to hammer on the door until it collapsed. They gained respect purely for that, people repaying U2's efforts by listening with an open mind. It was clearly not a front. U2 were openly enthusiastic about being on American soil and found that the people's response was rewarding.

The lack of cynicism in their live performance was essential and won great favour. In part, it was a tribute to the fact that they had not grown up within the confines of the British music scene and its inbuilt prejudices against the 'new world'. That U2 were less aware of and so less impeded by this background was to their advantage, even more so was the fact that they were a group from Ireland. The Irish people have a long-standing relationship with the United States that dates back into the last century when many emigrated there to try and make a worthwhile living, a better life than they felt would be available to them in their homeland. Irish people have come to recognize the USA not as a colossal power in the world, one that ruthlessly competes with them for world economic markets, but as a refuge from poverty and a place where your individual lot can be improved with luck and hard work, an Irish translation of the American dream. Through the potato famine of the 1840s, when people were literally starving at home, right through to the economic deprivation of the current era, America has been something of a promised land to the Irish, even paving a way to religious freedom or greater physical security for those beaten down by the Troubles.

Emigration has been a very real part of the Irish way of life for many years. It was the main cause of a halving in population from 8 million in 1846 to just 4.5 million in 1901 and, even after independence was gained in the south, it continued to drain the population. The UK and the USA have been the most popular destinations with the very strong Irish communities there making great contributions to their new countries. Bono is particularly fond of telling people that it was the Irish who built New York for instance. Therefore when U2 went to the States, they already had a considerable following among Irish 'exiles' who had heard about this rock 'n' roll band that, of all things, came from Dublin. Word of mouth certainly assisted U2 in winning reasonable crowds for themselves wherever they went, which was the only break they needed. By the same token, U2 didn't have any prejudices against the Americans and consequently refused to patronize them or their way of life since people from their own communities had been going out to live there for years. They knew about America and they wanted to know more about this land that was now home to so many of their countrymen.

Having got people to the gigs, U2 were able to cut across to a new audience, since Bono in particular refused to acknowledge any gulf between stage and crowd. Their most potent calling card in America, the one which initially gripped curious audiences who knew little or nothing about them, was their faith in rock 'n' roll as a medium of unparalleled power within popular culture. Though at times their music might express darkness, they were ultimately an uplifting band, something which caught the American imagination. *Boy*, obviously the staple of their live set, was a record of anger and pain, but it was also filled with love and with passion, the juxtaposition of these opposites giving the songs a fuller, more rounded definition which some Americans took to rather more quickly than had the British. Where contemporary British invaders carried gloom and despondency as their musical watchwords, U2 were not afraid of adding light to the darkness, accentuating both, making their songs a tangible reality with that more acute world view.

An extension of that positive philosophy came in the music itself. U2's playing was generally harder and more abrasive than much of the competition and, while a very original mix, there were echoes of other forms still playing about the perimeters of some songs, their hard-rock origins still occasionally floating to the surface. This gave audiences a reference point and U2 very definitely made the most of the opportunity, smoothing off some of the rougher edges and shaving away some of the subtlety of the recorded versions. Though this was a compromise of sorts, it was one worth making in view of the mountains they had to move in order to get their records played on radio stations, from where people could discover the other facets of the U2 personality in their own time. To get across to a first time audience, the statements had to be big and bold.

The Christian values that were tentatively on show in some of U2's music were again a little more attuned to an American sensibility than a British one. While UK rock fans tended towards agnosticism, or were at least wary of musicians who claimed overt allegiance to any faith, having long memories which helped them recall the Indian dabblings of the Beatles and the Stones in the 1960s, their American counterparts had grown up in an atmosphere where religion and faith were more common everyday subjects. Certainly they were currencies that had been abused and debased with fake evangelists demanding money and new religions springing up every day, but it was also a more openly discussed issue, one that was neither unknown nor embarrassing and one that was tolerated as a part of rock 'n' roll more so than in other parts of the world. By contrast, Britain, in its so far limited criticism of U2, had shrugged them off as post-pubescent Bible-bashers or used the condescending angle that they were merely troubled youngsters struggling through a phase of development from which they would eventually recover.

U2 played a canny promotional game, far more so than other potential 'invaders'. Just as they had ensured that everyone at CBS

Ireland was behind their first single by meeting everyone personally, U2 surrendered much of their free time in making themselves available to meet and greet any number of record company executives, radio DJs or other local worthies, interested to meet anyone who could have some bearing on the ultimate success of their American adventure and fully cognizant of just how much good they were doing themselves with their infectious enthusiasm. In return they got the full cooperation of the Warners staff, an organization committed to the success of U2 in America and pleased to have a new rock band with whom they could work, something which they weren't used to, having found many British bands surly and awkward. U2 were smart enough to make this marketing compromise to ensure that there was never any need to compromise the music, a lesson learned perhaps from the failure of the Boomtown Rats – Geldof, tiring of the endless round of handshaking and the pretence of enthusiasm, got a San Diego crowd to vent their anger on a collection of radio programmers who were seated in the stalls, trying to make up their minds on whether or not to play any of the Rats' music. Their records were instantly taken off whatever stations were playing them and their American career was virtually over. Bono did not intend to make the same mistake.

As U2 were trying to win fans and radio stations over to their camp, they were fortunate in hitting America at a time when radio formatting was beginning to open up. Punk and the new wave had generally been given short shrift in the States and the formulaic rock of the 1970s still held sway. The new wave was just starting to gain a tentative foothold as U2 arrived. The middle-of-the-road bastions such as Journey or Boston were being edged aside and there was an opportunity for 'alternative' music to be heard. Even so, getting that 'heavy rotation' slot was a very difficult hurdle to overcome, but again U2 had the right people in their corner. Warners were happy with *Boy* and felt that it was an album they could promote successfully and so awarded it a high priority across the nation, which took a lot of the strain from U2 and McGuinness, certain as they were in the knowledge that records would be available wherever they played, that the radio stations were being lobbied and that the Artie Fufkins were doing their jobs properly. That assurance provided the band with the freedom to play at their best, unhampered by other considerations.

U2 were able to benefit from this loosening up in radio policy and were able to force some stations to play them by virtue of the response they won at many live shows and their music, though very definitely a European style, had echoes of America within it. The anthemic quality of songs such as 'I Will Follow' did strike a chord even if these were at times misunderstood, which was to create serious problems for the band a couple of years later. For fans of 'alternative' music, there was something reminiscent of Bruce Springsteen in U2, just in terms of their attitude as much as musically, Springsteen not yet having became an AOR staple in the USA. It was ironic that U2's perceived link with the Boss did them some good, since the Boomtown Rats had suffered a few years earlier when 'Rat Trap' was dismissed as a Springsteen rip-off, although again, Geldof didn't help his cause by telling the Amerian press that Springsteen had ripped off Van Morrison in the first place. By 1981, however, a nod of approval from Bruce was the rock 'n' roll equivalent of a papal blessing and it added to the swelling number of people who were sitting up and taking notice of U2.

In years to come, U2's involvement, however slight, in the vanguard of the changes in American radio formatting would stand them in good stead. In 1981 they were one of the bands who provided disenchanted listeners with a focal point to rally behind. Bono admitted during the tour that 'it's a battle . . . We're over here knocking on doors hard and, if you have to come back a second time, a third time, a fourth time, a fifth time, those radio stations will fall, because when they come down and see a huge place basically sold out and there's been no radio play, they start thinking, "what is this?"' Fans, who as usual were way ahead of programmers, were able to overwhelm a station with requests for the new U2 record which would get them on the radio then start the ball rolling for other records by the group and then for similar groups who were away from the mainstream.

To say that there was a revolution in American radio would be a gross overstatement – now as then the stations are conservative purely because they depend on advertising revenue to keep going and naturally advertisers demand high audiences. Bands like U2 were able to open things up and that's one of the reasons why it was so vitally important that a band of their ilk cracked America as it's only by invading the mainstream and offering the alternative of real rock 'n' roll to a mass audience that any major change can be achieved. The success of U2 is directly responsible for other record labels taking chances on those artists who are currently being given some time to develop, like Jesus Jones, Ride or Lush, and to open up

America for home-grown groups like the late lamented Jane's Addiction or the Red Hot Chili Peppers. For alternatives to survive in these financially straitened times, some of them have to subvert the course of the mainstream. U2 did break the door down in the early 1980s and, as a result, have since received excellent media backing from people who might previously have been regarded as mavericks.

If you've won the first battle and are actually getting people to pay some attention, it would still all be to no avail without the music – remember Sigue Sigue Sputnik? Neither does anyone else. Fortunately, *Boy* was a record well suited to the America of 1981. As spokesman for the group, Bono was to talk very positively about the Americans he met on tour: 'I think in many ways Americans are innocent and more honest than us. They're very wide-eyed, it seems, but they make up their minds by instinct and I think that's very healthy.' Those were traits that *Boy* had espoused particularly strongly and its thematic continuity, its naïvety were aspects that appealed to an American audience, whose instinctive nature could only help U2. If U2 were having a bad night, the spark was still there. You might leave the show thinking they were a bit raw or rough-and-ready, but you could definitely see that there was something special about them, that when all the elements *did* fall into place they could take anywhere by storm. In Britain, audiences might try to intellectualize over U2's appeal and come up with very little except the endearing quality that four Irishmen chipping away at the darkness possessed, but, if you were prepared to take a U2 show or record on a gut level there was little else that was comparable to them currently on show in rock 'n' roll.

U2 benefited from reaching America as its radio network was improving, but they hit the country at a time when national confidence was at a low ebb and the people in turmoil. Conflicting emotions were at work in a country that had traditionally seen itself as the upholder of freedom, a land of opportunity and yet one which had a less than inspirational record over the preceding twenty-five years or so. While there was economic prosperity for some, there was poverty for many. The predominantly white middle-classes may have been free, but the predominantly black under-classes were kept under control by heavy-handed policing and the pernicious influence of drugs, allegedly flowing freely on the streets care of certain law enforcement agencies who used them as a tool to suppress any radicalism. If you were free to be a right-wing extremist and burn crosses on your lawn, there was a time when you could be jailed for being a Communist, and current society would still ostracize you. While some could afford a nice big house and two cars there were plenty who huddled together in cardboard boxes.

America entered the 1980s as a land bathed in guilt and soaked in blood. The young black leader Martin Luther King, a man of vision and integrity who hoped to lead his people to real freedom in the land of the free, had been gunned down in America. The young President Kennedy, who had promised to build a better, kinder country, had been gunned down in America. His brother, the Attorney-General and prospective President, who had pledged himself to the fight against organized crime, had been gunned down in America. While these strong, intelligent men who had the power, the will and the authority to bring about real change, were killed by America – a country which in a rock 'n' roll context also killed Elvis Presley, Jim Morrison, Janis Joplin and John Lennon – America involved itself in Vietnam, America sneered at the civil rights movement and America elected Richard Nixon as President who was then forced to resign on threat of impeachment after the greatest political scandal in its history. In an attempt to atone for its sins, America elected Jimmy Carter as President and then watched him struggle helplessly with the Iranian leadership as American citizens were held hostage by the Ayatollah Khomeini while their countrymen went to the polls. America had lost its self-esteem, its pride, its place. Post-Vietnam, post-Watergate, post-Iran, idealism was out – America wanted a strong leader who could kick some ass and so in November 1980 it elected Ronald Reagan, an actor who played this latest part to the full. America had never been more dangerous, a huge powerful military force looking for a military action it could win.

Reagan had re-introduced a gung-ho sensibility to the nation. He spoke eloquently and forcefully about re-establishing America at the forefront of the world stage, of economic growth, of the freedom to make money if you had the ability, of monetarist policy, of arming America to thwart the Soviet threat, of Star Wars missiles, of an exciting America that would lead the world in technology and of which people could be proud. If few of his policies bore any close scrutiny, his presentation was faultless and huge chunks of the population fell under his spell – this bumbling grandfather figure was somewhat comforting and the fact that he was larger than life, a hero of sorts come down from the silver screen to work for the good of the ordinary people, was a sure-fire winner. Ronald Reagan stood for the inalienable right of every American to be a reactionary, to revel in conservatism, to live in the fondly remembered world portrayed by Norman Rockwell and by Hollywood, a world which never actually existed. As Garry Wills wrote in *Reagan's America*, 'We are allowed to dream the wildest things, so long as we do not *think* anything new.' Ronald Reagan was the holder of what he saw as the sacred American truth, one that was never publicly articulated but which was true all the same – every man for himself. Wills again: 'For Reagan, economic motives are justifiable for the individual – people can "better themselves" by their own effort . . . but for a group to act from economic motives is somehow sordid and unworthy.'

Driven by this belief, he was able to present any acts that were concerned with the welfare of those worst off in society, such as the 'Just Say No' campaign organized by his wife, itself a ludicrously ill-thought-out crusade against inner-city drug abuse by people who had nothing else to live for, and so had nothing else to which they could say 'yes', as acts of supreme altruism, winning greater esteem for himself as well as winning the freedom for his administration to ignore social problems. Economic and social matters were not for the group to grapple with, but the individual. The unemployed should create jobs for themselves, the homeless build their own shelters or be protected by the good people of the community. These were not concerns of the Establishment, could not be catered for by group action. Reagan the altruist became the cavalry of the movies, riding in at the last minute to save the day, except the reality was of a few choice photo-opportunities and an obsession with the weapons of war. He was able to become all things to all people, he was a virgin canvas on which you could paint your own America.

There is another America, the America that U2 spoke of, the one that U2 saw attending their shows. This America was to be the basis of their success, the America that wanted to use its wealth in better ways than building bombs, that knew that nuclear missiles did not keep the peace, that held onto its moral values and refused to cheapen them, that did want to think new things, to dream new dreams, that did not want to live in some supposed golden age preserved in aspic around 1936.

But as the tide of Reaganmania swept over America, opposition fragmented to the point where Reagan was allowed to win the political argument and set the economic agenda almost unchallenged. Among younger people, those threatened and alienated by this turn to the right, there were differing reactions – some washed their hands of the debate and threw themselves headlong into their own careers, out-Reaganing Reagan in their drive for wealth at all costs, while others tried to keep alive ideals and hopes. In the 1960s, rock 'n' roll music had been an incredibly potent tool in that struggle but by 1981 rebellious rock had put on a suit and gone to the office, cleaned up its act and busily brown-nosed the taxman for any additional write-offs it might win – the 1970s yippies had become the 1980s yuppies. Idealistic acts like U2 were few and far between but, as in Britain, they were the right act for the time. Their openness, their questioning, their ability to get back up when they fell down were attitudes that were pertinent to those Americans who felt insecure and uncertain at their nation's declaration of war on the sick, the needy. The sense of community that a band such as U2 could inspire ensured that the overlooked need not feel quite so alone. If there was no political manifesto or alignment evident in the music, there was a very clear statement of understanding and sympathy in the music they played and how they played it. U2's idea of a revolution would begin with the individual, the individual who would recognize a responsibility to the group, not with the dogmatic slogan.

With a significant following behind them, U2 left America to make their eagerly awaited second LP. There was plenty of advice from critics and fans alike as to the tenor they should take, with many hoping that the direction that the world was taking would be central to the music. U2 were to confound people again with the music that made up *October* when it was released in the autumn of 1981.

chapter six

DEFIANCE

The cult of global fame is a particularly twentieth-century phenomenon, one made possible by the communications revolution but one
that is at times difficult to comprehend. The public and the media
confer the state of celebrity on a number of chosen people, be it
because they are talented, outspoken or simply because they're
strikingly attractive. How many people are there around today that
are instantly recognizable, absurdly famous and yet who don't
actually do anything particularly astonishing? What exactly have the
supermodels done other than observe strict diets?

Beyond those famous for being famous we have the category of
people whose fame has overwhelmed whatever it was that they did
in the first place. With some it is engineered that way – Madonna
for instance – while others such as Elvis Presley are overtaken by the
speed of events.

In terms of popular entertainment, a select minority are accorded
the label 'god' or 'goddess' – Marilyn Monroe was a legendary
screen goddess, Jim Morrison a rock god, words picked at random,
used thoughtlessly. Nevertheless, the fact that we use the word god
or goddess is particularly enlightening, a confession that however
much we might scorn the ancient civilizations and their superstitions
and peculiar rituals, we are no more sophisticated ourselves.

In the realms of rock 'n' roll, some of the greatest artists have
been transformed into theme parks. We live out our wildest dreams
vicariously through their actions. In observing Jim Morrison fulfilling his Dionysian desires, we who are imprisoned by the economic
realities of ordinary life get the chance to experience, second-hand
admittedly, the excitement of having the world at our feet. If they
then throw it all away and die, even better. They become immortal
and in return also allow us a sense of superiority. 'Look at Morrison,
the world at his feet and he pissed it all away. What a mug.'

Morrison is an especially intriguing figure in the whole fame/

content equation. 'The ceremony is about to begin' is a supremely picturesque view of just what the rock concert had become and what it has generally remained. Gigs, particularly at the upper end of the scale, become mass religious experiences – you can really start to question the direction events have taken when the press begin to compare the attendances at U2 concerts in Dublin with the crowd that the Pope reached there. The concept of hero worship has become just that, an act of worship with the band on the high altar before its congregation, eager for words of wisdom. Ultimately there is the delicious possibility of the final sacrifice, the cod-crucifixion as the star is destroyed by the stardom we bestowed upon him, drink and drugs taking him away, allowing us to play God for a moment, resurrecting him at will thanks to the wonders of digital technology.

The superstar deal works like this: we've given them all this money to live life to the full on our behalf, the least they could do is enjoy the bloody stuff and perpetuate our fantasies. Woe betide anyone who fails to live up to the dream – instant disqualification via the wrath of a whole society and a public who don't want your records/films/posters any more. Unless you're suitably penitent later, at which point the resurrection shuffle goes into overdrive and you too can hit the same nostalgia circuit as Eric Clapton where fans can beam down indulgently on someone who eventually sorted out his priorities. After all, the most celebrated piece of rock graffiti did once read 'Eric Clapton is God.'

When Lennon made his controversial remarks about Christianity and the Beatles in 1966 there was outrage, but his words bear scrutiny. 'We're more popular than Jesus now', later adding that 'we meant more to kids than Jesus did.' Substitute someone like Michael Jackson, or maybe Sonic the Hedgehog, for the Beatles and the sentiments might well stand today. In our alleged sophistication, in an age where we supposedly know all there is to know, in a time where there is no room for mystery, for the unknowable, there is also no room for faith in anything other than the holy trinity of sex & drugs & rock 'n' roll. With pop stars supplanting any of our religious symbols in the group mind, we are rarely at home with any substantial spiritual implications in our popular music, the few occasions when it does raise its head (see under Christmas Number Ones) generally being cause for serious squirming in the seat. Even Bob Dylan, the poet laureate, the sage of rock 'n' roll became the onion of rock 'n' roll with his Christian conversion and the series of unconvincing tosh that followed in its immediate wake, while Van

Morrison is perhaps the only writer to have consistently invoked religious spirituality and been accepted for doing so.

Religion and spirituality do not great records make or so the story goes. The incongruity of our gods – who we have appointed so that our will be done – talking about a higher power that we don't understand is all too much to take and so if there is any dabbling in that field, it's belittled, laughed at or ignored. Much better to take an interest in Madonna, a name which in itself is a brilliantly startling corruption of the great symbol of the Catholic church. That she should have become *the* female icon of our times is a bewildering irony that speaks volumes. That Madonna's book *Sex* should be such a runaway best-seller neatly encapsulates the high value (approximately £25) we place on physical gratification at the expense of mental and spiritual stimulation, forming part of the 'sex sells and everyone's buying' market economy. And if Madonna ends up looking like an extra from a skinflick, then she does us the ultimate service of illustrating the whole dehumanizing aspect of the sex trade. Who has a more powerful personality than Madonna among the celebrated? If she can become another faceless piece of ass for sale, doesn't that say something?

The 1980s merely served to harden those attitudes but they were very definitely at play in 1981. Rock music was supposed to be hedonistic or nihilistic, to play out the life of the self-proclaimed god and some-time Caligula, but without his self-restraint, and was required to stay in its particular ghetto. Only very well-established performers would be tolerated if they chose to move slightly beyond the perimeter fencing. New groups were certainly well advised to trundle down familiar pathways, especially if they were only just winning an audience and about to release a second LP.

By the release of *October*, *Boy* had been selling relatively steadily in both Europe and the USA, U2 were becoming a 'must see' live act and if a few critics were beginning to carp that the road had rid them of their subtleties and that they were teetering on the brink of rockism, they were very much in the minority. After they had recorded and finished their debut LP in August 1980, there had been barely a break in their schedule with gigs taking priority over all else, which was the way they had wanted it. U2 were very clearly a band in the ascendancy, one who, to the outside world at least, were on the brink of major league success with all the delights that had to offer – fame, money, girls, drink, drugs, in fact everything for which a rock band could hope, something borne out by the success of their latest single 'Fire', recorded in Nassau in preparation for the second LP, and which reached number thirty-five in the UK charts. It was therefore perplexing to a great many when U2 delivered a second album that was riddled with doubt, one of spiritual questioning along with a degree of evangelical proselytizing, but most of all one which seemed to ask whether being in a rock 'n' roll band was the best thing for them to do with their time and talents.

The Christianity question had increasingly raised its head as U2 made their way across the western world in support of *Boy*, to a point where the band and, as its spokesman, Bono in particular, were required to talk about their faith in interviews to a far greater degree than they were comfortable with – their music reflected their position. U2 were now the mouthpiece of Christian rock, which was a hopelessly misleading description of the band, if only because U2's music reflected the feelings of all four members and one of them was just as unsure about Christianity as the others were committed. Adam's input to the group was equally valid to that of Larry, Bono or The Edge and this misrepresentation of the band stems from one of the great misunderstandings about them. U2 were a real group and always have been. Their music derives from communal experience as friends in Ireland, as band mates, as people on the road together, as 'executives' at the head of the burgeoning U2 organization and as four men discussing anything and everything in the pub after work. The fact that U2 is a four-headed beast is central to everything about them and their work and so representing them as a Christian rock band was inaccurate, a great underestimation of their solidity.

If U2 have always remained as much a social grouping as a rock band, that's not to say there hasn't been friction between them, inevitably part and parcel of working in a creative environment and then being enforcibly confined together while touring. The record shows that the period around *October* was possibly the most strained, almost certainly for the simple reason that everything was new to them and they had yet to work out a viable method of coping with the unforeseen stresses and strains that being a part of U2 produced. In his book *Unforgettable Fire*, Eamon Dunphy paints a vivid picture of unspoken tension and disagreement on the road, with Adam being increasingly isolated as the others spent their time on the bus reading their Bibles and holding prayer meetings. Other accounts tend to portray things in wildly simplistic terms, with Bono, Larry and The Edge as Holy Joes – something which Bono denied, admitting that he admired pacifists like Martin Luther King and Ghandi because he himself found it so difficult to turn the other cheek – while Adam plays the Viking marauder pillaging his way across the continents.

Truth is of course slightly less clear cut than fiction. The whole period was a time of confusion for the band in general. Adam, if not a card-carrying Christian, was a straightforward, decent bloke who believed in treating people well and retaining his own integrity. He was fiercely honest with himself too, later telling the *NME* that 'I would have liked to have been part of the fashion scene that was going on in London . . . being the weakest member of the band emotionally, I wanted to do that but I couldn't . . . it would have trivialized what I was doing in U2' – a personal philosophy which allowed him to stand squarely behind the ideals espoused in U2's music. The very fact that he was set apart from the others in the group by virtue of their following of Christ when he himself was following his own code, was naturally upsetting, particularly as there had been some criticism of him as a musician in the press, which all served to alienate him from the others to a degree. This process was possibly exacerbated by the fact that the others all had steady girlfriends who joined them at various times on tour, thereby increasing the self-sufficiency of their circle while Adam was still 'footloose and fancy free'.

Much has been made of the possibility of U2 dispensing with Adam's services which is palpable nonsense. It does the other three a grave disservice, portraying them as one-dimensional God-botherers; like everyone else, they remain many people at the same time – friends, drinkers, chess-players, lovers, furniture, buyers, musicians, taciturn, outspoken, placid or aggressive according to circumstances and provocation. While their faith was vital to their lives, making their lives vital, it didn't mean that they threw out everything else. Adam was, first and foremost, a good friend and, like other friendships in any other walk of life, they saw the whole picture and were willing to ride with any disagreements as to approach, lifestyle or musical direction. Tensions there may have been, even perhaps anger behind closed doors on the occasion of some of his wilder adventures, but there could be no question of asking him to leave. Their unity was reinforced by their choice of album sleeve, when they decided to forgo the striking imagery that had instantly set up the atmosphere for *Boy*, instead using a group portrait taken in Dublin. It was not as obvious a reference and as clear a way into the music as the picture of Peter Rowan had been, but it did transmit two important themes – that U2 were together and would remain together and that the city of Dublin was central to their artistic endeavours.

If their Christianity was to have any impact on U2's line-up it was more likely to be in bringing things to a halt. The Shalom group was still an important part of their lives and their faith, yet it was a grouping which made it all the more difficult for the three to reconcile the contradictions about a life in the service of their God while at the same time being in a rock 'n' roll band. Shalom had become used to criticism in Dublin – a radical group such as theirs could hardly hope to escape it in a city largely defined by the Catholic church – but there had been internal strife too with Guggi and Gavin of the Virgin Prunes leaving Shalom, unable to sympathize with its demands, unwilling to give up their position as musicians. Was the submersion and surrender of one's ego so essential to the preservation of faith? Having rejected the rules of the organized churches, were not Shalom introducing a whole new collection of equally suspect regulations? In reacting strongly against certain kinds of religious fundamentalism had they not introduced their own, equally extremist, version of the Bible's meaning? The three men from U2 did not react so strongly as Gavin and Guggi but were nevertheless torn between the two ruling influences in their lives, their faith and their music. Ultimately, Shalom was to prove unsatisfactory in the demands it was to place on them, a community which, to them, finally betrayed many of the defects they had discovered in other organized religions, problems they were to allude to in 'Acrobat' from *Achtung Baby* some ten years later, when Bono admitted his desire to take communion if only there was '*a church I could receive in*'.

The tensions that surrounded the period up to and including the making of *October* are matters for their own individual consciences, matters on which the individuals in U2 have rarely been drawn. The Edge telling *Rolling Stone* that the situation was so complex, even he felt unable fully to explain it, Bono later speaking of a two-year period where they weren't sure if they wanted to be in a band at all, where U2 was a secondary part of their lives. The album triumphs, however, and remains a strong reminder that rock 'n' roll can survive on more than memorable riffs or catchy hooks. It's an enormous, sprawling album of prodigious emotional content. It's an album that remains too huge to be taken in with one gulp but rather one that has to be heard again and again before all of its intricacies can be fully appreciated. Above all it's an album of undiluted passion built around their own particular spark, a spark they had by now fanned into a flame. Isolated from the LP, the songs, with the exception of 'Gloria' and the title track, do not stand up as well as those on their predecessor, but as an entity it remains one of U2's finest moments, ranking along with *Achtung Baby* as their most deeply, nakedly introspective and richly rewarding album.

The resolution of their spiritual interests and its impact on their music is less than satisfactory on many of the songs, yet it is that very openness that makes them so exciting. At times the subtitle 'All You Need Is God' could be applied, a catch-all that is particularly off-putting to the uninterested or the plain non-believers and yet it's hard not to be carried along on the strident anthems or Bono's evangelical rush of adrenalin.

There are times when his enthusiasm is so tangible it becomes intoxicating. Despite that, the spiritual element does become overbearing at times to those not personally involved. The constant references to God did not leave too much room for other interpretations to be placed on the songs as U2, through its lyricist, betrayed the zealous appetite of new converts with their almost absolute concentration on Christ throughout the record to the detriment of its potential universal application, the quest for self-knowledge. Their faith was to remain central to their music, just as it did to the way they conducted themselves and the way in which the U2 organization worked, but on future outings it was rather more oblique, dealing in ethical values rather than spiritual specifics. *October* found them totally absorbed in the new fulfilment they had found in God and the conflicts to which this had given rise. Struggle was the essential element of *October*, a record which told of those issues most firmly on their minds when they were making it, all the more so since they were working with little pre-written music and a complete lack of words, Bono having had his briefcase stolen in America, which contained his notes and sketches for the album's lyrics. Robbed of his preparatory work, Bono was forced to write on the microphone under intense pressure, a pressure which brought out all his subconscious feelings, providing the album with its intensity.

For a record so obviously couched in spiritual terms, it is enlightening that the overriding theme was of failure and of getting back on your feet again, a musical extension of the closing words of Samuel Beckett's *Trilogy*, 'I can't go on, I'll go on' although *October* does not share Beckett's absurdist view of the meaninglessness of life. Time after time the album uses the image of failing, even using the title 'I Fall Down', an obvious depiction of their lives to that point, as people and as U2. Their willingness to make mistakes, to try to become a great band, to make live shows a more interesting and atmospheric experience had not always met with unanimous approval. There had been so many knock-backs from record companies, singles had sometimes failed, live shows had been a shambles on occasion, some songs hadn't hit their targets as directly as perhaps they might, but after each set-back U2 had got back up again, learned from their mistakes and become more defiant. The implications for personal lives were clear too – can an individual remain true to his values, his standards, can good actually triumph over evil within ordinary, fallible individuals or do we regularly fall down and fail to reach these spiritual or ethical goals? In the context of *October* this was central, a crucial admission from Bono and the others that they were not perfect despite their faith, that there was a constant struggle within to stay on their chosen path and that they would sometimes fall below the standards they set themselves. Without that declaration, the credibility of the LP as a whole would have suffered a mortal blow, U2's Christians coming across as men with all the answers when, in fact, as Bono often noted, they were simply men with a different set of questions.

October chronicled their spiritual awakening through to the point where the contradictions that rose from their position threatened to overwhelm them. 'I Threw A Brick Through A Window' grew from the protagonist's sudden realization that he had little direction in his life, that he wasn't going anywhere and was aimlessly drifting, a revelation brought about by catching sight of his reflection and not liking what he saw, another use of the mirror that had cropped up on *Boy*. Throwing a brick was a deliberately violent picture, Bono admitting the aggressive streak in his own nature and then turning that violence on his reflection in the hope of destroying that earlier character as he moved onto a different spiritual level through his newly found belief. Having been antagonistic – telling *Melody Maker* that 'I had a lot of hate' – experience had taught him that 'wherever you go in the world people are still flesh and blood ... if only they would realize and stop hitting each other over the head ... you can only make it stop in your own life.' It was a sentiment that he applied to the song, initially pointing the finger at himself and the error of his own ways, employing the biblical 'no-one is blinder than he who will not see' before embracing his fellow man, a brother whom he might previously have attacked. *'There is another way out of here'* holds out hope for pacifism and mutual understanding to win out over the all too easy option of aggression.

The title *October* was in part meant to reflect the cold cynicism that had gripped the world, maybe an admission that we had gone way beyond any 'summer of love' that a previous generation had enjoyed, conjuring up the autumnal darkness that coloured some of the music on the record. The harvest of the bright new technology of the 1950s and 1960s with all its promise had ultimately led to the construction of weapons of mass destruction. It caught a mood that was prevalent at the time, a recognition among those of a humanitarian bent that harsh, ominous years were ahead as the world's politics began to swing irrevocably to the right and that a nuclear, rather than a new clear, winter might be the more likely outcome and yet, in typical U2 style, it remained optimistic that spring would ultimately follow, perhaps with a reawakening to the spiritual side of human nature and a determination to fight back.

October was also chosen for its hard, industrial sound which captured the harsh percussive edge to much of the rest of the music. The title track itself was, in contrast, the most beautiful piece on the album, a calm, soothing presence in the midst of the storm, Bono's brief vocal particularly striking over a lovely piano piece from The Edge, the song itself a testament to the enduring nature of God and the kingdom of heaven. As earthly empires crumble, as the seasons come and go, God's message goes on. It's a beguiling vision and a touching exposition of a man's faith, Bono achieving a peace of mind and acceptance of his fate that is rarely touched upon elsewhere during the course of this restless record, although 'With A Shout (Jerusalem)' is again keen to proclaim a powerful faith in God. Even here though, there is the question of the future, the what do we do and how do we do it syndrome that they had fallen into. 'With A Shout' is anthemic in structure, a strident U2 song in the same vein as 'I Will Follow' which almost takes on the mantle of an evangelical hymn as it seems to call for a rededication to the word of God. Its lyric portrays someone overwhelmed by his faith and the power of the spirit that has overtaken him, one who wants to follow him *'who made me see'*, another allusion to his Road to Damascus experience and a metaphor which appears on three different songs, 'Tomorrow' and 'I Threw A Brick Through A Window' being the others.

The lead-off single for the album had been 'Fire', a song which seemed lost on its own but worked nicely in the context of the LP, reversing the perspective of the other songs as it almost explained their Christianity. The fire inside was the crucial point, a fire that wasn't dulled even by failure, a spark that each of them had within. The Holy Spirit was the obvious fire to which they referred, but it had equally clear connotations for the band. To the four of them, the most important thing about U2 and its music was that it was built around a spark which they had turned into a fire – they had begun with little musical ability but had immediately identified that there was something about the group that was special and now, as they matured as people and as musicians, it was still that particular spark that set U2 apart.

If ever there was a blatant invitation to jump to a conclusion, however erroneously, 'Fire' was it. The spark that started U2 was by association the early flickering of the Holy Spirit setting these young lads on the road to their destiny and here they were busily attributing their success to their faith alone. All of which sounds vaguely plausible if unnecessarily pious and hopelessly calculating. In fact, 'Fire', in keeping with the rest of the music, is far more instinctive, Bono telling *Melody Maker* that 'sometimes to think about it is to destroy it.' There was no master plan, no mission to turn everyone on to Christianity and certainly no desire to set themselves up as U2, rock band by holy appointment. The comparison merely drew parallels between the excitement they had as U2 and that they had found in faith. 'I think it's the spiritual strength that's essential to the band . . . I'm not standing up and saying, "Hey, you should be into God!" My own life is exhilarating through an experience I feel.'

Bono in particular seemed drunk with exhilaration and that was a weakness of the album. There was a distinct lack of any critical discrimination, which meant that it was ultimately flawed, although conceptually that was perfectly acceptable since it was an accurate description of mankind. Nevetheless, *October* ran the gamut from the sublime to the faintly ridiculous, leaving songs where U2 very definitely did fall down. Amongst that category was 'Scarlet', apparently an early choice for album title, in which Bono simply repeated the word 'rejoice' over and over again, backed by a thudding drum pattern which again called to mind Steve Lillywhite's work with Peter Gabriel.

To rejoice is to express great joy or happiness, a word generally used in a spiritual context as Bono was well aware. 'I used the word "rejoice" precisely because I knew that people have a mental block against it. It's a powerful word, it's lovely to say. It's implying more than "get up and dance, baby"' was his justification in reply to Lynden Barber's complaint in *Melody Maker* that the use of the word had grated. The strangest thing about the song was that the litany did not sound especially joyous, particularly in comparison with its use on the song 'Rejoice'. On 'Scarlet', Bono sounded more pensive than effusive, almost like a man trying to convince himself of his faith and its implications, whereas 'Rejoice' itself was the song of someone who had at last found some direction, some meaning to his life. It spoke of someone who had had no idea what to say or do, again a recurrent image of failure and doubt, until the circle was completed by his discovery of Christianity.

The doxology 'Gloria', a rock 'n' roll hymn of sorts, was anthemic, powerful and musically assured but Bono could only speak of his inability to express himself fully (so much so that he had to resort to Latin prayer) and his seemingly infinite capacity for failure and falling over time and again. There was a ring of the sackcloth and ashes treatment about some of Bono's self-flagellation, only for him to be ultimately redeemed by the love of God, the only way he could achieve fulfilment and perhaps, in the light of his partly Catholic background, absolution. The anguish that he, Larry and The Edge were going through was summed up in the promise that any talents they had would be used in the service of God – '*I'd give it to you*' – but therein lay a crucial part of the problem. Was the superficial world of rock 'n' roll the greatest contribution they could make or were there better ways of using their time? By playing music and entertaining people and perhaps giving them other things to think about, were they actually advancing humanitarian causes or were they using that simply as an excuse to allow them to do what they most enjoyed? Had they been given the talent to communicate with others for a specific purpose and therefore should they not be investing in those talents rather than ignoring them? Was it possible to square their lifestyle as itinerant musicians who, as popularity inevitably grew would be subject to assorted temptations as well as being submerged beneath large amounts of money, with their beliefs? Would they be able to survive success? Were their motives entirely selfless or selfish and was it all, at its roots, based on the gratification of their own egos beyond all else?

All these questions were an inherent part of 'Gloria' and of the album in general, though little pointed to a final reconciliation of the questions, questions that have become all the more important as success has piled on success. 'To be good at something, you have to be selfish and to be great at something you have to be greedy,' Bono told RCD's Bert Van De Kamp in May 1992. 'Without that greed, you won't make it, in the sense that you want everything for your music. That's why you should never look up to pop musicians – they're all egotistical bastards, they translate their pain into song – I know that I myself am not immune to it.' Frank Zappa was rather more blunt in his dismissal of that approach with 'Listen, I feel real bad, I'm hurting deep inside, so pay me!' but Bono's admission is pertinent to the creation of *October* where he wallowed in his confusion, calling to mind another later tongue-in-cheek confession: 'I'm happy to be unhappy.'

The only hint of some resolution to their anguish came on the final song, 'Is That All?', a piece which recommodified 'The Cry', a short song with a bristling guitar riff which The Edge had been using to preface 'The Electric Co.' on stage. As so often with U2's songs, there was more than one line to be taken with the piece, interviews revealing that they felt there was far more to music than just singing a tune to make people happy or sad, a trick that could be affected by any semi-competent showband back in Limerick. Music could, indeed should, be about touching the soul and moving the heart, as well as engaging the brain. 'Is That All?' was in that sense a welcome confirmation that a hard year on the road had not diminished their faith in rock 'n' roll as an important cultural medium, one that could be harnessed to present different ideas or ways of life in much the same way as a short story or novel might, an approach that had served Lou Reed well for most of his career, although U2 continued to use a more impressionistic, ambiguous vocabulary as opposed to Reed's general directness. Cynicism, the disease of the city according to Bono, had yet to claim U2 as victims, perhaps because they were well guarded from it by their Christian beliefs, and their belief in U2 and in rock 'n' roll. 'Is That All?' may well have been the closest that they got to resolving their struggle, a departure from the opening 'Gloria' and its offering of everything they had to give to the service of God to a conclusion wherein they asked if simply making music was all that He wanted from them, a personal application of the Biblical parable of the talents. As an answer to the raging storm that had gone before it, it was annoyingly simplistic, the tortured soul finding a solution that just happened to suit him down to the ground, but it did close the record on a positive note, which, after all the demons it had previously raised, was a fitting depiction of the kind of peace they had found in God.

Dublin in particular and Ireland in general appear to have been absolutely central to the making of *October*. Had it been made in a normal recording studio environment in the middle of London or New York, it would certainly have been a very different record to that which was finally released. The Irish influence was acknowledged for the first time in the use of traditional instrumentation on 'Tomorrow', where uilleann pipes were provided by Vincent Kilduff. The song opened as a lament, ostensibly concerning the funeral of Bono's mother and the grief and fear which it inspired in him, before it built into a stirring rock song, almost one of defiance, refusing to accept that the physical barrier that death creates will take away the love he felt for his mother while she was alive before, appropriately enough given the subject matter, Bono effectively commends her soul to God, again proclaiming his faith in Jesus Christ by reusing the 'making the blind man see again' image, and in the second coming. This belief that Jesus is coming back is an interesting addendum to 'Fire', the song which immediately precedes it and which alludes to the Book of Revelations, that part of the Bible which describes the circumstances which will lead to Christ's return.

'Tomorrow' did have another reading in terms of the Irish situation and is interesting for its oblique reference to the Troubles in the north of the country, the first that U2 had allowed themselves. Perhaps the memory of his mother's funeral had brought the religious divide into sharp focus again for Bono, who had grown up in a home that was split every Sunday by the two churches, or perhaps their world travels had brought home their Irishness to them and had given them the necessary perspective to look at the problems of their homeland afresh, but U2 were clearly beginning to broaden their own frame of reference and look at the world beyond themselves and their own lives.

In many respects *October*, a record of emotional spirituality, was an obvious starting point for looking at the ills that had befallen their country, for if the Troubles were ostensibly about the unification of Ireland, the initial partition and the resistance to change was built upon religious fervour and the antagonism between Catholic and Protestant. U2 had already declared themselves to be anti-religion, Bono going so far as to say 'I don't see Jesus Christ as being in any part of religion. Religion to me is almost like when God leaves and then people devise a set of rules to fill the space.' For men who had unlocked the spiritual side of their lives, who had actually found a living breathing relationship with God, religion had almost become the true enemy, dogma from the distant past that was tearing their own country in two, dogma defended with the gun by 'men of God', dogma that twisted the essential message of love given in the Bible. For an Irish band to embrace God so openly without speaking of the divisiveness of religion in their own country would have been hopelessly inconsistent and so the plaintive cry *'for the love of God'* on 'Tomorrow' was as much an exasperated cry aimed at those who abused religion as it was an expression of the grief he felt at his personal loss.

Sidestepping any condemnation of either side of the divide, 'Tomorrow' dealt with the fear that was an everyday part of life in Northern Ireland, where for so many the front door was their last line of defence, something to hide behind. Just as Bono was frightened to open the door to go to the funeral where he would be forced to confront the reality, the grim finality of the loss of his mother, across the border in the north people are frightened to open the door lest they usher in their own demise. The juxtaposition of his own loss and the fear of death in Northern Ireland painted a compelling picture – the black car parked outside the house was, in the personal sense, the hearse or the mourner's car while, in the violent scenario the song also painted, it could be the gunman's vehicle which would be followed days later by the official black cars. Somehow in the midst of their personal pain and that which they felt for their country, U2 were able to conjure an optimistic defiance from a song that was built on such bleak subject matter as it came to a rousing climax from its melancholic beginning – a property you could not attribute to 'Stranger In A Strange Land', a piece that owed much to the evocative atmospherics they'd introduced on *Boy*. *Hot Press* later termed it a 'picture postcard' and it does have the air of a travelogue, but at its essence is an ability to see the Irish question from the distance and perspective of a foreign country. Part of the song deals with a meeting with a soldier who asks for a cigarette, smiling from the other side of the road *'but that's a long way here'*, an evocation of the religious divide where on one side of a Belfast street can be Catholics, the other side Protestants, both at risk from zealots from each other's religion, a simple street divided by bigoted, irrational hatred. There is further mention of what seems to be a violent atrocity later in the song when Bono is unable to sleep after having been witness to some awful unrecorded sight, all the more terrible to the listener for the lack of detail. Just what was so dreadful that Bono couldn't bring himself to share the experience?

'Stranger In A Strange Land' was distinguished on *October* as the only song that fought shy of overt expression of their faith, instead evoking a strong mood of alienation that could be applied in many ways – it could simply refer to their attempt to grasp new knowledge and the flavour of their surroundings while on the run across Europe and America or it may even be a subtle acknowledgment of the tensions that were at play on tour. Maybe Adam was the stranger of the title, at sea with the spiritual fervour of the others, as Bono recalls the way things were when they were a more tightly knit unit. In its ambiguity it was a close relative to the songs on *Boy*, allowing any number of interpretations, but more than anything it seemed like a cry for help, the words of a band that needed to get its feet back on home turf to assess just what had happened to them and to make sense of the whole experience, to analyse the prizes laid before them and to decide which, if any, were of value – not wholly dissimilar to the sabbatical before the release of *Achtung Baby*, where they were to reinvent U2 in many ways, although the substance of the band remained intact.

Returning home to Dublin was both refreshing and taxing. They were able to meet friends and family again and spend time at home, but it also plunged them deep into the heart of the spiritual conflict that threatened the band's future. *October* is a very Irish record in its restless spirit, its romanticism, but most of all in its unselfconscious celebration of God, of doubt and of faith. The very idea that a British band could have made a record like *October* is unthinkable. Their upbringing would almost certainly have left them too embarrassed to talk about matters of the soul, a subject rarely discussed in any real depth in the nation's schools and one which has little bearing on the everyday consciousness of much of the population. Spiritual conversation is almost as great a taboo as sexual conversation in the Britain of Victorian values, Victorian economics and Victorian attitudes and if any band had been sufficiently concerned to bring the subject into their music in any obvious fashion, they'd have been laughed off the pages of the *NME* and back into the obscurity from which they'd surfaced.

Irish attitudes to religion were different. It is untenable to present it as a country of liberated religious outlook where all creeds are treated equally – this is after all a country where a civil war is effectively being conducted along religious lines, an ethnic struggle which has echoes in the horrific present-day problems which face the former Yugoslavia. Roman Catholicism is very much the religion of the nation and the decrees of Rome play an influential part in the running of the country. Short of the inevitable suspicion that exists almost everywhere between different religious and ethnic communities, there is religious freedom of sorts, with the essential exception that the beliefs of the Holy Roman Church are enshrined in the laws of the land, something which has immense implications for the personal freedom of other religious groups, such as the non-availability of abortion and contraception for instance. U2 stepped into that particular arena in February 1991 when they paid a fine of £500 on behalf of the Irish Family Planning Association after it had been found guilty of selling condoms in Dublin's Virgin megastore.

Nevertheless, if Ireland is by no means perfect in its religious freedoms, it is at the very least a nation which accepts the existence of a spiritual side to life far more than Britain does. A subject that is out in the open does not threaten or frighten in the same way that one kept under wraps does. It becomes a perfectly natural topic of conversation or discussion without being forced or seeming precious. From that base, U2 were able to give full vent to their explorations, their beliefs, their doubts and their failings.

Dublin was the place where they could get their feet back on the ground again and use the time and space they were afforded there to develop, away from the glare of incipient fame. The locals remained stoically unimpressed by the success that the band was beginning to experience, an important steadying influence that prevented putative performing egos overwhelming them, a process further enhanced for the three Christians by the Shalom sessions. The very setting was rather more inspirational, too. While parts of the city were run down there was great beauty in the surrounding countryside, the elemental images on which Bono so often thrived, the hugeness of the natural world inspiring the big music they wanted to make. Having toyed with the idea of following the drain of Irish musicians to London, they had decisively rejected it, instinctively realizing that Dublin was an important part of their muse, was a factor in separating them from other bands whose music was shaped by the grimness of life in a metropolis like London, where the stench of decay was all around. Bono was later to concede that 'it's not urban music, it's more to do with hills, rivers and mountains.' Dublin had its own inner-city troubles, its own drink, drug and violence problems, but for all those faults it was a far healthier place, a more creative city, one which encouraged experimentation and adventurous artistic behaviour as well as fostering an epic sweep of romanticism, U2's most seductive card. The Edge was to talk about Irish groups leaving home and losing whatever was originally special about them, becoming just another rock band, saying, 'I've seen so many Irish groups move to London and just lose touch with whatever vein, creatively, they were locked into at one stage in their career. I think it's tragic. Not that I don't like London ... but I think for an artist it's absolutely the wrong place to be.' Dublin to Bono is 'a warm place and that's the beauty of it. People here aren't afraid to make a fool of themselves ... you need that lack of inhibition to be creative. You've got to be prepared to jump off the deep end.'

Such acceptance from their home town was a double-edged sword of course. If they were encouraged to make a record that honestly depicted the group state of mind without any fear of ridicule or disapproval from those closest to them, it did encourage an element of self-indulgence to creep in, a problem exacerbated by the speed at which they had to make *October*. When one recalls that they had been on the road almost constantly for eighteen months, they were lucky to have the bare bones of even a couple of songs when they entered Windmill Lane Studios again, a paucity of material which wasn't helped by the theft of Bono's lyrical notes. In order to meet the October release deadline they had set for themselves, they had to work quickly. But Bono in particular caused problems as he wrote words live on the microphone, not a process ideally suited to speedy and efficient working practices.

If Larry, The Edge and Bono were all caught up in the strength of their still relatively new-found faith, then it was right and proper that a band who had stood up for being real should give some space to singing about this faith. Sadly, since time was pressing, the ideas hadn't been fully digested and there was a lack of variety in them that hampered the power of the album. Although they had opened themselves up to doubt as much as to faith, it was the latter that generally won the day, overbearingly so at times, the ambiguity which had so characterized *Boy* notable for its absence. If they were lyrically short, it did sometimes seem all too easy for them to resort to praising God or bringing in the 'blind to see' metaphor, which was becoming a little tired by the end. Ultimately the decision is with the listener – did the pressure give rise to a touching, emotional, passionate record or did U2 end up with a half-decent half-finished album? Looked at dispassionately, it wasn't until the next album, *War*, that they struck a balanced and more palatable view on their Christian values, often exposing them in a wider moral, philanthropic worldview. And yet U2 are not a band that can be looked at dispassionately, are not a band to be ignored – one to be loved or loathed certainly, but never ignored. Commercially the record broke little new ground and radio stations, particularly in America, were less than keen to take the album, but to those willing to seek it out it simply betrayed that there was no great master plan, just a desire to make honest, instinctive music for the moment, Bono later recalling John Lennon's view of the muse to *Hot Press*: 'He was saying, "Well, this is it, what do you want – no music or the truth? Because if I lie, the music will choke on itself." That's the choice.'

Musically they were not lacking, a virtue that kept many fans happy when they might otherwise have been disappointed by their direction, and as Neil McCormick later pointed out, 'as a hard-rock unit, U2 had never been this cohesive, this tight, this professional,' a sound to which they had initially asked Dick Evans to contribute. 'I did turn up during the recording of *October* and was asked to do some guitar but I think there was a bit of a communication gap about exactly what was wanted. I was into heavy fuzz and feedback at the time so I spent a few hours recording all these backwards guitars and half-speed guitars but it got dropped in the mix and didn't finish up on the record.'

The rigours of the road had added layers of technical competence to the unquestioned originality of expression that U2 had, a general improvement even if they did at times repeat the mistakes of their debut record and confuse speed and bluster for spirit and emotion. The foundation of the album was Larry's drumming. That was what kept U2 in check as a rock 'n' roll band according to Bono, and it was true to say that Larry adopted a role similar to that which Ringo Starr had had in the Beatles. While Adam worked on the melodic bass lines which he favoured and The Edge spent his time experimenting and innovating, heading off into uncharted waters, Larry's drumming was the rock solid foundation to which everything eventually returned, occasionally taking a leaf from Phil Collins' book with thrashing drum figures on 'Scarlet' and 'I Threw A Brick Through A Window'.

The most vulnerable member of the band during recording must surely have been Adam. The concentration on Christianity must have been cause for concern as U2 began to travel down a road alien to him – if there was no possibility of him being eased out of the group, there was a chance that he might finally find himself unable to stand behind U2's philosophy if it continued down this overtly evangelical path, a galling prospect for the man who had been the prime mover in establishing the group in Dublin in its early days. His response was to come up with some excellent bass lines, work that was especially dramatic and absolutely in context on 'I Threw A Brick Through A Window' and 'Stranger In A Strange Land'.

Adam's work on *October* summed up the whole mood of the band – defiant. If the others were determined to stand up and be counted as believers in God, Adam was prepared to stand up as a creative force with his own distinctive muse. U2 as a band would not be swayed from making the music they wanted, from saying the things they felt and would defy the vagaries of fashion to do so, even if that meant ignoring more commercial sugar-coated melodies and obvious pop.

One thing that The Edge didn't serve up on guitar was obvious pop, but again he was the musical focus. *October* didn't see him moving too far from the territory that he had made his own on *Boy*, but the refinements he made were always satisfying, at times startling. The incorporation of the coruscating riff from 'The Cry' into 'Is That All?' has already been remarked upon, but there was much more to enjoy and admire. There was the searing melodic work that made 'Gloria' his most potent offering yet, the incendiary slicing through 'Fire', while the keyboards he contributed to the title track served to expand further U2's seemingly limitless horizon of possibilities. Often soaring and inspirational, the optimism inherent in much of his work on the album served to throw Bono's confusion and anxieties into sharper relief, adding greater depth and context to the songs and making them all the more fascinating, portraying an inner confidence that, although the making of *October* had been a real examination by fire, it was one that they had come through and one that would leave them all the stronger.

The U2 camp might have become more resolute and closer as individuals than for a while, bonded together as they had been in the heat of the battle for *October*, but still there were doubts about the future progress of the group and what it should be doing, if anything. The Edge, Larry and Bono did have a meeting with Paul McGuinness where they expressed reservations about embarking on as rigorous a touring schedule as they had endured the previous year, perhaps recalling some of the tensions to which it had given rise. Bono later recalled in a *Sounds* interview on the release of *The Joshua Tree*, 'it was all part of the personality crisis as to whether making music was all a waste of time when we should have got on with the real problems.' A compromise was arranged with the shelving of plans for a tour of Australia and Japan in the new year, giving the group more time to spend at home, looking at the domestic problems of their city, going on to use interview space in the press to discuss the situation in Dublin, at times appearing to be drawn towards taking an active rather than passive interest in the affairs of their home city. Bono admitted that 'some friends and I went into a centre for itinerants in Dublin and offered our services. The social workers look so worn out there. One told me that the people they're trying to help are so crazy, so arrogant that it seems impossible . . . I can only give myself to it – I don't have very much money but I do have to justify it to myself and to my conscience.'

Bono had taken steps already by confronting Garret Fitzgerald, the leader of the then Irish opposition party, Fine Gael, in the departure lounge at Heathrow Airport and continued to buttonhole the garrulous politician on the flight to Dublin. Though they refused to join or endorse any political party, a stance they've maintained, Fitzgerald was a personality to whom they could give a qualified level of support since his policies were of a liberal bias, favouring some element of reform of the nation's position on divorce and contraception. Keeping in contact with him, Bono and the rest of the group invited Fitzgerald to visit the Windmill Lane studio while they worked on *War* on what was the final Friday of the 1982 general election campaign. When the votes were counted the following week, Fitzgerald became Taoiseach, defeating the incumbent Charles Haughey and his Fianna Fail party. It would be overstating matters to a ludicrous extent to say that U2 were important in the engineering of his victory, but the photo-opportunity can have done Fitzgerald little harm with a younger generation of voters.

If Fitzgerald had ulterior motives in his courting of Ireland's rock idols – and how many politicians don't have ulterior motives? – did U2 have a similar vision of their alliance with the country's prospective leader? *Hot Press* was quick to note that 'rock as an industry may have suffered from its shyness in fighting for its interests' – by becoming bosom pals with the new Taoiseach, maybe U2 were playing their part in the lobby that was looking to perpetuate the very favourable tax situation under which artists operated in Ireland. By virtue of the Artists and Writers' Dispensation from Income Tax, their tax-free income has been considerable and must have added to the undeniable attractions of staying in Dublin. Whatever the reasons, be they philanthropic or otherwise, Bono was quickly invited by Fitzgerald to take part in the Select Goverment Action Committee on Unemployment. Despite his initial interest and commitment to the idea, Bono soon quit after attending a meeting and discovering that he could not communicate in 'committee-speak'. 'I just felt that if they were going to talk about unmarried mothers, I wanted an unmarried mother to be there and talk. I wanted to put flesh and blood on the statistics.' But his passion and loquacity, his desire to bring in those actually affected by unemployment and let them give their point of view, ran up against a brick wall built by those administrators who were keen to preserve the rules and regulations of committees.

Garret Fitzgerald is not the only politician to have realized the advantage to be gained from associating with U2, which is why they have generally kept any overt allegiance to a particular party to a minimum. On the Zoo TV tour of America in 1992, U2 played a small but significant part in the campaign to remove George Bush from the White House. At every available opportunity, U2 mocked the incumbent President, Bono even taking to telephoning him every night from the concert stage without any success. What was undoubtedly a nice publicity coup for the band, getting them additional column inches in the ordinary press, became a little more serious as the year-long election campaign wore on and Bill Clinton gained his party's nomination. Playing 'I Still Haven't Found What I'm Looking For', Bono would regularly add that 'I hope you get the President you're looking for, or we're all fucked!' Eventually, on a national phone-in radio show in August, just over two months before America went to the polls, Clinton responded to a tongue-in-cheek invitation to call in and spent some time talking with the band. Quizzed on America's position in the world and his attitude to censorship, Clinton used the platform intelligently, though Bono's performance was equally impressive proving there was a great deal of substance behind U2 and the current Zoo TV façade.

Governor Clinton's campaign was expertly run and there can be little doubt that he benefited greatly from the fact that he was an almost constant frontrunner in opinion polls, enabling him to take a relaxed attitude and perform with the composure that made him look like a President long before he was actually elected to the Oval Office. The American people were further drawn to Clinton as he rode out the storms that the press endeavoured to create over draft-dodging, marijuana smoking (to inhale or not to inhale, that is the question) and alleged marital infidelity. Every bit as important, Clinton's was the first presidential campaign to directly target young American voters and inevitably popular music was instrumental in that attack. Some well-wishers were more vociferous than others, with REM's Michael Stipe sharing a platform with Clinton's running mate Al Gore for instance, but U2's partial support was also helpful. Breaking from previous tradition, they were more blatant in their support than in just giving a simple endorsement of Clinton's personality, but then they had to to have any effect – Bush's personality rating was so low that Hannibal Lecter would have triumphed over him in any straight popularity contest.

Fighting shy of actually telling people to 'Vote Clinton', a declaration that would have left an Irish band skating on thin ice in America, they did go so far as to tell him 'from all of us, you sound like a President', while their outspoken criticism of Bush and his predecessor Ronald Reagan did give those who were interested a pretty good idea of where they stood. In their new role of supreme pop ironists, on their 'Who's Gonna Ride Your Wild Horses?' single they did, however, include a cover of Credence Clearwater Revival's 'Fortunate Son', a song concerned with dodging the Vietnam draft, one they had originally intended to plague Vice President Dan Quayle with at the previous US election. Further to that, they later held a 'summit' of sorts with Clinton, where they apparently discussed possible American initiatives to help ease the situation in Northern Ireland, Clinton having already floated the idea of sending an envoy to Ulster should he go on to win the election. This led to a gaffe from Bush which sent his popularity ratings with younger voters plummeting further when he suggested that in foreign policy dealings he would speak with the likes of Major and Yeltsin while Clinton could go and talk to Boy George! What was intended as a put-down of his opponent merely proved to the young audience that he was hopelessly out of touch. It may appear a trivial, trifling matter, but to a country looking for young, vibrant leadership, one searching for a Kennedy figure, a comparison that Clinton's aides were keen to play up to, Bush looked all the more like yesterday's man. In a land where the 1960 election was allegedly decided by Richard Nixon's inadequate shaving technique, public relations were as important as international relations and, as far as young America was concerned, Bush was dead meat, an impression given further credence when Clinton used a *Rolling Stone* cover feature to great personal effect, coming across as concerned, able and willing to meet the great challenges that faced an America in decline.

MTV was a part of the equation too and again U2 cropped up time and again with brief soundbites from the concerts which showed them hounding Bush mercilessly, following the different line of attack required of them by their new shape. Rather than the righteous anger of the 'Joshua Tree' tour and what was portrayed as the finger-wagging 'outside it's America', this time U2 used sarcasm and ironic wit to castigate the President, employing the latest video technology to portray him as a bumbling buffoon. This was backed up by Clinton's own excellent performance on an MTV questions and answers session where he spoke to young people sensibly and attractively about the issues that concerned them. The final piece of the MTV jigsaw was the series of *Rock The Vote* public information films, a general nationwide campaign in which U2 were again involved – the U2 party line was 'we don't tell you who to vote for, but we do ask that you use your vote.' *Rock The Vote* was an enormous success in encouraging young people actually to register to vote and so enable their voices to be heard as part of the democratic process. There can be no doubt that the campaign hurt Bush and helped Clinton into the White House as young people flocked to a man who was at least within touching distance of their own generation. U2 ended the campaign by instructing people via the video walls at their gigs to vote for Frank Zappa, but it is certainly true that they played a small part in the mobilization of the youth vote and its role in the subsequent removal from office of George Bush.

Direct 'political' action from the band was not always quite so well received however. In May 1986, during the hiatus that followed the 'Unforgettable Fire' tour, Dublin played host to almost everyone who was anyone in the Irish music business, all of whom came to play their part in a concert called Self Aid. The show had been arranged in the main by Tony Boland, a producer from RTE, in the aftermath of Live Aid, as an attempt to address the terrible unemployment problem that plagued Ireland, to give a platform for those experiencing the harsh realities of the situation, a situation that has now reached the point where 1.3 million people in Ireland live below the poverty line. If anything, it was designed as a day of recognition as much as of hope. Christy Moore, Van Morrison,

Gary Moore, the Pogues and a host of other acts were on the bill but, inevitably, U2 spearheaded the line-up which went under the banner of 'Self Aid – Make it Work.'

Just as in the UK, the mid-1980s saw Ireland experiencing a period of very high unemployment, a crisis which, again as in the UK, does not seem likely to be solved and which persists to this day. In Ireland however, there is a very different resonance to unemployment – it is set in a historical context dating back many years in a nation that has traditionally been one of Europe's economically poorer cousins even if culturally it has been especially rich. Eventually, many grow weary of struggling to find work in a country that cannot provide it and which often appears unwilling to try. The result has been the constant flow of economic migrants flooding out of the country to find work elsewhere in Europe or in America, a situation already discussed. While Irish parents have become used to rearing their children for export they naturally don't welcome the fact that their family might be strewn across the globe rendering normal communication impossible. Not just a catalyst for social ills, unemployment in the Irish sense also splits families.

Not only does that migration hurt families, it destroys the spirit of regeneration in a country that needs fresh ideas. In *Wide Awake In Ireland*, John Waters discussed this aspect of the problem. 'The real tragedy of modern Ireland is that the younger generation who should by rights be challenging the country's political leadership is being siphoned off to emigration. In the past decade (the 1980s) a whole generation has been wilfully let go. Ireland has, apart from a brief period of hope in the 1960s and 1970s, been a society with an almost constant absence of the vital generation which would give it a cautionary kick in the pants at the appropriate moments and, because of the survival of the 1960s generation after their sell-by date, their own particular obsessions have continued to monopolize the national agenda with no sign of resolution.' In that regard, not only has the unemployment problem in Ireland meant the absence of new ideas, the very staleness of the debate that remains – contraception, divorce and abortion – has created its own cultural vacuum from which the young want to escape even if they could get work at home. As Waters notes, 'those with better things to talk about must find a different place in which to talk . . . for whatever reasons [the Irish] are a people who have constantly lacked a crucial piece of our lifeforce.'

That loss of the young to the outside world has disturbed Irish culture to a great extent. The difficulty that grows out of that is that Ireland exports its problems and so has no need to address them, now finding itself out of step with much of the West on those issues which seemingly occupy so much of its time and which emanate from its religion. Ireland's stance on abortion and contraception has remained unrelenting simply because it has never really been a problem as those to whom it is a burning issue are effectively forced out of the country to search out that freedom elsewhere. Now in the post-AIDS era, when contraception is such a vital issue, Ireland has not evolved a position to cope with it since it has spent decades sweeping the problem under the carpet. Professor J. J. Lee commented in Waters's programme that 'we [the Irish] grossly under-analyse and there is a thought deficit. Until we address it, we can't arrive at the strategy required to cope with the inadequacies.'

Since emigration was the cornerstone issue of the show, U2 were one of the artists who caught the mood correctly on the night, using their own as well as other people's songs to illustrate the point with a caustic reading of 'Maggie's Farm' taking the honours.

' "Maggie's Farm" was right on the day because emigration is the most difficult underground problem in this society,' commented The Edge, indicating that the Irish people like it just fine at home, give them jobs there, not across the water as guinea pigs on Maggie Thatcher's farm for her doomed dogmatic experiment where jobs were not in any more plentiful supply anyway. At Self Aid, U2 were angry – a state which suits them best – were fiery, compassionate and bitter at the way in which their compatriots had been sold down the river. Bono later said, 'I just wanted to *be* that anger', the anger felt by those consigned to a life on the dole, those left without hope.

Other social ills could be laid squarely at the door of unemployment, too, particularly the rise among younger people of alcoholism and drug abuse, phenomena that had spread down to the youngest members of society, children openly sniffing glue on the streets of Dublin just as they did in hard-core inner-city areas of England or America. For those reasons, U2 endorsed Christy Moore's view of Self Aid as an event that'd do no harm and might do some good. Bono spoke later to *Hot Press* about the show and the reasons for U2's involvement. 'I knew there'd be certain politicians watching the programme and I didn't want to let them off the hook. Because the truth of it was that a lot of people were *on* the hook because of their policies.' By attracting a huge national TV audience for the day, Self Aid was effectively an advertisement of the bitterness felt by Irish people about the economic situation in the country, particularly with regard to unemployment. The show was heavily promoted in advance and then took almost an entire day's TV coverage to say 'No more!' As John and Yoko had used the worldwide press coverage they got for their bed-ins as an advertising campaign for peace, Self Aid was an advertising campaign for job creation, and as a protest rally and a celebration of the wealth of indigenous talent that was available, it was perfectly admirable in its intent and a great success.

Where controversy raised its head was in its charitable aspect. People were asked to send in money that could be used to help job-creation schemes and prospective employers were to call in with vacancies which would then be offered on screen during the show so that the unemployed could phone in for interviews, etc., after the weekend. In this regard, Self Aid was a more questionable activity. To ask for financial help from private citizens in order to help the unemployed certainly sailed close to the wind marked 'patronizing and insulting'. To treat people who were unable to get work, generally through no fault of their own, as charity cases was degrading and misleading. The unemployed were and are made up of people with a whole variety of skills from manual labourers through skilled engineers to nursing staff or administrators. None of them were asking for handouts. What they were asking for was a government policy that actively sought to create new jobs for them to do, a truism that is still pertinent.

The argument against the 'charity' aspect of the show was very simple. No handouts were required, it didn't actually create any new jobs and it simply acted as useful advertising for those firms involved, many of whom were actively cutting, rather than recruiting, staff. The argument also ran that by trying to raise money, by treating unemployment as an unavoidable human tragedy of a sort similar to that in Ethiopia which Live Aid had sought to help, the Irish government was being let off the hook – there's nothing to be done, so let's feel sorry for the unemployed and salve our consciences by handing out a little charity. While Bono felt that his performance had tried to keep the politicians on the hook, The Edge did express his reservations. 'It was a gestural thing that was all about hopes and aspirations and very little about real answers . . . did anyone really benefit in a job sense?'

U2 had lent their organization to the event, with Paul McGuinness becoming one of the trustees involved in the distribution of the money that came in. Those facts, allied to U2's profile in Dublin, made them the public figureheads of the day and put them firmly in the firing line when the brickbats were being hurled. In a piece published in the week leading up to the gig, *In Dublin* carried a cover story by Eamonn McCann entitled 'Self Aid Makes It Worse'. It was an eminently sensible, necessarily cynical, piece – which has since been reprinted in Dunphy's *Unforgettable Fire* – that carried the arguments that could be ranged against the day, indicating just why it could have a negative effect. Putting across the other side of the argument was certainly valid amid the mutual back-slapping that such events engender, but what caused the real stir was the fact that the cover sported a photo of Bono with the headline 'Rock Against the People'. Understandably, bearing in mind the philanthropic intentions U2, and for that matter the other artists and organizers, had in playing the show, they were upset to be the focus of such bile and indeed, during a snatch of 'Candle In The Wind', Bono made his feelings clear with *'They crawled out of the wood-work/Onto the pages of cheap Dublin magazines/I had the grace to hold myself/I refuse to crawl.'*

That the band were so visibly upset by comments that they at least partially condoned says a great deal about the image they had of themselves. U2 were Dubliners and fiercely proud of it, seeing themselves as men of the people. There's little doubt that many of their fans felt similarly about them. To many, U2 were their mouthpiece, expressing their hopes and aspirations, fear and frustrations. Doing so without taking on any of the bullshit trappings of rock 'n' roll stardom meant that they were still the kind of blokes you could rap with at the pub or at a gig. Most of all fans felt that they *understood*, even if they didn't. In a nutshell, that was part of the Self Aid problem, one which U2 themselves tried to dispel when Bono admitted from the stage that he didn't know how it felt to be unemployed, to stand in line for a dole cheque, had no conception of just what a soul-destroying, dehumanizing, desolate existence it can be. But still Dublin demanded answers of U2. *In Dublin* magazine, speaking from the intelligentsia's standpoint, felt that U2 should understand that only governments and not charity could create jobs, possibly implying that U2 should have opted out of the show on principle, in that way creating a greater media stir and perhaps focusing the spotlight more firmly on the politics and the long-term answer. As an act of political solidarity, there is a case to be made for such a line of action: as humanitarians hoping to show compassion and to give hope there could be no such case to answer. A refusal to play at a show where Irish artists had gathered from around the globe would have been an affront to the people of their own land and as great an insult to the unemployed as the acts of charity were.

McCann's article was trenchant in tone and astute in its comprehension of political and corporate machinations. By contrast, U2 were politically naïve and, to an extent, were happy to flaunt it. Given their powerful position they were understandably unwilling to endorse political parties or philosophies and, although their ideologies were broadly to the left, they refused to ally themselves with any movements, wary of the way in which they might be manipulated. To add to the contradictions of their position, U2's very success was proof positive that the capitalist system did actually work. Here were four ordinary lads from Dublin, who, by virtue of hard work and the creation of a commodity that a lot of people wanted, had achieved great material wealth. That you could come from the heart of nowhere and yet reach the summit of a richly rewarding profession was the personification of the capitalist dream and so it would have been awkward for U2 to refute the values of such a system. It would also be true to say that, in the 'emotional positivism' they had preached, it was possible to interpret, or misinterpret, different messages to the simple one of 'don't give up.' Their anti-cynicism line that stood up so well against the doom-laden music of their contemporaries could also say 'you too can do what U2 have done.'

It's one of the great principles of market economics and capitalist philosophy that anyone can make their way in the world if they identify a gap in the market. If four blokes from the Dublin streets can become the world's biggest rock 'n' roll band, then anyone can do it – U2 were a great advert for capitalism. What this line of thought fails to recognize is that there's only room in the market place for a certain number of plumbers, accountants, car mechanics, rock 'n' roll bands, designers, etc. Not everyone can be a success, not everyone has the skills, the health, the opportunity or, just as importantly, the good fortune. It is the prevailing economic climate, a climate that is controlled by government, that decides the availability and demand for work, not the dream of an individual. Self Aid's proclamation of do-it-yourself, while perhaps useful in trying to restore pride to those out of work, was in reality nothing more than a pipe dream. While in theory some of those watching might have been able to start their own small businesses, the vast majority would not have the wherewithal to do so, being short of the capital or the skills (an area where Self Aid was trying to make a difference) or, more importantly, the opportunity (an area where Self Aid could do little).

Self Aid, for all its noble intentions, was a flawed idea. Where it did score points was in the platform it gave for expression of humanitarian compassion, a forum that U2 used well. Always concerned with the social conditions in the inner city they had left behind, they used some of their accumulated sums to good effect, both anonymously and by the public support of events such as Self Aid. More important than such displays was the sense of conscience that informed their music, the sympathetic rather than disapproving tone they took when dealing with drug addiction on 'Bad', for instance. Peter Gabriel's preferred description of his occupation for the purposes of his passport is 'humanist' and that's a description that could equally be applied to the members of U2. Bono articulated anger and passion, talked about the tragedies of unemployment, in song painted vivid, haunting pictures of the personal strife it can cause. If there's to be a debate about the quality of people's lives and the economic circumstances that dictate their future, we need to hear words that bleed, words that cut through meaningless statistics and touch the heart. Unemployment can and does destroy lives. No job, no hope, no money, no future is the real world, the only world for many, many people and that feeling needs a passionate, angry voice. At Self Aid, U2 provided such a voice. And yet . . .

Anger and passion isn't enough and logical expression needs to play a part. An understanding of some of the issues above and beyond the human cry for help is an essential part of solving any problems. There's a fine line between the passionate speech being stirring and being embarrassing. Bono found himself falling on both sides of the line at times and U2 did need to acquire a greater degree of political understanding for them to make their point more incisively in future, but they were at least trying. How many other artists could have inspired this kind of debate in the mid 1980s? Very few, which made U2 all the more valuable and their naïvety all the more disappointing. U2 were not politicians and in song wrote about human frailties rather than philosophical ideology. But they were, like it or not, spokesmen of sorts for the friends that hadn't left Mount Temple for a life of adventure but had found themselves resigned to a life on the dole. They expressed their anger at Self Aid just as they had expressed their doubts and aspirations on *October*. Even then, with just two albums behind them, they had constructed a loyal, burgeoning constituency of their own who were prepared to open themselves to new ideas and experiences. The follow-up single to *October* was 'A Celebration', a title which spoke volumes and which demonstrated just why U2 were special – they were part of their own crowd.

'A Celebration' was released in March 1982, a single deliberately recorded as a separate entity away from their albums, and one which indicated a move towards a more measured combination of rock 'n' roll – a more aggressive rock 'n' roll at that – and Christian faith. Driving in on a wailing repeat guitar figure that was becoming something of a trademark, U2, a group caricatured as true believers, declared their belief in all manner of things, facing up to the unpalatable realities of life, specifically looking at the world's seemingly irreversible drift towards nuclear disaster, to which they reacted with typical defiance. The Establishment and the vested interest do exist, *'but they won't overpower me'* nor, by extension, the U2 audience. Bono commented to the *NME* that 'a lot of people got angry about those lines . . . but all I was saying was that the realities of the bomb must be faced. It showed our idealism wasn't being dissipated in the way that the idealism of the 1960s just got blown away in the breeze.' 'A Celebration' was the most blatant expression yet of the strong bond which existed between fans and band, an expression that the concert experience in particular was a celebration. Niall Stokes from *Hot Press* noted that U2 had immense faith in the 'quality of the ordinary people' despite barbed comments from some quarters that they were wallowing in the mire of the uninspired, allowing themselves to be held back by the average. Ignoring that kind of superiority, U2 recognized the extraordinary strength that was so often to be found amongst the ordinary people and it was almost as if they had been vampirishly drawing on that strength to help keep them on course when their personal doubts had threatened to derail the train.

'A Celebration' did seem to be just that, a celebration, a record that suggested that U2 had survived *October*'s difficult birth and were again looking to operate as a rock 'n' roll band that commented on the world as they saw it. The B-side, 'Trash, Trampoline And The Party Girl', seemed to bear out the new relaxed mood in the band. Removed from anything else they'd committed to vinyl, it was a bizarre song based on acoustic guitar and the slowed down drum-track from the A-side which came about when they discovered they had left themselves just two hours to record a second song for the single. Some strange synthesizer accompaniment from Bono added to the disjointed guitar sequence, giving the whole song a surreal aspect complemented nicely by Bono's odd lyric that was again improvised on the spot and which he later described as being about Adam, though he declined to elaborate further. As a release it was, in its way, more interesting than 'A Celebration', illustrating the growing confidence that U2 had in themselves in the studio and the spontaneity which often yielded some of their finest moments. An unpolished demo of sorts, it was a precursor to some of the material they would arrive at when making *The Unforgettable Fire* with Eno and Lanois some two years later.

chapter seven

SURRENDER

America had made its mark on U2 when they toured it in their insatiable hunt for new fans when *Boy* was released, but it had had little direct influence on the songs for *October*. When they went back to promote that record, events very clearly did filter into what was to become their third album, *War*. Returning for a month in November 1981, they then spent two further months there in February and March of the following year, including a brief stint supporting the J. Geils Band at a number of arena shows, U2's first experience of the venues they were to make their own a few years later. On that particular jaunt, they had planned to play a major part in the famous St Patrick's Day parade in New York by playing live on one of the floats, but the band had to pull out when it was revealed that Bobby Sands had been made an honorary grand marshal of the day.

Sands, a member of the Provisional IRA, had been imprisoned in the top-security H-Blocks at the Maze Prison in Northern Ireland. Following an intermittent but long-running campaign of non-cooperation by prisoners who were arguing for the reinstatement of 'political prisoner' status, status that they had effectively been granted in the 1970s, in October 1980 seven men had gone on hunger strike at the Maze, a strike ended by negotiation in December of that year. It was resumed amid allegations of 'moral blackmail' on the part of the government in March 1981, with Sands as one of the hunger strikers. During the course of his protest, he was elected as MP for Fermanagh and South Tyrone at a by-election in April 1981, before he finally died of starvation in May 1981. To some of the Irish community 'exiled' in America, Sands became a hero, a martyr, a contemporary emblem of the 'revolution' against the British government. NORAID, an American organization that busily raises money to help the activities of the IRA, were instrumental in elevating his status still further, quickly grasping his potential as a fundraising symbol.

U2, as a group who had always rejected violence, whatever the cause or provocation, were unable to take any part in the celebrations surrounding the day of their patron Saint, while the parade embraced a man who had advocated terrorist activity as the road to a united Ireland.

This was not their first brush with the zealous behaviour of Irish Americans and their romantic espousal of the struggle back home, having met such exiles on their travels and having money virtually thrown at them for them to then pass on in order to support the IRA. Bono recalled that in San Francisco, 'I walked out of the backstage door . . . and there were thirty or forty people waiting for a chat and for autographs and I was scrawling my name on bits of paper. I got this one piece of paper and was about to write on it and something in me said, "Hold on a second." The paper was folded and when I opened it there was this big dogma thing looking for signatures. I was about to sign my name to support some guy I'd never heard of, an Irish guy with Republican connections.' This as much as anything else forced them to look again at the situation in their country, to evaluate their own response to something which hadn't seemed important to them before and to redefine their own behaviour on stage and on record. U2 were very clearly and very passionately an Irish group, but that was being increasingly misinterpreted as tacit approval for the tactics of the IRA, which could not have been further from the truth and which gave real cause for concern.

Over the course of two years' worth of press coverage, the 'Irish Question' had inevitably cropped up on a number of occasions, with the band constantly being quizzed on their apparent reticence in writing about the Troubles. The stock answer was that they were from Dublin, they weren't affected by the day-to-day realities of the situation in Northern Ireland and that just because they were an Irish band, they weren't going to trot out some half-hearted song to placate those people who wanted to be able to put U2 into a pigeonhole. Borders and territories were something U2 stood against – they were humans first, Irishmen second – and they refused to fall into the trap of writing about a topic that didn't move them sufficiently strongly simply because it was expected of them. Whatever else might be said of U2 at that time, love 'em or loathe 'em, they were honest in their songs and would condone no hypocrisy.

By the time of *War* they had altered their stance to justify the writing of 'Sunday Bloody Sunday', among other songs on the album which referred to the Troubles, by saying that, OK, the bombs don't go off in Dublin, but some of them are made there.

For an Irish band to write a song called 'Sunday Bloody Sunday' was a bold move open to misinterpretation and yet it was a song that U2 *had* to write, all the more so in view of the album they were planning to make. America and the Irish exiles they had met there had forced the decision on them, making them step back and realize their own nationality and the implications that had. It was also time to point the finger at those Irish people living in a far-off land with their romantic ideas of a united country brought about by an armed revolution. These weren't the people who were being torn apart by life in the firing line, these were the people who lit the blue touchpaper with their money before retiring to a safe distance to watch the explosions. Their identification with U2 was not welcomed and the group had to make a statement to that effect. 'Sunday Bloody Sunday' was part of that statement, *War* was the complete story.

'Sunday Bloody Sunday' was the song which elicited the strongest response, the most powerful emotions and the biggest misunderstandings. A recurrent theme of *War* was the repetition of historical mistakes, of people rooted in traditional, unthinking hatred, striking poses handed down from previous generations, no longer caring why or what for, '*too right to be wrong*'. A fresh approach, a break away from history, was something for which Ireland was crying out – an end to rebel songs, an end to Orangemen parades, and a new beginning with open minds. '*How long must we sing this song?*' was U2's angry response to the adopted entrenched roles. And yet Ireland's problem according to some is its *lack* of historical perspective. Waters' BBC series argued that Ireland does not have a fixation with the past and that it is consequently relegated to repeating it because it has never understood it fully, in part because of the break-up of family units by enforced economic emigration. It is a trait that shows itself in the political life of the nation too. Politics grew from the civil war in Ireland and so it 'did not express itself in ideological terms – your politics like your religion were determined before you were born . . . the old tribal model of politics has gone its merry way. The result is a fossilized political system incapable of absorbing the aspirations of a now modern electorate.'

The nationalism that so fired Ireland through the first part of the century has had unexpected, unwelcome effects, too. Waters again: 'We are stuck in a nationalist groove, still astounded by our lack of chains. The energy expended in dislodging the British was so great that there was very little left to imagine the national condition in 1921 ... the images of Irish possibility froze at that point. There was no energy left to liberate it.' It is at this impasse that some of U2's rage is also directed, the destructiveness of violence on the collective imagination of the Irish people and their culture, the way in which it consigns them to an unpromising future built from a still scarcely believed triumph

Before anyone even heard the song, the title 'Sunday Bloody Sunday' demanded some response, 'Bloody Sunday' being the name given to two of the most shameful days in Irish history. The first came on 21 November 1920 when, in the aftermath of the early-morning murder of seven army officers, three ex-officers and two members of the Royal Irish Constabulary, British troops had opened fire on a football crowd gathered in Dublin's Croke Park and murdered fourteen people. The second took place in Londonderry on 30 January 1972, three years after British troops had gone into Northern Ireland to restore order and protect the Catholic population, when paratroopers killed thirteen Roman Catholic demonstrators who were on a civil rights march that had been prohibited by law, a law which they refused to recognize. Within two months, direct rule of Northern Ireland from Westminster was introduced, replacing its own government which had operated from Stormont Castle. 'Bloody Sunday' was clearly an emotive phrase to be handled with care. In order to tear down the heavy burden of history – a history which, it is said, it would best serve the Irish to forget and the British to learn and remember – and to point out its irrelevance to the situation in Ireland in 1983, U2 commandeered that phrase in the same way that 'rejoice' had been recaptured on *October*. Picking their way through a minefield was a U2 trait that won admirers even as they were blowing themselves apart on controversy and misinterpretation. The *Boy* cover, 'Twilight', the allegedly apostolic rock and religious fervour of *October* had all led to criticism, but the passion with which each statement was made broke down borders that other listeners might have erected against such subject matter. 'Sunday Bloody Sunday' was no exception to that tradition and remains their most contentious song.

As with so many U2 songs, the lyrics reached out to touch upon a number of issues and so were open to misinterpretation, whether wilful or accidental. What rooted the song in the territory of the Irish question was the musical backing, from Larry's opening blast of military drums through to the furious aggression of The Edge's guitar, flashes which exploded into the song with venomous force, to which were added complementary lines on electric violin, a folkish element which made the Irish connotations all the more blatant. This was a happy accident in that Steve Wickham, the violinist in question, had simply bumped into The Edge when he was getting the bus home from a writing session and had offered his services to the guitarist. From its initial composition though, the song took on a life of its own and at times threatened to become something bigger than U2 themselves.

As had been the case before, U2 were not willing to come out in support of any side. The question here was one of humanity ultimately winning out over the gun. Standing against the rule of violence, they typically translated the carnage into personal, rather than political, language. The images were of families torn apart, broken bottles and dead bodies littering the streets of Belfast, the futility of armed struggle and the poisonous cancer of hatred that disfigured the island of Ireland, the '*trenches dug within our hearts*', trenches that would surely make unification unworkable, the legacy of distrust a potentially unconquerable obstacle that might render it impossible for those on either side of the divide to work constructively together in the future, the inevitable first requirement of any peaceful political settlement.

In the same way that other rock musicians had had confused views on matters of political import in the past, U2 were less than clear on their own position except insofar as they categorically condemned violence of any kind, The Edge giving the best summary with, 'You may be prepared to stand up for your beliefs, but to kill someone then I'd rather die than do that.' Thankfully sparing us the agit-pop sloganeering of the Clash, they were, however, guilty of sitting on the fence, offering little that was positive in the way of alternatives. No one would sensibly expect a rock group to answer a problem that has raged in one form or another for centuries, but to refuse to ally themselves to any line of progress other than the laudable but limp 'live in peace' was disappointing, especially when Adam was to admit in a later interview that 'Sunday Bloody Sunday' is its original form had been 'harder hitting'. He said, 'We realized that would have placed us in a very awkward situation in terms of what we could do after that. I think it started out very vitriolic and became a very humane non-sectarian viewpoint, which is the only responsible position . . . to add to Northern Ireland's divisiveness would be exploiting other people's misfortunes.' Ironically, in taking that broad humanitarian approach they did little to distance themselves from the tag of Republican sympathizers that many were keen to attach to them. In concert Bono was forced to declare that 'Sunday Bloody Sunday' was not a rebel song, not a Republican song, but a song that asked for the past to be forgotten and a new peaceful future won. This was a recognition that lyrical ambiguity might not always be a good thing.

The naïvety that had served them well on *Boy* was, with 'Sunday Bloody Sunday', coming back to haunt them. Failing to make their stance abundantly clear had made it very easy for mischief-makers to misconstrue the message of the song and portray U2 in the wrong light. A band who looked to break down barriers, to cross borders, were not likely to be territorial in instinct. Bono had admitted that he would like to see a united Ireland but said, 'I get scared when people start saying they're prepared to kill to back up their belief of where a border should be.' A song that was designed to say that U2 were sick of the killing and of the hate was one which to some extent backfired and it was to take the length of the *War* tour to clear the air. There the intensity of U2's performance, coupled with the use of white flags on stage to represent the idea of surrender and an end to fighting, made the song more clear cut.

Even so, a simple hope that the violence would end coming from a professed, if lukewarm, Republican raised other issues, although the very nature of such a reserved response exposes a conundrum at the heart of Irish politics, a matter which John Waters identified in his radio series when he said, 'Our horror of the IRA, far from helping us to resolve anything, has simply caused us to cop out. Unable to grapple with the the concept of violence and the armed struggle, Irish nationalism has been surrendered to the IRA and cannot be dealt with until it has first been reclaimed.' Without the gunman would there ever be any prospect of a united Ireland, could it ever come about other than as a political solution inspired initially by violent means? By extension were not those Republicans who opposed violence simply living in a fool's paradise, unwilling to condone the actions and atrocities perpetrated by the IRA but ultimately happy to accept the united country even if it were to be achieved by war-like methods and guerrilla tactics? Should it not also be called to mind that it was men not dissimilar to the

Provisional IRA of today who actually won independence in the first place and, where those men had been praised as men of conviction, perhaps simply because they won, their latter day equivalents were rightly vilified for the perpetration of wanton violence that might conveniently and similarly be forgotten should a united Ireland be won? While U2 might be accepting Gandhi's maxim that 'an unjust law is itself a species of violence, arrest for its breach is more so,' should they not be advocating viable alternatives on either side of the border in actions of civil disobedience? Wouldn't a refusal to pay taxes or to take industrial action or to mount protest marches concentrate the minds of the politicians? As it is, the only voice that is consistently heard in favour of a united Ireland is that of the terrorist and the bomb. The peace-loving majority appears to be broadly silent or at the very least devoid of any ideas, perhaps from the fear of speaking out and running the risk of being unjustly associated with the IRA.

While there might be many in the predominantly Catholic Republic who were keen to see a united Ireland, was partition such 'an unjust law'? What of the views of the Protestants who comprised more than half of Ulster's population (Catholics taking roughly a third of the population share)? What of their doubts as to religious freedom, their economic strength and their personal safety when independent of Britain? What of those who actually wished to remain loyal to the Crown? What would their future be in a united Ireland? Surely they might regard unification to be every bit as unjust. The Irish question remains a minefield, with solutions seemingly as far away as ever, a situation which on a wider scale does not bode well for the possibility of the European Community working together as one state. The one thing that should be said is that while borders are being dismantled across the Community, as the Berlin Wall has been demolished, there seems no sensible movement towards a peaceful solution in Ireland that would lead to the removal of its own psychological wall between the North and South as well as the geographical absurdity whereby travelling north through Northern Ireland eventually leads you into the South again!

Sinn Fein, the political wing of the IRA, does have an important role to play in the eventual solution of the troubles – their weakness lies in their failure to condemn those planting bombs in the name of freedom. Sinn Fein's leadership comprises many intelligent, articulate spokesmen but it is a sign of how far out of touch with ordinary people they have become that at Westminster elections in Northern

Ireland, their share of the nationalist vote has dropped from 40% in 1983 to 30% in 1992, a function of the revulsion people feel for the terrorist outrages – in the south of the country, Sinn Fein accounts for just 1.2% of all votes.

'Sunday Bloody Sunday' has been almost a millstone around U2's collective neck and yet it has also been the setting for some of their finest moments, as well as leading indirectly to U2's fascination with the work of Martin Luther King, which would surface on their fourth studio album, *The Unforgettable Fire*. At Live Aid it drew upon a wholly different interpretation, being a general condemnation of war (the civil war in Ethiopia being a major factor in the famine there) and the terrible impact it can have on lives away from the front lines. It almost seemed to have been composed for the occasion, with the lines *'Today the millions cry/ We eat and drink while tomorrow they die.'* As a piece, 'Sunday Bloody Sunday' is quin-tessential U2, U2 in microcosm, gathering together all the parts of the jigsaw into one package – the anguished voice railing against the enemies of humanism; the failure, as the meaning of the song was misinterpreted; the song's eventual acceptance and success in the live setting; the spiritual doubt expressed in terms of its questions as to the benevolence or otherwise of human nature; the spirituality which shone through in the contradiction between the violence of a bloody Sunday and the greatest victory of Christianity, Christ's resurrection on a Sunday.

'Sunday Bloody Sunday' was a song which continued to evolve as U2 refused to allow it to stagnate or become just another 'greatest hit' in a cabaret show. To ensure it retained its spirit and sentiment, it was regularly rearranged and, by the time of Self Aid and the 'Joshua Tree' tour which followed it, the opening drum blast and caustic vocal had been replaced by a gentle guitar opening that turned the song into a lament for lost lives and for a beautiful country disfigured by blind hatred, a setting that was its most appropriate. On that tour, Bono was regularly to use the middle of the song as a forum for a bitter diatribe aimed at the men of violence of whatever cause, taking in the Irish Americans who even now spoke to him in glowing terms of the revolution back home.

If 'Sunday Bloody Sunday' captured much of the essence of U2, one performance of it defined 'the band of the 1980s'. Forget Live Aid. Forget Self Aid. Forget the Amnesty Tour. Forget *The Joshua Tree*. The evening of 8 November 1987 gave rise to the moment that gathered together all the multifarious strands of the musical and emotional beast that up to that point had been U2 and crystallized them into one powerful, desperate, definitive statement of pain, anger, confusion and hopefulness/hopelessness of such force that, just maybe, that band's energy was drained forever, an impression borne out by their later re-emergence as something so different, at least on the surface, as to be an entirely new entity. The screaming intensity of Bono's vocal and the searing savagery of The Edge's guitar during that particular performance of 'Sunday Bloody Sunday', coupled with Bono's passionate condemnation of the mindless sectarian violence, were the ultimate display of the group's commitment to peace and understanding over the Troubles.

The occasion was just another gig on the American tour in support of *The Joshua Tree*. However, this wasn't to be any ordinary show. Before they went on stage, the band learned of yet another bomb outrage, 'a wild act of terrorism', in their home country. A Remembrance Day parade in the small town of Enniskillen had been the inexplicable target of another callous, cowardly IRA attack, an attack which they were later to concede had been 'a mistake', where young and old alike had their lives devastated and destroyed forever when a terrorist's bomb exploded during the course of that parade. Eleven people already lay dead, many more crippled and dangerously ill in hospital, when U2 took the stage. The fury that they felt, as once again their homeland was the centre of brutal, senseless violence, was channelled into a painfully intense concert, climaxing in 'Sunday Bloody Sunday'. But this was just one show in front of a few thousand Americans, many of whom understood little of the Troubles in Ireland, whilst fewer cared. What impact could these words from an American stage have?

> And let me tell you something. I've had enough of Irish Americans who haven't been back to their country in twenty or thirty years come up to me and talk about the resistance, the revolution back home and the glory of the revolution and the glory of dying for the revolution. Fuck the revolution! They don't talk about the glory of killing for the revolution. Where's the glory in taking a man from his bed and gunning him down in front of his wife and children? Where's the glory in that? Where's the glory in bombing a Remembrance Day parade of old-age pensioners, their medals taken out and polished for the day? Where's the glory in that, to leave them crippled for life or dying under the rubble of a revolution that the majority of the people in my country don't want.

Fortunately it wasn't just any concert, because Phil Joanou's camera crew, busy filming the band for the movie that was to be released as part of the ultimately flawed *Rattle and Hum* collection some twelve months later, had chosen to record that particular gig. By capturing this emotional evening, an evening filled with rage at another mindless terrorist atrocity, and then bravely deciding to include it within the finished movie, Joanou and U2 transformed the significance of the event from a parochial incident into a statement with international resonance. This was no longer directed at those few thousand paying customers but at a global audience of millions who would later witness it at the cinema or on home video. In both Northern Ireland and the Republic, a great proportion of the population would see that performance, hear this heartfelt condemnation of violence. And those words weren't confined to the film. No, they were splashed over the press the length and breadth of both countries, as terrorist death threats rained down on the group for their uncompromising anti-violence stance. Anyone on either side of the border around the release date of *Rattle and Hum* would have found it difficult to miss out on just what U2 had said and done.

Surely then, many impressionable youngsters, ripe for the picking by the warring factions, would have the wanton stupidity of it all brought home to them. The strength of U2's position and the influence they could wield would certainly hammer home the message that violence was not the way, that it was the way of the coward and those of low principles, that peaceful negotiation was the only way of ensuring a lasting solution. While a mere rock group would not cause those already recruited to think again, while it might be unable to bring about political change, one as powerful and as influential as U2 could make a vast contribution in mobilizing opinion against the violence, so starving the hatemongers of their lifeblood: future converts.

Take a walk around Belfast. It's a fine city set in rolling hills, filled with some beautiful buildings, populated by honest, decent people, as friendly as any you could ever wish to meet. Head down any road away from the city centre though and you'll find walls awash with graffiti: 'JOIN THE STRUGGLE'; 'SMASH THE IRA'; 'PROVISIONAL IRA'; 'FIGHT FOR YOUR FREEDOM'; even 'U2'. You won't find any that say 'FUCK THE REVOLUTION'. Naturally enough, part of that is down to the fear that anyone found responsible for painting such a slogan would soon find their balls nailed neatly to their knees, a fairly strong deterrent in anyone's language, but the real key is that attitudes have not changed, no one's mood has been turned around enough to say 'fuck the revolution'. Walk down some of the 'no-go' streets of the city and the atmosphere of hatred can be so thick and heavy that it will physically drag you down, like walking into the teeth of a howling gale. There's a suffocating tension, a feeling of battle lines drawn in the air, the impression that the most minor spark could ignite a huge powder keg of barely suppressed violence. Most obvious of all is the knowledge that the hatred and mistrust of the 'opposition' on both sides is so ingrained that it will take a hell of a lot more than a well-intentioned rock group to change attitudes in this part of the world.

The realization that music cannot change the world, cannot on any major scale bring people to understand that violence is not the way is the final nail in the coffin of the dreams of the 1950s and 1960s. Then love was going to save the world, triumph over evil, allow us to be more sympathetic to the plight of our fellow man, all achieved by the cleansing tide of popular music – 'All you need is love/All together now!' The man responsible for that anthem, John Lennon, reported from the trenches dug within his own heart that the dream was over as early as 1971 but for many hope sprang eternal, the fire still flickered, bursting gloriously into flames from time to time in order to protest over Vietnam or to widen public consciousness on the shameless constitutional racism perpetrated by South Africa, but now it seems extinguished forever. Music cannot save the world, cannot change the world, may no longer have any place in the world other than as an accompaniment to washing the dishes. Rock 'n' roll stop the traffic? Maybe. Rock 'n' roll change the world? No.

Yet U2 still 'justify the term rock 'n' roll', as Bono put it, and rock 'n' roll has rarely been more riveting, more compelling and more moving than that performance even when it was reduced to the small screen. Passionate honesty is a quality that cannot be manufactured but, in a world where it has become a debased currency, it is all the more striking when it makes a reappearance. Over the course of their live career, Bono had been U2's greatest strength and their biggest weakness. Never having mastered the art of strapping on the mock sincerity of the politician, his homilies from the stage often sounded forced and hollow, he himself admitting that 'it can backfire and U2 can fall on its face,' one of the great ironies of a media age where lies and superficialities sold to us by 'great communicators' sound more genuine than naked truth. On this occasion however, the powerful emotion engendered by the situation transcended his usual self-consciousness to result in a forceful and obviously heartfelt statement.

But if music at its most powerful can achieve so little in global terms, where is the future for music in a radical, political sense? Indeed, does it have one? Is it in the huge events held in support of Amnesty International? While helpful and necessary chips taken away from the implacable monolith that is apathy, the media jamboree which they inevitably become in the quest for new members and donations means that, at times, their message can be obscured or lost. Perhaps the time has come to resign rock 'n' roll to the Easy Listening bins and use it as yet another cheap thrill, a quick fix, a bite-size unit of entertainment. Do we have a lifetime of ersatz music ahead of us, banalities which say nothing to me and countless others about our lives as they could or should be? Is this better than the real thing?

If the medium cannot bring about change, then with the global decline in intelligent, articulate cinema at the hands of the corporate mafia, it does remain perhaps the only mass 'artistic' forum where people can express themselves to an international audience. What then is the way forward? How can music be influential in making us more aware of our lives, ourselves and the ways in which we can improve matters?

The underlying amorality of the human condition has always been fair game for popular culture, though it is often treated as a grotesque – perhaps rock 'n' roll's fatal error in its 'political' moments has been to assume that humankind is basically benevolent and keen to do the right thing, when the great film directors of recent years, such as Scorcese or Coppola, have been more authentic in their treatment of these decades of expedient brutality. Some have given it more mature and considered thought, but it remains comparatively rare for an articulate rock group to investigate it in depth, still rarer to juxtapose that with the sensory overload that the modern world imposes upon us all, to replace naïve idealism with unsentimental realism. With the reinvention of U2 that arrived with *Achtung Baby*, they have confronted that dilemma head on. Realizing that sermons from the mount were too much for many to take, that the form of expression was given greater coverage than its substance, understanding that the huge sweep of their music was building a vast audience of people who had little time for the ideas that they were trying to discuss or convey, Saint Bono and the rest of U2 renounced their canonization and spent two years stripping down their Frankenstein and rebuilding a leaner, fitter, harder vehicle, which met their requirements perfectly and distanced them from the caricature that was constructed around them. Bono confessed, 'People try to turn (a U2 gig) into a political rally and I get nervous about that.' The new machine was one wrapped in darkness, bombarded by irrational obsessions, consumed with doubt, tortured by deep-seated fears, guzzling gas from the new technology deli and ultimately laughing at the absurdity of pampered, limo-riding rock gods, taking the part of Jiminy Cricket against a bewildered generation's elephantine Pinocchio. In the midst of a wretched nightmare as we crave the morning's light, aching for the relief that never comes, there lurks a little piece of *Achtung Baby*. That recognition and the accompanying shift in emphasis has seen U2 focus on the enigma that modern life has become. With that new concentration, they may have helped give rock music a future in the 1990s and beyond, a more incisive politicism since 'it deals with the human heart, betrayal . . . which in the end (is) where you must start, you've got to start with your own hypocrisy before you start pointing it out in politicians,' as Bono told London's *Time Out*.

It's a metamorphosis that has surprised and confused but is based in very many respects upon the music they were making around *War*, and particularly in 'Sunday Bloody Sunday', and so it's highly appropriate that it was a seismic reading of that song that seemed to signpost their shift in musical and visual direction, U2 being required to point out the differences between the music and the musician more clearly. In the early 1980s they had to fight hard to bring idealism back into music, to stare down the Broadway trend in popular music and make rock 'n' roll mean something again, Bono explaining to *Melody Maker*'s Ted Mico, 'People think, "Oh yeah, there they are, U2 marching off to war. There goes Bono running all over the stage. And unlike Mick Jagger, Bono doesn't do it with a wink. *That's* the problem. Bono actually *believes* in the people that come to the concerts and believes in what he's doing. Oh how embarrassing. Oh dear oh dear!" The problem with the 1980s is that people stopped believing in rock 'n' roll – to believe in it has become something to scoff at.' U2 stood up and said that it's OK, even necessary, to be idealistic in such times. 'Sunday Bloody Sunday' was an important part of that process, however unfocused it might have been.

And it was an unfocused piece, especially when taken out of the setting of *War*, an album designed to be 'a slap in the face' of the bland wallpaper muzak that (dis)graced the charts at the time. 'We're angry with the present nonchalance of music, (*War*) takes on the friction but it has a lot of love in it, makes people want to fight back,' as Bono described it. It was a record with which U2 stood up to be counted and which captured the mood of the times. *War* was a brave choice of title but it conveyed a sense of much of the subject matter and was virtually a motif for the year 1982 when it was written and recorded, a year where conflicts raged around the globe in places as far apart as the Falklands, the Middle East, South Africa, Poland, Northern Ireland and Central America. In that context, a cry for an end to fighting was the only logical response. After the more atmospheric and impressionistic arrangements that had made up much of *Boy* and *October*, U2 made a far more direct, aggressive record that centred itself on struggle, looking at war in its broader sense, mental tensions as well as physical confrontations, Bono pointing out that '*War* could be the story of a broken home, a family at war . . . an emotional thing between lovers.' *War* set its face against the violence that was endemic in society, the blurred lines between fact and fiction where 'one minute you see someone being shot on *The Professionals* and the next you see someone falling through a window after being shot on the news . . . we're becoming so used to the fiction that we become numb to the real thing.'

The uncompromising nature of the album was caught by its sleeve design. Peter Rowan, the boy, was again shown on the cover, adopting the same posture he had taken on their debut album, but it was very clear that things had changed. Where folding his hands behind his neck had seemed relaxed on *Boy*, now it was a position of submission, a boy who had been forced to surrender. Where his eyes had been wide open and innocent, now they were wild and belligerent, filled with anger, while his lips were cracked and scratched, portraying him as the victim of violence. The two and a half years that had passed since *Boy* had seen him grow into a world that was not as awe-inspiring as it had seemed in days of yore but one which was only too willing to take advantage of him. He had grown up physically but mentally, too, no longer content to be anyone's fool. If he was held in physical submission, his spirit was clearly unbowed. His transformation mirrored that of a band from Dublin that had travelled the world and had seen the prizes on offer, the temptations that had destroyed many rock 'n' roll bands before them. Not only that, but it put a human face to the traumas of war.

War might be fought with tanks and guns but its tragic consequences could be measured only in terms of the human price it exacted.

The complementary aggression of much of the music came from a desire to crack, if not break, the U2 mould. As a band which had grown without roots, U2 had sculpted their own highly identifiable sound, The Edge being the main creator of that. His expressive use of effects such as his echo unit, the high soaring clarity of his playing and his subtle use of repeat figures were fast becoming an oft-copied style and a personal cliché. As a group who had always aimed to avoid clichés in their music and their lifestyle, the time had come to reassess their position and investigate different avenues of sound.

As a part of that search, they had approached a number of different producers to work on the record, including Jimmy Destri of Blondie and Sandy Pearlman, who had worked with the Clash and Blue Oyster Cult, and at one stage the idea of having a different producer for each song was seriously considered. Eventually though, sufficient change in musical emphasis was coming from within the group itself and in order to help with the transition they asked Steve Lillywhite to return to the fold and make *War* with them. Lillywhite had a self-imposed rule of only making two records with any artist, but for U2 he was willing to make an exception since he was keen to capture them as a more confident, mature band.

Lillywhite's input was naturally vitally important, but it was The Edge who signalled the new direction. Restricting himself to fewer effects, he turned to playing a more traditional rock guitar, setting himself the daunting, but exciting, challenge of reinterpreting a style that had been dominant for twenty-five years or more and extracting fresh life from it. It wasn't to everyone's taste, with the *NME* accusing them of running 'aground on rock', but it did give a new lease of life to what could have become a jaded, stereotypical sound, essential for a group attempting to turn rock 'n' roll into a three-dimensional form once more. On 'Like A Song' The Edge employed a Byrdsian riff, steel guitar on 'The Refugee' (the released version of which was their original demo remixed by Lillywhite), impressive harmonics on 'Surrender', acoustic strumming on 'Seconds', and he opened 'Drowning Man' with a guitar part that sounded as if it might have stepped out from Yes's 'Close To The Edge', but the tour de force was 'New Year's Day', quite breathtaking in both beauty and intensity as the guitar took a back seat to Adam's ominous bass line before bursting to life on brief, incisive incursions.

All of this was a radical departure for a guitarist who had

inspired a hundred imitators, but it was only to be expected from such a fine musician, a man who justified that term every bit as much as U2 justified the phrase 'rock 'n' roll.' If not a great technician, not a classically trained guitarist, The Edge was and remains an inspirational innovator, one whose music comes from within rather than one who composes as a technical exercise, relying on flash techniques to create a stir. Others were busily creating a legend around his playing, but The Edge simply occupied himself with playing the guitar and developing new sounds. Bono has often introduced him, tongue-in-cheek, as Jimi Hendrix, but the comparison does stand – Hendrix was a bolt from the blue in the 1960s, a sound from nowhere, just as The Edge was in the 1980s and now the 1990s, his determination to push back the boundaries implicit in a comment to the *NME*: 'I want U2 to be a band that takes risks. I hate this idea of U2 as a nice safe band.'

Just as the guitar on *War* had essayed a raw-boned sound that suited the subject matter, the rhythm section followed suit and took the band into new territories, with 'Two Hearts Beat As One' and 'The Refugee' dancing to a funk beat that owed something to New York and to labelmate August Darnell, aka Kid Creole. U2 were not shy of employing his backing singers, the Coconuts, and his trumpet player, Kenny Fradley. It was a bold experiment which didn't always work as well as it might have done but which was nevertheless an interesting departure from the tried and trusted. The strength of *War* was its directness of approach. The upfront attack from Adam – who was expressing the influences he was taking from the reggae with which he surrounded himself on tour – and Larry was an integral part of that, just as it was vital that they reined themselves in for the more sensitive songs like 'Drowning Man', a calm in the midst of a storm which made the strident nature of a piece such as 'Like A Song' all the more effective. The musical experimentation was also a metaphor for Bono's lyrical subtext – the world should not consign itself to mindless, thoughtless repetition of the past, but should build a new future from the present. The resultant music seemed more nervous, hesitant, less assured than before, reflecting the tension in the outside world.

For songs which aimed at universal targets as much as autobiographical issues, it was important that the music reflected the harsh nature of the topics on which they commented, but in so doing the sonic density did obscure the themes of some of the album, that of hope and the struggle for love in an unsympathetic climate. To many casual observers *War* became U2's political manifesto, when it was more accurately their reaction to the oppressive and depressing events of the previous year.

The burning issue of the time was the nuclear debate, with the Campaign for Nuclear Disarmament (CND) gathering momentum, as the global superpowers were seemingly engaged in a never-ending arms build-up. There was a sharp deterioration in relations between the USA and the USSR as Reagan rejected détente in the aftermath of the Soviet invasion of Afghanistan, terming theirs an 'evil empire', the same Hollywood jargon that led to his love affair with a defence initiative called 'Star Wars'. In a volatile situation, a new cold war was ushered in by the crisis in Poland in 1981, a crisis which proved to be the precursor of the winds of change which blew with such force across Eastern Europe at the end of the decade.

Poland, a member of the Warsaw Pact, was a nation under strict Soviet supervision, having already lost territory to them at the end of the Second World War, after the Soviets had liberated the country from the Germans. Having felt the full force of Nazi atrocities in the war, when six million Poles, half of them Jews, were murdered in concentration camps, its people were then subjected to a harsh regime, religious oppression and economic disaster. By the mid 1970s food prices had spiralled, a hardship exacerbated by shortages which necessitated lengthy queueing for the most basic of commodities.

Strikes broke out through Warsaw in 1980, the hotbed of unrest centring on the shipyards of Gdansk. Permission was given by the government for free, independent trades unions to be formed. The result was Solidarity, forged under the leadership of Lech Walesa, a devout Catholic. Solidarity blossomed into a 10-million-member organization and caused great concern in the Soviet Union, then led by Leonid Brezhnev. Martial law was imposed by the leader of the Polish Communist Party, General Jaruzelski, in December 1981 at the behest of the Soviets, who also undertook military manoeuvres on the Polish border. This all called to mind the scenes that had preceded the Soviet invasion of Czechoslovakia in August 1968 in the aftermath of the 'Prague Spring' initiative and its resultant easing in the restriction of civil liberties. Under martial law, Solidarity became a proscribed organization and its leaders were arrested. Jaruzelski then instituted a Military Council which ended in fifteen deaths and 10,000 arrests over the first five months of 1982. Walesa, who had become the public face of the unions' struggle for freedom and recognition, remained imprisoned until November of that year, which enforced a lengthy separation from his wife, also his staunchest supporter.

As an encapsulation of the type of fight which U2 were addressing with *War*, it was grist to their mill and indeed the song that was most clearly influenced by it, 'New Year's Day', became the first single from the album, setting the audience up for what was to come. As a song, 'New Year's Day' did not carry any specific mention of the conflict in Poland, but that situation was a subliminal reference point and the most obvious example of the subject matter. It came to represent the defiance of the human spirit under provocation and persecution, the strength that can be gathered when **two** join together as one, a spiritual unity which can help them face the world even when they might be physically apart. '*Though torn in two we can be one*' in the specific sense referred to that spiritual closeness which kept Walesa and his wife together prior to any physical reunion, but it was also part of a motif, a thread which ran through the songs, the concept of two people acting as one, 'the only starting point from which anything productive is likely to ensue' as Liam Mackey described it. If two people acting, thinking and living as one were possible and indeed, essential, then the obvious great leap of faith towards whole peoples, entire nations, acting as one together became a flesh-and-blood idea rather than a theoretical concept from a human relations laboratory.

In that sense 'New Year's Day' was a song of hope and optimism, but it also had a fatalistic air of resignation, '*Nothing changes on New Year's Day.*' Adam described the song as an 'acknowledgment of Solidarity . . . we were just saying that no matter how much people try to change the situation, things are always more or less the same at the start of every new year,' although, in a strange twist of fate, martial law was lifted in Poland on New Year's Day 1983. This threw what was ostensibly a song about individuals under stress ever further into the 'political' arena, when the only real comment had come in the final verse, one later omitted from concert performance, where Bono railed against the obsession for money, twisting our sense of superiority over the past, the feeling that we live in some 'golden age', into the truism that 'gold' is almost always the reason we go to war. In Poland, what money there was was in the hands of the state, and Solidarity were simply after their share, a share of the money that the ordinary people they represented were creating by their labours, a corner fought by the labour movement against avaricious owners for centuries.

In moments of delicious black comedy, we were treated to the spectacle of Margaret Thatcher sending her best wishes to Walesa and Solidarity in the fight against communism, adjudging them to be engaged in a righteous fight against those who would suppress freedom – this from a Prime Minister who dedicated herself almost entirely to crushing trades unions in her own country, culminating in the miners' strike of 1984/5 when she drove a wedge into Britain's most powerful union, the National Union of Mineworkers, causing a break-away organization to be formed in preparation for the decimation of an undefended industry announced in the closing months of 1992.

Gold as the catalyst for war was an undeniable sign of our times, particularly in the West. It became of paramount importance therefore that the impact of global decisions on individuals was brought to the forefront of debate, making recognizable just how elusive the concept of 'freedom' had become. While in the West it was referred to in terms of economic freedom, in many countries of Eastern Europe or Central America the people were searching for freedom of expression, freedom of movement, freedom of thought.

Revolution became a fashionable word, even a fashion accessory in the early 1980s – every university had an Anarchist's Society that met regularly at the same time each month while their favourite rock bands adopted combat chic and pretended to be guerrilla units – but any practical radicalism was quick to fizzle out. Where once rock 'n' roll had stood united, manning the barricades against war in Vietnam, it too had become fragmented, its young followers engaged in tribal warfare of their own. Where rock 'n' roll had once promised real revolution, it now wore it on its sleeve in perfectly matching shades to complement the season's other essential garments, mouthing empty platitudes to win admirers and commercial success. But where was the substance? This was not a music to change lives, it was a music to change wardrobes, wardrobes that became a theatre of war as the young created elitist cliques, using clothes to distance themselves from one another. A community of shared experience and mutual distrust of the Establishment that expressed itself through rock 'n' roll was now a community of dissent that couldn't commit itself to anything but the ritual dislike of other styles of music. It was around this emptiness that 'Like A Song' was based, although it was equally clear just where the real targets lay should you wish to extend the metaphor to an outside world engaged in violence that was rooted in historic conflict.

'Like A Song' was an alarm call and a call of alarm, an attempt to wake those who would bicker among themselves to the wider truth they chose to ignore, and an expression of disquiet at the direction the pop culture was taking. If the old guard was beyond redemption, too set in its ways to see sense and discard the foul heritage of hate and mistrust purely along traditional lines, then the future would have to be won by the young who did, after all, have a greater stake in that future. There was a 'prophet in the wilderness' feel to the song, Bono articulating an immense rage against the apathetic among his generation who were missing the opportunity to change the world and hold back the tide that was threatening to sweep away basic human rights across the planet, a world that was living under a mushroom cloud of fear greater than at any time since the Cuban Missile Crisis. Bono expanded on the idea: 'It's very important that people make a stand. It's interesting that youth culture has been divided into pockets like punks, mods, whatever, so they're too busy arguing among themselves to tell governments what they think. I'd like to see a change in that. Music should break down barriers not set them up.'

The vocal diatribe was all the more powerful when, in conjunction with the aggressive rock backing provided by Larry's pounding drumbeat and The Edge's glorious jangling guitar, which he interspersed with a slashing rock riff, a call came for a real revolution, a revolution in mind that could change the state of play, not a safe revolution that hid behind a badge and a poster of Che Guevara. A decade later, U2 concerts would proclaim, 'It's your world, you can change it,' a sentiment at the heart of 'Like A Song', a song to get people off their backsides and fighting back with words and ideas. The old answers were not enough. Where were the new Karl Marx, the new Martin Luther King, the new thinkers? Where were the people of soul, the people who cared and would care for those in need of help?

'Like A Song' was undoubtedly the angriest song the band had recorded to that point, sneering at phonies, spitting at the uniform of rebellion, kicking down the walls of traditional divides. Did anyone actually want truth from their rock 'n' roll any more? Did anyone want a sound that could change their lives? Did anyone want debate or did they just want wallpaper music? U2 were one of the final flourishes from a music that had once meant something, that had once been an attitude with a cause. They had to sing their songs because they had something to say, something worth listening to, in a medium that was capable of touching millions. Few others have come along with a similarly powerful belief since U2, and perhaps only Morrissey and REM have actually succeeded in transmitting their faith in rock 'n' roll music as a force for good, or at least as a medium with a point to make, rather than just more entertainment. '*Like a song I have to sing/ I sing it for you*' were the words of artists who wanted to make a difference. While they were laughed at as pretentious waffle, why shouldn't rock music aspire to the level of the short story or the film as a conductor of emotion, especially in such times of dislocation? Rock 'n' roll had been the voice of sanity of all humanity. Now it was the voice of Armani. 1983 was a year where people had to grow together not apart, to draw strength and avert the dangers that seemed to lurk in a dark and foreboding future. 'Like A Song' was a showcase for all the frustrations that U2 felt – rock 'n' roll's current impotence, their own inarticulateness, their place in an industry that added to the divides even in a seemingly trivial manner, their inability to stop the fighting, their helplessness. Its core philosophy was hammered home in its closing seconds, when The Edge blasted through the main riff to 'Two Hearts Beat As One'.

War was an album of hope, but it was realistic, too, and had to deal with the bleakness that was enveloping the world as people really did live in fear of the mushroom cloud and the mutually assured destruction that was, allegedly, keeping us safe. As Bruce Kent, CND's general secretary in the first half of the 1980s was to put it, 'preparing for a suicide is not a very intelligent means of defence.' The siting of US Pershing missiles in the UK put extra coal on the fire of debate in this country and, by virtue of geographical proximity, Ireland too, while the rest of Europe mobilized itself on anti-nuclear marches, seemingly without the assistance of any major-league musical acts.

In the song 'Seconds', U2 had another angle on the scope for atrocity which the bomb had opened up – terrorism, an inescapable conclusion for anyone with an interest in the problems of Northern Ireland. While it might then have been the stuff of low-budget sci-fi horror movies, it could not be denied that the possibility existed for terrorist organizations to assemble some kind of nuclear device and hold a nation to ransom – '*you can assemble them anywhere*', even in Times Square perhaps. The power that would bestow on terrorists would be incalculable, as the zealots with a cause could pull the strings from the government's hands and run the world. If the

Establishment might protest that their security measures were unbreachable, making it impossible for the necessary materials to fall into the wrong hands, they said the same about airline security before Lockerbie, they said the same about the safety standards at nuclear plants before Three Mile Island, and astonishingly they still say the same – with a straight face! – about Sellafield. No security system is impregnable and, when the superpowers are busy selling the technology used in nuclear armaments to some of the less stable countries of the world, the possibility of a terrorist splinter group wreaking havoc cannot be ruled out – the World Trade Center mean anything to you?

If the world seems unstable now, it's positively relaxed compared with the early 1980s, a time when warmongering was the first requirement of any world leader. Ronnie had an 'evil empire' to deal with, that empire occupying itself with the occupation of Afghanistan and preparing to let the tanks roll over Poland should it prove necessary. The only thing you needed to know was who to hate and how much, something brought home by a TV documentary shown in 1982 called *Soldier Girls*, a look at women in the American army, an excerpt of which was used in 'Seconds'. 'They were being wound up, chanting away, "I'm gonna be an airborne ranger, I'm gonna live the life of danger,"' recalled Bono for Radio 1. 'Then the Sergeant Major said how he'd been turned into a killing machine.' The idea of people being turned into machines to be pointed at any opposition and then told, 'Kill!' like a pack of dogs does tend to question the idea of civilization and whether it might not be a good idea.

In spite of its subject matter, 'Seconds' was a blackly comic song, a kind of 'Doctor Strangelove sings the Beatles' anthem, with The Edge taking the lead vocal, though it was hard to distinguish him from Bono. A surrealist stance on the absurdity of nuclear arsenals was perhaps the only way to cope and 'Seconds' was to presage *Achtung Baby* and particularly Zoo TV, of which Bono said, 'I really understood surrealism after the Gulf War. It seemed like the only response. I understood how Picasso couldn't paint human faces after the war.' 'Seconds' contained comic asides about a new dance craze 'the atomic bomb', a barb used as a corollary of 'Like A Song', and aimed perhaps at the way youth culture had drawn a veil over involvement, opting instead for trends, cliques and self-indulgence on the dancefloor. Similarly buoyant on the back of the acoustic strum that The Edge mapped out was the central refrain '*It takes a second to say goodbye,*' which called to mind the popular image of Reagan with his finger on the button ready to pull the plug on the world without a second thought. 'Seconds' was an important indication that, although U2 chose to use their voice and their power over an audience to address serious topics that really did mean something to them, thereby spurning the bubblegum and ear candy that otherwise filled the charts, they were not humourless, strait-laced puritans who would refuse to laugh at a joke for reasons of higher morality – U2 were enjoying their success despite an image to the contrary – but 'Seconds', like 'Trash, Trampoline & The Party Girl', was an isolated expression of any musical humour.

Image versus substance was one of the wars which U2 waged in the early part of their career. Their early albums were a very conscious, deliberate attempt to return some thought to the rock 'n' roll agenda, to elevate the music to the status it had enjoyed a decade or more earlier, a reaction to the foppishness of current pop music, its Broadway trend. While the music was not in any way contrived – it was too vehement for that – they were very careful to ensure that they were portrayed in a particular light. At the heart of their image was a non-image, a reflection of the truth at the centre of U2, but this was not presented as a whole; there were things very clearly held back. Although they were good-humoured and usually easy to get on with, they took great pains to come across as believers in a cause, artists who were driven to make their music and who had the utmost respect for their fans. Long gone were the mischievous days in Dublin when U2 were playful as well as serious. Now there only seemed room to engage people spiritually and intellectually, which resulted in the later backlash descriptions of the band as one-dimensional characters who were forced to carry the weight of the world on their shoulders.

There were flashes of humour in live performance and in interviews, but these were few and far between, seemingly kept in check lest any whimsicality should devalue the music or dilute their drive. It was an image that they preserved on video in the snows of Sweden for 'New Year's Day', later to appear with furrowed brows on *The Unforgettable Fire* – although Adam couldn't quite keep an occasional smirk off his face – then being photographed in the desert for *The Joshua Tree*. U2 as serious young men was a jealously guarded picture since it did appeal to an earnest audience who shared their concern at the drift of rock 'n' roll and were keen to welcome back 'the big music'. In that sense, U2 manipulated a public picture of themselves every bit as much as Duran Duran or Spandau Ballet, while maintaining the ability to sidestep any accusations of narcissism until much later in their career when they were aimed at egos allegedly out of control rather than any preconceived imagemongering.

U2 may have been altruistic in intent and in their musical view, but they have never been naïve as far as the business and marketing side of their career has been concerned. Journalist Tony Fletcher noted in 1984, 'U2 are run with a military precision that I for one have never seen matched.' Despite the harsh criticism of independent bands towards those signed to big record companies there is little wrong in that. Far better that a band control its own destiny together with its company than that it have to continue playing the Camden Falcon, consequently changing nothing.

Exercising such tight control over all one's affairs does have its potential pitfalls however. In a business that's as obsessively concerned with the maintenance of a level of 'street cred' as rock 'n' roll is, it can lead to accusations of megalomania, can portray the band as executives in distressed jeans and can squeeze the humanity out of their operations. The Edge admitted in 1984, 'That is the biggest single threat to this group: money. You've got to be so aware of the dangers of losing what you've got due to this thing called money. I think the most significant thing about our new position is that we can do what we want creatively.' The money and attendant power have not always necessarily been used in what many would consider the wisest or the most sympathetic manner.

There have been regular squabbles in Ireland over the ticket prices for U2 shows. They chose to see out the 1980s with a series of shows at Dublin's Point Depot, a move which provoked outrage in the city when ticket prices were announced, the prices eventually being reduced as a result of that pressure. Similarly, in 1993 early promises of a free Zoo TV Outside Broadcast in the city were not realized, the imposition of a cover charge of £10 being mooted to an equally lukewarm response before the gig was finally cancelled because of fears as to crowd safety. Instead three conventional, i.e. ticket-paying, shows were drafted onto the itinerary in the Republic. It is important to remember that, while U2 have privately put money back into their own country, have helped create better facilities at Windmill Lane, thereby attracting foreign talent and giving home-grown artists a start, have founded their own label to help those newcomers and have given Ireland more publicity than any Tourist

Board could hope to across the world, they are required to labour under a number of insoluble difficulties. Firstly, they are monstrously successful and therefore wealthy people in a relatively poor country. In addition, they did benefit quite enormously from tax advantages given to artists by the Irish government, which meant that they were allowed to keep a huge proportion of the money they generated, far more than an equivalent act in the UK would have been able to. While they might voluntarily plough some of that money back into their country and their city, they enjoyed a privilege that the ordinary man or woman scraping a living did not have, so why did they have to charge their own people so much? And the press always like to have an excuse to engineer a nice backlash.

These minor spats have soured relations between U2 and their native land a little, yet Ireland's reluctance to grant U2 a sainthood has been a saving grace for the band. Brendan Behan eloquently expressed the situation in 'Richard's Cork Leg' when he wrote, 'The English and Americans dislike only some Irish – the same Irish that the Irish themselves detest, Irish writers – the ones that *think*.' Likewise, James Joyce described his country in *A Portrait of the Artist as a Young Man* as 'the old sow that eats her farrow,' yet that very refusal of Ireland's to welcome the success of its offspring has given perspective to the band. Had they resided in the USA during the phenomenal success they enjoyed through the 1980s, one would have had to fear its impact on them. In a land where success was demanded and lauded to the skies, the seductive trappings that they now trash with Zoo TV may have overpowered them and their music, a danger they had already alluded to in 'Stranger In A Strange Land' on *October*.

More important in terms of the international rock 'n' roll constituency was the Negativland affair which broke out at the end of 1991, a considerably more complex set of circumstances than was reported at the time, but one which did very real damage to U2's reputation on the alternative scene. This was particularly damaging bearing in mind that it preceded the release of *Achtung Baby* by a month.

Achtung Baby was to be a relaunch of a very different U2 that was apparently hoping to recapture the devoted, alternative audience that typified their early ascent to prominence before *The Joshua Tree* and *Rattle and Hum* had hurled them into what Bono termed 'Kevin and Sharon territory . . . an audience that's just into big bands' (another revealing glimpse of what lay at the heart of U2's self-perception). When they finally took *Achtung Baby* on to the road,

Bono was heard to remark that the album might shed some of the 'pop-kids' that U2 didn't need anyway, and the whole record was presented as avant-garde; the album might well rank among their finest work, but U2 were now far removed from the alternative scene, as much by their success as by their music, and could not hope to return there. The indie bands didn't want them, unfairly, if healthily, treating U2 with the same disdain that U2 had reserved for ELP fifteen years earlier, while the mainstream that U2 had found themselves in was ready to forgive any excess because they sold records, put bums on seats and kept radio ratings high.

Even so, while taking to laughing at their previous persona they seemed to long for the music to be taken as seriously as it had been before success obscured it rather than be treated as the object of scorn simply because it was popular with the world outside the cloisters of rock 'n' roll criticism. U2 seemed to covet the image of the alternative, college-rock band and the prestige that bestowed, ignoring the fact that they, like virtually every other band in history, had deliberately aimed for the global acceptance they now tried to reject – remember 'Desire'? (It also conveniently ignored a very high profile advertising campaign for *Achtung Baby* which included a number of prominent billboards featuring the gaudily painted Trabants that had become the official mascot of U2 in 1991 and a heavily repeated national TV ad.) That, however, was the deal. Fame and alternative cachet were mutually exclusive commodities unless you happened to be REM, a critical oddity that must have been a bitter pill for U2 to swallow. For a band that wanted to be considered as an alternative again, suing an independent label was not a great start, although it wasn't acutally U2 themselves who took any action.

Negativland were an underground band out of San Francisco who dealt in satirical observations, using sampling technology to construct their music. Their September 1991 release 'U2' was a remixed, considerably altered version of 'I Still Haven't Found What I'm Looking For', mixed into which were snatches of conversation from Bono and Casey Kasem, best known as the host of the TV show in the UK *America's Top Ten*. The waters became muddied because Negativland felt that, since the song was a satirical parody, their use of it was protected by US copyright law, a stance backed by their record company SST. Warner Chappell, the company who have licensed U2's material, weren't happy with the decision, in part because they felt that, since almost all the song had been used by

Negativland, it now went beyond the realms of parody. Things weren't helped by the sleeve, which featured U2's logo in enormous letters, a picture of the U2 spy plane and 'Negativland' in tiny type at the bottom. Island Records took out an injunction to stop sale or distribution, leading to an out-of-court settlement whereby SST and Negativland agreed to pay a fine and costs prior to attacking the other side for preventing free speech, eventually following the lead of Iran – an intriguing application of the principle of free speech – in decreeing a, presumably satirical, fatwa on the head of Bono.

In the middle of this were U2 themselves, who had had little to do with the case, Paul McGuinness apparently seeing the record's funny side. U2 tried to persuade Island not to seek payment but Island were not willing to allow the legal costs, estimated at anything between $55,000 and $70,000, to go unpaid, SST then demanding total recompense from Negativland who, unsurprisingly, chose to leave the label. When the dust had finally settled, the perceived situation was U2 as control freaks tracking down every last penny they could get their hands on, with Negativland and SST the unfortunate victims. In reality, U2 had no involvement in the lawsuit and endeavoured to get Negativland off the financial hook, yet the suspicion still lingers that U2 should have done more and that they could, indeed should, have underwritten the legal expenses them-selves, understanding Negativland's innovative and experimental stance as well as appropriating some very positive publicity into the bargain. After all, that kind of money would be small beer to an act of their stature and they knew what it was like to be on the receiving end, having been forced into paying an out of court settlement for copyright infringement when Bono included a snatch of 'Send In The Clowns' on the live version of 'The Electric Co.', released on the initial pressings of *Under A Blood Red Sky*. To allow a lawsuit which was, at least as far as the public were concerned, being conducted in the name of the band was not rock 'n' roll – rock 'n' roll bands sued their managers, promoters or record company, not one another. Any lingering benevolence that certain sections of the press or the 'independent scene' in general might have felt for U2 and their possible altruistic activity was destroyed by the Negativ-land fiasco. Whoever said the world was fair? For U2 it was also proof positive that, whatever they might do, critics had cast them irredeemably into just that 'Kevin and Sharon territory' and would beat them accordingly at every opportunity, something Bono plainly understood, sending a hatchet to *Melody Maker* critic Everett True, inveterate U2-hater and shameless self-publicist, prior to him reviewing an American show on the Zoo TV tour.

If in this instance U2 felt the brunt of what were perhaps unwarranted accusations, these were the inevitable consequence of their ambitions and achievements. U2 and Paul McGuinness were quick to realize that a band like U2 needed a big stage in order to create change from within the industry. They were willing to make some compromises to ensure artistic freedom and a worldwide following, the essentials for communication of ideas. Playing up to an image was part of that process of compromise, but U2 did at least control that representation of themselves, a vital break with the past and a step forward which has created space for artists such as Jesus Jones, who are presently conducting their affairs in a manner reminiscent of early U2, although naturally updated for the times, controlled and monitored by the keen intelligence of lead man Mike Edwards. Not only were U2 writing about war, they were waging war on the cumbersome music industry. The Edge said, 'We're not scared of (the music business), we're just determined that our ideals and principles will not go under or be compromised for convenience sake.'

U2 were uncompromising in their musical output, and 'The Refugee' was an example of that, propelled by a powerhouse funk rhythm and savage in its condemnation of the futility of war and the way in which people can be caught up in it, fittingly the last of the songs that could be termed broadly activist or political in intent. There is no specific reference in the song as to who is the refugee or why, though there are hints at economic refugees – particularly pertinent to an Irish band – or a refugee from abuse at home. The obvious explanation, a refugee from physical war, is examined with a man going off to war without knowing why, a pointer towards conscientious objection and to the numbness in which people are conditioned to live, blithely going off to fight purely on the instructions of their government without questioning the motives or reasons behind it. Adam later said, 'They get caught up in the glamour of going to war – there is no glamour, it's nasty and ugly.'

The most intriguing element of the song is the constant refrain of a promised land that the refugee will find, the promised land of America, land of plenty to generations of U2's countrymen and women. At first America does appear to be the answer, the escape route to security, but the song then turns that idea on its head as

Bono gives it a distinctly different pronunciation: 'Amerika.' Amerika, the land of the bigot, the land of the trapped, the land of the downtrodden, the land of the mad gunman, the land of corruption, the land that was a source of many of the world's problems, a land that lived uneasily with its neighbouring America, truly a land of promise, of hope, of dignity, of integrity, God's country, a force for good across the world. The world's most powerful nation split in two, again a strong analogy for the struggle which *War* built itself around. For Bono, 'going to America was a real culture shock. It was inevitable it came out in the work.' He added, 'Amerika, that's y'know eight channels, that's Ronald Reagan, that's pistols and the Ku Klux Klan. But I'm interested in America which is open-space, which is new-found land.' 'The Refugee' was a summary of that attitude, dreams trying to stay alive against all the evidence to the contrary.

'Drowning Man' took a similar position but in the setting of a more traditional love song, the lyric noting the volatility of the times and the stresses inherent in maintaining a relationship in the midst of modern day turmoil, but a more hopeful song, as this time the love that lasts forever manages to endure such travails. It's an aching portrait of a man sustained by love against all the odds. The sensitivity of the lyric is dealt with sympathetically by the musical accompaniment, an ethereal, fragile piece of atmospherics that proved to be the forerunner of some of the material on *The Unforgettable Fire*, but it's a song out of place, out of time with the rest of the album. Bono was adamant that *War* had a lot of love in it because he, as lyricist, was in love, having married his long-time girlfriend Ali in August 1982 at a ceremony in Raheny. This commitment had given Bono an anchor, as U2 were in the eye of a mounting hurricane, and gave him something on which to focus beyond U2 and the music industry. This was to be followed in July of the following year when The Edge also got married to Aislinn O'Sullivan, whom he had first seen in the audience at a U2 show in Dublin early in their career. Understandably, then, there was a strong thread running from these personal alliances – amplified by Larry's long-term relationship with his girlfriend, Ann – into the music, along with fears for the longevity of such bonds, the chance of them remaining unbroken by the pressures of the outside world which try to destroy fidelity, pressures exacerbated by the position of celebrity that went hand in hand with success as a rock 'n' roller.

'Two Hearts Beat As One', the album's second single, took that struggle as its theme, with the plaintive cry '*Is this love out of fashion?*', an acknowledgement of the invidious influence of external society on the lives of individuals as well as a scathing attack on the blind following of trends which was a divisive force in the world, as 'Like A Song' had already shown. Bono's performance was that of a man being pulled from all sides to the point at which he had nothing to cling on to but his love for another, a vivid picture of the destructive capacity of life in the 1980s. The confusion rife in the lyric also covered the tension created by the undercurrent of the violence which was so prevalent. While to the rational mind there might be no simple solutions to the troubles that beset Northern Ireland other than long drawn-out discussion, others could see an answer in the deep red of spilled blood on a Belfast street. 'Two Hearts' beat a tattoo of contradictions, a time where sanity was no longer an objective reality but a subjective concept, a time built on shifting sands, a time where the only answer was to hold on tightly to each other.

War did give hope and did try to energize some positive response, to begin the fight back against whatever forces of oppression were attacking, be they personal or political, but at times it was oddly resigned in tone, adopting a fatalistic acceptance that things might not get better, that there might not be any other way out of here, a far cry from previous U2 records. The album's thrust was distilled into a closing trilogy of songs that were in part spiritual refusal to be beaten and bowed but also an admission that the will to resist might ultimately be exhausted.

The first song of the three, 'Red Light', was another love song but, where love had given hope of redemption on 'Drowning Man', it was now spurned as the protagonist tried to blank out human contact by immersing herself in a city. Bono sang of the wretchedness of existence when there's no will to go on and life boils down to the despairing sanctuary of escape, an escape that's impossible – where can you go if you need to '*leave yourself behind*'? The only conclusion was a suicide attempt from the top of the tower blocks that symbolize so much of the sanitized emptiness of the times. A suicide, the most desolate cry of despair, and yet for some an inevitable consequence of the overwhelming impact of those late twentieth-century information/ambition overload blues where not even love could save everyone, a hammer blow to those believing in the word of God, yet an act that increases with every passing day as life is reduced to an unceasing futility.

'Surrender' was just as much a subject of the songs as 'war', harking back to the difficulties U2 had undergone in preparation for *October*. Larry had by now left the Shalom group, feeling that its regime was no longer right for him, almost that it was alienating him from his own faith, causing him to be too judgemental of others. Prior to the recording sessions for *War*, The Edge had gone through another long-drawn-out period of soul-searching in an attempt to arrive at a logical compromise between his faith and his day job. Later interviews suggest that his personal answers lay in the very irreconcilability of the two, coupled with the incipient doubts which lie at the heart of any intelligently held belief. He was to say that 'every faith is always undergoing a crisis' and 'I think the sort of spirituality I believe in transcends religion, leaving it looking stupid. I've given up thinking about Christianity or spirituality in terms of religion.' For a band whose members were seemingly always on the brink of leaving in its early stages, it's worth remembering that, unlike the bands who hid behind their haircuts, U2 tried 'to put our life into (our records), we write about what's going on around us and in us.' Consequently it could be a nightmare to actually make the albums because everything surrounding their construction was so intense, making personal choices more difficult and personal crises harder to resolve – art feeding off life feeding off art.

'Surrender' was, albeit in a more restrained manner, an extension to the spirituality of *October*, dealing as it did with the search for God and the submission of ego, along with the Christian concept of going through the experience of death in order to be born again. On 'Surrender', the search, indeed any search for a meaningful existence, was set in the context of city tension, in this case New York, the presumed setting of 'Red Light'. Another recurrent theme in U2's work, the dehumanizing excesses of city life were vividly portrayed in a city that never sleeps, where artificial lighting provides a brighter night than there is day, where neon signs pound the consumer into submission as individuals surrender to advertising or surrender themselves in the quest for money in a soulless 'concrete jungle', a jungle constructed over years of public submission to the powers that be. It's a song which captures the alienation of tiny people under the huge skyscrapers, the struggle for fulfilment, particularly spiritual fulfilment, in a world designed for material gratification, something particularly apposite to Reagan's vision of America where more and more incentives were being given to the highest earning members of the population at the expense of the worst off, creating a society of haves and have nots. New York was a monument to that, the imposing skyscrapers of Manhattan dedicated to a business community while the parks and alleyways of the city were host to down-and-outs, drug addicts and drunks unable to cope with the demands of modern life, having been denied any chance of playing their part in its development.

Following on from that, 'Surrender' again hinted at suicide as the only way out for some, far away from the adolescent obsession with it on *Boy*. Here the song portrayed a desperate woman unable to make any sense of the modern whirl, the insidious influence of the all-consuming fire of the big city on family life, the advertising which tries to take you away from its drudgery, the city as energy vampire – '*The city's desire/To take me for more and more*' – until Sadie, the song's protagonist, surrenders herself to the inevitable and is destroyed by it, unable to cope with its pressures, trapped by the material promises that had turned into a spiritual nightmare. The final surrender, the final breaking of the individual's will when there is no other way through the odds stacked against you, the final admission of utter helplessness.

In the light of 'The Refugee', which had gone before with its stinging condemnation of Amerika, there was an ominous suggestion that the Sadie of 'Surrender' was actually 'The Refugee' herself and that, having fled from physical conflict to the promised land, she now found herself overwhelmed by the way of life in New York. The challenge for positivists like U2 was to accept that this happened and that they and many like them were voices in the wind calling for change that was not yet on the horizon. Their power lay in providing a soundtrack of inspiration, a letter to all the individuals that bought their records, a message of hope, of understanding and of community.

In that regard, the album closed on a fatalistic note, but one which held optimism for the future. Although U2's spiritual preoccupations continued to inform their music, there was less of a blunt concentration on that sphere than on *October*. The closing piece, '40', carried the most obvious allusions to their faith, as it took lines from Psalm 40, a Psalm of David, its serenity after the raging storm of the album, and particularly after the bleakness of 'Red Light' and 'Surrender', perhaps indicating the inner peace they had found in their faith, a personal place to which they could retreat in the chaos of modern life. It was a device they employed to good effect on *War*, following the ultra-aggressive 'Like A Song' with the atmospheric

'Drowning Man', the all-out assault of the former accentuated by the soothing mood of the latter. 'My ambition for U2 has always been to push it to its limits – the most aggressive music ever made and at the same time the most sensitive,' Bono told *Hot Press*. The placid atmosphere of '40' did belie its recording process, as the band were running late at Windmill Lane – the song was being mixed as Bono was actually recording the vocal so that they would be able to get out of the studio on time. The Edge termed '40' 'a monument to U2 in an instant.'

The refrain *'how long to sing this song'*, which had also been used in 'Sunday Bloody Sunday', neatly encapsulated the album's plea for new solutions to combat the divisiveness of the day and to rid ourselves of the stale status quo. It also brought the final trilogy of songs to an end with an air of resignation at the impotence of the individual and with the fond hope that one day U2 will no longer have to sing this song. It was a sensitive juxtaposition of a line from their music which they believed to be a God-given gift, and a line from the Psalm itself, 'And he hath put a new song in my mouth, even praise unto our God.' When could we dispense with the mindless hatred of rebel songs, of ritual bigotry, and sing a new song, a song of celebration and of life? The use of the Psalm also put meat on the bones of the pat vision of 'U2, Christian Rock Band'. Bono said, 'The Psalms of David are the blues. I get great comfort from that.'

Bono presumably took great comfort from the fact that *War* entered the UK charts at number one, a vindication of their deeply unfashionable and yet highly effective stand on touring. As Bill Graham vividly explained, 'U2 knew they had made hostage a fiercely loyal audience, certain to immediately support their next album.' The UK was a very important market for U2, who used it as a barometer of credibility and relevance. While the UK music market had many faults, it was also the home of people who were as passionate about their music as the band were themselves, an audience who knew their rock 'n' roll and could see through the bands that weren't for real. The UK audience had also been the first step beyond Ireland for the group and it was their early support, allied to friends in the music press, that had given U2 a high profile right from the start. Reaching number one on release in the album charts was a heady moment indeed, but characteristically they refused to dwell on it and began to look at the challenges ahead, the key one being a return to America.

October had been an album that failed to advance U2's popularity in America to any great extent, although their tour in its support had added new converts to the fold, just as every tour was to do. *War* was going to have to perform a great deal better before U2 could be considered to be a band of any importance in the world's biggest musical marketplace. It was not simply a question of figures; U2 had to crack America for their own sakes, Bono having already predicted, laughingly perhaps, a great future for the band over there. U2 could be defined as a new communication medium in many ways, a group to beam across borders and kick down barriers and, because of that, they had to reach out to the largest audiences – it was their raison d'être. A group that was all about the power of the individual could only succeed if it could talk directly to those individuals with their music. Without an audience in America U2 would be a failure, for it was in America that the shots were called for the rest of the world. America played the tune, others danced, and so to effect any change American audiences were the ones that mattered most, for it was clear that U2 did still see themselves as a group who could make a difference. Bono grudgingly admitted, 'Half of me says, "I know I can't change the world," and there's another half of me that, every time I write a song, I want it to change the world . . . I do know that music's changed me and I know that in Vietnam music helped change a generation's attitudes.' To take the first steps towards mobilizing themselves, those American audiences needed a flag to rally around.

Flags were an integral part of the *War* tour. While the band played before a huge backdrop that featured the album sleeve picture of Peter Rowan, at the back of the stage were three white flags, flags which articulated the theme of surrender, flags of truce, non-violent flags. In a world torn apart by wars over the siting of border posts and the decisions as to what flag should fly where, the white flag was one not tainted by bloodshed, one of sanity, one of innocence, one of peace. While an overly simplistic notion of the sort U2 were fond of, it did suggest that, if that were the only flag, the world might not have so many problems and while U2 were still an underdog in the international scheme of things it was a strikingly vivid piece of symbolism.

U2 were in the ascendancy, but their tendency to fall down was as strong as ever and the flag became a problem on numerous occasions as they became caught up in the conflicting emotions that America inspired within them. By 1983 Ronald Reagan had been in the White House for two and a half years, during which time America had undergone a recession that had rocked its economy. Where Reaganomics had succeeded, in the same way as Thatcherism had before it, was in the protection of the middle classes, the higher earnings groups upon those support he relied for electoral votes. America grew into the reality that had seemed inevitable under Reagan, a house divided between those who tasted the fruits of success and those who were trampled underfoot in the rush. U2 saw both aspects of the country on that tour, travelling through the poorest districts into the best-heeled and out again. Americans reacted in disparate ways to the economic difficulties. Among those who benefited there were pangs of conscience at the way in which their fellow citizens were required to suffer, while among the suffering the understandable, yet destructive, politics of envy were never far away. America's young were a cameo of those emotions. Some chose to deal with it by dedicating themselves to achieving good academic grades and joining the workforce at the highest level possible, others dropped out or were betrayed by a system which refused to give them a chance because of their lowly circumstances, others became radicalized and politically aware or active, particularly on the college campus, the hotbed of U2 support, while yet more bought the happy hedonism that was pushed at them by MTV, beer commercials, etc. America, a land that had prided itself on its status of pre-eminence across the globe had had to deal with twenty years of internal problems. Reagan had achieved the first goal of his Presidency on the day he took office by talking as if the past hadn't happened and America was still God's own garden, but that belief was beginning to dissipate in the country at large.

In times of governmental crisis, there is always one last card to play, that of patriotism, and it was one that Reagan traded on with relish. A choked 'God Bless America' and a quick snatch of the national anthem could always guarantee a sympathetic response at home and, if that wasn't enough, Ronnie's increasingly warlike stance against the Soviets did take away attention from the troubles at home, which made a certain percentage of the population feel good about their homeland. Reagan was far from the complete idiot that was so often portrayed and he recognized the value of 'feel good' politics above all else, devoting himself to that cause as much as any other.

However 'feel good' politics often descend into obsessive jingoism, an attribute that, necessarily, formed American foreign policy.

Recall the words of former President Warren Harding: 'I don't know much about Americanism, but it's a damn good word with which to carry an election.'

America desperately wanted to feel good about itself – that after all was what the country was built upon. It was a time to push away the homeless and the unemployed, social deprivation, drug abuse and institutionalized racism, and celebrate being American. Bruce Springsteen was compelled to release 'Born In The USA' in the following year, just prior to the election, to vent his frustration at the direction the country was taking and the pernicious influence of the 'me-me' administration on ordinary decent values, only for the song's meaning to be completely misunderstood and then hijacked as a national anthem for a new era of American greatness that Ronald Reagan was busily ushering in to being. Previous material from Springsteen had always represented the blue collar worker, but 'Born In The USA' was an especially savage attack on a country that had sent its boys to fight in Vietnam and then didn't want to know them when they got back, refused to house them, took their jobs away from them. 'Born In The USA' was blatant in its scathing attack on the values that now ruled the nation and the world, and yet people were so keen to jump on to the patriotic bandwagon that the government was constructing, they completely missed the point, headed directly for the (ironic) chorus and chose to wear the song as a badge of pride.

U2 suffered similar misunderstandings in their visit to America a year earlier, in part because of the new music they were making, music that had a more toned muscularity to it than anything they had previously recorded. Even though numerous artists down the years have gained reputations for the serious intent or intelligence of their lyrics, it is still the musical performance which first captures the interest of the casual listener, who may then become more enamoured with the artist and their viewpoint later – it ain't just what you say, but the way that you say it. U2 already had an audience that had been forced, by virtue of their being an under-ground band in terms of the limited commercial success of the first two albums, to seek out their music. This was a committed, partisan audience who were drawn towards U2 for the whole package which they provided. With *War*, new fans were drawn to the flame, some of whom simply liked the piano introduction to 'New Year's Day', some who just wanted to see the latest 'big thing' from across the water, some who liked the way Bono sang or The Edge played guitar, many who just knew a good rock 'n' roll band when they heard one. Although it was a great thing for U2 to break through and reach more and more people, there was an effect on the band and their performance, a lessening, initially at least, of the dramatic communication between what had been an entirely sympathetic audience and group.

As it seemed in keeping with the prevalent celebratory aspect of American culture, the anthemic nature of the material on *War* caught a mood for which it had not been designed. With the video for 'New Year's Day' in heavy rotation on MTV, the shots of war atrocities that formed part of it almost became aspirations for a segment of the audience who were looking for America to stamp its authority on the world again – while no one actually advocated open warfare, a little morally appropriate military action might not go amiss. U2 on horseback (even if The Edge's horse was ridden by an extra for filming purposes) looked like men off on some crusade, maybe off to war as much as they appeared men appalled by its prospect, despite the snow-covered background which presented a symbol of surrender, its virgin white as untainted as the flag of truce. If you added the surface stridency of the songs to that cocktail, aggression might well come across more powerfully than the sanity and sensitivity, particularly to first-time audiences. This was the very antithesis to the emotions U2 were looking to promote and yet, paradoxically, a misapprehension that did U2 no harm at the box office. With Bono being surprisingly described as a chest-beating singer in the tradition of previous British invaders such as Led Zeppelin's Robert Plant, U2 needed to be aware of the tightrope they were walking, the grimy waters of hard rock excess waiting below. This gave an undeniable frisson to their live performances – sometimes they strode the wire with consummate ease, at others they sounded hollow, pompous, out of their depth, Bono especially bereft of ideas.

A proportion of the new audience did register a lack of interest as U2 moved into larger venues across the States, a throwback to the early club days in Dublin, to which Bono responded in similarly over the top fashion, demanding feedback, demanding the crowd's attention, actions liable to backfire as they had done in the past. Happily U2 were generally able to rise to the challenge and communicate as they would like, but things did get out of hand at times. In his urge to engineer a reaction, Bono would pace the stage – already there was no stage in the world large enough to fence in this irrepressible, relentless energy – and would often eventually find himself in the audience. On the many occasions that it worked, it was a supremely assured piece of theatre and an expression of a shared understanding of the music. There were times when Bono simply passed a white flag into the crowd and watched it being passed around the auditorium from front to back, then back up to the stage again. This element of commitment to their ideals, a highly unfashionable attitude in America at the time, and the value they placed on the crowd as a vibrant, equal partner in the success of every gig, was a cornerstone of their success in winning new converts. The concert they staged at Denver's Red Rocks arena perfectly encapsulated what U2 were all about.

Looking for a suitable landscape to shoot a live concert film, Paul McGuinness' directorial eye was taken by the undeniably splendid amphitheatre that was Red Rocks, a site in the middle of the Rocky Mountains with a relatively small capacity of 9000 but which appeared to be double that size, with its stage placed among huge red boulders that gave the whole scene a timelessness which made it a quite unique venue. If Cecil B. De Mille had made concert videos, he'd have shot them at Red Rocks. It was a venue which immediately bestowed an epic grandeur to any artist able to play there. As a break with the lame orthodoxy of filming a band playing a run-of-the-mill show in a run-of-the-mill ice hockey arena, Red Rocks was ideal as a surrounding for the scale of the musical that U2 were performing, making the subtle point for the benefit of the industry supremos that U2 were just too damn big to play indoors, there was nowhere big enough to hold them. Again, as an example of McGuinness' sharp business mind, Red Rocks was an inspired choice, instantly lifting U2 into the top division of live concert draws, at least in the minds of the public. If a band gave a performance on that scale, then they had to be as big as Springsteen hadn't they? The Red Rocks phenomenon was a self-fulfilling prophecy – U2 looked like a top grossing act, so therefore they must be – which eased them into the biggest stadia across America when they returned for the 'Unforgettable Fire' tour two years later.

Red Rocks was a gamble, in that it consumed the bulk of the capital U2 had built up over three years, but the potential impact made it a chance worth taking, particularly once Tyne Tees Television, in the shape of *The Tube*, came on board, giving technical assistance and a guaranteed TV slot back in the UK. This time, though, the elements, so often a starting place for Bono as a lyricist, conspired to thwart all of U2's endeavours to set up the show. Rain poured for days in advance, making the transport of the band's equipment to an already remote venue a barely surmountable problem. Even then, once the gear had arrived the rain continued to fall, soaking the stage, putting the concert in doubt purely from the safety aspect. U2 were offered a nearby indoor arena from which to do the show but, once those fears had been dispelled, they maintained their faith in their original vision and ploughed ahead with the promise that they would play indoors for free the following day for anyone who had a ticket for Red Rocks and had been beaten back by the incessant rain. An announcement to that effect was broadcast on local radio networks, but by mid-afternoon on the day of the show, Red Rocks was beginning to fill up with hopeful fans ready for the concert.

As history has shown, U2 rode out the storm brilliantly, giving as fine a performance as any other on the American tour, which left them with that rarity of the modern age, a live concert video that actually captured the excitement and atmosphere of the event. Indeed it was as much the atrocious conditions as anything else that gave the band the perfect situation for delivering a spellbinding concert, for just as the songs were concerned with physical and mental struggles, so was the gig itself. As many a school teacher has said over the years 'adversity is good for the soul' and the soul at the heart of U2's finest compositions shone through. Red Rocks was all about capturing the moment, a U2 speciality. Everyone concerned, the road crew, the promoter, the band and their management and the audience, had moved mountains to keep the show on the road. The meteorological gloom that shrouded the venue, with only flaming torches at the side of the stage to provide any light, was a tangible atmosphere that bound the participants before the artists had even taken to the stage, an atmosphere which demanded reciprocation from the group.

As soon as they hit the stage, U2 gave evidence that they were in complete control, masters of this eerie environment. It was a vindication of the concert as an art form in itself, and of U2's commitment to it, one of those rare occasions when the audience and the band were able to feed off one another's excitement, one another's adrenalin, until there was no distinction between stage and audience. It was left to Bono to make that connection all the more apparent when he pulled a girl from the crowd to dance with him, and by the time they concluded their encores, with '40' still ringing around the rocks, U2 were confirmed stars in America, an impression which was swiftly reinforced when the Red Rocks video was aired on cable television across the nation.

In retrospect it was ironic that it was a TV appearance that finally catapulted them to the top of the tree, TV having been the enemy of U2 since their inception. As Bono explained, the small box in someone's living room wasn't conducive to receiving the best impression of U2's wares: 'U2 have always looked silly on TV because, in the great tradition of Irish theatre, U2 have always played to the back of the hall, so the TV is far too close . . . we just look well over the top on TV. U2 are a live band and when you see this guy breaking his heart on TV it's too much.' Red Rocks itself provided the appropriately momentous context for U2 to reach a TV audience, and the concert footage had a similar impact in the UK when given a repeat screening on *The Tube* to coincide with the release of its companion live album *Under A Blood Red Sky*, another example of their sure grasp of marketing strategy, calling to mind as it did Red Rocks' ambience. The budget-priced mini-album, riding on the back of the quite astounding *Tube* film, introduced U2 to a vast new audience in the UK as it peaked at number two in the middle of the cut-throat Christmas market, a major achievement which confirmed their new status, although artistically the album was rather disappointing. Eschewing the attractive option of releasing a simple Red Rocks soundtrack, they took the songs from a number of venues on the *War* tour and as a result the album lacked cohesion as well as the adventurous, restless spirit that was such a vital part of U2 shows and had certainly been part of the Red Rocks concert. It did nevertheless capture a point in time that was particularly threatening to the continued artistic development of U2, as the success of *War* and the more and more hysterical crowds they drew were blunting the music. Bono confessed to *People* magazine, 'When the energy of the crowd is so brutal, the spirit of the music flees and all you're left with is crashing drums and clanging guitars.'

The success of the live video and album had helped push those negative excesses of the tour into the background, circumstances which had threatened to engulf them. Many of the difficulties stemmed from an insecurity in the new larger arenas, allied to an overwhelming desire to prove themselves capable of dealing with them, a drive which sometimes toppled into over the top stage-craft as the band's emotions were channelled through Bono' performance. U2 had always prided themselves in the strong empathy that existed

Top left: U2–4. (*Retna*)
Top right: Exploring the music. The Edge at the Baggott Inn, Dublin, 1979. (*Paul Slattery*)
Above: Out of control. Bono and Larry. (*Retna*)

Opposite page: Surrender, 1983. (*Paul Slattery*)
Opposite page (inset): Outside it's America. J.B. Scott's, New York, 1981. (*Retna*)
Above: War correspondents. Tube, 1983. (*Erica Echenberg / Redferns*)

Left: Gavin Friday and Dik Evans of the Virgin Prunes. (*David Coro*)
Top: Mother's the word. Larry Mullen Jnr, New Y[o]
1987. (*Pictorial Press*)
Above: Wide awake. Live Aid, 1985. (*Retna*)

: Close to the Edge. USA, 1987. (*Pictorial Press*)

ve: Bass: the final frontier. Adam Clayton during the Joshua Tree tour, 1987. (*Pictorial Press*)

op: The Dalton Brothers ride again. 1987. (*Pictorial Press*)
oove: Rock 'n' Roll stop the traffic. San Francisco, 1987. (*Retna*)
ght: The director of Rattle And Hum, Phil Joanou, 1988. (*Pictorial Press*)

Above: The Rock 'n' Roll circus. USA, 1992. (*Retna*)
Right: Introducing the Mayor of Love Town.
Bono and B.B. King, 1989. (*Retna*)
Below: I'm Trabbie, fly me. USA, 1992. (*Retna*)

Top left: Adam with fiancée Naomi Campbell. (*Pictorial Press*)
Top right: Elvis Presley and America. Lakeland, Florida, 1992. (*Retna*)
Above: U2 react! Sellafield, June 1992. (*Retna*)

between crowd and band, but now the back row was twice as far away and it had to be reached too, Bono often trying to press the flesh as well as touch the soul. The most obvious manifestation of what might later be termed 'tour madness' came in at Los Angeles' sports arena, when he went onto the balcony and jumped around twenty feet into the arms of fans waiting below. Frighteningly, his example was immediately followed by other members of the audience. Bono remembered, 'There may not have been people to catch them . . . the place had gone berserk – what if somebody had died?' To add insult to potential injury, the flag he carried into the audience was ripped to shreds by frenetic fans presumably looking for a souvenir, the final violation of what U2 were there to represent.

These forays into the audience were quickly forcing Bono into a tight corner since they were becoming a much talked about part of the show, something which people came to see as much as the band, as hysteria was beginning to mount. The serious aspect of U2's work was becoming obscured by the singer's desperate need to communicate and the irresponsibility to which it sometimes drove him. Bono would regularly hang his head in the post-gig inquest, vowing never to do it again, but the following night he'd be clambering over speaker stacks or jumping into the crowd once more. In that respect, there was no little relief when the tour ended without any injury.

The 'War' tour was undeniably the one that put U2 into the position of global respect and popularity which gave them the freedom and opportunity to take the twists and turns of the second half of the 1980s, but their new-found prominence was not without its drawbacks, some self-inflicted. The most obvious problem was that a proportion of the audience and of the media were coming along to join in a crusade, to march off to war on the back of stirring anthems. U2 were starting to attract a crowd that was not interested in their messages of faith, love and doubt but latched onto the hard, powerful edge that they had added to their songs. This was a development begun on the *War* album itself and then completed by the emotional performance of them which almost took U2 into the realms of hard rock as again U2 were guilty of mistaking physical force and musical volume for the passionate realization of an artistic vision. There was an aspect of the 'Oi!' scene coming into focus in U2 concerts as those among the crowd who drew other things from them began to gain supremacy – hard driving rock songs equal hard mindless hedonism – culminating in the aforementioned flag fiasco in Los Angeles.

This was something which U2 had brought on themselves in no small way. Their love of the huge, simple, symbolic gesture, which was such a strength before a devoted crowd, was a weakness before an audience who were less caught up in the other baggage that U2 carried with them and had less idea of their humanitarian stance. The waving of a flag, even the white flag, could easily be construed as Bono leading his army of followers into war rather than away from it, particularly in the large arenas they were playing at the tail end of the tour where a less committed audience was given access to the concerts. At times *War*, an undoubted artistic and commercial success, was overshadowed by the trappings that it had forced upon them. 'Surrender' began to sound like hollow, cosmetic sentiment, a blast of pomposity in a swirl of noise and 'Sunday Bloody Sunday' seemed to be the rebel song it categorically was not, inspiring the occasional anti-British tirade from segments of the audience who thought they were expressing solidarity with the Irishmen. The religious cartoon that had surrounded them on *October* had been dispelled by the album that was *War*. The tour foisted another cartoon upon them, one that would prove harder to shake: U2, the self-righteous rockers, waving a flag of emptiness in the air, while violence, however inadvertent, regularly threatened to erupt as frenetic fans overwhelmed with evangelical fervour rushed the stage, the 'born-again storm-troopers' as they were termed by one newspaper.

Gestural music may be an eminently sensible approach to attacking social issues, avoiding the suffocating trap of political bias, but sincerity thus expressed does not always translate as accurately as activism. This was to become part of U2's future challenge as *War* closed the book on the first chapter of their evolution, an expressive development paradoxically ushered in by the most impressionistic, intuitive musical statement they had yet recorded.

chapter eight

DISLOCATION

'There is a danger in being a spokesman for your generation if you have nothing to say other than "help!"' Bono's thrust during the interviews that surrounded *The Unforgettable Fire* may have rung true with the impassioned followers that U2 had collected over the years, but to those whose only contact with the band had been through the *Under A Blood Red Sky* video it sounded like career-enhancing humility. Could this be the same guy who had been screaming from the rock 'n' roll pulpit a year earlier, the man who spat fire and brimstone and seemed to be pointing the finger at the sinners below with righteous indignation? It was a misrepresentation that U2 had come to recognize and unwittingly conform to, Adam eventually agreeing that 'the *War* tour was very up and aggressive and a bit like a football crowd and you play up to that sort of approach ... we keep repeating that the music is much more important than the musician. Maybe on the 'War' tour it was the other way round.' Bono took the football analogy further when discussing U2's position post *Rattle and Hum* with John Waters, but the sentiments apply equally to U2 post *War*: 'We further confused the matter by being artists who are seen in some quarters as like a football team and so we went along for a period with carrying the torch, the flag, whatever, and then you start to realize that people are into you without even knowing or having any under-standing of your music. It's like supporting a football team and you don't know who's playing on the team or what the strategy is or what competition you're even in, you just know it's a football team, and that started to frighten me of late and I started to be wary of that.'

Musically they had completed a cycle with the release of *War*. They had emerged from Dublin, travelled the world, recorded some impressive songs and carved a niche for themselves. *Under A Blood Red Sky* was an exclamation mark that proclaimed just how far their journey had taken them, but it was a double-edged sword which threatened to hang the cult of personality around their necks to the detriment of their music. Bono spoke of the period after the end of the 'War' tour as one of rebirth, as though U2, having laid concrete foundations, were now ready to build upon them in earnest.

War had been the first U2 record to address the world beyond a group of four lads from Dublin – it had been a very necessary departure for a band that might otherwise have choked on itself, that might have become too self-referential and too introspective to mean anything to anyone outside. Like its two predecessors, it had been an instinctive record with few preconceptions prior to their entering the studio and yet its outspoken hard rock attack on the powers that be, the idealism and optimism that bubbled at the music's sources, had put them at the forefront of a new rockist movement. Soon there were dozens of bands with the U2 sound but without the U2 spirit. For a band that was only in favour of movements of one person, that was a lonely and dispiriting place to be, a place where manifestos, expectations and requirements tried to bind the creative spirit and shape it for its own ends, a place that attempted to encase the heart of U2 in stone, leaving them to deal with only their new enforced political obligations. It was a place U2 had to leave behind as it threatened to rob them of the humanity that was the very soul of their music.

Looked at from the vantage point of late 1983, the three studio albums that U2 had issued displayed a certain continuity of approach and yet *War* was very clearly out on a limb, disparate in nature from the opening salvo of their career, particularly in its live incarnation. *Boy* and *October* had revelled in the mystery the songs were shrouded in, songs that gradually gave up their secrets with repeated airings, subconscious lyrical allusions suddenly reaching out from the grooves to grab the listener by the throat, odd lines of guitar that betrayed more about the songs' aims than did the words. If *War* had a serious fault line amidst its undeniable strengths it was in the head-on attack that had been employed, leaving less to the imagination and Bono standing on a platform that he did not want to use. An understandable desire to comment on the state of the world, even in a deeply personal context, had had an enervating effect on the music and had meant the submersion of U2's poetic heart, the epic romanticism that had so vividly coloured their early work. *War* was music of a primary colour made with the primary colours of rock 'n' roll, bass, guitar and drums. Before that, they had mixed those primary elements to create new colours, new shades, new subtleties. In that originality lay U2's spark, a spark dulled by a lack of enterprise. None of which meant that *War* was anything other than a very fine album, just an uncharacteristic one, one removed from the ancestral line. They took that on board, Bono noting, 'We started out as a group innovating in the three-piece format . . . we wrestled with that. Whereas *War* was a deliberate stripping-down into the three-piece format.'

To come down from the mount in order to allow themselves the artistic freedom necessary to make the music they required of themselves was an awkward transition but an exciting one. It was a conundrum made all the more troublesome by virtue of their abiding interest in maintaining a relevant stance on external issues without resorting to the broad-brush approach of *War*. As had so often been the case, America was to provide a hint as to how that marriage could be engineered.

During their trek across the States, they had discovered the Chicago Peace Museum, a living, breathing exhibition dedicated to the work of the peace movement. Having been asked to donate some work, U2 agreed to provide the stage set for *War*, with its backdrop featuring Peter Rowan and the accompanying white flags along with the original handwritten lyrics for 'New Year's Day', for an exhibition on the efforts of musicians in the cause of peace, naturally entitled 'Give Peace A Chance'. Visiting the museum, U2 were particularly taken aback by an exhibit entitled 'The Unforgettable Fire', a Japanese national treasure that was normally housed at the Hiroshima Peace Memorial.

The roots of 'The Unforgettable Fire' exhibit were set down in the mid-1970s when Iwakichi Kobayashi, a survivor of the atomic bombs that turned the cities of Nagasaki and Hiroshima into a ghastly monument to mankind's inhumanity, drew a picture that illustrated his memories of the nuclear holocaust. Japanese television broadcast his work and asked for more from similar survivors, and this ended in a collection that exceeded a thousand pieces within a few months. It was necessarily grim but eloquent. Struck by the message in the work, the Chicago Peace Museum received permission to show sixty of the pictures in their museum, the first such exhibition outside Japan. It is difficult to describe the emotions such a display stirs, from wonder at the resilience of the human spirit to revulsion that such actions could ever be countenanced, let alone executed. British MP and political diarist Tony Benn visited the larger Hiroshima site with its more extensive exhibition in August 1983.

'There was a huge model of Hiroshima just after the bomb was dropped, showing absolute devastation except for a few buildings that survived. From the ceiling hung a black rod, at the bottom of which was a red blob showing where the epicentre was. Next was a vivid scene of a life-size woman with her hair standing on end, bleeding, with the skin burned off her and another woman with a burned child. Behind them was a massive backdrop of Hiroshima burning. There were samples of girders which had melted and children's little luncheon boxes containing food scorched by the bomb. There were some granite steps which had been outside a bank with the permanent imprint of someone who had been sitting there when the bomb fell. It was terrifying. I wrote in the visitor's book. "Every child in the world should see this museum" . . . No sane human being could possibly assent to the use of bombs a thousand times as great as that.' Just as interesting were Benn's recollections of a meeting with the Hibakusha, the victims of the bomb. 'An old lady . . . now seventy-three, was terribly badly injured and couldn't stand upright. She was working near Hiroshima in August 1945, for the military, and had been 1.1 kilometres from the epicentre of the explosion. She had seen the flash. She had been trapped in wreckage, was unconscious for two days and had suffered blindness, loss of hair, bleeding gums, fever and diarrhoea, and loss of power in her fingers and toes. All her organs were affected. She said, "I try to lead a normal life. My father died of acute leukemia in October 1945. I had breast and kidney cancer and operations for cataracts. My fingers and limbs still tremble. I can barely walk. And," she said very quietly, "I so much resent the production of nuclear weapons. Atomic bombs have made no positive contribution to the world."'

Whatever the rights and wrongs of the dropping of the atomic bombs on Japan – and, even if the use of nuclear weapons seems indefensible, one has to remember that the Japanese were the aggressors who had effectively declared war on America with the bombing of Pearl Harbor and had carried out barbaric atrocities of their own during the war, and that the lives of thousands of allied troops on the front line in the Far East were saved by the attack – there can be no other response than to say, 'Never again.' And to keep on saying it.

You don't have to be confronted by the appalling reality of war to understand how hateful it is, but exhibits such as 'The Unforgettable Fire' do throw the intellectual arguments into sharp relief, bringing the whole idea down to a gut-level comprehension. As far as U2 or any other artist committed to the furthering of the peace movement is concerned, such an arresting use of art to communicate the awful reality can only increase their belief in the relevance of their own artistic endeavours. For U2, the subconscious aspect of their music gained greater focus on the back of such an exhibition since so many of the images used in the paintings were elusive and yet spoke so volubly of the torment and horror that had been visited upon the people of the two Japanese cities. A music that did not speak directly in a manifesto style was the escape route from the confines of *War* but was not in sentiment a radical departure from their earliest work. It was a step that would court disapproval in that U2 were appearing to stand on the fence by not directly and unambiguously addressing 'issues', but the music itself would decide just what U2 would do, not outside considerations of vanity.

It was strange therefore that *The Unforgettable Fire* was portrayed in some quarters as U2's most obvious attempt at social awareness to date. This too was a legacy of their visit to the Peace Museum in Chicago, which also held a display dedicated to the work and memory of black civil rights activist Martin Luther King. The event which changed King's view from hope to one of active radicalism was the Los Angeles riot of 1965 in the all black district of Watts, a riot which went on for six long days and left forty people dead. Veteran news reporter Charles Wheeler who has written at length about the civil rights struggles in America recently drew striking parallels with the Los Angeles riots in 1992 after the Rodney King trial fiasco: '(In 1965) what concerned the urban masses was the lack of jobs, public transport, medical care, brutal policing and the inability to break out of the ghetto – in a word, the issue was poverty. As in 1965 the trigger was fierce policing; as in the '60s the deeper cause was the sense of hopelessness in the ghetto . . . there is an expanding middle class of black Americans. But there is also an exploding underclass, sullen and rebellious, trapped in poverty . . . If you ask Martin Luther King's former associates what he would think of the plight of ghetto blacks today, they'll tell you that if he had lived, the movement for economic equality would not have been stopped in its tracks.' King's unequivocal rejection of violence in any form, even in self defence, was a line that U2 adhered to without question and so it was not surprising that they felt so strong an empathy for the man of peace who was gunned down on 4 April 1968.

The Chicago Peace Museum was not U2's first brush with the work of Martin Luther King, Bono having already spoken of him in connection with the writing of 'Sunday Bloody Sunday', expressing his fond hope that a man of King's stature and belief would emerge from the troubles of Northern Ireland to give it new vision, a man who could help resolve the insoluble conflicts. The message of King was to become a recurrent theme of U2's work and their association with such an explicit symbol of pacifist resistance did ensure that the message of songs like 'Sunday Bloody Sunday' could never be misunderstood again. It was undeniably fulfilling that U2 were later able to make a further concrete gesture of solidarity with King's work and his memory when they opened their tour in support of *The Joshua Tree* in Arizona a few weeks after its Governor, Evan Mecham, had attempted to repeal the 15 January holiday that was celebrated in recognition of King's achievements. The group were in favour of cancelling the shows in Tempe upon learning of a boycott by black artists but ultimately decided to go ahead with the concerts, first insisting that a statement attacking the Governor's action was read out before they took the stage, thereby raising the temperature of debate – a real and impressive use of the power of a number one band. Governor Mecham was later removed from office by impeachment.

There were two eulogies to King on *The Unforgettable Fire* and between them they caught the spirit of both the new and the old U2. The album's first single release came in the form of 'Pride (In The Name Of Love)', which was an undeniably moving, powerfully emotional statement of the belief that living in the name of love is the only way forward, the only hope for a better world, although it is only in the final verse that the words really convey King's strength of purpose, the embodiment of his famous words 'if a man hasn't discovered something he would die for, he isn't fit to live.' In spite of the stirring musical accompaniment, which is celebratory in the extreme, there is a sense of melancholy transmitted in lyrics which also allude to Christ's betrayal – do all men of peace, of vision have to die before their message can be heard? Even in the midst of pacifist activity, must there always be hatred and violence? It was the best-expressed record yet of their spiritual beliefs, although in so saying, it is merely perpetuating a misconception about U2 and such spirituality, implying that they ladled so much into one song, a different amount into another, leaving one 'spirit-free', which is plainly absurd. U2's belief in Jesus and in another dimension to life beyond the merely physical was on show in all their music, all their actions, all their words – the things they wrote about, the morality they tried and sometimes failed to uphold all indicated how vital a force it was in their lives. Equally important was the way in which they opened themselves to doubt and were quick to point out their own inadequacies on a personal and musical level. Belief didn't make them supermen, simply more human. The Edge noted to *Melody Maker* that 'we've seen a lot of the falsehoods (of faith) and rejected them so I think we're probably more temperate than we were a while ago.' In keeping with that, 'Pride' was a song of passive, passionate resistance in the face of forces of division, a song that upheld principles whatever the provocation.

'Pride' also reminded them of the most valuable asset in their musical armoury, their positive approach. 'I originally wrote "Pride" about Ronald Reagan and the ambivalent attitude in America,' said Bono. 'It was originally meant as the sort of pride that won't back down, that wants to build nuclear arsenals. But that wasn't working ... I was giving Reagan too much importance. Then I thought, "Martin Luther King, there's a man." We build the positive rather than fighting with the finger.' As a piece of music, 'Pride' could have found a place on *War*. The rhythm section was still dynamic and punchy, the guitar rang out loud and clear, the whole song being anthemic in structure, a rough, tough slab of rock 'n' roll – you could almost see Bono waving a flag as he sang it. While it was an obvious hit single, it was a woeful decision that allowed it to be released as the first song from an album that was expected to break the back of the U2 sound. While 'Pride' did contain a subtle shift in atmosphere, it was so subtle that it largely passed everyone by, leaving U2 looking as though they were tramping down a well-worn track and playing the percentage game. Perhaps it was a case of everyone wanting to ensure that people bought the forthcoming album, not wishing to shock prospective punters with something that was too left field, but it did close a lot of minds to the album with the result that a number of reviews simply said that there was no new U2 sound and that *The Unforgettable Fire* was U2 playing 'as safe as houses' as *Sounds* put it. It was a mistake that they were not to repeat at the outset of the next 'reinvention' of U2 prior to *Achtung Baby*, when they warmed people up for the new material with 'The Fly', a far braver choice than the more obvious 'One', which would undoubtedly have been an even bigger hit.

To make a statement on both their admiration for King and on the new music of U2, 'MLK' might have been a better choice as a single. 'MLK' was built around sonorous banks of synth sound, sending out billowing clouds of music through which Bono's tender, breathy vocal, possibly his best performance, cut like a shaft of sunlight. 'MLK' was effectively a lullaby, an elegy for a fallen leader whose message would not be forgotten, whose life and premature death would not be in vain. As a testament to the strength of passive resistance and to the struggle for good and for love in which we should all engage our energies, it was every bit as moving as, more so than 'Pride'. By removing any obvious lyrical content that could be construed as political, U2 allowed the music to strike at the listener's subconscious and the song only gained greater strength from that decision.

Martin Luther King became, in those two songs, a symbol of both sides of U2's musical coin – the triumphal exposition of a 'cause' that stood shoulder to shoulder with the visceral, indefinable punch of their work which was their version of the emotional impact that 'The Unforgettable Fire' exhibit had made, a connection emphasized on the 12-inch sleeve for 'Pride', where a quote from King was included: 'I refuse to accept the cynical notion that nation after nation must spiral down a militaristic stairway into the hell of thermonuclear destruction. I believe that unarmed truth and unconditional love will have the final word in reality. That is why right temporarily defeated is stronger than evil triumphant.' Quite accidentally, U2 had engineered a position where they could forgo the occasional histrionics that touring *War* had inflicted upon the music without leaving behind the important worldwide issues that had come to fascinate them.

In order to make the new music that these disparate, yet complementary, elements required, U2 needed a period of reassessment before they entered the studio. A three-year relationship with Steve Lillywhite had seen a maturing understanding, one which had rescued *October* in particular from being a record that might have been unrecordable with anyone but a trusted ally at the console. With *War*, the inventiveness of approach remained and Lillywhite played an instrumental role in stripping away the traditional polish of the recording studio to expose the naked rock 'n' roll sound underneath, a sound that was conceptually perfect, providing the musical slap in the face that was intended. However, U2 were a band that always looked to cover fresh ground and to change the ingredients that would make up the album.

There had been talk of new producers prior to both *October* and *War* but these ideas had not come to fruition, Lillywhite bailing out the band on both occasions. As with any long-term working association however, a degree of staleness did start to creep in simply because the band knew the sort of things that Lillywhite liked to hear, he knew the type of sound they wanted, and so certain parameters were established at the outset, songs being subconsciously shaped and directed to match a preconceived pattern. As U2 wanted to approach their fourth studio record in an iconoclastic frame of mind – Bono was fond of saying that after the 'War' tour, U2 disbanded and then formed a new band with the same name and the same members but a different approach – it was absolutely essential that changes were made on the other side of the recording desk so that the old U2 could be cremated, leaving their new sound to rise from the ashes. Where the bold broad brush had characterized *War, The Unforgettable Fire* was to be fashioned from a more delicate wash of colour.

Boy was a record that stood out from the crowd by virtue of not only its irrepressible enthusiasm, but also its intelligent and articulate employment of atmosphere and musical textures, the creation of a new palette that often centred around a minimalist approach which allowed new shades to break out from repeated figures. It was a side of U2 that was particularly attractive but one which had been usurped by the more pugnacious frame of reference they had increasingly come to work within, the atmospherics and the humour being generally relegated to B-side status. The energy of U2 was well documented, the textures were not. It was time to redress that particular balance with the aid of a new producer and for that role there was no one better qualified than Brian Eno, the doyen of 'ambient' music, in tandem with Canadian studio owner Daniel Lanois.

Eno had begun his musical career with Roxy Music, initially as technical adviser before becoming a synthesizer player, but preferred to call himself a 'non-musician', allegedly the reason for his split from the group in 1973, two non-musicians in any one band apparently being one too many (the other was Bryan Ferry). Eno then set up a very healthy solo career, notable mainly for its pioneering spirit and keen intelligence as well as the application of unorthodox recording techniques seemingly based on the theory of entropy. Collaboration was a key aspect in Eno's own artistic development as he worked with like-minded spirits such as Robert Fripp, John Cale, David Bowie, Devo and Talking Heads. He still had time to make his own records, like 'Another Green World' and 'Taking Tiger Mountain By Strategy', before creating a whole series of ambient albums that included 'Music For Films', 'Thursday Afternoon', 'Possible Music' and 'The Plateaux Of Mirrors', to which was added a further minimalist alliance with pianist Harold Budd. By 1984 it was hard to reconcile this professor of intellectualized, highbrow music for minorities with the androgynous member of Roxy Music who had gone on to make avant-garde rock music in the mid-1970s. How could someone who appeared to take such a studied, almost mathematical angle on writing and performing music possibly work in combination with an instinctive, raucous rock 'n' roll band?

Much of the answer lay, yet again, in the very fact that neither U2 nor Eno, particularly Eno, were the people that they were seen as being. Eno was seen as a scholarly presence – he was once described as a 'continual refiner and redefiner of the role of theory in making rock' – but this belied his relaxed approach to working in the studio. He did bring a fresh dimension to recording, an intelligent decisiveness towards sessions, and was happy to change things around if they were not working, throwing a creative spanner in the works to make Bono reappraise a vocal or to coax Larry into changing the set-up of his drumkit. The seeds of the successful alliance between Eno and U2 could perhaps be seen in Eno's truly ground-breaking work with Talking Heads and their leader David Byrne. A neat swap eventually took place, with Steve Lillywhite producing Talking Heads' 1988 album *Naked*, Byrne making *My Life In The Bush Of Ghosts*, a very early 'world music' venture, with him and commending his sense of adventure and sense of humour, important ingredients in U2's own music. Interestingly, *My Life In The Bush of Ghosts* was based on 'found' sounds from radio broadcasts, an approach very similar to U2's use of found visuals during Zoo TV. Where Eno was concerned, the conventional rules of rock 'n' roll did not apply and this was the lift that U2 required to help them capture their flights of imagination as they were coming to mind. Spontaneity was all-important, an attribute on which both band and, perhaps more surprisingly in view of his reputation, the producer were agreed. The following quote from Eno, taken from

David Gans' book *Talking Heads*, says much about his approach and its attractiveness to U2:

'When I first began working in studios, I became aware of the panic effect that accompanies the high cost of studio time. I noticed that one becomes progressively less inclined to engage in experimental activities that might not lead anywhere (and) focuses on the safe bet ... so the Oblique Strategies began as a list of aphorisms intended to check the headlong flight down the path of least resistance by suggesting side roads that might prove more interesting. The first one I wrote was "honour thy error as a hidden intention," a reminder not to have too fixed a view about what was appropriate in a given piece, to accept the possibility that sometimes the things one doesn't intend are the seeds for a more interesting future than the one one had envisaged. My technique at this time (1979) was to scan the list regularly during recording sessions to see if there was an aspect of approach that I might be overlooking. Most of the Oblique Strategies deal more with approach than with specific techniques, so in that sense they imply a philosophy about working ... some chosen at random in true Oblique Strategy style: overtly resist change; emphasize the flaws; reverse; discard an axiom; mechanize something idiosyncratic; do something boring; cluster analysis; change instrument roles; you don't have to be ashamed of using your own ideas; it is quite possible (after all); take a break; remove ambiguities and convert to specifics.'

The prospect of working with a producer who was so willing to confront the orthodox and challenge studio basics and therefore to try something different, to introduce a random element into proceedings, was almost a literal translation of a U2 concert, where so often Bono might throw things off course by doing something completely off the wall that might or might not work but which could take a show down a completely new path. More importantly, it was also an empathic statement with the whole U2 approach to music, all four constantly trying to kick away preconceptions that could hem in their collective imagination. At a time when U2 very definitely wanted to step back from the band they had created, a radical such as Eno was the ideal guide through the new territory.

It's fair to say that in the wealth of words that have spewed into the press about U2's post-1984 success, many have dwelled on Eno's importance, even to the detriment of U2's input, but far less has been made of Daniel Lanois's contribution. Since *The Unforgettable Fire*, Lanois has come increasingly to the fore in modern music, having worked with Peter Gabriel, Bob Dylan, the Neville Brothers and Robbie Robertson as well as establishing his own solo recording career with *Acadie*, a beautiful album that was well received by critics and audiences alike. To use a ready cliché, his music has a very organic quality, ethnic traces that sometimes place it on the edge of folk music, again a trait that appealed to U2, Bono having noted that 'I was thinking that in the 1990s people won't be listening to electronic music – who wants electronic music in an electronic age? The music of the 1990s I believe will be ethnic music, black music, soul music, reggae music, cajun music – this will be the music of the future because it has a humanity that city dwellers will need.' While not a quote to remind Bono of in these post-'Fly' days, it did capture a growing interest in traditional music that can be felt on songs like 'A Sort Of Homecoming' or the Van Morrison influences on 'Bad' and 'Promenade'.

Among Lanois's other talents was an aptitude for capturing atmospheres, essential when the group was to record songs like '4th Of July' and 'Elvis Presley And America' which were atmosphere and little else, while it is the texture of 'A Sort Of Homecoming' that makes it such an affecting piece. As a talented musician in his own right, Lanois was able to follow the flow of musical ideas sympathetically, able to respond to the needs of the musicians intuitively. In the rush for spontaneity that U2 were engaged in, it's also worth recalling that Peter Gabriel has been surprised again and again at Lanois's ability to get a sound together very quickly in the studio, enabling him to 'catch the magic'.

Given then that Eno and Lanois were the obvious men for the job from U2's perspective, what was it about U2 that attracted the producers? Since Alan Parker's 1992 film, *The Commitments*, the idea about the Irish being the blacks of Europe has become a tired, overused cliché, but like so many clichés it does have a degree of truth in it. Whether it be categorized as soul, emotion or whatever, the spirit of abandonment in U2's live show could reach a pitch where at times it could equal the joyous fervour of a Pentecostal meeting, where songs could create the same inspirational feelings that great gospel music might. On record there had always been a certain tension that had prevented U2 from reaching that peak, but in concert there was an intuitive punch that went straight to the heart. Eno in particular had been less than impressed with the music he had heard from U2, but once he had met the group he was intrigued by the spirit they had in the camp, the way in which the band operated and by the enthusiasm with which they spoke of their music. Eno had lost interest in most mainstream rock music and had apparently spent his time immersed in gospel music but the way in which U2 spoke of their songs was a very good European approximation of that strain of music, something which Eno was quick to pick up, identifying U2's 'abundance of lyrical soul'.

In keeping with the new approach, U2 had decided to leave their traditional home at Windmill Lane, at least initially, and make the record in Slane Castle, County Meath, where the owner, Lord Henry Mountcharles, was happy to allow them the freedom they required. The natural acoustics of many of the castle's rooms were perfectly suited to U2's new determination to capture a live sound on record as opposed to the orthodox studio wisdom of recording in a 'dead' room and then attempting to inject life into those sounds with technical wizardry. The Edge explained, 'We would go into a very live room and try . . . to tame this wild sound, something with natural excitement. It worked in many ways because I think there are sounds on this album that we just couldn't have got from a studio.' Adam agreed, pointing out that 'we got a lot of benefit from those loud cavernous rooms,' although the castle ballroom almost got the better of them, Edge adding, 'That turned out to be almost too wild for us because the roof was thirty foot high and it's just a huge oval dome.' The music did betray a greater off-the-cuff element but there were incredible technical headaches for the U2 crew to cope with as U2 used different rooms for different effects and qualities of sound. In the midst of these difficulties, Lanois's enthusiasm and Eno's decisive control helped maintain morale as U2 relaxed into the sessions, even undergoing a day of naked recording with the liberal use of gaffa tape preserving their modesty.

The laid-back attitude which they employed for the duration of their stay at Slane had an enormously beneficial impact on a number of the songs, creating an environment in which certain songs like 'Promenade' could be written and recorded, songs which would not have survived the tense atmosphere which prevailed during the recording of their earlier albums. 'We rediscovered the spirit of our music and a confidence in ourselves,' noted Bono. 'The emphasis was on the moment in this recording, on the spontaneity. It's like that Irish tradition, the Joyce thing – when you're relaxed you're not inhibited.' Where passion had been the clenched fist, the billowing flag and the angry shout, by sitting back and letting the music flow, U2 had become yet more intense but able to dispense with the clumsy trappings that had usurped their songs.

The Unforgettable Fire is undoubtedly the most elusive collection of material that U2 have recorded. Trying to grab hold of any of the songs to tie them down is like trying to catch shadows. At the heart of that intangibility lies the enduring appeal of the record as well as an explanation of the themes that characterize it – it is a work imbued with a powerful spirit, that appears momentarily time and again, coaxing, pushing, dragging the music into new corners, different landscapes, fresh vistas. The album sleeve set the tone for the music, a brooding atmospheric sepia shot of the derelict Moydrum Castle in County Westmeath which was accompanied by a photo of the band members with the castle in the background. Appropriately, the four men were out of focus in Anton Corbijn's photograph, a pictorial approximation of the sketchy, blurred music they had made. The creepers which covered the castle walls also intimated that, while kingdoms come and go, there is always new life ready to take over. If western society was in its death throes, a pessimistic attitude underlined by the selection of the album title, then the light at the end of the tunnel was the hope of rebirth in another form. Their poetic lyricism did indeed seem to usher in visions of the end of materialism which would be replaced by the same sort of deeper spirituality which Van Morrison had written about on 'Inarticulate Speech Of The Heart' in particular.

The kind of spirituality which listeners had come to expect from the band was most obvious on the songs relating to Martin Luther King, but it was at work elsewhere, a flame that ignited songs and led U2 to a tacit recognition of a muse beyond themselves which was shaping the record for them. The Edge confessed that 'that's the thing I feel passionately about music, that it's not me, it's not U2 creating this great art. That's why I can be so arrogant – or seemingly arrogant – about what we do, because I don't think it's us essentially. There's something that works through us to create in this way . . . there's an undercurrent to most music . . . and you open yourself up to that.'

That U2 were simply a cipher for other forces was one of the lyrical strains to 'Indian Summer Sky', a song which Edge once described as 'autobiographical of U2' without being able to put his finger on his reasoning. As Bono sang of a power blowing directly through to his soul, it was easy to equate that with The Edge's words, just as when he sang of coming up for air *'to swim against the tide'* there were clear parallels to be drawn with U2's defiant anti-fashion stance and their highly individual approach to their work. The most obvious example was Bono's lucid depiction of the spark that had set U2 on their way, though even here there was an admission of the trials and tribulations in keeping that muse alive when day to day life was invaded by external considerations which evolved from their celebrity and success.

The Unforgettable Fire was an album which saw U2 return to their roots in terms of their commitment to freeing the subconscious, sculpting with atmospheres as they had done on *Boy* rather than delineating ideas in a precise, exact manner as they had on *War*. The match of lyrical and musical ideas was interesting in that sense, making a crucial contrast with the songs that had gone before. The music that U2 had written, especially in terms of The Edge's guitar work, had often been pictorial and impressionistic and the combination of that with similarly impressionistic words gave the whole album a dreamlike sonic quality that was undeniably seductive. It also gave Bono the opportunity to explore more than one train of thought in any given lyric, a freedom he had deliberately denied himself on 'War'. 'Indian Summer Sky', for instance, did hint at some of the pressures U2 were under, but more than that it was a requiem of sorts for the demise of the Native American Indians. Bono spoke of their spirit remaining within the concrete jungles that had been constructed on their homelands, being forced to metaphorically come up for air by returning to the remaining forests, the few areas not yet blighted by the rapacious greed of American industry.

Although U2 had always been interested in the music of the elements, this album saw them taking the roof off the studio or the concert hall so that it could be played beneath the sky, the music so all-encompassing that it couldn't be physically contained. This harked back in part to their outdoor experiences with *War* and their desire to fill the wide open spaces with a resonant music suited to such a setting, but the very natural flavour to the music they were creating required Bono to convey that feeling in his lyrics. The living world contributed to his vocabulary for the album, but again he chose to write about struggles within that setting, in this case the fight for survival facing the Native Americans, a people with whom the Irish have some affinity. Perhaps it's an empathy growing out of being the underdog, perhaps there are spiritual ties in that both are peoples who are at peace with the natural world around them or perhaps it's because both have lost at the hands of larger, not greater, nations.

Those bonds were demonstrated in the most atypical song on the album, 'Elvis Presley And America', of which John Waters said, '(It) doesn't sound Irish, but it is – a cross between English, Apache and Connemara Irish.' It is also a bewildering, ragged piece of glory that is paradoxically the most bewitching and the least impressive track on the album, which belies its unprepared origins. '"Elvis Presley And America" was recorded in five minutes,' Bono told the *NME*. 'Eno just handed me a microphone and told me to sing over this piece of music that had been slowed down, played backwards, whatever. I said, "What, just like that, now?" He said, "Yes, this is what you're about." So I did it and when it was finished there were all these beautiful lines and melodies coming out of it. I said, "I can't wait to finish this." He said, "What do you mean finish it, it's finished."'

From the historical perspective and that of the rabid fan, 'Elvis Presley And America' is an exciting insight into U2's work in progress, but as a coherent statement on a record destined to be played over and over again, it has very clear limitations. To criticize a band of their influence for taking such bold steps into the unknown and for realizing something so experimental would be churlish, but it has to be said that further work might have been advisable. Bono's mumbling vocal delivery is an attempt to convey the later period of Elvis when under heavy sedation as he grasped desperately for words he couldn't remember. In a sense that's fine but they did pay the inevitable penalty of impressionism. An abstract musical painting, or 'tapestry' as the buzz word of the time would have it, does not always cut across as accurately as intended and many found the song wilfully obscure and impenetrable, some even suspecting that Bono was taking the rise out of the King. It would be fair to say that, had it not been for the title, it would have been difficult for outsiders to discern any real connection with Elvis. The title promised much – indeed there might have been a decent novel to be had from such a title – but the song was frustratingly thin, giving the impression that it was included purely for effect to show that U2 weren't so uptight about themselves after all, that they were loosening up.

Once you make the effort to home in on what Bono is doing, the song takes a kind of shape, hinting at Elvis's genius – he knew exactly how to stand, how to hold the mike, how to sing, how to move yet *'no one told you how.'* Elvis made up his own rules, wrote his own story and was an instinctive performer who eventually was consumed by the destructive side of America, a man who tasted the material fruits of his success only for them to bite back and leave him with an insatiable appetite for pills. In that sense, in the ultimate consumer society, people become little more than a can of cola or beer to be thrown away once it's empty and replaced when you need another shot – *'You're through with me but I'll know that you'll be back for more.'* America in particular, but also the world in general, seems more comfortable with icons, be they Elvis, Marilyn, Lennon or Dean, once they're dead and manageable.

Extending that argument further, 'Elvis Presley And America' can also be seen as a veiled attack on Albert Goldman, Goldman representing the outside interests who still feel threatened by the unorthodox danger and unpredictability of rock music and who are consequently determined to relegate rock 'n' roll to the status of entertainment for the intellectually and culturally retarded. Goldman of course made his name with a biography of Presley which portrayed him as a mumbling incoherent wreck who couldn't possibly have anything to contribute to society, before he moved on to John Lennon, giving him the same treatment. Goldman's poison-pen letters got under the skin of U2 and on *Rattle and Hum*, they blasted back more directly with 'God Part 2', calling Goldman a 'curse', pointing out that instant karma would account for him *'if I don't get him first'*. In interviews, Bono was even more fulsome in his condemnation of a man who has built a career from picking fights with dead men. 'The more dangerous thing about his books is that he's trying to write off the culture – he's a New York intellectual who's trying to write off Elvis as the *idiot savant*, John Lennon as a screwed-up guy, he attempts to write off rock 'n' roll, which is an expression for people like me who didn't get a university education – it's all we've got.'

Fire was the overall theme of a broken, fractured record that was wildly elemental in construction and tone. Within each song the idea of an 'unforgettable fire' could be applied, be it in the nuclear winterscape that pervaded 'A Sort Of Homecoming', the fire that propelled a man as great as Martin Luther King, the fire in U2 itself or in Elvis, a fire which eventually claimed him, the fiery strength of the Native Americans, but, most pervasive of all, the devastating, unquenchable, destructive fire of heroin. The preaching style of which they had sometimes previously fallen foul was put to one side and their document of drug abuse sounded like a forlorn, desperately human cry of anguish rather than the notes of a social worker.

'Wire' was the first to broach the subject, with a music so physical and yet so ethereal that it ran a vicious assault on all the senses, a bombardment that was frightening in intensity and in its disorientating blast. It was a song that seemed to be born out of Slane Castle, a ghostly piece that featured disembodied voices shrieking from out of the woodwork, tormenting, agonizing, apocalyptic almost and vivid in its depiction of the horrors of drug abuse. It is a song to hear through headphones, but not in the dark! The playing is venomous, the guitar striking jagged intravenous lines, Adam's bass by turns threatening and angry, but it is in the use of background voices that 'Wire' is most startling, an aural approximation of cold turkey. In its vituperative attack it hits home, a scathing demolition of the drug and its pushers, an indictment of the society that leaves its youth with nothing to live for beyond the chemically induced buzz – the corruption of willing innocents.

Dublin, like so many other inner cities, has seen rampant drug addiction in recent times, a phenomenon that has gone hand in hand with rising levels of poverty and youth unemployment and the systematic planned destruction of housing communities. Old houses are pulled down, the people living within them forced to move out to tower blocks in the suburbs, the inner city itself becomes run down, business leaves because of the environment, jobs go, the family unit breaks down since it has already been divided – these are tales that could be told in any city across Ireland, across the UK and in America. Once the heart has gone, only a shell is left. Once there is no pride left, the easy way is down. Well-meaning schemes that endeavour to prevent drug-taking seem to miss the point: drugs have to be replaced in the lives of the addicts and the would-be addicts by something that makes them feel better than the drugs do. When there's no job, no self respect, no hope, no future, oblivion for a while is an alluring respite. Whatever else might be said, it is hard to deny that, in the early stages at least, a heroin high dispels all the worries, all the anxieties. Until there is a way out of those root causes, drug abuse and the attendant social problems it brings will remain. Social deprivation is the surest route to a drug problem, a matter addressed by eminent Irish poet Brendan Kennelly in 'Eily Kilbride', taken from *The Book of Judas*. Eily Kilbride is a child from Cork city whose parents are out of work, who only knows the realities of rundown city life. Eily Kilbride, a child like so many others today:

Who went, once, into the countryside.
Saw a horse with a feeding bag over its head
And thought it was sniffing glue.

These are the horizons of so many who know only their small piece of ground and who become easy prey to the dealers. These are the only horizons towards which those people are allowed to look – only a cast-iron will and determination can ignore the moneyed trail that results from drug dealing, only someone with something better to live for can ignore the sensory escape via a quick fix. 'Wire' attacks the dealers and the cause, the predatory instinct of those who attack the weakest, but it's also a terrifying cautionary tale for anyone getting involved in heroin, the cold fire. The imagery flashes across the surface, leaving fractured lines that have to be pieced together, but there's real vitriol in the sentiment expressed – the recurrent theme is the chill of addiction, the cold, soulless, emotion-less life on drugs, the emptiness that is there between fixes. '*Cold in his eyes*' is a line that is later echoed in 'The Unforgettable Fire', an affecting depiction of the coal-black empty eyes of the junkie. It's not just another right-on story to fill out the record either, but a tale hewn from the bitter experience of friends taken over by their habit leaving a heart of stone.

People being torn in two by circumstances and external forces had long been a staple of U2 material and it recurred again on both 'Wire' and 'Bad', two very different perspectives on the same addiction. 'Wire' was a game of Russian Roulette – is the next hit the final one? The heroin soul deep within, always tempting its shell to inject more and more, to take the biggest gamble. '*Place your bets*,' laughs Bono unnervingly. Is it time '*to win or lose*'? Heroin, in this context, is a Judas, the traitor's heart a cold fire encased in ice that razes all obstacles to the ground. Having seduced his victim with a kiss of freedom, he exacts his powerful revenge, either in the taking of the life, the reduction of it to meaninglessness or, at the very least, by inflicting the savage agonies of withdrawal. The closing lines of the song suggest a successful dismissal of the habit – '*Here's the rope, now swing on it*' – the rope, having previously exposed the veins, now being offered to Judas to hang himself. Any precise reading of such a schizophrenic track is impossible though, for the rope around the addict's arm is essentially no different from a noose around the neck. The only obvious emotion is rage at heroin, at the conditions which encourage its use and at betrayal, a subject which was to feature more and more in various guises in U2's later work, particularly on *Achtung Baby*.

The Joshua Tree allowed Bono to explore the sentiments behind 'Wire' and 'Bad' once more. 'Running To Stand Still' was a more fully rounded realization of U2's anger and frustration at the way in which their own city had been betrayed by its politicians, by its city planners. The setting for that song was Ballymun, a district in Dublin which has, over the years, become notorious, synonymous with street violence and trouble in the same way that many inner city areas in Britain are – kids in Ballymun are quite candid about the fact that there is no future for them in Dublin. There are few jobs in the area itself and it's a place where your address goes before you. A Ballymun postal address, as is freely admitted, is one that means trouble and leads to potential employers, of whom there are far too few to go around, ignoring the letters of application. Of course, like everywhere else, Ballymun is made up of the good and the bad, people who want jobs, want to work, want to create a future for themselves, but they have to fight all the harder to get a fair crack of the whip since the headline of Ballymun is trouble, violence, drugs, crime. Places like Ballymun, and they exist all over the world, become self-fulfilling prophecies, ever-decreasing vicious circles feeding voraciously on themselves and from which it is almost impossible to escape. People say there's trouble in Ballymun and so inevitably there will be since the people there are so frustrated with the way they're painted and the way that that then takes away their opportunities, which frustrates them still more.

'*I see seven towers, but I only see one way out*' strikes deep to the heart of the inner-city malaise, the seven towers being the seven high-rise blocks that disfigure the Ballymun skyline, a skyline that lay just beyond Bono's childhood home in Cedarwood Road. When heroin is the only way out, things have gone too far and U2's anger with their national politicians was wholly justified since it was an anger aimed at giving a kick in the pants to those in power and consequently an anger aimed at rebuilding rather than simply tearing down.

'Bad' looked at the prison of addiction but seemingly from a different standpoint, that of someone forced to look on helplessly as a friend succumbed to the drug. It was a surging, slowly building song constructed from a soothing bass line, a radically different drum sound and an echoing, insidious guitar figure that eventually reached a peak as the subject tried to drag himself back from the brink – '*I'm wide awake, I'm not sleeping,*' a refusal to go back to the living sleep of addiction, an echo of the '*longest sleep*' line in 'Wire'. Bono again sang of a person tearing him or herself in two, the split personality that heroin encourages, where a friend is no longer a friend but a person so desperately driven by his craving that he will steal or lie or cheat to get the necessary funds to buy more.

In the creation of a mental landscape, Bono's work on 'Bad' was quite superb. There are no overt references to heroin or to drugs, but there is no doubt as to the intensity of pain he is singing of, the personal surrender not, this time, of the ego, but of one's very soul, the letting go of the everyday misery for a few brief moments. The very brevity of the effect is almost as terrifying as the consequences of drug use. That people should be prepared to go to such lengths, to debase themselves so shamelessly, to betray friends, family, themselves for a moment's release from the world is so complete an indictment of contemporary society and its emptiness for so many people that it almost beggars belief.

Faced with the escalating drug problem in their own city, U2 took action more concrete than simply writing songs and began privately and quietly to sink some of their own money into Dublin, be it in community projects or, as in the aftermath of the Croke Park show in 1985, by making a substantial donation towards the construction of a rehearsal space at the City Centre development for Ireland's up and coming bands to use. This was a subtle yet important distancing of themselves from the ethic of the individual which they had previously espoused, taking on a more collective responsibility, accepting that society's problems need group responses. 'God's chosen band', as many would choose to portray them, have to walk a very fine line in their own city – any actions that would portray them as the bountiful, munificent old boys done well doling out slops to the proles have to be avoided, but it was very important to put something into the community and the country that nurtured them.

In that regard, involvement in some music-related activity was probably the best step they could take since it was a venture close to their own hearts. As one of the biggest groups in Europe, and with the USA catching on quickly, U2 were able to strike a blow for the talent of the future within their own land.

In many ways, simply remaining in Ireland was a big enough

statement for U2 to make – that a band could emerge from this island, could grab the attention, the hearts and the minds of the world and yet write, record and live within Dublin city was almost beyond comprehension. That they gave resources, financial and administrative, to the construction of a better infrastructure was excellent, but of greater value was simply that they legitimized rock 'n' roll as a serious activity worthy of community interest – maybe you could make a career out of the electric guitar after all. To prove it, in 1984, U2's Mother Records opened its doors for business in Dublin, its debut release being 'Coming Thru' by In Tua Nua, a band who then went on to support U2 on part of their 'Unforgettable Fire' tour.

The basic theory behind Mother was to provide groups with the opportunity to go into Windmill Lane Studios and cut a single as a calling card for major label interest in much the same way that the 'U2–3' EP had been used, an idea that had first been floated by Bono in 1981. Mother was not restricted purely to Irish groups, although inevitably there was that kind of slant to its output, but its creation was a clear attempt to put another stepping stone in place to smooth the path from a garden shed in Cork to a deal with Virgin Records and it gave artists another goal to aim for, a measure of their progress. It also allowed U2 to indulge their own personal musical tastes, bringing them heavy criticism including the accusation of cultural imperialism, U2 allegedly trying to dictate the growth and tastes of rock 'n' roll in Ireland, with Sinead O'Connor going so far as to say, 'There isn't a band in Dublin who could get anywhere if they aren't in some way associated with U2,' to which The Edge replied, 'Sinead is not in the business of communicating facts, she's in the business of creating news for herself.'

Larry is the member of U2 who has ultimately been the most closely involved in Mother's development and he has gone on record as saying, 'It's not a money-making thing, it's basically U2 trying to give younger bands a hand; it's no big recording deal, there's no big commitment, it's just a step up.' Bono added that 'before Mother there was nothing or nobody you could turn to for advice . . . hopefully, now people don't feel that same lack of help and that same pressure to leave the country before they're really ready for it.' The story of Mother to date has been one of ups and downs. When a band has got its act together and is ready to grasp the opportunity that comes its way, as the Hothouse Flowers or Cactus World News were, then Mother has worked successfully and impressively in providing that vital first rung on the ladder. At other times it has failed, often because of its own inadequacies – setting up a label that only works in one-off deals does not give promotion or distribution staff much incentive, knowing that a successful act will end up elsewhere – and sometimes because of the failings or misinterpretations of those artists on the roster. Some were totally uncommercial in any conventional sense and were never expected to have a hit single immediately – Operating Theatre for instance – but others treated Mother as a bottomless pit from which recording expenses were paid, looking at the company as a charity, a misunderstanding of the whole Mother ethic.

Mother works on the basis that U2 have operated on – you don't get anything for nothing. If you want some success, you have to work for it within sensible parameters. Mother has provided total unknowns with not only an opportunity to make a record with complete artistic control in a good quality studio and without having to sign a long-term deal that might become a millstone around the neck, but has also provided some insight into how larger companies operate, the importance of keeping to budget, the way in which promotional activities work, etc. In a sense, Mother plays a finishing school for being in the band business that could help both artist and management, U2's altruism only extending as far as giving artists a chance they wouldn't otherwise have had. Beyond that, Mother is supposed to be a real record company – any benefits you get from it are down to you. When the Hothouse Flowers single came out, they toured extensively and worked the record damned hard to get it the notice it received, while other bands just waited for the single to come out and do the work for them.

There were faults aplenty with the organization of the company, many of which centred around the ever-increasing demands put on U2 by the growth of their own career, thereby allowing them less and less time to devote to Mother. This ultimately meant that things didn't get done as quickly or efficiently as they should have been, bands that might have been signed weren't, artists on the label were left frustratingly in the dark. There were colossal cock-ups, too, such as the unavailability of The Painted Word's single anywhere in the UK, including their home town of Glasgow. Many of the initial administrative problems have been ironed out over the course of time and Mother has recently begun to widen its horizons towards giving bands longer-term deals, it has sharpened up its A&R stance and is generally beginning to look more impressive.

That U2 have such a close relationship with their homeland, even if it is not always reciprocated in full, is an important part of their music, and that was especially so on *The Unforgettable Fire*. The fractured imagery they employed so densely on the album hinted at a rootlessness that seemed to gnaw at them, perhaps the inevitable consequence of their itinerant, kinetic lifestyle as travelling musicians, a lifestyle which, while it may have had detrimental effects on their home lives, did unquestionably heat the creative molecules. Two songs in particular touched on physical as well as mental dislocation, 'A Sort Of Homecoming' and 'The Unforgettable Fire' itself. The title song was a disparate collection of mental pictures, almost phrases snatched from a dream, or perhaps more accurately, a nightmare. Although the title relates to the attacks on Hiroshima and Nagasaki and there is a faintly oriental mood to the music, there is no other tangible evidence of nuclear devastation in the song other than the apocalyptic vision of the mountains disappearing into the seas below and the reference to a dry and waterless place, which might be calling to mind those cities after the bombs had gone off when the survivors couldn't find sufficient water.

That aside, the troubles of this song seem to be altogether more personal, a journal of thoughts flashing through a troubled mind, a stream-of-consciousness attempt at exorcism. The coal-black eyes are again quoted in the song, ice-cold rivers hinting at further preoccupation with the drug culture, but this time the singer seems to be on the edge of his own precipice – *'don't push me too far'*. This time, and it's a suggestion that crops up again and again, almost subliminally at times, throughout the record, the singer is trapped, is within a cell of some kind. The subtext of much of the album is 'let me out of here!' If characters like Presley or the addicts on 'Bad' or 'Wire' are trapped by a fire beyond their control, it might be reasonable to conclude that U2 are equally prisoners of their own creativity, their own desire to communicate and their own fame. There is a strong undercurrent of dissatisfaction with the U2 lot, though it's impossible to tell whether that is an artistic sentiment, as they tried to break into a different style of music, a resurfacing of the old doubts as to their calling or just a general disenchantment with the rock 'n' roll lifestyle. The pull of home life is strong on this song and the record in general, a point emphasized on the opening track 'A Sort Of Homecoming', a point made in the very Irish feel to the song. U2 had begun to take an interest in traditional music, a form that they had perhaps looked down on in their youth but one from which they were now able to draw inspiration. A feel for roots music would come to the fore more strongly on *The Joshua Tree*, progressing into the blues and early rock 'n' roll on *Rattle and Hum*, but the folkish base that they were to use to great effect was first more fully realized on *The Unforgettable Fire*, presumably since it acted almost like a letter from home while they were on the road, the storytelling aspect and the strong emotional connection of the most powerful folk music striking a chord of similarity with their own ideas about the effects good songwriting should have.

'A Sort Of Homecoming' was a sound of the times, a music that conjured up the seeming fragility of life labouring under the auspices of the superpowers. It was a passion play which took place before the backdrop of a nuclear winterland, the *'fields of mourning'*, but one which touched earlier conflicts, too. Its inspiration lay in the poetry of Paul Celan, a Romanian poet who had killed himself in 1970, unable to house any longer the inner conflict of his personal survival as an agnostic after his family had perished in the concentration camps of Auschwitz (a plight also hinted at in 'Pride' with its reference to a man caught and held by a barbed wire fence). The horror of his life in death was vividly transmitted by Bono's own poetry – *'no spoken words, just a scream'* – as he tries to simultaneously reconcile his own doubts, his own faith and his own work.

Catholic guilt is an important constituent of U2's music and there are constant reminders as to just how fortunate they are when compared with their contemporaries. That has in no way reduced their need to belong and that is the fiercest emotion conveyed in these songs, that U2 are part of a generation that has to wake up and turn things around. The references to coming home are more than simply geographical but point to a consuming desire to find a resting place, a safe haven, maybe a refuge from the pressures and contradictions of being in U2. In with a certain resignation there are mixed doubts and uncertainties as to their own faith and their own worth and an aggressive assault on those frustrations – the layers of guitars scratch and kick, Bono spits out his words vituperatively, seemingly in an attempt to cow those doubts into submission, before accepting that that doubt is a central part of any living faith, that without the struggle, the faith is worthless.

The Unforgettable Fire was a record of U2 in transition, not simply musically, but as people. The spiritual fervour which had driven them through their previous records, while not diminished, was a more temperate influence on their existence, the lessons that it had taught them having been absorbed more fully. Bono, in particular, was less uptight about his beliefs and was beginning to loosen up in performance and on record, unleashing a torrent of original ideas as a result of the lessening of the pressures he placed upon himself. No longer the evangelist, no longer fighting the bland forces of wallpaper muzak and not willing to become the spokesman of a generation, he was able to give rein to his subconscious and allow his lyrical soul a greater freedom. He was ready, however, to note the changing circumstances in which U2 and the world outside found themselves.

Prior to *The Unforgettable Fire*, U2's music had been an undeniably rich and absorbing mixture, but one which had been largely inward looking, notwithstanding the occasional blasts on *War*. Individualism had been their creed and that U2 still prized the sanctity of the individual was not in doubt, but there were subtle signs that they were beginning to recognize the need for greater collective action to protect those people that formed the heart of their songs, the people used and abused by society before they were cast aside. Bono, for instance, noted on TV's *World In Action* that another lyrical strain in 'Bad' was used 'to wake myself up, to see what's going on around me. I'm part of a generation that needs waking up.' *The Unforgettable Fire*, like all albums, was old news by the time they took it on the road. It had a germ of their new mood of activism about it in 'Pride' and 'MLK' along with hints of social realism on 'Wire' and 'Bad', but to call it a political record would be misleading. It was poetic, ethereal and aesthetically pleasing but it was not a call to man the barricades. *The Unforgettable Fire* was an unfocused album, one that points the way to a new method of operations for U2 and new subject matter but which has not quite reached fruition. It was a boldly experimental record from a group that was understandably advised by their record company to play safe and look for the hit album, yet that willingness to make mistakes and come up with some songs which failed to hit their targets was a vibrant part of a rounded package.

Mistakes were very definitely made – '4th Of July' is little more than an undistinguished piece of soundtrack music looking in vain for a film and trying a little too hard to conjure up echoes of 'Another Green World'; 'Promenade', while engaging, was slight and insubstantial and 'Elvis Presley And America' smacked of self-indulgence – but the importance of the album was the opportunity it gave U2 to develop an identity that would stand them in good stead through the second phase of their existence. The Edge became immersed in creating musical textures and unleashed an orchestra of sound that moved him further to the forefront of the U2 sound in characteristically unobtrusive style, not allowing himself any flash guitar histrionics but simply continuing to employ new treatments to the sounds he could coax from his instruments. Adam was able to pare down his hitherto extravagant bass playing, replacing it with a greater simplicity, thereby achieving a greater degree of cohesion with Larry, whose playing was equally transformed by the ideas that Eno and Lanois put to him, such that he became a far more emotive and less purely technical drummer.

While the finished results were broadly satisfying, at least insofar as they saw U2 breaking free of a mould, it was another hard record to make. There were teething troubles at Slane Castle, both technical and attitudinal, as everyone was getting to grips with the new surroundings and the new personnel on board. These then turned into problems with the new style of recording. Adam, in particular, was uncertain about the piecemeal style of recording, complaining that nothing ever seemed to be completely finished and instead there were lots of songs hanging around in assorted stages of undress. The perfectionist streak in both band and producer took the final stages of recording, held at Windmill Lane, right up to the eleventh hour, when a halt had to be called since Eno was committed to another project and U2 were due in Australasia for a concert tour set to begin in the closing days of August 1984, a month before the album was ready to go into the shops.

Australia and New Zealand were two of the few places left on the globe that U2 had not played before and unfortunately their shows there did not showcase the new material to any extent simply because of the short rehearsal time they'd left themselves with having worked so long on the record. Songs that had been constructed and arranged purely for vinyl were impossible to recreate on stage since they were far too elaborate – it needed a far greater time period for the band to trim away the studio frippery and rearrange songs like 'The Unforgettable Fire' for live performance. They were not able to do this until they had returned to Europe, where they were now checking into the largest arenas on the continent, including Wembley Arena and Dusseldorf's Phillipshalle.

It was a very different live show that U2 had decided to put on this time. Gone were the dramatic backdrop and the white flags that bordered the stage, gone were the melodramatics that Bono had indulged in, gone was his walk into the crowd. This time, U2 were far more in control of the power they had as a live unit and the performance was all the stronger for the restraint they displayed. Assured of the strength of the music as well as the size of their following, U2 no longer had to kick the door down to win attention; people were kicking doors down to get in to see them. The minimal stage set suited the greater ambient atmospherics that the music was capable of engendering and indeed the potent simplicity of the set-up was something from which REM drew inspiration for their arena tour in support of *Green*, REM actually supporting U2 on some of the outdoor dates at the tail end of this tour.

Arenas were a fresh challenge to U2, especially in the UK where so many people had a natural prejudice towards bands that appeared at Wembley Arena. U2 were confident about their chances of success, however, The Edge going so far as to say, 'I really think that, of any band making the transition to arenas or stadiums from theatres, we have the best chance because I know that the people in the stadiums will be the people that we've seen in all the theatres. I've no apprehension about them – we're just gonna rewrite history concerning the stadiums.' In terms of the popular perception of the arena show, it's probably true to say that U2 did open a lot of minds to the experience. They were again fortunate in being the right band at the right time with the right audience. U2 entered stadiums on the crest of a wave in terms of confidence as *The Unforgettable Fire* was the album they were most pleased with, they were enjoying the new freedom in the music and were playing well. The response of audiences indicated that they had no need to worry about acceptance; tickets sold at a phenomenal rate and so they were relaxed enough to enjoy the shows without having to go over the top as they had on *War*. Finally, the new music was custom-built for arenas by virtue of its scale and scope, music that could reach the back of the biggest halls without losing its impact. U2 blazed a trail that made arena shows credible.

Their most lasting legacy to the arena was the attitude in which they made the leap – like so much else in the U2 story, they succeeded by going against convention. The normal book of rock rules would state that you win in theatres by being intimate and scaling down any theatrics whereas in arenas you need to pull off heroic poses, have a huge light show and any other eye-catching devices you might think of. It was either a fortunate accident or a piece of alarming insight that caused U2 to do the opposite. In theatres, U2 were wildly exaggerated, in arenas they were anti-heroic and yet these were approaches that worked, possibly because they were so unique. The arena shows stood or fell on the music alone, not on a multi-media extravaganza, in itself a confirmation of U2's belief in the new path they were following despite some heavy press criticism that they were becoming overblown.

It's true to say that U2 were, and perhaps remain, rather precious about their music and are desperate to stay in complete control of every facet of their activities. By actually achieving that total control they created a credibility paradox. In the past when acts like the Clash or Dexy's Midnight Runners published manifestos which said they were in charge of all their affairs, it was acceptable simply because everyone knew it wasn't true. Their posturing was the kind of rhetoric that the press wanted because it was supposedly heralding a revolution against the Establishment, when they knew, as we all did, that no such revolution was taking place and, since the journalists owed their living to the maintenance of that very Establishment, they were happy to see a safe revolt that didn't threaten the Winter Palace. When U2 came along demanding and winning total autonomy over their affairs, it introduced a real conundrum – they had done the apparently impossible and by so doing had set dangerous precedents. They were a band that had isolated themselves to a marked degree from the vagaries of fashion and the whims of the trendsetters by having watertight publishing and recording deals, renegotiated in the run-up to the release of *The Unforgettable Fire*. U2 actually could do just what they wanted. This inevitably meant that they had become capitalist lackeys and were bleeding younger artists dry by taking all the money from the pot, that U2 were motivated by the idea of being 'big' and nothing else. While there can be no denying that U2 have been very quick to make intelligent deals that have seen them do very well financially, this particular accusation holds little water since they could have been far better off had they left Island for another label in 1984. U2 were simply able to do what other bands weren't because they hadn't sold their souls to get any kind of deal and because they had put the money aspect of their career second behind artistic judgements, correctly reasoning that if the artistic environment was right, the sales figures would then look after themselves.

To many U2 took themselves too seriously, but there was a lighter side that came across during the live shows. Unable to refrain completely from audience contact, Bono would frequently drag a girl from the front rows for a brief dance around the stage and had even taken to calling aspiring guitar players up on stage to play with the band. The message was obvious. No matter how big the venue or the stage, there was still to be no gulf between audience and group, Bono still had to reach everyone. On the larger screen that they were now performing on he sometimes floundered and was left looking stupid, but his forays were generally well-received by audiences across the world. These moments aside, U2 did seem to hold on to their music very tightly, almost as if they were afraid to let it fly, afraid that it might be trivialized by outsiders. The serious nature of their work, coupled with their status as one of the very best live bands in the world – *Rolling Stone* made them 'Band Of The 1980s' in its 1985 awards, recognition of how far they had penetrated America's consciousness – made U2 obvious benefit fodder and it was in those circumstances that they cemented their hold on greatness.

U2 had regularly and quietly put their money into charity projects over the previous few years and had played a few benefit shows too. As 'the band with the conscience' there were many causes that wanted their time and many causes to which they wanted to contribute. There was a degree of reluctance on their part simply because there were noxious connotations to the whole charity syndrome, with certain artists using them as platforms to boost flagging careers or to re-promote a back catalogue. One call for assistance which they were unable to refuse came from Bob Geldof in the autumn of 1984 as he and Midge Ure tried to organize a benefit single to help with famine relief in Ethiopia under the blanket title of Band Aid. Bono and Adam attended the studio session and were part of the roll call that featured on 'Do They Know It's Christmas', a single which changed the face of fundraising forever.

Geldof's desire to bring about change via the medium of popular music was a dramatic change from his previous stance and indeed the way in which he would think of music after Band Aid had run its course. Indeed if there was a group that did think rock 'n' roll might make a difference, it was U2, a band diametrically opposed to Geldof in so many ways, yet one with whom there was a definite empathy. Both were emphatically Irish artists, though Geldof had fled the 'Banana Republic' as he termed it at the first possible opportunity, both wrote songs about real people and both were stubborn bastards who wouldn't lie down quietly and disappear in the face of setbacks. Geldof refused to stand idly by and 'watch another child die in my living room' as Michael Buerk's moving BBC News reports brought the full scale of the tragedy home to each and every person in the country. Through Geldof's tireless enthusiasm, the record did as it said it would – it saved lives. Bono commented, 'For Bob Geldof, the sight of little bits of black plastic actually saving lives was a bit of a shock. He had always thought of pop music as something wonderful in itself but nothing more than that. But I wasn't quite as taken aback by the success of it all. The 1960s music that inspired me was part of a movement that helped to stop the Vietnam War and there is no reason why contemporary music cannot have a similar importance.'

There was another closeness between U2 and Geldof which goes far deeper than simply being musicians working on such a vital project. Over the course of the Live Aid phenomenon the following year, Ireland distinguished itself by giving more money per capita than any other country in the world, a remarkable accomplishment for a country in such a state of economic impoverishment that the Self Aid concert was required the following year. The response to disasters since then has been equally impressive and there is something about the nation that allows it to respond so magnificently to the disadvantaged. Current Irish President Mary Robinson sees it as a function of the painful heritage of the nineteenth century. 'The generosity of the response to Somalia, Bosnia and others is a reflection that there is a very strong folk memory of the potato famine in the 1840s – I'm certain we identify with developing countries.'

As Ireland was so philanthropic in its participation in the Band Aid project, it was no surprise that U2 played an important role in its successor, the Live Aid concert in July 1985. By this time, they had taken *The Unforgettable Fire* around the world to rapturous response and had filled all the biggest indoor arenas before moving on to outdoor shows at Milton Keynes bowl and back in Croke Park. U2 were undeniably one of the hottest tickets in rock 'n' roll and had to be on the bill. There was no chance of them turning down the show and, on the day, U2 captured the spirit of the global jukebox more than did any other artist. They were passionate, compassionate, tender, angry and fiercely committed but refrained from any hackneyed gestures or inappropriate song selection, allowing the music to speak for them. Some had expected Bono to make a speech from the stage, but on this occasion he was wise enough to keep his own counsel. U2's collective statement on Live Aid came in the form of a press release which the press chose not to use. 'U2 are involved in Live Aid because it's more than money, it's music . . . but it is also a demonstration to the politicians and policy-makers that men, women and children will not walk by other men, women and children as they lie, bellies swollen, starving to death for the sake of a cup of grain and water. For the price of Star Wars, the Mx missile offensive-defence budgets, the deserts of Africa could be turned into fertile lands. The technology is with us. The technocrats are not. Are we part of a civilization that protects itself by investing in life . . . or investing in death?'

U2's original idea had been to play three songs, 'Sunday Bloody Sunday', 'Bad' and 'Pride (In The Name Of Love)' but, inevitably, things did not go according to plan. After a fiery 'Sunday Bloody Sunday', during which the *'no more'* chant took on obvious new connotations, 'Bad' was ushered in with deceptive calm before Bono seized the occasion and gave it its most human moments, the musical moments that, along with Bowie's 'Heroes', stayed in the mind longest after Live Aid had ended.

Unable to accept the huge distance between stage and crowd, Bono went into the photographer's pit and pulled a young girl from the audience, dancing slowly with her for a few moments before embracing others, underlining the need for solidarity in the face of such terrible crisis – everyone was doing their bit, not just the people on the stage. 'Bad', the song U2 used to wake themselves up, to broaden their vision of what was happening around them, was a song which opened the eyes of the watching millions. U2 had cut through the pious platitudes spouted by mealy-mouthed politicians, had dispensed with tired intellectual argument and with simple emotion had said, 'We are all the same, we have food, they don't, please help.' U2 were the band that defined Live Aid by going beyond a simple crowd-pleasing ritual – they *involved* the crowd, an act which also defined the new activism within rock 'n' roll circles. U2 were also now the biggest rock 'n' roll band in the world.

Live Aid, the triumph, was very nearly Live Aid, the end of the road. Bono later conceded, 'The next few days were the blackest depression. I saw the TV film back and I thought I'd made a big mistake and misjudged the situation. I thought, "That's it." I thought I had to leave the group. This thing where I was ending up in the audience had gone so wrong for me . . . I always resented the stage as something that would try and contain us and the music. But it ended up looking wrong, like I was coming down off our pedestal to the masses. I didn't mean to do it at Live Aid. After that I went out and just drove for days. I couldn't really speak to anyone. This whole thing of whether I wanted to be in a band or not came back to me. At Live Aid the whole question of Africa and the idea that millions were dying of starvation brought back the stupidity of the world of rock 'n' roll . . . I met along the way at a place called Newross a sculptor, a man in his fifties or sixties, and he was working on a piece, a bronze. And he'd been watching his TV, the Live Aid thing, and he described it all by saying that there was a different kind of energy coming off the TV set. The figure he was doing was of a man, a naked man, and he called it 'The Leap'. He said to me he was trying to capture the spirit of the day but the part of it he wanted was our part, the U2 piece. I thought to myself, "If a person who's so removed from rock 'n' roll can understand that, maybe it wasn't such a big mistake." '

Bono tried to make some sense of the Live Aid effort and the personal success he and the band had reaped from it by visiting Ethiopia with his wife Alison, where they worked on a World Vision educational relief project for a month, a visit he surprisingly managed to keep away from the press so that he could avoid the 'pop star saves the world' rubbish that the daily tabloids were now busily printing. Bono post-Live Aid was now the new Springsteen as far as the dailies were concerned and that paradox is something which seems to have had a great impact on the way U2 behaved during the period either side of *The Joshua Tree*. By helping the starving millions, U2 had reactivated their back catalogue, made an astonishing amount of money for themselves and, by virtue of their performance at Wembley, had opened the group up to a huge new following for whatever else they chose to release in the future. Although U2's own response to charity appeals was well known and it was fair to assume that a sizable proportion of that increased turnover found its way into the coffers of the appropriate causes, it was nevertheless a real problem of conscience for them to wrestle with. The only response was to make the best music and do the best shows possible, since anything beyond that level is, at least in part, out of the group's direct control. They were now the biggest band in the world, all the commercial dreams they could ever have had had come true, even if the final piece of the jigsaw had not come in the way they had anticipated. Nevertheless, there appeared to be a strong element of, not so much guilt, as a recognition of a greater responsibility that had been passed on to them to speak out on behalf of what they considered to be worthwhile causes and to use their position as world-renowned rock stars to talk about issues that concerned them – as Delmore Schwartz wrote, in dreams begin responsibilities. Maybe it was an act of atonement for the hideous sin of accumulating wealth, for there certainly was an hedonic streak to the Quakerish austerity of their behaviour, but the way in which they comported themselves seemed to suggest that it was impossible for them to have a good time if there was any suffering of any kind going on anywhere in the world. While this was probably not an accurate reflection of the mood in the U2 camp at the time, since any band with a number one album and single in most countries of the world would have to be pretty stupid not to be having a good time, even they would be hard-pushed to point to any attempts at humour or a more light-hearted approach during *The Joshua Tree* jamboree, a period where guilt again seemed to triumph over joy. The obligation that they seemed to feel they had towards the disadvantaged did seem to be more important than the music which had thrust them into the spotlight at times but it did also give them the opportunity to give their voice to some of the most vital causes of the day.

Even in 1992 with Zoo TV and the supposedly greater detachment they felt towards causes -- an impressive marketing trick if ever there was one, Larry getting the opportunity to tell *Vogue* (*Vogue*!), 'After ten years saving the whale it's like, forget the whale, remember the bank account!' – U2 were still happy to become involved with Greenpeace on one of the few issues that unites all of Ireland, an opposition to the proposed Thermal Oxide Reprocessing Plant (THORP) at Sellafield, just south of Workington on the northwest coast of England. Admittedly, instead of the earnest press conferences from days of yore, U2 now had to dress up like 'complete wankers' to make their point, but the point was made all the same.

Sellafield, formerly known as Windscale before the powers that be decided that, on its transfer from the Atomic Energy Authority to British Nuclear Fuels Limited (BNFL) in 1971, a change of name might make a nuclear processing plant appear more user-friendly, is fascinating in the perception people have of it. For instance, in the *Hutchinson Encyclopedia*, its entry baldly states, 'The plant is the world's greatest discharger of radioactive waste: between 1968 and 1979, 180kg of plutonium was discharged into the Irish Sea.' It then refers the interested reader to another entry on nuclear accidents, where the 1957 fire at Windscale, when the core of a reactor was destroyed, is discussed. Sellafield is defined, and not only in reference works, purely in terms of its danger to human health, not by the work it does. This before the introduction of Sellafield 2 – appropriately, even the name sounds like a disaster movie – which is set to increase the levels of radiation to incredible levels.

Sellafield 2 represents folly on an unimaginable scale. The Irish Sea is already the most radioactively contaminated sea in the world, an obvious enough reason for U2's involvement in the campaign to stop the discharges. If the go-ahead were to be given, BNFL's own figures, which generally err on the side of the optimistic, state that discharges into the air and sea could increase by up to 2000 per cent, while Greenpeace figures indicate that at full capacity the whole plant will be sending out 11.48 million curies of radioactivity each year (the accident at Chernobyl released 50 million curies in total). The proposed emissions over ten years will give the same level of radiation dose to the world's population as that from all the barrels of radioactive waste dumped into the oceans from 1960–1982, an activity then banned because of concerns over the levels of radiation such behaviour would lead to. Sellafield's current safety record, which BNFL is keen to broadcast to all and sundry, palls into insignificance against the fact that the occurrence of leukaemia around the plant is ten times the national average, adult leukaemia rates along the north Lancashire coast are three times the national average, cancer rates along the Irish coast are twice the national average.

The supposed logic behind Sellafield 2 is that it has been built to work on the more sophisticated and more toxic fuels from the pressurized water reactors which now make up the majority of nuclear power stations. The idea is to import around 600 tonnes each year for the next thirty years for the plant then to separate the uranium and plutonium for re-use, leaving the waste to be disposed of. The first absurdity is that plutonium, which was to have been used in a new line of fast-breeder reactors which never passed the prototype stage, is thoroughly useless except in the construction of nuclear weapons, something which is supposedly unnecessary in the new peaceful world which we are supposed to have. As a result, there is widespread worry among the world's governments that these increased levels of plutonium will fuel an escalation in the number of nuclear weapons. Secondly, when, over recent years, ships of all shapes and sizes have been sinking at terrifyingly regular intervals, what happens if a ship transporting radioactive material to and from

Sellafield runs aground? It should be noted that enormous quantities of the waste fuel are transported on normal roll-on-roll-off ferries. Shipping plutonium back to Japan – enough to make thirty nuclear bombs – is a journey fraught with danger, not only running the risk of the ship going down but also of being hijacked. Large amounts of fuel are also transported by road and rail across Britain. Anyone who uses the M6 regularly and sees the number of incidents involving overturned lorries might like to consider the effect if one such lorry was carrying plutonium. Goodbye Birmingham. BNFL and the industry in general dismiss such worries, insisting that the flasks in which the material is carried are strong enough to withstand any accident, but when the result of just one accident could be catastrophic, is it worth believing them? Environmentally and financially, Sellafield 2 makes no sense whatsoever, its cost having escalated from initial estimates of £300 million to £1.8 billion, with an additional £1 billion required for associated waste treatment facilities. Germany, one of the main contractors, seems increasingly likely to stop sending its waste to Sellafield, which will create an even bigger financial disaster.

These appear to be powerful arguments against the opening of Sellafield 2, but no one in power seems to be taking them seriously, trying to push the scheme through without so much as a public enquiry. Having already spent £2 billion on the scheme, the government is keen not to be seen to back down, although slightly more encouraging noises have been heard as the campaign has progressed. Nevertheless, the whole Sellafield 2 operation is a shining example of just why it is that people have less and less time for politicians and, more worryingly, the democratic process. Sellafield is something that most people do not want and even if the plutonium it generated were still appropriate for energy production it wouldn't be wanted when coal mines are being closed left, right and centre. When a government can impose VAT on domestic fuel and call it an environmental measure which encourages energy conservation and yet allows the THORP project to go ahead, might it not be pertinent to question which shade of green defines their policies – an environmental green or greenback green?

U2's presence at the forefront of Greenpeace's 'React' campaign has many threads to it. Firstly as long-standing contributors to Greenpeace, they had an obvious line of involvement. More than simply a reaction to a global issue however, the noxious nature of Sellafield was a deeply personal matter. As Dubliners, they live 130 miles from Sellafield. Bono reminded the audience at the benefit show held at Manchester's G-Mex Centre that 'it's a lot farther to Number 10 Downing Street!' There is a very real sense of bitterness in Ireland towards the British government on the Sellafield issue, a depth of feeling which, in many quarters, actually exceeds the antagonism felt over the unification question. In many ways for the Republic, Sellafield represents yet another attempt at British imperialism even after independence – Sellafield is damaging Irish interests just as the British have done for centuries. (It's instructive to imagine the outcry in this country if a nuclear plant in Cherbourg were spewing out radioactive waste to contaminate the south coast of England. To its credit, the Irish government has consistently led protests against Sellafield.)

The British government sanctions operations which eventually lead to the systematic poisoning of the Irish coastline. Bono lives on that coastline, 'right next to where all that crap is washed up', and has two young children whom he would dearly love to see play on the beach. He cannot allow them to do so since the British government have chosen to contaminate that beach. That beach might kill them. At the very least it might seriously damage their health, even though Sellafield doesn't carry a government health warning. This seems like a very good reason for getting angry.

The 'React' campaign did also fit into their plan of attack on the 'causes' front. Having been the 'band with a conscience' for so long and having been so closely identified with Amnesty International, it was time for a change of tack. There was a very real possibility of U2 being the benefit band appearing at every show, thereby diluting their potency as spokesmen for particular efforts. Familiarity does breed contempt, as Sting has unfortunately discovered. By concentrating exclusively on Greenpeace and the Sellafield issue throughout 1992, U2 were able to focus their attentions on one subject, were not drawn into debate that would be detrimental to the way in which they had now chosen to operate as a group since, however wrongly, Greenpeace was seen as being a far less political organization than Amnesty International, and were able to even the publicity odds a little – BNFL employ the biggest advertising agency in Britain and spend millions on portraying themselves as a caring, family organization that is no more dangerous than the local Women's Institute Sewing Circle. Greenpeace could obviously never compete on a financial level, so the publicity that U2 won was invaluable.

The whole campaign, from U2's point of view, began in the spring of 1992, when they announced plans to play a benefit show on 20 June for Greenpeace against the proposed THORP plant, choosing Manchester's Heaton Park as the outdoor site since it, like Dublin, is 130 miles from Sellafield, although eventually the show was transferred to the G-Mex arena in Manchester's city centre and was held on the 19th. U2 were supported by Kraftwerk, B.A.D. II and Public Enemy. The gig was intended to preface a Greenpeace demonstration at Sellafield the following day, a rally which U2 had agreed to attend. Having already given their go-ahead to the demonstration, which would have to take place on BNFL property since they had already bought up all the available land around the site, amounting to 3225 acres at present, BNFL then chose to take out an injunction to prevent such a rally taking place, a High Court judge, Mr Justice May, cancelling the concert, agreeing that they were within their rights to withdraw permission. BNFL's reasoning was that, having anticipated an attendance of 300 when the rally was first mooted by local pressure group CORE (Cumbrians Opposed to Radioactive Environment), the likely number of people arriving had escalated to 15,000, a direct result of U2's decision to attend, a decision drawn to BNFL's attention on 3 June, two days before they changed their minds over the demonstration. BNFL expressed its concern over public safety should a concert take place on land that was not suitable, adding a sanctimonious press advert on 18 June saying, 'What we will never do, however, is to allow our commitment to public safety to be compromised. Either by ourselves or by others.' As Bono was to say, 'They cancelled a peaceful demonstration because they said they were worried about public safety. Public safety – that's just a joke coming from them. These people are responsible for the deaths of innocent children.' Greenpeace were more temperate if no less angry in their choice of language: 'BNFL do not own the Irish Sea or the air we breathe yet they pollute it with impunity and reach for a writ if anyone dares to protest.'

BNFL's case seemed to rest on the back of Greenpeace having applied for an entertainment licence for the site; obviously a concert was being planned. In fact, Greenpeace were instructed to apply for the licence by the authorities and protested in vain that they had no need for one. The entire injunction episode does not smell of roses, but of small brown rodents, and turned Sellafield into an issue of free speech as much as one of environmental concern. BNFL quite clearly did not want the adverse publicity that a huge demonstration such as the one planned would have attracted, so one can only imagine that they had something to hide or were not keen on Greenpeace getting the opportunity to broadcast the pollution figures to a national audience. The fact that BNFL is owned by the government and that they had little difficulty in gaining an injunction from the judiciary to prevent a peaceful demonstration is surely just one of life's funny coincidences.

U2's involvement in the whole affair, which went on as they were playing their first British concerts in five years, did mean maximum publicity in all the newspapers, both tabloid and broadsheet. Having been thwarted by the courts, U2 were still in a position to assist Greenpeace by staging their own demonstration along with Greenpeace activists on the day that the original protest had been scheduled. Although Greenpeace were not allowed on BNFL land, as had already been pointed out BNFL did not own the Irish Sea and so the demonstrators were able to walk on the sand up to the level of the high water mark – not BNFL land. A total of sixty demonstrators, including U2, went ashore at 7 a.m. on inflatable dinghies sent out from the Greenpeace ship *Solo*. They were able to erect 700 placards over a three-kilometre line reading 'React – Stop Sellafield' and put up hazard-warning tape to mark a 'free speech exclusion zone'. As an exercise designed to extract mass publicity, it was a photo-opportunity *par excellence* as the sartorial elegance of the rock star was replaced with white anti-radiation suits and sunglasses as U2 dragged several oil drums filled with mud from Ireland contaminated by Sellafield's discharges and dumped these at the high water mark too, before attempting to spell out 'Help' semaphore style, *à la* the Beatles. The band used the opportunity to spell out the potential damage from Sellafield 2, Bono adding, 'The stuff in these barrels is already ten times over the allowed radiation limit. We won't let them gag us and get away with it.' While U2 did help Greenpeace to make their point forcibly, garnering mass exposure across TV, radio and newspapers alike, they did run up against the implacable face of the British government who, at the time of writing, are still to sanction a proper public enquiry. Maybe if Bono had walked on the water rather than coming into the beach by boat, people might have paid even more attention.

Having decided to endorse Greenpeace during the 1992 round of U2 activity, it was ironic in the extreme that they found themselves embroiled in a freedom of speech issue. It is freedom of speech and the right to a conscience that is the core of Amnesty International's work, work that was a cornerstone of the public perception of U2 and indeed their actual output when they recorded *The Joshua Tree*.

chapter nine

A CONSPIRACY OF HOPE

'Guilt over joy' is a phrase oft bandied around in connection with U2 and is one that became almost inextricably linked with *The Joshua Tree* and the tour that accompanied it, yet there is real joy even at the heart of the darkest music on that record, some of the songs bubbling over irrepressibly. 'Trip Through Your Wires' is just a blast, 'I Still Haven't Found What I'm Looking For' finds real consolation in doubt and 'Sweetest Thing', which found itself consigned to the B-side of 'Where The Streets Have No Name' is, quite simply, a thrilling pop song. In musical circles it had become axiomatic that U2 must be, above all else, 'uplifting'. Perhaps this was due to the clarity of The Edge's glorious guitar work, the driving force of the rhythm section or the anthemic choruses in their best-known songs, such as 'Pride'. Lyrical ambiguity had played a part, too, and even while they were taking a more and more studied and restrained view of the spiritual side of life, the celebratory aspect of their faith had generally come across more powerfully than the doubts and fears which riddled them in equal measure. They were pieces that were in the jigsaw but that were hidden underneath the box. Although *The Joshua Tree* saw U2 holding a few cards close to their chest, some of their previous equivocation was kicked soundly into touch as they began to express more fully a three-dimensional world-view that came from their increasing maturity both as people and musicians. Taking a leaf from the rootsier sounds which were beginning to influence them, they chose to be more revealing. The, some might say unreasonable, optimism that had clouded their judgement in previous songs seemed now to have dispersed, providing a more realistic and rounded view of the human state. And yet, the joshua tree alive in the desert was itself, amongst other things, an undeniable symbol of almost unquenchable optimism

Musically, the genesis of *The Joshua Tree* could be found in many incidents, some going back to the recording of *The Unforget-*

table Fire, although naturally every U2 record will hark back in some way to all its predecessors. *The Joshua Tree* was almost a reaction to the ethereal nature of *The Unforgettable Fire* and the atmospheric textures that The Edge had captured on his soundtrack to the movie *Captive*, a project undertaken with the assistance of Michael Brooke, the inventor of the infinite guitar, which was to be important in the construction of U2's fifth studio record. Having explored such ambient forms to their logical extreme, U2 now wanted to experiment with a different style.

The attraction which U2 had begun to feel towards traditional Irish music has already been remarked upon, but that was just one facet of a changing appreciation of the music that had existed in the years BC (Before the Clash). Where previously the band had looked askance at anything pre-1976, with the exception of obvious staging posts such as the Beatles, Bowie, the Who or the Stones, they were now beginning to realize that there was a wealth of music that demanded their attention. Delving into roots music, the obvious first route was via the folk songs of their own land, a pathway which Clannad had already constructed for them with their consummated marriage of the contemporary with the ancient. 'Harry's Game', perhaps Clannad's best-known piece, was regularly played at the end of U2 concerts as people left the hall, in what was effectively a mark of artistic respect for fellow countrymen and women. Inevitably perhaps, the idea of a collaboration was mooted, with Bono eventually singing a duet with Maire Ni Bhraonain in December 1985 for their album *Macalla*. The song, 'In a Lifetime', was an undeniable artistic success that was typically Clannad in style and yet had very definite traces of U2 in there as well and was an outstanding track on an album that was almost timeless, 'Caislean Oir', the opening piece, being especially outstanding. For U2-watchers, 'In a Lifetime' did point a different feel that the band might be looking towards, one which had origins in the strong depiction of moods on *The Unforgettable Fire* but which moulded those more fully into a more traditional song structure.

Ah yes, the song! Suddenly U2 had discovered the song! Despite having racked up somewhere in the region of fifty original recordings, U2 only now decided that they should be writing songs. Their euphoria in uncovering this seemingly hitherto unknown musical form was a little overdone, particularly if you were prepared to think back to 'Pride', 'Sunday Bloody Sunday', 'A Day Without Me' or 'Gloria', but the point had some validity. A lot of U2's music was built around a 'sound,' often from some new avenue that The Edge had been exploring. That kind of 'sonic sculpting' had reached an obvious conclusion with *The Unforgettable Fire* and the treatments that Eno and Lanois helped to apply to the music they had written. Bono was the main culprit in a sense because of his renowned reluctance to write words in advance of going into the studio. His sketches that were so often written on the microphone allowed him to tap into his subconscious with real results but this method was equally likely to leave him struggling. While it would be unfair to accuse U2's music of a lack of melody, the very fact that their songs were not arranged in the more conventional sense around a lead vocal did lead their music into unfamiliar territory that was atypical of popular music in general. While this meant that in their early work they really were unique – a phrase used too loosely, but one which does have relevance to U2 – the very lack of rules also paradoxically placed constraints on the sounds that they could create. Simplicity was not something facilitated by their method, although the signs on *The Unforgettable Fire* showed that they were beginning to move in that direction, Adam and Larry, particularly, holding the torch.

Clarity of lyrical image was vital to *The Joshua Tree*. Where previously Bono had left listeners to scrabble about in his words to find some sense of illumination, this time there were powerful events and emotions that he wanted to portray without fear of misunderstanding. It was a process begun in part on his visit to Ethiopia post-Live Aid, where he and Ali had helped an educational relief project, returning to realize that he had gained far more as a man than he had given during his time there, allowing him the perspective to come to terms with his position in a rock 'n' roll group and the real value of a band like U2 in the modern world. It also gave fresh perspective on the courage of the Africans in the midst of tragedy – the wealth of laughter and the proud dignity that he found in Africa brought home to him the mental obesity of the West: 'I had no culture shock going to Ethiopia but I did coming back and I started to ask myself some real fundamental questions about the way I was living in the First World as opposed to the Third World. The people I left behind me had such a strong spirit and that really shone in my memory, whereas I came back to this big fat spoilt child of the West and I started to get confused, seeing our cities as wastelands. Even though we aren't physically impoverished I started to see that we're spiritually impoverished.' Those were the emotions that drove the first song on *The Joshua Tree*, 'Where The Streets Have No Name'. Musically, it suggested a wide-open desert landscape that was the ideal setting for a lyric that juxtaposed Bono's distaste for the claustrophobic city existence and the savage backbiting it engenders.

On his return home in August 1985, Bono spent a day in Dublin before getting the call to jet off to New York to take part in the Artists Against Apartheid 'Sun City' project organized by Little Steven Van Zandt. Initially, Bono was there simply to add vocals to the 'Sun City' song along with other artists such as Springsteen, Lou Reed and Run DMC, but things took another turn. Reunited with Peter Wolf of the J. Geils Band, whom U2 had supported in American arenas in 1982, Bono found himself in a recording studio where the Rolling Stones were making a new album, *Dirty Work*, with Steve Lillywhite at the helm. During the course of the evening, Bono heard John Lee Hooker for the first time, which set the tone for an evening where Mick and Keef ran through the Everly Brothers back catalogue, followed by the blues standards they'd cut their own artistic teeth on. When Bono was eventually asked to play one of his own songs he was lost without Adam, Larry and The Edge, putting another nail in the coffin of U2 music rather than U2 songs. It was a process that Bono had begun at Bob Dylan's open air show at Slane Castle in August 1984, when he joined Bob Dylan on stage to sing a couple of songs including 'Blowin' In the Wind' (to which he didn't know the words). Having made a virtue out of rootlessness, having indeed created a band out of that rootlessness, U2, and Bono in particular, were looking for a tradition to plug into it, a desire heightened when, to Bono's patent embarrassment, he discovered that Dylan knew far more about traditional Irish music than he did himself! That was a gap in the band's knowledge that was being filled on the road during 'The Unforgettable Fire' tour when they played that music to give them a sense of their homeland while they were away, but it was a search that led them into other traditional types of music such as gospel, courtesy of Eno's huge collection of gospel records, and then eventually into the blues.

Friends back in Dublin had been gradually introducing U2 to the blues, but it was the meeting with the Stones that really inspired Bono. It came at a good time, as his enthusiasm for music had been renewed by his work in Africa and the space it had created away from rock 'n' roll. In the spirit of the music he had heard Keith Richards playing, he went back to his hotel room and, not having slept for two days, wrote 'Silver and Gold', which was so strong a piece, particularly in the context of the AAA project, that despite being recorded very late in the day it found its way onto the 'Sun City' album with musical accompaniment from Richards and Ron Wood. 'Silver and Gold' ultimately found its way on to *Rattle and Hum*, a vicious live version spoiled only by Bono's absurd exhortation to The Edge to 'play the blues', Edge responding with U2's own interpretation. Unfortunately, although Bono was clearly lost in the spirit of the song and of the occasion, and made the comment tongue in cheek, on the record it sounds patronizing and faintly ludicrous, one of the more obvious reasons for the U2 backlash that *Rattle and Hum* created.

Bono discovered that Richards was still lost in his love for his music and found that to be an added inspiration, but it was the music that he heard there and was beginning to delve into on his own which tilted the balance towards the song form taking precedence on the forthcoming U2 album that he was soon to return to Dublin to help write. It fitted the lyrical direction he was interested in pursuing at that time, a desire to write words that told gritty, harsh stories of real experience that were not clothed in impressionistic imagery, requiring a powerful, direct music to reflect that. At the same time, the others in the band had had their fill of atmospherics and were looking to simplify their playing, Larry, in particular, being a devotee of the archetypal pop-song format. That simplicity, that classic R. & B. style was the ideal vehicle for the issues that U2 were reacting to in their music.

Live Aid had kick-started an active streak in U2 that had hitherto been submerged, breaking out only in the form of occasional benefit concerts and the odd broadly political pronouncement in favour of humanitarian causes. The Artists Against Apartheid project was a further push along this road that Bono embraced wholeheartedly – after all how could any man of conscience stand idly by while a political system existed that was built upon discrimination against the colour of a man or woman's skin? Self Aid came next – after all, how could any man of conscience stand idly by while a political system existed that was built upon discrimination against men and women who were unemployed? Last, but not least, in this run of benefits was Amnesty International – after all, how could a man of conscience stand idly by while political systems existed that were built upon discrimination against those men and women who had a conscience? As Bono was to point out to *Sounds* in 1987, 'You can fall asleep in the comfort of your own freedom. We can't right all the wrongs but we can find people who can help to do it. If Amnesty International are doing it, why not lend support to them?'

Amnesty International had long been a passionate commitment for U2, their interest having been raised in the early 1980s with the series of Secret Policeman's Ball concerts. Since they had become involved through entertainment they needed no convincing of the important role that it had to play in spreading the message of an organization like Amnesty. Amnesty's problem, particularly in America, was that it was seen as a political organization and, more specifically, communist in bias. (Amnesty is, in fact, independent and impartial, it does not take sides in conflicts between governments and opposition parties and refuses to favour any political ideology or religion. During the Gulf War, it found examples of human rights violations by almost all countries involved.) In the USA, a country of 170 million people, there were around 150,000 members of Amnesty in 1985, a total that was simply inadequate, not only from any philosophical viewpoint but also financially since, because of its autonomy, Amnesty will not take any government donations, all funds having to come from members. Amnesty's International Secretariat, its nerve centre, runs at a basic cost of something like £90 a minute. The executive director of Amnesty, Jack Healey, felt that a consciousness and fundraising crusade was wildly overdue and, bearing in mind the success of other events like The Secret Policeman's Ball, concluded that a tour across the States to celebrate Amnesty's twenty-fifth anniversary might work a miracle. As long-term supporters of Amnesty, having already donated proceeds from a New York show the previous year, U2 were an obvious choice as a headline act and all the more so post-Live Aid since they were now able to attract stadium-sized crowds on their own. On approaching Paul McGuinness and the band in August 1985, Healey was promised two weeks of their time for an American tour the following spring. (Maybe it didn't hurt that Healey was born in America into an Irish family!)

Professionally, when the moment came to go on the road for Amnesty, the timing was hopelessly wrong as they had just begun to get their songwriting underway again, but there was never any question of reneging on their promise to Healey. Amnesty is the kind of organization that seems to have that effect on a multitude of 'entertainers', for want of a better word. The question therefore is 'Why are people so devoted to that cause?' One of the most obvious connections for writers and performers is that so often they are helping their own kind. In many countries of the world, the freedom of speech that bands like U2 take for granted is forcibly withheld. There is no freedom of expression, no freedom of thought, no freedom to criticize governments, no freedom to live your own life. It is often writers who attempt to break these barriers down and who, with depressing and distressing regularity, find themselves imprisoned for their pains. As a gesture of artistic solidarity across the globe, Amnesty is an obvious cause for songwriters with an eye on the social and political world.

More than that, Amnesty is irreplaceable as a means of monitoring the worst excesses of excessive administrations. It seems to be the only remaining organization that is actually concerned with upholding the provisions of the Universal Declaration of Human Rights. The declaration is so obvious in content that you wonder why it ever had to be written down, until you remember that these basic freedoms are being violated all over the world. Some of the articles include the right to life, liberty and security of person; that slavery and slave trade shall be prohibited in all forms; that all are equal before the law; that no one shall be subjected to arbitrary arrest, detention or exile; that everyone is innocent until proven guilty; that no one shall be arbitrarily deprived of his property; that everyone has the right to freedom of thought, conscience and religion; that everyone has the right to freedom of expression and opinion; that everyone has the right to freedom of peaceful assembly; that everyone has the right to work and to protection against unemployment and the right to form and join trade unions. These are basic human rights that are being abused in virtually every country of the world but, as Bono pointed out in 1987, 'the notion that there are people in the world still being tortured on the scale of Nazi Germany is a truth that is still being resisted.'

Along with many other artists, U2 felt an obligation to bring these truths home to people, but there was still more to their commitment to Amnesty. The workings of the organization and its very ethos were attractive to the band. Not simply caught up in the philosophy of individual freedom, Amnesty International gets involved in the day-to-day practicalities of the struggle. Its three-point mandate is clear. It seeks the release of prisoners of conscience, i.e. people detained anywhere solely for their beliefs and origins, who have not used or advocated violence. It works for fair and prompt trials for political prisoners. It opposes the torture or execution of prisoners. The non-violence clause is especially important and was particularly appealing to U2, who, while always welcoming the release of Nelson Mandela, for instance, were never able to give full public support to the cause because of his refusal to condemn violence. While the desire to take up arms is wholly understandable in such a desperate situation as that faced by the victims of apartheid, a point Bono made on 'Silver and Gold', pacifists can never agree to the use of physical force. Pacifists must not however indulge themselves in hippy-dippy idealism, wearing flowers in their hair and telling everyone, 'Well, wouldn't it be so great if we were just nice to one another y'know?' They must use tactics of aggressive opposition such as peacefully campaigning to force their governments to see the wisdom of economic and political sanctions, to ensure that countries which enact such atrocities are isolated from the rest of the world, that their violations are publicized as loudly and as regularly as possible and to ensure that there should be no refuge for those who seek to perpetrate these evils. Pacifists must seek to spread the word, to educate others and to create a world climate where those who would contravene these international laws will themselves be brought to justice. Amnesty International, winner of the 1977 Nobel Peace Prize, is an important forum for such people.

To U2, who believe in the power of the individual, Amnesty has further values to commend it. If the idea of U2 is very much one of 'don't follow leaders,' then the way in which Amnesty encourages its members to become active in their own right is perfect. By virtue of its 'send a postcard save a life' operation it actually empowers individuals to make a stand against tyranny and oppression, it gives individual members the chance to let their voices be heard; it is in a sense a step towards a true world democracy, where the voices of all the individuals can make a difference. Writing letters to governments is still Amnesty's basic weapon – a civilized solution to a barbaric problem – though of course that has evolved over recent years. In urgent situations, such as imminent executions, a network of volunteers can send hundreds of faxes or telexes within hours to appeal for the prisoner's life. Members often lobby governments or ambassadors of other nations, arrange petitions, rallies, marches to raise public awareness of Amnesty, its work and the people that it seeks to help.

Families are also helped by Amnesty as this moving letter testifies. It comes from the brother-in-law of a 'disappeared' social worker in Guatemala, asking for more information. 'The information that you send me will be like a motor, a dynamo that will make my sister stand up ... Your information will be like telling her "Look, we have worked, we have fought, we have done all that was humanly possible."' It was the plight of these disappeared people that prompted the closing piece on *The Joshua Tree*, a moving song called 'Mothers Of the Disappeared', a kind of companion to Sting's 'They Dance Alone'. Rather than an indictment of the behaviour of the governments of Latin America, it was a very human treatment of the suffering endured by the women of those countries, whose children had been taken away by the death squads for opposing the government line, 'disappeared' being a euphemism for murdered. The song was inspired by Bono's visit in 1986 to El Salvador, where he had met with some of these mothers who had lost their children. His words capture the overwhelming sense of loss along with the faint hope that one day they may return – *'we hear their heartbeat'* – while the ominous, slowly building power of the music vividly described their hope in the midst of the struggle. This is perhaps the most inhuman kind of torture on earth; the mothers of the disappeared are left to mourn their children's passing but are unable to bury them, are unable to go through the essential human ceremonies that mark a final letting-go of loved ones. They continue to fight their oppression and continue to campaign for answers about their children's fate, Amnesty giving them an important platform from which to work, for without those answers they can never be at peace.

Amnesty International is about a greater truth than shades of political philosophy. It is about freedom and it is about hope. Every now and again the press will print a story about Sting or about Peter Gabriel or about U2 or about Dave Stewart or about Lou Reed – at best, their activities for organizations such as Amnesty International will generally merit a brief postscript to the article, sometimes used to portray them as benevolent eccentrics. Sometimes, there is a cynicism that stinks – phrases like 'career-enhancing', 'bogus humility', 'empty platitudes', 'champagne conscience', 'messianic megalomania' (especially for Bono) and 'ego-massaging meddlings' are employed to indicate that the artist in question doesn't really understand what they're doing, is only in it for the extra sales or is wasting his time. The undertow is Goldmanesque – rock 'n' roll is for idiots, play it safe and stick to filling the dance floor. Rock 'n' roll has no place dealing with higher issues and Amnesty only soils itself by its association with emotional and intellectual retards.

Cynicism is, of course, very fashionable and the pieces are

undeniably witty and clever. But fuck 'em. Sometimes the performers have been overwrought and sincerity has looked like bullshit but then as a culture we are so shocked by the spectacle of real faith, of real belief, that we become embarrassed and our only recourse is to mock. That we should live in a world where barbarism on a medieval scale still goes on is frankly disgusting and degrades us all. If it takes a pop star in a stretch limo to put that message across, then hail, hail rock 'n' roll.

There is cause and effect in rock 'n' roll, the facts clearly prove it. The clearest exposition came with Amnesty's American tour in June 1986 which went under the name 'A Conspiracy Of Hope', the title a direct and optimistic play on the covert operations of the governments who rule by fear. The tour stretched across America, playing shows in San Francisco, Los Angeles, Denver, Atlanta, Chicago and, finally, New York and featured U2, Sting (reuniting with the Police on some of the gigs), Peter Gabriel, Lou Reed, Joan Baez and the Neville Brothers. The final show at New York was a true American multi-media jamboree before a crowd of 55,000 in the Giants Stadium and millions more on MTV, radio and other TV shows. Additional guests like Fela Kuti, who had himself been released from prison following Amnesty action, Joni Mitchell, Robin Williams, Miles Davis and Bob Geldof arrived to lend support to the final show too.

As a consciousness-raising event the tour was a triumph with Amnesty stalls, petitions and literature everywhere within the halls and across MTV's coverage but, more importantly, much of the music the artists selected was apposite to the cause and made a deeper, subconscious impression on the crowd than did the well-meaning spiels on screened public service announcements by the likes of John Huston or Meryl Streep – the lasting impression was that of actually having seen a clip of Meryl Streep rather than what she was saying. If, on the other hand, crowds left the arena humming 'Biko', 'Driven to Tears', 'I Shall Be Released' or 'Pride', connections between the song and Amnesty's work could be made more power-fully over a period of mental incubation.

U2 were by now *the* band to see, this being America's first chance since Live Aid. They didn't disappoint their banner-waving followers, playing a selection similar to that at Self Aid a couple of weeks earlier, including the cover versions that proved that they could at last play other people's songs (an impression refuted by the execrable version of 'Paint It Black' released in 1992). U2 went from

'MLK' and 'Pride' into 'Bad', the song everyone had come to hear, and then 'Sunday Bloody Sunday', this time directing the increasingly adaptable song towards the world's trouble spots like Beirut and Nicaragua, before closing with 'Maggie's Farm' and 'Help!' There could be no mistaking the conviction with which they played and it was a conviction to which fans responded – all over the USA, there were U2 fanzines and fan clubs who began to organize petitions to help prisoners of conscience, were holding events to raise money for Amnesty or for Third World causes, probably the biggest compliment ever paid to U2 in that people were inspired by the music and the public face of the band to become involved in humanitarian causes on their own behalf.

It was also an important antidote to the feeling that 'event' shows create, that the vast bulk of the crowd are there simply because it *is* an event. Amnesty International were able to prove that it was far more than that and give similar fundraisers a new lease of life. By the time figures were in, Amnesty membership had doubled and they had raised $2.6 million as well as increasing interest and awareness of Amnesty's work and importance – vital since the struggle for human rights is a very long way from being won. Recent Amnesty figures point to more than 1.1 million members in over 150 countries along with more than 6000 volunteer groups. That these numbers are maintained and then increased is essential when one looks at the work Amnesty had to do in 1990, when it worked on in excess of 3200 cases involving 4500 individuals. Action actually began on 1683 new cases, 1609 being closed. It issued 134 major reports on violations in 62 countries, ranging from the killing of children in Brazil and Gautemala, to torture in Senegal, mass executions in Iran and mass imprisonments of political prisoners in Chad. In 1989, prisoners of conscience were held in 71 countries; torture and ill-treatment were reported in 96 countries; deaths reportedly from ill-treatment in custody occurred in 40 countries; extrajudicial executions were reported in more than 40 countries, disappearances in 20. There are more statistics, equally chilling. Yet cold statistics often fail to move. That is why efforts such as 'A Conspiracy Of Hope' are so important – they put statistics into an emotional context and can move hard hearts far more than another report on another human rights violation.

It's clearly absurd to suggest that U2 only sell records because people believe in their humanitarian stand rather than because The Edge is a great guitar player, but a large portion of their success with

The Joshua Tree was based on the fact that they were able to articulate the emotions of those who felt that there was a better kind of world to be built and who sympathized with U2's rage at the iniquities of modern life. U2 had a far wider constituency of common ground and like-minded spirits than did the political figures of the day. Financially, 'A Conspiracy Of Hope' did U2 no harm, priming people as it did for their return to the world stage a year later, but the real rewards were on a personal and artistic level. On those levels alone, it probably is true to say that U2 gained at least as much as they gave to Amnesty International.

One of the greatest attractions of the tour for all the artists on board was the opportunity it provided actually to meet some prisoners of conscience freed by Amnesty's work. For Bono, one such chance came not at the concerts but in the Latin Quarter of San Francisco, when he and Lou Reed went to Mission Street to look at the anti-American slogans and murals that covered its walls. During their visit, they met Chilean artist Rene Castro, who later provided the stage set for U2's Love Town tour in 1989–90. 'At first he didn't pay me much attention until he discovered the Amnesty connection. Amnesty saved his life. He'd been captured when Allende was killed and they had the military revolution. He was tortured. They bored a hole in his chest. He was in the stadium with Victor Jara when he had his fingers cut off and then, eventually, was brutally murdered. Amnesty International had got him out and people from the Latin American community came to our gigs and Rene Castro sent me some of his paintings and eventually I was asked to go to Nicaragua and El Salvador.'

Central America was to be an important theme on *The Joshua Tree* even though it caused further disruption in the album sessions. Nevertheless, that visit was a vital creative force for Bono, one which set the direction for some of the album's lyrics and helped the band work on the most compelling track they had yet written. 'Bullet The Blue Sky' was a sound that helped U2 revitalize rock 'n' roll and prove that it was still an important contemporary medium. Nicaraguan democracy was under threat from America, supposedly the upholders of the democratic way, since it was America that was providing the money to arm the Contra-rebels who were opposed to the socialist Sandinista government there, which was led by Daniel Ortega, a regime which had been given economic assistance by Reagan's predecessor Jimmy Carter. Reagan revoked the aid and accused the Sandinistas of trying to overthrow the administration in

El Salvador, an interesting instance of the pot accusing the kettle of being a particularly dark colour since he was busily trying to undermine the Nicaraguans, including, by 1984, mining their harbours. Reagan's administration actively supported the Contra rebels, who were already known to have executed prisoners, killed civilians and used enforced conscription and who, unsurprisingly, had minimal support among Nicaragua's people who, in 1985, returned the Sandinistas to power in democratic elections. This flagrant misuse of democracy (i.e. voting for the wrong side) so enraged the Americans that in June 1986, not content with channelling funds via the back door to the Contras as part of the Irangate scandal, the US Congress chose to provide $100 million in military aid. American troops were involved in similar meddling in El Salvador, where their brief was to prevent any communist parties coming to the fore, to the extent that the 1982 elections were boycotted by all left-wing parties and voting eventually took place amid scenes of extreme violence. The USA then continued to help the government fight the socialist guerrilla movement despite the fact that countries such as Mexico and France recognized them as legitimate political parties with whom the government should negotiate.

Bono's visit to Central America in 1986 came at the height of the fighting and the sights he saw just bled into the words he was writing. He later described 'Bullet The Blue Sky' as an attempt to exorcize his own fear. 'Salvador looks like an ordinary city. You see McDonalds, you see children with school books, you see what looks like a middle-class environment until you go twenty miles out of the city and see the villagers and the peasant farmers. I was outside on my way to a village and the village was bombed and it scared the shit out of me. I didn't know which way to run. They were mortaring the village and there were fighters overhead . . . and this little farmer says to me, "No worry, ees over there." He was going through it every day of his life and he'd learned to live with it . . . Troops opened fire above our heads while we were there, just flexing their muscles and I literally felt sick. The idea that the people at our concerts in America, their tax was paying for these instruments of torture was something I hadn't quite come to terms with.' Bono returned home to tell The Edge, 'I want you to put El Salvador through your amplifier.' And he did.

The sound that comes out of the speakers when you play 'Bullet The Blue Sky' doesn't so much jump out as leap out, put its hands to your throat and pin you to the wall. Edge's vitriolic guitar swoops and dives around an enormous drum pattern from Larry to create an immense, monolithic sound that is mesmerizing. It was one of the angriest, most expressive pieces of music that rock 'n' roll has produced since Hendrix had mauled 'The Star Spangled Banner' into submission almost twenty years previously and was a similarly scathing and unequivocal condemnation of the greed of America and the lengths it can go to to protect its own interests. The closing line was a barbed comment that not only attacked Reagan but U2's American constituency for sitting back and allowing this to happen. It was a rallying call to those who slept through this Central American scandal and a warning not to believe the disinformation spread by the press and the White House briefings who pretended to know nothing about Irangate. Corruption was not restricted to military juntas, it was alive and well and living in Washington DC, too.

'Bullet The Blue Sky' evolved musically from a long, dark, improvisation, although the writing sessions had seen the band initially working on a purely experimental basis, compiling between twenty and thirty pieces of music which they began to work on in more disciplined fashion when Eno arrived on the scene – clearly the Eno/Lanois production partnership had worked well with U2 on *The Unforgettable Fire* and it was a relationship that obviously had much more creative mileage in it. In order to catch all the musical moments, the band experimented with a new style of recording, as Adam explained: 'We taped a lot live and set up so that we didn't have to stop and start so much – we worked it that we could do an hour's recording before we had to change tape reels by slowing the tape down – we set up to serve the musicians.' By having that extra freedom, the band allowed themselves the luxury of losing themselves in whatever piece they were working on without needing to think unduly about any technical considerations. The result was to create a generally looser, simpler sound that gave the music a potent, live feel, an additional power that was the closest they had come to replicating their strength in concert in the studio.

Part of that live strength was a result of employing the best people they could find to work with them on the technical side. For a band that put such a reliance on its live show, it was crucial that their road crew be of the highest order as well as being in tune with the musical direction of the band. Over a period of time, U2 had pieced together a crew of people who were widely recognized as 'the business', a crew that had coped with Bono's excursions into the crowd and across balconies, with Edge's ever increasing battery of guitars, keyboards and effects, that had seen them through the trials of Red Rocks – their triumph in actually putting the show on was an even greater one than the band achieved in playing – Live Aid, recording in the strange setting of Slane Castle or in Adam's house and who had been equal to every challenge. One recent addition to what was an extended family was Greg Carroll, a Maori who had become involved with U2 when they had played in New Zealand in 1984 on the first leg of 'The Unforgettable Fire' tour. He and Bono became particularly close, to the point where he became Bono's personal roadie. During the writing of *The Joshua Tree*, he went out on Bono's behalf and was killed in a road accident.

The loss of a close friend gave the group a view of their own mortality and also fresh perspective on the band business. Adam admitted, 'There are more important things than rock 'n' roll . . . your family, your friends and, indeed, the other members of the band – you don't know how much time you've got with them. I'd rather go home early than stay up all night mixing a track.' The song they wrote about Greg Carroll, 'One Tree Hill', was tender, moving, charged with emotion, yet never sentimental. It was a loving tribute to a great friend which included one breathtaking line, death as *'the cold enduring chill'*, as well as a closing section which sounded as if it were some kind of primal therapy for the band, each pouring their all into a few seconds before an elegiac coda closed the song in the same peaceful mood they had employed on 'MLK'. When they chose to dedicate the record to Carroll's memory, it was an act that expressed their love and gratitude to all those who had helped them along the way, be it in physical terms or be it their families tolerating the absence of their children, brothers, lovers.

The Joshua Tree has come to be considered as an album obsessed with America, which gave rise to a certain tension within the music they were making. Bono in particular had been attracted to an American sound, the blues music he had become used to on his travels having taken hold of his imagination, while The Edge was still working on a music rooted in a similar sensibility to that on *The Unforgettable Fire*. This neatly balanced Bono's excesses in the other direction, although it did give rise to some initial difficulties, The Edge remarking, 'There were two opposing directions. Bono was fascinated with blues imagery and America but his heart was elsewhere, these twisted love songs like 'With Or Without You' and 'Luminous Times', which was what I was more interested in because what I was writing was more European, textural.' Interestingly, by the end of the sessions, Bono and Edge had swapped roles, Bono arguing for the more European music, Edge excited by the American style. Meanwhile, the key to the greater accessibility that *The Joshua Tree* gloried in came in no small part from Adam and Larry – whose bass drum it was that rooted U2 in rock 'n' roll according to Bono – who were keen on maintaining the strides made on the previous album. One of Lanois' maxims is that the closer the physical proximity between drummer and bass player when playing, the better they will work as a unit. If that's the case then Adam must have been sharing the drum stool, because the solid R. & B. kick they gave the songs made U2 music for the feet as well as the head and heart at long last. As the first rule of music marketing said, if you've got an audience by the feet, their wallets are sure to follow.

There was a very obvious intent on the part of U2 to capitalize on the new status they had achieved over the course of the preceding years. Naturally enough, they wanted to sell as many records as possible because, after all, they are professional musicians and that's how they earn their living. But there seemed to be more to it than that. The production that Eno and Lanois employed, the additional mixes that Steve Lillywhite performed on a handful of songs gave the music a surface radio-friendly sheen that had never been so blatantly in evidence before. The album gave a hint of a very deliberate, calculating move towards the mainstream in order to mess around with it, to change things from within the monster itself. There had always been an obsession within U2 with the appalling state of chart radio, especially in America, something they had been keen to put right. The only way to put it right was to ensure that their records got played there. In order to achieve that, *The Joshua Tree* saw U2 making some minor concessions to the format, something made all the easier by their commitment to the classic song structure. By writing within that strict limitation, a useful restriction that was almost liberating as a reaction to the absolute freedom they'd given themselves on *The Unforgettable Fire*, it was as though they'd happened on a mainstream formula by accident.

Going into *The Joshua Tree*, U2 knew that whatever they released would get some airplay on AOR radio stations in the States because of their status within the industry, but to breach commercial radio they would be forced to record a more obvious kind of song. The whole situation became one of trade-offs. By simplifying they might be seen by their hard-core support as compromising their integrity but they would also be able to reach a lot more people with their music. Those who believed in the importance of popular culture could not hold an elitist position, but must instead endeavour to attract as many people as possible. This is not to suggest that U2 deliberately decided to make a bland record in order to reap financial benefit – *The Joshua Tree* with songs of the stamp of 'Exit' or 'Bullet The Blue Sky' is proof positive that they did not do so – but it is difficult not to conclude that they chose to concoct their own 'conspiracy of hope' for artistic reasons.

The music on the album really did have something to communicate, some ideas and ideals to discuss, challenges to lay down. To hit their existing audience who might want to hear 'Son Of Unforgettable Fire' would be preaching to the converted, people who had already been made aware of issues like Amnesty, like the problems of unemployment, people who weren't afraid to admit to their own personal doubts or crises of faith in themselves or in their god. To restrict themselves to just those people and to just those ideas would lead to creative atrophy. After all, they had thrown the rule book away after *War* and it was now time to do so again.

In a country like America whose popular music was defined by corporate sponsorship, renegades like U2 who have carved out a huge popularity on their own terms had to cut across to ears that might otherwise be tuned only to REO Speedwagon and their ilk. To attract those people was another invigorating challenge for the band but it was also an essential step on from 'Sun City' and 'A Conspiracy Of Hope'. There remains in the unusual sonic cohesiveness of *The Joshua Tree* a strong feeling that U2 had discovered how to infiltrate the mainstream and were deliberately doing so purely in order to attack from within – once casual listeners had been drawn in by the admittedly lush sound of 'With Or Without You' or 'I Still Haven't Found What I'm Looking For', both of which made number one in America, they were hit by lyrics that were very different to the standard chart fodder, Bono pointing out that 'there's something exciting about subverting Top 40 radio because the sort of songs they play on the radio don't have much relevance to me.' Just when Middle America wasn't looking, U2 hit them with a song about Central America, the social implications of unemployment or the general state of their country. 'In God's Country' is a song which echoes REM's 1984 song 'Little America', in that it shows America both good and bad from a tour bus window. Millions heard 'In God's Country' from the nation's number one album and doubtless some of those paused for thought; it was an audience of college students who heard REM's underground record and they had already stopped to think – REM had to wait a little longer to win their wider audience and make points with pieces like 'Finest Worksong', released into a more receptive climate which U2 had helped to fashion.

Just because the songs mean something and bear close scrutiny does not mean that U2 are on a crusade to save the world – does Martin Scorsese have to be denied a sense of humour because of films like *Taxi Driver*? The answer is clearly no. His work, while a vibrant part of the whole man, is just that, a part rather than the whole. The same is true of U2. Bono speaks of feeling like a postman when people mention the message in U2's music and that being in U2 really gives him and the others licence to do just what they want. Who is stupid enough to say that that's a miserable kind of existence especially when their contemporaries queue up to receive their 'pocket money' from the dole office? However, it would be equally wrong to deny that U2 make very serious music and that they are all the more vital for that. 'Social politics' is but a part of their overall sound, but it is an exciting, important part.

Now, on *The Joshua Tree*, they chose to look at another side of human life. Having dwelled on the spirit and on the socio-political in the past, they now began to uncover the sexual, sensual dimension as a challenge both to themselves and to their well-established enthusiastic audience, who might feel that love songs were not worth the tape they were recorded on. Moon-in-June love songs per se were not something for which U2 had much time but 'relationship' stories were something that had increasingly begun to interest them, perhaps a legacy of seeing the strength of relationships in the most severe adversity in Central America. 'Rock 'n' roll is obsessed with sex in the back seat of a Chevrolet,' remarked Bono. 'Now I'm sure sex in the back seat of a Chevrolet is pretty good for those involved but I'm more interested in writing about relationships beyond that point. I'm interested in the mental conflict of a relationship,' stories explored in songs such as 'With Or Without You', 'Red Hill Mining Town' and 'Running to Stand Still'. A take on the kind of work Springsteen did in his song 'The River', which took a relationship past the altar, Bono's fascination with that kind of battle came to a head on *Achtung Baby*, where it permeated almost all the songs on the record. On *The Joshua Tree* it was but one ingredient.

The Joshua Tree was undeniably the most mature of U2's albums but it was not a record that could be fully appreciated in total isolation. During recording, they put together around twenty songs and there was. heated debate about the final track listing. Rather than release a double album which would undoubtedly have been too much for listeners to take in, the album as it stands coming close to being overpowering, they decided to reinvent the role of the single, adding the extra songs as B-sides. Of these seven additional tracks, some were obviously experimental and almost incomplete but the majority were the equal of virtually anything on the final album. In looking at *The Joshua Tree*, some consideration has to be given to that music.

Looking at those pieces, it becomes far clearer just where Bono was heading lyrically, giving a far stronger indication of what kind of ideas would form *Achtung Baby* four years later, since they were mostly relationship songs with savage twists. Had these been on the album, replacing things like 'Bullet The Blue Sky' and 'Mothers Of The Disappeared', the reaction to U2 might have been very different since the album would have become far more intimate. Bono might not have been pushed into the role of the new messiah that his passionate condemnations of America, apartheid and human rights violations on those songs led him into, but it would also have made for an unbalanced record. Things were probably not helped in that regard by the almost biblical vocabulary of floods and fire which Bono employed and by the very title of the album.

The Joshua Tree had many readings as a title. There was the optimistic defiance of life going on in the desert, there was the image of the desert itself, conveying the personal and political wasteland of 1986, and there was the slightly ludicrous sound of the title. Apparently Larry was too embarrassed to let his girlfriend know the title and Bono reckoned it was the sort of title that would sell three copies. There is another angle to the title too, which was never discussed at the time presumably because it sounded even more absurd than the title itself. The joshua tree itself in legend takes its name from the way in which the branches reach up to heaven, supposedly like Joshua in the Bible, arms raised in supplication. Joshua was, of course, the successor to Moses and led his people into Canaan, the Promised Land of the Israelites. The first city to fall was Jericho, where music brought the walls tumbling down . . .

Bono was instrumental in the selection of the title, Edge remembering, 'We were driving on this desert road and saw these weird-looking cactus things. The driver said, "they're joshua trees," and I caught this look in (Bono's) eye and he came up and said, "This would make an amazing title," and eventually we said, "Yeah, let's go with it."' An indication of U2's increasingly relaxed approach came in the same interview when Edge admitted that shooting the cover pictures in the desert 'was a good excuse to go somewhere we hadn't been!' This change in attitude was beneficial to the music but was not transmitted by the way U2 were presented to the world. *The Joshua Tree* features yet more startlingly powerful images from Anton Corbijn's camera, but it has to be said that the framing of the cover shot sets the listener up for a musical version of an Ingmar Bergman film, a contrast to the impression of 'Carry On U2' that the collage cover of *Achtung Baby* conveyed. Packaging has become more important than the goods these days, a point U2 were keen to make, since although *Achtung Baby* was a darker, heavier, infinitely more intense scrawl than *The Joshua Tree*, U2 are now thought of as being lighter in tone. The moral of the story is get your cover right.

Evidence of elaborate Bergmanesque metaphysical imagery was not found on the album, however, since it chose to deal in harsh, sometimes base language. 'Trip Through Your Wires', a real hootenanny marked by a rough-and-ready blues harmonica part, rejoiced in its sexual and spiritual confusion. There was the spiritual sense of rebirth in love, the hope in a desert landscape and the yearning for someone to share life with, but this time Bono admitted that his intentions might not always be honourable and that the citizens of Arizona might do well to lock up their daughters after all. That same sense of duality could be found in the object of his desire – and to hear Bono singing so lasciviously of desire was a shock in itself – '*angel or devil?*' Was she his salvation or the agent of his damnation? More importantly, so wrapped up was he in the sensual experience, did he care any more? Is sex itself dirty? Only if you do it right.

The Unforgettable Fire had seen U2's first excursion into the darkness of the human soul on an individual rather than corporate or political level but *The Joshua Tree* took that several stages further with its powerful merger of the sacred and the profane, the spiritual and the sensual, the angel and the devil. 'Trip Through Your Wires' smouldered, not with indignation but with a sensual passion. Owning up to their own personal shortcomings, admitting that they were not saints, nor exclusively sinners either, U2 put on a human face of human frailty more overtly than at any other time, showing themselves to be men who needed to share their lives with others but who were unable to control the consequences. The music was not made by saints, not by evangelists, not by the righteous (although there were musical traces of the Righteous Brothers) but by four

Dubliners who saw the murkiness of their own souls and understood that they were prey to the darkness in the same way that those around them were. 'I Still Haven't Found What I'm Looking For' was further indication of that joyous confusion.

For U2 to tackle a gospel song might have seemed unlikely but this was a marriage made in heaven, Edge admitting that 'the subtle sexuality of gospel music attracts me. It's strange and twisted because that's far more what it's all about.' 'I Still Haven't Found What I'm Looking For' was a tale of spiritual search and the side-roads along the way, the temptations which anyone can fall prey to, a song with a restless and glad spirit, one that was affirmative in its doubt, suggesting that it's important not to have the answers to life, the universe and everything, that the search is all. It was an opportunity for Bono to own up to the fact that 'I'm not a very good advert for God! If ever there was a sinner, there's one here in me!' The song was one with a 'but' at the end of every sentence. 'I believe but,' 'you set me free but.' Christianity was a great thing and an important thing in Bono's life, but there's a girl over there . . .

The music of the blues had helped Bono, in particular, find his position in the lineage of rock lyricists and find a heritage and a language which he could draw upon – Robert Johnson's *Blues falling down like hail*' were words he felt he could have written and that led to a brutality in some of the lyrics which enabled him to work sexual politics into the mix. 'I've come to the realization that . . . all the singers that inspired me over the last twenty years are, for the most part, people with similar spiritual concerns as myself and similar confusion and chaos in their lives. Whether it's white singers like Bob Dylan, Van Morrison or Patti Smith or black singers like Marvin Gaye or Stevie Wonder and going back to Aretha Franklin you can see they could never separate the spirit from the soul.' The sexual guilt factor that those artists had struggled with was the boxing ring in which Bono the writer now found himself, trying to own up to his baser instincts and trying to engage the higher mind for the sake of a monogamous relationship.

Further courage to articulate that position was taken from the very fact that the people whom they admired were not always spotless in their personal lives. J.F.K. was not a model of sexual propriety, neither was his brother Bobby, but hand in hand with that went the knowledge that they were two of the greatest political and humanitarian figures of the twentieth century. Angels and devils. John Lennon, a musical hero, was a genius who used every opportunity he had to talk about himself, his own lack of what a previous age would have termed 'moral fibre', the turmoil that went on in his personal life, which included a violent temper that could be vented upon those nearest to him – who else could have written a song like 'Crippled Inside'? And yet Lennon was an impassioned campaigner for the peace movement, wrote its modern day anthem, gave aid to a directory of charities and wrote some of the greatest songs in the history of popular music. Angels and devils. Then there was Martin Luther King whose own private life did not bear the closest of scrutiny. Yet he remains the most potent symbol of a moral crusade, not based on intolerant fundamentalism but on equality, justice and freedom. Angels and devils. Within the same man. After all, you gotta sin to get saved.

Although *The Joshua Tree* was not a concept album in any sense the sequencing of the record worked particularly well, with each song having some kind of relevance to what had gone before. 'With Or Without You' attacked the subject of personal relationships head on. It portrayed the singer as being torn between life without love on the one hand and life in an unworkable relationship on the other. 'With Or Without You' was the first evidence of Bono, in his role as singer, being on the receiving end of a one-sided partnership and taking an almost masochistic delight in it. Musical history has seen rock 'n' roll strap on its traditional macho trappings and look for a convenient site for conquest in a series of testosterone-fuelled one-night stands. U2 were more interested in the spiritual conflict that preceded them and the mental conflict that followed. They wanted fever.

'With Or Without You' furthered that direction and investigated the violence of love. Love as the closest emotion to hate, power the closest to submission and sadism the closest to masochism. Bono revealed that 'it was interesting to me because I see it in myself and in other people around me. Love is a two-edged sword and I didn't want to write about romance because that doesn't interest me as much as the other side.' Love is not just wine and roses, it's claws, teeth, nails and steel, it's the divinity of union and the profanity of carnality. The concept of sexual and spiritual manipulation runs throughout 'With Or Without You', mind games run riot where the singer is required to wait forlorn on a bed of nails, finally realizing he is caught between the devil and the deep blue sea in a relationship which he needs desperately and yet which brings nothing but pain. Dahlberg wrote that 'what men desire is a virgin who is a whore' and that madonna/harlot-style duality of the woman is called into play on 'Trip Through Your Wires' and on so many of the other songs on *The Joshua Tree*, but on 'With Or Without You' it is love itself which has been perverted, maybe by modern-day pressures or maybe by the protaganists themselves.

There's an underlying tension to the song that suggests that all love ends in betrayal simply because human nature is such that people must break their promises – it started with a kiss, did Judas think it would come to this? Whatever the cause, they are locked in a relationship that is eating away at them both but which neither can do without. Live readings of the song were often ended with Bono adding the 'chorus' from Joy Division's 'Love Will Tear Us Apart', a precise summation of his own song. The suffocating, paralysing tension within the relationship was beautifully caught by what was becoming a U2 musical trademark, the dramatic, gradually building swell of sound that slowly ups the heat to bursting point before, instead of climaxing, it fades out. What a metaphor!

The corruption of love and the inequality of relationships was central to 'Spanish Eyes' too, the B-side of 'I Still Haven't Found What I'm Looking For'. Musically, the setting was perfect, a sweaty, throbbing R. & B. stomp with a pounding rhythm section and a sparkling guitar, with Bono singing like the hardest working man in show business although he could only feel good within the context of his pain. Where 'With Or Without You' had achieved a balance in its own impossibility, here she was holding all the cards with Bono spluttering furiously at the injustice inherent in '*I need you more than you need me*,' admitting to both sexual frenzy – '*forever in heat*' – and emotional desolation in her absence – '*she's gonna turn the daylight on*.' It was an interesting turnround to see the man on the receiving end, him in turmoil, he the one being kept on a lead and forced to, if you will, smell the glove. The taunt and the tease of the emotional cat-walk was stripped down from the heavy-metal associations of stockings, suspenders and motorbikes, a cartoon replaced with reality as the woman called the tune and Bono helplessly acquiesced because he could do nothing else. The physical strength of the actual emotion and the spiritual impact of the sexual act were too great an addiction, one that he could not disentangle himself from no matter what the personal cost – '*you picked me up to put me out on the street*.' It'll end in tears but, in the meantime, it's all he will allow himself to see, ignoring the certain knowledge that he'll be kicked aside someday. In the meantime '*I love the way you talk to me and I love the way you walk on me.*' 'Spanish Eyes' is a hymn to a dream of absolute fulfilment set against a backcloth of an unattainable reality and as such is a kind of precursor to 'Mysterious Ways' on *Achtung Baby.*

Bono's lyrical drift at this time was towards a bitter-sweet torch song so it couldn't have been more appropriate that Roy Orbison was to record a song that Bono and Edge wrote especially for him around that same period. 'She's A Mystery To Me' had most of the ingredients that had souped up 'Spanish Eyes'; the woman who leads the singer into dangerous, uncharted waters where he might be reborn or drowned. Yet it's that very air of danger, the knowledge that he might be torn apart, that so attracts him – *'darkness in her eyes that so enslaved me.*' The bewitching quality of this woman has so taken control of his soul that he no longer cares about his fate. Like the card player going into the gambling house, he doesn't care that the game is crooked because 'its the only game in town.' Most telling of all, after *October* and its constant repetition of the love of God making the blind see again, the love of a bad woman has the opposite effect: *'If my love is blind, I don't want to see*', again an emotion that finds its own logical conclusion on *Achtung Baby* in the savagely bleak 'Love Is Blindness'.

If the singer's continuing obsession with the woman despite his ill-treatment at her hands is one intriguing line of discussion, then so too is her treatment of him. The 'my woman done treat me bad' tenor of these songs is a little too insistent to ring completely true, so the question is how much of Bono's grief is self-inflicted. There is a guilt over the joy in the physical expression of love which threatens to overwhelm the spiritual dimension of the man, a contradiction which he seems incapable of resolving. That he seeks his pleasure in such inhospitable circumstances suggests deliberate self-flagellation in the face of original sin. The sackcloth and ashes approach seems to apply, just as it did around his spiritual awakening on *October*, but now, as atonement for the sexual fulfilment he finds, he allows himself to be mistreated, to be walked on, to be pulled apart. His only sanctuary comes with the night, the only meaningful time of the relationship being when they can communicate on a physical level, for when the morning arrives *'our heaven turns to hell.*' It's a poignant depiction of love gone wrong, of love in a void where, despite the trials and tribulations, he has to hold on because without her he is lost, a reference to the situation in 'With Or Without You'. In the admission of his weakness and of her indispensability, he hammers the last nail into his own coffin, handing all the cards over to her, allowing her carte blanche since he cannot live without her. In that way, he encourages her to treat him badly, which further enslaves him since it is to that very darkness in her that he is attracted, perpetuating a vicious circle from which he cannot escape, from which he does not want to escape and which he feels he deserves. He wants to be her dog.

The pleasures of the bedroom also form the basis for another B-side, 'Deep In The Heart', a disturbing song built around an ominous thumping bass line. Again, love is blind, but this time there's a lustful desperation for love in Bono's voice that is compelling and a little frightening, almost calling to mind the mania of 'Exit'. A steamy, sensual swamp romp of the kind that Maria McKee performed so forcefully on her eponymous debut album, it pulled in many strands of U2's current preoccupations and allowed lust free rein in their midst.

The theme of love under pressure and the fight for love in a world that sets its face against it is portrayed almost as a forlorn struggle but one which has to be fought. As in Woody Allen's *Annie Hall*, despite the anguish, the pain and the ultimate futility of so many relationships, Bono still needs the eggs. To that end, 'Sweetest Thing' is a thrilling, life-affirming, heartbreaker of a pop song. Based around a gospel-style piano and rumbling, tumbling bass riff, it remains the greatest single U2 never released, maybe their most enjoyable song ever. The decision not to release it as such was taken, according to Bono, because 'we're scared of having hits with untypical songs.' Even so, to relegate it to the role of filler on a single, thereby reducing its potential audience, was incomprehensible. Bono is the hapless victim of unrequited love, but still he doesn't care, love this time being its own reward. Bono's love is blind, he's the raincloud in her skies of blue, she makes him crawl when he wants to run, she greets him with ambivalence when he wants love, he's losing her, but still *'ain't love the sweetest thing!'*

Love as a pure emotion stacked up against lust as a marketable commodity was a source of some of the conflict in Bono's lyrics but for the most part he was happy to admit that his libido was claiming victory over the litany as the most powerful life force. Clearly it was an attempt to point out that he and the rest of the group were creatures of the flesh every bit as much as creatures of the spirit and that maintaining a balance between the two was a full-time task. The spirit may have been willing, but the flesh is always weak, Bono acknowledging to *Time Out*, 'The same person who is capable of high ideals is also very capable of base acts.' In 'Sweetest Thing', the final *Joshua Tree* track to be released, he tried to balance the equation with a song about a love that was as much a spiritual longing for the other person as a sexual one, though of course the two were inextricably linked. While that may be hard to reconcile, U2 celebrate that union of the flesh and the spirit over the course of the songs despite the fact that the relationships they cover are all in assorted states of disrepair. Gone was the unfettered optimism of 'Two Hearts Beat As One' and the love that they had promised would last forever in 'Drowning Man' no longer seemed to provide the happy ending they wanted. Even so, love was the only response to life and to their own Christian leanings, as the B-side 'Luminous Times (Hold on to Love)' was to suggest.

As with all the other love songs of the period, nothing was straightforward in 'Luminous Times' and Larry's dramatic drum pattern hinted at a sinister undercurrent to the song, but the overall thrust of the song was of love as redemption, a cleansing, purging power that was the only way ahead even in the most trying of circumstances. She was once more the source of his troubles, the overwhelming force in his life that impacted upon everything, occupied his mind and yet was again the siren on the rocks. *'She is the waves and she pulls me under'* is a line that illustrates just how caught he was between his flesh and blood existence and the higher ground of a purer kind of love, admitting that he loves her because he needs to make that emotional sacrifice, he needs to be in love to experience it as an idea as much as he has to have any physical attachment. Against some of these other songs, which could perhaps be construed as misogynistic in tone, it's an important revelation of his own inadequacies and the way in which he uses and exploits women as ruthlessly as they exploit him. It's a nasty piece of work although its saving grace is in its attitude of love being the final redemption, preventing it descending into the savagery of REM's 'The One I Love', released later in 1987.

Love as salvation it may be, but there is a negative side to the concept that cuts through 'Luminous Times' and which is most convincingly articulated on 'Exit'. 'Exit' reads like a short story and, in common with a number of pieces, has more than a trace of Lou Reed about its construction, although in this case Patti Smith gets a look in too. It's a contemporary story along the lines of Raymond Carver's work although its conclusion is unclear, Bono himself admitting that he doesn't know whether it's about a suicide or a murder. It's irrelevant to the song because the violence within it is so vividly painted, the mounting desperation of a man pushed to the end of his tether so that he has no recourse left other than the gun. In that regard, there's a corollary with 'Silver And Gold', where the prisoner has been pushed to his limits and, on a wider scale, Black South Africa has exhausted its own patience and is ready to strike back at its oppressors.

It's a very American story where a man's vision of love is corrupted until he realizes that it can be equally as destructive as it is rejuvenating. With Edge's blistering guitar treatment midway through the track, the most obvious reference point is the Beatles' apocalyptic 'Helter Skelter', the sound on 'Exit' is so twisted and evil and thoroughly abandoned, almost psychotic. A man who has to remain awake '*to drive the dreams he had away*' is obviously the victim of derangement, maybe the kind of 'religious possession' that America seems to throw up on a regular basis. Here's a man who has lost the fight for a meaningful faith in the increasingly Godless world that surrounds him, someone who has lost any kind of contact with the real world, living some twilight existence within his own imagination, to the point at which his warped perception of reality is the only one which exists. For a song from a man who wanted to believe in the redemptive powers of love, it seems to take a swipe at the religious fundamentalism of Reagan's America, where the morality that he supposedly stood for is a morality of the comfortable, of the rich, of the secure, a morality that spits on the poor and the sick, a morality that allows the mentally ill to roam free because no one is willing to take responsibility, a morality which has no time for love. It's a poke at a society whose higher echelons pretend to despise violence while all the time they carefully nurture the environment that causes that violence to multiply, an environment which inflicts wounds on people as a matter of course, which drains their humanity and forces them into unthinking acceptance of the status quo since that is the only way to deal with reality. It has been said that a nervous breakdown is the only sane way to cope with an insane situation and that kind of dementia was the root of 'Exit'. Sadly, 'Helter Skelter' associations came further to the fore when a fan was supposedly driven to commit murder by the song, an unwelcome echo of Charles Manson's response to McCartney's song.

Mindless, indiscriminate violence looms increasingly large on our city landscapes as we seem to fall victim to some end of the millennium psychosis, but the careerist killer mentality does seem to be a particularly American phenomenon. Perhaps it's just that America is so vast that by the law of averages it has to house every extreme of behaviour, both good and bad, perhaps the simple hugeness of the country dwarfs people to the point at which they lose their identity and are forced to hit back or maybe the fact that America was the first nation to taste the benefits of the consumer society means that it is just further advanced down the road of decay. Whatever the case, U2 remained rooted like rabbits in the headlights of the American juggernaut. They'd already discovered that it was the richest of nations in its cultural mix, the most wide-reaching in terms of ethnic background, the most open, innocent and childlike in its response and yet almost the most conniving, dangerous, and ruthless country on earth. The Edge described 'Exit' as 'the American nightmare' and that was a vein which ran through 'In God's Country'.

Kicked along by a country-tinged folk guitar, The Edge obviously having enjoyed rooting through Bono's newly acquired blues collection, America was personified as the Statue of Liberty, effectively the upholder of the American constitution and the welcoming figure for legions of immigrants. Through the ravages of the late twentieth century her dress was in shreds, the values she stood for similarly distressed. Like the woman in the other songs on and around the album, Liberty was both angel and devil – '*like a siren she calls to me*' – just as America remains the Promised Land for so many across the globe and yet it's the poisoned chalice too. America as the country of Martin Luther King and of Ronald Reagan is an unfathomable conundrum and U2's postcard home could do little but point out the inconsistencies and the dangers of God's country.

'In God's Country' was a song so rich in language and musical images that it could barely contain all its ingredients, but the finished brew was splendidly full in taste, *The Grapes of Wrath* on acoustic guitar. In its very title it pointed an accusatory finger at the fundamentalist moral majority on a self-appointed, self-opinionated crusade against an evil empire because God told them to do so. When the man with his finger on the button rather than on the pulse thinks that the sin of the flesh is a greater enemy of mankind than a nuclear warhead and that God's message via America is to uphold a strict code of morality, one could only hope that the newsstands of Moscow were never to be flooded with issues of *Playcomrade*.

So much of the warped side of America emanated from the

rejection of original sin and the resultant 'past' of American history. Reagan and those of like mind simply dismissed the idea, choosing to view his country as a clean slate upon which their own dreams could be etched, employing what William James termed a religion of 'healthy-mindedness' where sadness is the real enemy of human nature, not sin. Such a view requires an almost unsustainable, certainly an unrealistic, sense of blind optimism. It suggests that no man's actions impinge on the life of another (tell that to someone who has just been mugged) and that we can all act in a perfectly independent manner without fearing that any unfortunate conse-quences will be visited upon innocent parties. This is of course the view that Reagan propounded on the principle of trade union activity as against philanthropic measures and one which dovetails beauti-fully with his reconstructionist attitude to his own life – for Reagan, everything *is* a clean slate. Ironically, the difference between 'healthy-mindedness' and the doctrine of the Fall is an interesting reflection of U2's own spiritual journey. On *October* there was a blinkered optimism about their faith that everything would eventually turn out fine if you only believed. By *The Joshua Tree* things had changed and they were well aware of the sin within everyone and the struggle between the two conflicting forces. The joy remained at the heart of their music but the songs were sadder in tone, reflecting a greater breadth of experience.

Reagan's rampant optimism that somehow, an invisible hand will come along and guide everyone's independent actions for the greater good of the community is, of course, at best misplaced or at worst an evil manipulation based on a knowledge that certain groups will benefit at the expense of others. It is also the basis of the market or capitalist system, the basis of American economics and the basis of a 'haves' and 'have-nots' American society. It was only fitting therefore that the TV evangelists should prove to be the greatest of all capitalists, Bono castigating them for 'stealing money from the old and the sick' from the concert stage throughout 'The Joshua Tree' tour. The controversy that surrounded the funds generated by these TV evangelists and their eventual use has long ceased to be news, but still it goes on, still they promise a place in the sun if you give God the money he needs. *'The greatest gift is gold'* ran the song and it was upon that principle of greed that modern American economic policy in the hands of the Reagan administration was based. Small wonder that the Statue of Liberty might be considered the siren on the rocks, for the American dream was one which lured so many to self-destruction in their search for economic security in a dog-eat-dog nation.

Perhaps the most worrying aspect was the way in which parts of America had gone to sleep in the 1980s, Edge noting that 'you go over and ask people how on earth he got selected but no one admits to voting for him.' Reagan's persistent optimism in the face of all the facts, his refusal to listen to any criticism of his policies, since that meant holding a pessimistic view which in turn meant talking America down, did actually cut through to many, many Americans who were suffering at the hands of his policies and who decided to vote for him again because he seemed genuine in his beliefs. The gravest danger was that many could see the difficulties they were facing but chose to ignore them because they really did think Reagan represented the cavalry and that at the last moment he would lead some kind of charge over the hill to save the day. Even in the face of Irangate, the belief in Reagan never wavered, Bono suggesting that 'they're a very open people . . . that leads them to trust a man as dangerous as Ronald Reagan. They want to believe he's a good guy.' Garry Wills studied this further in *Reagan's America*, concluding that 'the power of his appeal is the great joint confession that we cannot live with our past, that we not only prefer but need a substitute . . . even young people have accepted his version of the past as their own best pledge of the future. Visiting Reaganland is very much like taking children to Disneyland where they can deal with New Orleans cut to their measure. It is a safe past with no sharp edges to stumble against.'

America did fall asleep in the comfort radiated by Reagan and, as so often, it required outsiders to see the extent of its decline and comment upon it. The Amnesty tour played a vital role in that and the music of the following years was also instrumental in revitalizing the youth of the nation to look again at the sickness from which their country was suffering, an illness that grew from the policies of their government. U2, as the biggest band in the world in the late 1980s, had their part to play and did so effectively with powerful critiques of the nation in songs such as 'In God's Country'. Careful, however, not simply to paint a nation as huge and diverse as America as an 'evil empire', they also showed America as liberty, the defender of freedom, a nation of hope and potential.

A land of dreams that destroys its dreamers is a daunting concept, especially when that nation is the most powerful on earth, but they do die in the search for the other side. Martin Luther King told a meeting in Memphis on 3 April 1968, 'I just want to do God's will. And he's allowed me to go up to the mountain. And I've looked over and I've seen the promised land . . . so I'm happy tonight. I'm not worried about anything. I'm not fearing any man.' Once he'd seen the other side, King was an even more dangerous man to the powers that be. Within twenty-four hours he was dead. Silver and gold was a perennial theme of *The Joshua Tree*. Worldwide oppression was rooted in economic power and the refusal to allow it to pass to those who deserved it and earned it. In America, Lincoln had been assassinated after abolishing slavery, Bobby Kennedy had been murdered because of his aim to defy organized crime and because he stood between Nixon and the White House. Once Nixon was installed, business would return to normal among the companies who take advantage of their workforces and their customers. Working conditions and safety standards could slide, the rich could pay lower taxes while those lower on the economic scale suffered. At the end of his life when talking about 'my people', Martin Luther King was not talking exclusively about Black America, he was talking about the economically disadvantaged, he was preaching socialism, social and economic justice for the working classes of America, the homeless, the unemployed and those in poverty. In a society in constant retreat from real Christian values to one based on stock market values, those who missed out on the materialistic boom were left with nothing. How could they find faith in a world where a spiritual God had been replaced by the monetary god and the all-encompassing language of the greenback?

Such a plight inevitably led to a disenchantment with political solutions, causing people to respond with the gun, gang violence, drug abuse – U2 picked up on that ideological vacuum on 'In God's Country', Bono calling for *'new dreams tonight.'* The old political answers of left and right were no longer enough to answer the complex chain of questions that was besetting the world at the end of the twentieth century. Capitalism had grown from the eighteenth century, socialism the nineteenth, both to deal with an industrialized economy, not the computerized, machine-intensive systems which we now operate within. U2 were perfectly right to draw attention to the impact of failed systems of government, were intelligent enough, indeed valuable enough, to draw the general problems into the realms of the personal, the specific relationship so that they could touch people's hearts far more deeply than could unemployment statistics or talk of the merits of a planned or market economy ever could, yet this also began to push them into a corner in the same way that *War* had done.

The problem became one of timing. The period of 1986–87 was an absolute wasteland politically, with Reagan marching on in America despite the early rumblings of the Irangate saga, Thatcher winning another term of office in the UK on the back of an alleged boom in the economy which the majority of the country north of Watford missed out on. There was fighting throughout Central America, talks between Reagan and Gorbachev on arms reduction had broken down, there seemed to be no political initiatives to help the victims of African famine and the world's political parties appeared to be thoroughly bereft of any convincing ideology to help carry the world into the challenges of the next century, so busy were they fighting the dogmatic battles of capitalism against socialism that had become irrelevant thirty years earlier. As the world looked for hope, the only signs of optimism came in the form of rock 'n' roll – Band Aid, Live Aid, 'A Conspiracy of Hope', Artists Against Apartheid had all been expressions of disgust with the way in which the world was run, a rejection of old values and a general looking ahead to a time of new ideas and greater justice. There was undoubtedly a degree of nostalgia for the golden days of the 1960s when Dylan, Lennon, Townshend, Hendrix, Baez, CSNY and the Band had, so the legend went, single-handedly stopped the war in Vietnam, and a hope that the new crop of 'socially aware' artists might be able to work similar miracles. U2 were in the vanguard of that movement, as Bono's occasional pronouncements from the stage proved, and with the death of political leaders of any standing they were being promoted as the leaders of a generation behind whom people could stand. Yet they were far from equipped to take on the mantle, even had they chosen to do so, since, politically, they were deeply confused, or at least innocent.

Bill Graham raised the point of political belief during a *Hot Press* interview that coincided with the release of *The Joshua Tree*, having already discussed it at some length, most perceptively, in his album review. 'Could and should their politics be more explicit? U2 presently content themselves with a liberal moralism that's alert both to how planet pop limits local language and the fact that their potential American constituency cannot, by any stretch of the imagination, be equated with *NME* readers ... as a lyric writer, Bono may still be erring on the safe side of coded ambiguity.' Bono's reaction was to attack the concept of liberalism while refusing to put anything in its place: 'I'm more interested in the man as opposed to men . . . I think in a funny way the country gets the party it deserves, that it has choices. I think men choose the system they live under in our age . . . I don't know what the alternative is in Ireland. Ireland seems so politically absurd, that the main parties all have the same policies and the Labour Party which is my own background . . . if we go by the elections, the Labour Party doesn't mean anything at this point.' (In the light of the Labour Party's renaissance in the 1992 election under the leadership of Dick Spring, Bono's views on the role of the Labour Party may well be rather different now.) There was also an understandable reluctance not to let themselves slip into the traps that the Clash or Billy Bragg had fallen into, whereby they had become so widely regarded as being heavily politicized it was difficult for their music to be seen in any other light.

Asked to replace the system with something better, Bono was left to offer: 'I'm more interested in what you might call a revolution of love. I believe that if you want to start a revolution you better start a revolution in your own home and your own way of thinking . . . for me, the future lies in small-scale activity. For instance, commitment to a community like U2 are committed to Dublin.' Laudable ideas, but commitment to communities is ultimately controlled by government in terms of financing unless you happen to be wealthy philanthropists like U2. The arguments that had raged about their naïvety in their involvement with Self Aid still persisted, in that they said nothing that advanced the cause of any opposition to the status quo but, more dangerously, they made political apathy a reasonable stance. Bono later admitted, 'It's a dangerous idea when you slag off all politicians. Then people stop voting and start feeling impotent in the political process.' One of fate's great ironies is that when U2 were supposedly the political band that was going to save the world in the late 1980s they had not worked out any credible position, yet by the time they were perceived as rock 'n' roll jokers in 1992 they were politically sharp and more active in a constitutional sense via the 'Rock the Vote' campaign in America.

If anything, U2 did seem to have realized that denigrating political activity was unwise, as the words of Dr Noel Brown indicate. John Waters, in his series *Wide Awake In Ireland*, interviewed Dr Brown, the politician who is credited with the eradication of tuberculosis from Ireland in the 1950s, something Waters regards as the greatest achievement of seventy years of Irish independent government. Brown's view of the changing social fabric of the cities is thought-provoking, frightening and rather sad: 'We are in transition from a very rigid doctrinaire, authoritarian, deeply conservative sectarian society to one which alas has no particular vision. I remember working as a psychiatrist in the high-rise flats in Ballymun and I used to work with the young curates there who were idealistic young men. We had a conversation about twenty years ago – they said to me that the old extended family had broken up, they'd been put into the high-rise, they'd lost the grannies and so on, all their connections, and so you had young marrieds whose marriages were going on the rocks because of unemployment or incompatibility or whatever. The general feeling of the curates was that they hadn't the same control as their predecessors so the one said, "We've lost them." Then turning to me, the politician, he said, "But you haven't won them either." There was some structure to society then, I don't think we're moving into one now – the level of politics is so shoddy, shabby, unstructured, I don't see where they're going, any of the parties. I've come to the conclusion it's almost a one party state, there seems little difference. That's a highly dangerous situation.'

These were worries that were being echoed across the world as people were reaching a point where they could not have faith in anything, least of all themselves, and so these were not problems unique to America, but they were painted on an undeniably broader canvas and a grander scale over there. In U2's home country, economic difficulties had created their own social problems, giving Dublin a drug problem that was far worse than that, for instance, in London. 'Running To Stand Still' was set in the Ballymun Dr Brown spoke of and was a song about a relationship collapsing under the strains of economic desperation and, ultimately, drug abuse. That drug abuse was the symptom of a deeper malaise, a gnawing emptiness that ate away at so many city dwellers. Adam perceptively pointed out, 'In its simplest form I've always seen heroin as a very evil thing . . . so I can assume that anyone who takes it has a similar fear. To actually have their back so much against the wall, to be controlled by it, is something I can't understand. I haven't been that close to the edge . . . to imagine the next stage is pretty much impossible.'

A song of desperation born out of economic inadequacy and social deprivation, it cut to the soul with its graceful instrumentation despite an awkward, clumsy lyrical opening that evoked a stumbling drug-induced haze which was stretching a relationship to breaking point. The lyrical poignancy of the song speaks volumes for the desperate nature of the situation and the need to see through heroin eyes, if only for a few fleeting moments to get away from the real world. Bono approaches the lyric from a sympathetic, understanding attitude to drug use, a message underlined by the delicate, almost folk-based treatment it receives musically, creating a supportive mood with the characters in the song. It was an attitude that featured heavily on 'Red Hill Mining Town', perhaps the hardest-hitting piece on the record and another song about life under the stress of economic difficulties.

More than that, though, it drew attention to the spiritual as well as the financial beating that unemployment inflicted upon people. In a world constructed upon the work ethic, an idea sold to generation after generation, an idea that says you must work for a living, you must fill your time with gainful employment, you must above all have a job or you're nothing, mass unemployment suffered on the worldwide scale is a psychological as much as an economic problem. Modern industrialized civilization is built upon the idea of having a job to the extent that people are what they do for a living. When that living is taken away, what do you become? Employment has effectively supplanted religion as the central life force and so where do we go when there are no jobs left and unemployment is low on the government's priority list?

In Britain, a last ditch attempt to preserve employment was the miners' strike of 1984–85, an industrial dispute which lasted twelve long, bitter months.

The dispute began after the appointment of Ian McGregor, formerly head of the British Steel Corporation at the time when it shed thousands of jobs, as Chairman of the National Coal Board and the subsequent closure of the Cortonwood colliery in Yorkshire, announced in March 1984 and timed so that any action would have to run through the summer when demand for coal would be at its lowest. (Cortonwood had been assured of a future of at least five to six years in March 1983.) The NUM had already resolved at delegate conferences to take strike action if a major closure programme was imposed and Cortonwood was seen as a step on the road towards that, despite government statements to the contrary. The level of trust that could be placed in their word was to be seen in the number of collieries that were closed after the return to work took place and in the continued decimation of the industry which continues even now. The strike itself was nasty, acrimonious, savage and, at times, violent. The Police were forced to take aggressive action against lawful, and sometimes unlawful, pickets in an increasingly vitriolic spiral designed to paint the unions in the worst possible light with the rest of Britain. Trades unionists may not disappear in this country but many found themselves in court on charges that had no foundation. The government continued to feed the anti-NUM fire, with the then Chancellor Nigel Lawson announcing in July 1984 that more than £300 million had been spent on the strike but that 'even in narrow financial terms it represents a worthwhile investment for the nation.'

The miners were gradually starved back to work since those on strike received virtually no money during the dispute, compelling miners to scab against their own kind and even provoking the creation of a breakaway union, the Union of Democratic Mineworkers, whose strength was founded largely in the then unthreatened pits of Nottinghamshire. What had begun as a show of solidarity and of strength ultimately broke families apart under the economic and mental strain the strike imposed on them. Brothers would no longer talk to one another because one of them had gone back to work to get money for his children, husbands and wives couldn't sleep together any more because they were so at odds with each other, men lost their dignity and self-respect as they lost their jobs, women lost their husbands' spirit, left only with a broken shell.

Tony Parker, a journalist, visited one of the communities six months after the strike had ended to find that wounds had not even begun to heal. The town, which he called Red Hill, was based around a pit that was scheduled to be closed, though no mention of that had been made at the time of the strike, the first hints coming at the very end after Red Hill had proved to be completely behind the union. Parker had been a conscientious objector in World War II and had served down the mines for the duration of the war. He understood the mining community and his interviews revealed a strike very different to that portrayed by the media. The fierce pride in their community came through time and time again, a human face to the political warmongering. There were men in their mid thirties who told him, 'If they close the pit they're closing down my life,' there were tales of false imprisonment, tales of lives ripped apart without the people concerned having a chance to fight back. The book closed with a comment from a young school-leaver that said it all: 'The people in the government ought to come up here and talk to people and see what they've done to their lives.'

At the end of the day, it's the impact on real people and their real lives that acts as the catalyst for any kind of meaningful change. The best attack on the insular, self-satisfied values of those only concerned with lining their own pockets was to show how savagely their greed affected the lives of ordinary people. 'Red Hill Mining Town' was a song that concurred with that maxim and which was graphic in its account of a man losing his self belief, clinging on to his wife for some sort of support as their *'love runs cold'*, destroyed by external pressures. 'Red Hill Mining Town' addressed itself not only to their turmoil but to the destruction of working class values, the loss of trades, skills that had been passed down from father to son. Whole communities, entire villages were and still are based purely on coal mining, almost every job in an area depends directly or indirectly on the success of the pit. To close the mines means closing a community and a closed community is the first step towards the social problems that 'Running To Stand Still' spoke about, the problems of unemployment having been a way of life in Dublin for far longer than they had in Britain – 'Red Hill Mining Town' could have been subtitled 'Mothers of the Dispossessed'. Although some might have wanted U2 to discuss the political impact of the strike, they served the unemployed better by tackling the human side and shaming those with work into thinking about those less fortunate, saying, 'Is this the kind of society we want?', leading listeners to think about the wider issues the lyric implied. The connection was made more powerful when U2 regularly played a very straight-forward live version of Peggy Seeger's song 'Springhill Mining Disaster', a tale of the same kind from an earlier age when the price of coal was *'bone and blood'*. Music might lead to political change only through an emotional revolution.

Bono had thrown himself into blues writing and the detailing of relationships under threat, but the other thrust of his writing at the time was economic injustice and the principle of the love of money being the root of all evil. 'Silver And Gold', the song written for the 'Sun City' project and later released as a B-side to 'Where The Streets Have No Name', tackled apartheid within those reference points, indicating that the racist aspect of South Africa's struggle hides an even more deeply rooted problem, that of financial elitism. For White South Africa, to dismantle apartheid means to provide Blacks with opportunities, education, jobs and the right to make money at the White man's expense. At its heart, that is one very strong reason for apartheid. The Whites have money and a very comfortable lifestyle and have absolutely no intention of sharing it with anyone else. That interpretation also puts South Africa into a wider world context – the treatment of the miners in Britain during the strike was a subtle kind of apartheid in that their basic rights were denied them. The reason? Money. Historically, what was the reason for the slave trade? Money. Why did South Africa get away with their evil form of government for so long? Because the West has generally refused to apply stringent economic sanctions. Why? Money.

U2 might have reinterpreted the form, but they were still playing what was recognizably the blues, spiritual songs to exorcize emotion. To take the blues back to the USA was the next challenge to maintain the cultural flow of ideas that had gone on for hundreds of years. Although U2 were the biggest band in the world, they felt themselves to be a group with a faulty education. The time they were about to spend over there provided the chance to fill in some of the gaps and learn some more about their craft, like an Open University course you got paid to do. Then someone decided to film the whole thing . . .

chapter ten

ROCK 'N' ROLL STOP THE TRAFFIC

From the band's point of view, *Rattle and Hum* was probably an artistic success and a commercial disaster, an odd state of affairs for one of the fastest-selling albums ever released and one which was reviled by critics who had had their fill of the U2 overload. However, there can be little doubt that *Rattle and Hum* was, in part, an attempt to shed some of the 'Kevin and Sharon' audience that did not appeal to them and to bring themselves the artistic freedom they had had before every move they made was subject to universal scrutiny. How better to dump the U2 sound that had characterized *The Joshua Tree* than to take on the air of a rock 'n' roll revival show, releasing new songs that were totally out on a limb in terms of the current musical scene along with some highly suspect cover versions. By now, however, U2 were the proud, if not delighted, wearers of the emperor's new clothes – if it had *that* logo on it, buy it anyway.

That was a public attitude that broadly summed up the whole *Joshua Tree* experience, particularly on the road in America. Wherever U2 went everyone wanted a piece, from local to national TV, newspapers, magazines (U2 took the cover of *Time* magazine), radio stations, manic fans and curious observers. U2 were the hottest ticket across the States throughout 1987, which forced them into a hectic schedule of arenas and stadiums, criss-crossing the country in the spring and then again into the autumn and winter. While they were required to maintain a similarly frenetic pace during their European tour in the summer, they had wisely invested in a plane which was at their personal disposal, enabling them to return home whenever the itinerary permitted, giving them some sense of a real world outside the eye of the storm, a luxury impossible in America as word of the band spread across the country like a bush fire. In America they were there to be prodded and poked as much as appreciated as a very good, possibly great, rock 'n' roll band. It was perhaps only in America that a band such as U2 could have stood out so clearly from the others around them, only in America that they could be deified. It's also an indication of a country that is relatively so young, one that has so little history of its own when compared with Europe, that the great figures of America come so often from popular culture.

Interview followed interview, Bono in particular seeming to spend all his time talking to the press, which might not have been so taxing had it not been for the fact that the lines of questioning seemed exclusively to feature Amnesty International, Martin Luther King, Solidarity, American foreign policy, religion and Northern Ireland. The music didn't seem to get a look in, particularly the 'personal' songs that had been included on *The Joshua Tree*, since everyone wanted to talk about U2 the phenomenon, not U2 the rock 'n' roll band. By the time the tour was reaching its close, U2 were suffering from an advanced state of cabin fever, tour madness run wild, leaving them with some kind of identity crisis.

The question has to be why were U2 in such a state of relative disenchantment? After all, in America, *The Joshua Tree* reached number one, and two singles, 'With Or Without You' and 'I Still Haven't Found What I'm Looking For', also scaled the summit of the charts and they were enjoying playing live to such huge crowds across the country. The external pressures undoubtedly began to take their toll. Adam confessed, 'I was in a very bad way. I couldn't believe it, I'd actually got to the point where I couldn't talk any more, people wanting things all the time and all you got back was TV.' It was, however, a situation that U2 and their organization had brought largely upon themselves in their overt courting of popular success. Based on the original desire to communicate and to create a sense of shared community with a large, committed audience, U2 had made themselves available for interviews with all the media on a ridiculous scale, seemingly willing to talk all day, every day, partly to sell more records and win a greater audience, partly to sell the intelligence that was at work behind the music, but also to explore other issues that they felt deserved an airing. For all the later protestations that U2 were formed in line with the classic rock premiss, i.e. get rich and get laid, U2 always had far more on their agenda than that and were keen to use their position to promote ideas as much as themselves.

U2, by 1987, were as successful as any band has a right to be but, while they enjoyed some of the fruits of that prosperity, the struggle to deal with success became more important than their music for a time, calling to mind The Edge's warning at the time of *The Unforgettable Fire* that money was the greatest danger to the band. On 'The Joshua Tree' tour, U2 were so constantly on the defensive about their wealth and their position as musicians with a global audience, they became more uptight than a duck's ass, which is, as everyone knows, watertight. They were being strangled by their position, by the Catholic guilt associated with their ascendancy at a time when their contemporaries were on the dole, and by their own inability to come to terms with what they had achieved materially. Perhaps the hardest problem to deal with came with the necessary handing over of sections of their career and their future to others, however trusted those people might be. For a band that had tried to make every decision about itself down to the most inconsequential level, indeed to a point at which they could be accused of preciousness, this loss of power was particularly difficult to handle but it was logistically inevitable, the five-piece Feedback that used to cadge lifts from Edge's mother having mutated into a rock band that required well over a hundred staff just to get it on the road. It was not an easy transition and indeed they still kept a very tight hand on the rudder, understandably so, yet in so doing they made matters even more fraught. Prior to the tour in 1987, things had reached the point where Larry, for instance, was spending his free time working on the merchandizing arrangements, ensuring that the quality of the T-shirts was maintained. While it was this kind of attention to detail that had won them such a devoted following, Bono was already speaking about the attractions of irresponsibility, simply to give themselves a little more freedom in what he termed 'a tidal wave of a year'.

In true, 'caring, sharing' U2 style, as the tabloids might have had it, they did not fully let go the reins of their responsibilities and so allowed themselves to be pulled in every direction by all kinds of conflicting demands, both in terms of business and publicity. That U2 more than fulfilled their obligations in pushing sales of *The Joshua Tree* could not be denied, but they had to try to do more than that and spent extended periods taking the weight of the world on their shoulders. Again, that was their choice, Bono finally admitting in 1993 that they were 'trying to keep so many balls in the air and it took so much energy . . . trying to do the right thing: Oh we've been put in this position, we better not fuck up, we better use our position for some good.' It was an exhausting pace that they therefore set themselves and not one they were always able to maintain, their final refuge being that there was always someone else in the group whom an individual could pass on his share of the work to for a couple of days if he was going under. The film *Rattle and Hum* might have had many flaws but among its good points was the way in which it illustrated the close bond between the group members, proof that The Edge, Adam, Bono and Larry were a real band and, perhaps more important, real friends who could rely on one another to get themselves through the trouble spots of a hectic tour.

The fact that they were in America did little to lessen the mood of manic intensity that surrounded them. Bono was loath to sleep during the course of their tour in case he might miss some action in the breakneck pace at which life was lived in centres such as Los Angeles and New York, while in the South the band were keen to soak up the atmosphere and the stories of what they considered to be the heart of the nation, as well as taking on the musical influences of places like Memphis or the environs of the Mississippi. The action that surrounded the U2 bubble fascinated the band, who were drawn to the interesting spectacle of a great nation in a state of decay where seedy clubs, hard-core pornography, poverty, guns and drugs dominated whole sections of cities that, in the daytime, buzzed to the sound of commerce and industry. Yet in those clubs, in those potential no-go areas lay America's most intriguing stories, lives lived on the fringes of the material society, stories of people getting by, struggling to pay the rent but having more soul, if you like, than those who by day inhabited the skyscrapers and made their multi-million-dollar deals. For a writer like Bono, this subtle blend of the carnal and the ethereal in the face of adversity was a source of hope, in that so many of these people were able to remain unbroken in spirit, but also of anger that they should be denied their piece of the American Dream.

These people were the detritus of what William Burroughs termed 'America After the Bomb', a nation which he saw as having sold its soul for global power, sacrificing its innocence as the price. Insofar as that related to America's establishment, that was a reasonable summation of a nation which, if the then Secretary of Defense is to be believed, bombed Hiroshima and Nagasaki not to hasten the end of the war but in order to establish a position of strength against the Soviet Union before the war ended, establishing its supremacy in terms of its nuclear arsenal. In the towers of steel where life and death decisions were made on the strength of the dollar, innocence had dissipated long ago, the movers and the shakers of the Western world being perfectly well aware just what they were doing to the people, the environment and the future. Beyond those people, however, were people who had become an underclass, whether it be the middle class with unattainable aspirations who had been sold the dream of riches and were willing to believe in it, the working classes who lived in fear of their jobs and their future, and finally the poverty-stricken for whom day-to-day survival was the only question that meant anything. These were people in America who, by night, would often mingle with one another on the neon-lit strips of the inner cities, looking for different cheap, instant thrills to help them cope with life. Burroughs' work looked at these themes, described by his biographer Ted Morgan as 'the individual's powerlessness against state control, the feeling of being manipulated by unknown forces, with tormented characters fearing unidentified dangers, the need to connect sex and violence, the sense of doom relieved by gallows humour.'

While evidence of this set of mind was readily available, particularly in the increased use of violence, both domestic and otherwise, as a substitute for real power over an individual's own life by forcing the will of those weaker than one's self, it's also true to say that many people retained their spirit, that they refused to be cut down by the powers that be. Some may have chosen to do so by simply rejecting life as it was portrayed in the adverts and opting out via drink or drugs, some by simply ignoring the outside pressures and living their own lives, some by fighting back politically or socially. What was clear was that there was a very strong subculture made up of people who were not of the Establishment and were resolutely ploughing their own furrow. More than ever, America was a country split down the middle, particularly in the wake of the Irangate scandal. In so many ways the one nation of the West where dreams could become reality, a land that was in so many areas unspoiled by progress, America was also a land in decay and one whose recent unenviable moral record was seeping further and further into everyday behaviour. The battle between the two parts of America was more intense than it had ever been while U2 were on tour there in 1987 and that frantic pace and the depressingly low level of intellectual argument for change clearly had an effect on their music and on their state of mind.

Although these external forces were, at least in part, responsible for some of their disillusionment, the greatest difficulty was artistic, since they were a band in the midst of musical transition. There was a very real concern that, although they might well be the biggest band in the world, they didn't feel themselves to be the best. As is so often the case, a period of turmoil gave rise to an eruption of artistic energy and the four members of the band spent much of their precious free time ensconced in hotel rooms or during soundchecks working out new songs. They regularly spoke of this being the first time that all four members of the group had been on fire together at the same time since the very earliest days of the band and it was true to say that the roots music that they were soaking up across America was making a formidable impression upon them, driving them to write and write. However, as the finished results on *Rattle and Hum* tend to indicate, this was something of a false dawn as their enthusiasm clouded some of their critical faculties.

Nevertheless, the music of the blues, gospel and even jazz became a lifeline to a band that could so easily have found itself jaded by the mania that went on beyond their control. Even the material they were playing was beginning to have a detrimental effect on them at times, Bono admitting that 'members can get a bit out of control on a tour and forget where they've come from and who they've left behind ... you can start to live out the music a little too much sometimes, where the demons you're exorcizing in the songs sort of follow you home. And they follow you home to what is the padded cell of a hotel room.' On several occasions in the new songs that were to form a part of *Rattle and Hum*, Bono sang of finding some kind of salvation in the blues, that the blues were a life-saver for him and the others. Having had the less enjoyable side of the music industry brought forcefully home to them over the course of *The Joshua Tree* period, they were able to gain a necessary injection of enthusiasm in discovering this new kind of music. The Edge noted that they'd fallen in love with music again and it was clear that they found a greater pleasure in exploring this heritage than they did in playing 'I Will Follow' for the umpteenth time. Bono even had to confess that he no longer had any idea how to approach a song like 'New Year's Day' and that U2, in that sense, were in a state of distress from which they had been rescued by the likes of Billie Holiday, Elvis Presley and B. B. King. This new burst of writing was an essential kind of therapy, as Bono pointed out to Bill Graham when discussing the then embryonic *Rattle and Hum* album: 'If we can't play the old songs then write new songs. It's our only way of surviving and getting through the tour. I don't care if people don't like it . . . you may not like it, U2 fans may not like it – but we need it.'

The Joshua Tree, while a commercial awakening for U2 in America particularly, a record which placed them firmly in the upper echelons of rock 'n' roll history, was also the end of another phase of their development, in much the same way as *War* had been. The political overtones that some of their music carried had been seized upon by a hungry press corps anxious for a new angle on rock 'n' roll that was provided by these 'God-fearing boys with a social conscience' and it was this that was becoming the most famous thing about U2's music. As The Edge was to put it succinctly in a *Hot Press* feature: 'It's much more emotional than political . . . we're not social workers. We're a fucking rock 'n' roll band!' The time was right to ditch those wearisome political connotations, the weight of having to save the planet, and to allow the music and the lyrics to follow a direction in which they were most interested, bringing things down to the level of two people rather than a global consciousness. On 'So Cruel', from *Achtung Baby*, one line from Bono has him torn *'between the horses of love and lust'*. That was the emotional terrain that so much of *The Joshua Tree* had been written on, its B-sides in particular, and was an area that Bono was especially drawn towards, one far more emotional and thus one which made far better raw material for songwriting.

To do so, they were required to debunk the whole U2 myth, something which they might have felt capable of doing with their mutation into a very loud folk group – they even kicked against the rigours of touring by playing support to themselves as country and western stalwarts the Dalton Brothers. To write new songs in that style and in the style of the blues music that was currently inspiring them would be to kick the accepted, successful U2 style into touch and to be able to progress unhindered by the demands of such an enormous audience and the attendant fame. Like David Bowie five years earlier in the aftermath of *Let's Dance*, artists who had had a huge underground following were now mainstream fodder. They didn't like it and they were unsure how to cope. They were also beset by the idea that being such a big band automatically meant that they were worthless, that they had become hollow and they were keen to shed that particular burden, too.

If that was their intention, as subsequent pronouncements indicate, with hindsight the decisions that were made in a period of weeks and which finally led to the *Rattle and Hum* mediafest look ludicrous. The pace of life within the U2 circus and their detachment from the real world outside must have contributed to a complete lack of objective judgement in recognizing just how these releases would be viewed. To release a double album was one of those challenges that every group eventually has to face down but it's a step that always invites criticism of self-indulgence. That was a problem that U2 could have neatly sidestepped without too much difficulty or loss of credibility – and credibility remained very important to them – but when you add to that a feature film with all the attendant promotional hype which makes a record launch look as extravagant as the advertising budget for a local jumble sale, and then a book, you're asking for trouble. In part, this may have been a deliberate strategy to destroy the shield of invincibility that the band now seemed to wear but it was more likely a complete loss of perspective that saw them agree to the whole jamboree. Admittedly it was an important time to capture on film, firstly to replace the artistically redundant *Under A Blood Red Sky* video and also because, whatever else might have been going on around them, as a band they were firing on all cylinders, making it worthwhile to capture that burst of creativity, hopefully putting a greater accent on to the music that was sustaining them through the pressures of the tour. To that end, they decided to try to take the emphasis away from U2 and share the spotlight with some of the elder statesman from whom they were learning. What had been intended as a humble gesture, according to Bono, was understandably perceived as a huge effort at self-aggrandizement, a statement which boldly proclaimed that U2 were now up there with the gods of rock 'n' roll history.

It's virtually impossible to address one of the releases under the *Rattle and Hum* banner in isolation, since the film and the record became virtually interchangeable, and yet they were radically different animals which, looked at separately, had much to commend them. Taking them together it was all too much and U2 suffered the inevitable critical backlash and, while *Rattle and Hum* sold in vast quantities (more than 5 million double albums within a year), it was noticeable that there was less public fervour surrounding the release of *Achtung Baby*, suggesting that those who had flocked to hear *The Joshua Tree* and then bought *Rattle and Hum* on trust were not all delighted with their purchase.

For a musical form that came into existence to rip up all the rule books, to be irreverent, sexy, irresponsible and wildly individual, by the late 1980s rock 'n' roll had certainly taken on a lot of conventions that its acts were required to play up to. A period of sex and drugs, a period of atonement, a megatour followed by a megasilence and then a mega-album, the big live double album cash-in that was as exciting as listening to paint dry, unless you happened to be the band's accountant. The challenge for a big band like U2 was to tear down those rules and respond with individuality intact, another extension of their desire to use their position to mess around with the conventions of the day and so do the right thing. *Rattle and Hum* was their attempt to beat the system and an effort to play down their own importance. Instead of the superslick studio-enhanced shine of typical live records by big rock bands, *Rattle and Hum* was a ragged collection of hurriedly scribbled picture postcards from America which looked at that country and at the band. To discard some of the excess baggage that had been foisted upon them was vital in order to reach perhaps the most essential truth about U2 and their work. U2 are not important because they sell millions of records, although it is important that they have achieved such success. U2 are a popular music phenomenon not simply because they make phenomenally popular music.

U2 remain the most important, with the exception of REM perhaps the only consistently essential rock 'n' roll band of the past decade, because the music in all its glory, with all its mistakes, with all its yearning, with all its overambition, with all its passion, with all its underachievement, uncertainties, its successes and failures, reminds us all of our own human frailty. It is music made by ordinary men in an extraordinary situation who have rarely forgotten their roots, not by superstars or machines. The music is the only message that U2 have to deliver and, by late 1987, no one was paying much attention to that. The time had come to make a noisy, aggressive, rock 'n' roll record that could shake, rattle and hum the wider audience into listening or walking out. The obvious answer was to release a deliberate anti-statement, a record purely about music. Releasing a book, record and film simultaneously did make a statement though – it said, 'We're U2, we're important, give us the money.' The substance got drowned in the hype and even less attention was paid to the music this time around.

To a degree, U2 were lucky that this was the case, for while the music stood up reasonably well as songs it was far less ground-breaking than the material that people had come to expect from them. While you couldn't fault U2's idea of reinventing a tired old concept, the live double album, while they were trying to give greater value for money from a soundtrack to the film they expected you to see too and while in the age of the big production number it was nice to see the very biggest band reviving the rough-and-ready punk ethic of 1976 – even if it was in part an attempt to boost their own credibility with the new breed of iconoclasts who had succeeded them – there were two fatal flaws. Firstly the off-the-cuff nature of the project was undermined by a massive publicity campaign and the attendant tie-in with the movie, advertising that served to heighten an already feverish degree of public expectation. More seriously, the quality control department hadn't been consulted and so, as a piece, *Rattle and Hum* the album was shambolic, ranging from the sublime to the faintly ridiculous. Its greatest drawback was that it was made by a group that sounded a bit like U2 but which didn't have the same level of invention as previously shown. That U2 had already entered the pantheon devoted to the rock 'n' roll greats was not in dispute, but they had entered it on their own terms by sculpting a sound, a mood and a direction that was very clearly all their own – they owed some debts to various inspirations, but basically, U2 records were unique until someone copied them later. On *Rattle and Hum*, U2 didn't sound like U2, which might not have been a bad thing had it heralded a step forward as *The Unforgettable Fire* had done after *War*. Unfortunately, they did sound like a lot of other people from days gone by. The rock 'n' roll storm they kicked up gave rise to some good songs but generally they were songs that could so easily have been done by other artists, not a criticism that could have been levelled at 'Bad' or 'Exit' or 'I Will Follow,' for instance. Where U2 had always sounded like nothing else on earth, they were now very definitely of this planet, the earthy sound and emotions owing much to the popular music masters of the past.

In his series *Wide Awake in Ireland*, John Waters describes Ireland as a nation 'of vast energies, wild enthusiasm and exhilarating possibilities'. It was in that spirit of wild enthusiasm that U2 seemed to lose their musical plot. Bono in particular had often spoken of boring people senseless by spending an entire day discussing some new discovery with an almost childlike enthusiasm, a genius for abandoned enjoyment that the repressed English lock firmly away at the age of around thirteen to move on to a more 'mature' way of life, thereby explaining why artistically U2 have been way out in front of any British competition. The Irish still retain the capacity to be excited by new sounds, new ideas, new experiences while their more cynical counterparts remain stoically unimpressed. For *Rattle and Hum*, U2 were swept along in the tidal wave of 1987's hectic schedule and kept afloat by a tidal wave of enthusiasm for this 'new' music.

The 1987 tour and their continuing exposure to roots music was reminiscent of the new wave explosion of 1977 when the Hype were exposed to these new sounds from Talking Heads, the Ramones, the Clash, Television et al. At that time, when they were learning to play and trying to form a group of their own, these influences and earlier ones such as Bowie were discernible in their own music, which was not immediately particularly original. However, by the time they had struggled through Dublin's small rock scene to win a degree of prominence in their own city, prior to going on to a wider stage beyond Ireland, they had had three full years to absorb those sounds and mould them into their own highly individual style. As a band on the run across America in 1987, they were adding these new rhythms, these new colours to their music simply by aping them, not absorbing them – there was little time for them to do anything else. With *Achtung Baby* it is clear that excavating rock's roots was a worthwhile exercise since it has given U2 a broader palette with which to work, but releasing their fledgeling experiments before they had completely absorbed the rudiments of the form was not such a great idea. Some of the material on *Rattle and Hum* might well have been better served as a series of one-off singles like 'A Celebration' had been post *October*, pointing the way ahead, expanding their horizons in a more relaxed situation.

The songs that were released did have an air of inspiration about them, they were not pedestrian muso plods by any means, but it was an extremely lazy, sloppy record by U2 standards, The Edge even admitting on its release that the record was 'just treading water, it's only a fraction of what we can do.' U2 were guilty of falling asleep in their own comfort, be it the comfort of their position or the comfort of a settled life in Dublin away from the rock circus among people who they knew and loved, sequestering themselves away from the harsh realities of the world and artistic inspiration. There was comfort too in the knowledge that they were unopposed as the best and most successful band of their kind – Echo & the Bunnymen were in decline, Simple Minds had never reached the same level of commercial or artistic success, New Order and the Cure were largely European institutions, the Smiths had come and gone and there was no real challenge. While U2 had not viewed making music as a competition, there can be little doubt that, had some of those bands remained a part of the scene, U2 would have been spurred into a creative reaction, professional pride preventing them releasing sub-standard material. As it was, the ride was easy.

The prevalent state of mind in the U2 camp on 'The Joshua Tree' tour was captured accurately by some of the music which also poked a hole in the side of an America that was not at ease with itself. The album opened with a truly dreadful run through of 'The Beatles' 'Helter Skelter', a dirty Paul McCartney rocker – possibly a comment on the unreal U2 cartoon that was busily being constructed, just as one had been created around the Beatles painting Paul as the cute balladeer – on their *White Album* which, by the time U2 had finished with it, was calling for mercy. Bono proclaimed, irreverently, that they were stealing the song back from Charles Manson, but if he'd heard what they did to it, he wouldn't have wanted it back. That said, the very disarray in which it was performed was an excellent introduction to the mayhem that was encompassed by the four sides of the double album, the song lending itself to a depiction of nightmarish mania. U2 were in the middle of a hurricane of their own creation, fending off the press, dealing with all the problems of making a major movie, to which were added additional problems which Bono had with his voice in the early stages of the tour and injuries he sustained when a light fell on him during rehearsals and then when he slipped on stage and injured his shoulder (hence the shoulder harness during the filming of 'I Still Haven't Found What I'm Looking For' in Harlem). The helpless hamster on a treadmill of 'Helter Skelter' set the tone beautifully, although that was lost in the rush of condemnation that followed Bono's mentioning of U2 in the same breath as the Beatles, the first of many, large erroneous conclusions that were jumped to.

The next came with 'All Along the Watchtower' – Oh my God, first the Beatles, now they rank themselves with Dylan and Hendrix too! Once more, the motivation was slightly simpler, although it led to the most famed piece of U2 tour madness, an original outbreak that put the old rock 'n' roll habits of trashing hotel rooms and driving cars into swimming pools into the shade. In an attempt to break out of their schedule, U2, while on a free day in San Francisco, decided to borrow some gear from the Grateful Dead, set up on a flat-bed truck and play a free concert in the business centre of the city. An indication of the po-faced reporting that U2 had to endure – although anyone who is photographed stone-faced in the desert deserves everything they get – came when, in the wake of the previous week's financial crash, Bono dubbed it the 'Save the Yuppie' concert and asked people to donate briefcases. This was then seriously reported as a group of concerned musicians who were always on the look out for a good cause trying to help the local businessmen. Small wonder that Bono went slightly berserk and spray painted 'Rock 'n' roll – Stop The Traffic' on a piece of sculpture which he later described as 'cosmic debris'. While the artist felt that Bono's action was in keeping with the spirit of his work, the local authorities who owned the piece were less than pleased and threatened Bono with charges, a piece of opportunist politicking that was finally dropped. 'Stop the Traffic' had become a pet phrase during the tour (along with the self-explanatory 'only in America' at each new absurdity encountered on their travels), one which had grown up around the video shoot for 'Where The Streets Have No Name', when U2 played on a rooftop and literally stopped the traffic.

The song they opened the free show with was 'All Along The Watchtower', apposite to the occasion for the line *'Businessmen they drink my wine, plowmen dig my earth/None of them along the line know what any of it is worth.'* Allegedly none of them knew the song prior to actually playing it, although press reports from a Lyceum show in February 1981 suggest that it was played as an encore with Pete Wylie of Wah!, and the film shows the group rehearsing in their trailer behind the stage, trying to get the words and an arrangement together. To learn something minutes before putting it on your record was a splendidly off-the-wall idea that deflated the bubble but it was seen as affectation by those who had the knives ready. It's a piece that works well on the album the first few times and the spirit it creates does endure, but it's better seen on the film where the whole release that it gave to the group is very evident, the sense of leaping off the treadmill for even a few minutes. 'It does become a prison,' Adam opined. 'The bigger you get, the smaller your world becomes and you get cabin fever.'

Throughout what is an intense and powerful movie for all its faults, the stage acts as a refuge for the group away from everything else that's happening around them. For two hours every night, the stage was their escape from the pressures and an effective and essential safety valve, something which the live cuts on film and record amply demonstrate. Like so many of the new songs that were included on the album, the live songs chosen were aggressive, incredibly belligerent and sometimes a little disturbing, 'Exit', for instance, reaching monstrous proportions in the movie and both 'Pride' and 'Bullet The Blue Sky' far surpassed their studio incarnations on this album. The live shows came from deep within the heart of darkness and so it can be little wonder that the mania of 'Helter Skelter' was such a strong motif for *Rattle and Hum*.

The only sense of a breather on celluloid or on the album comes in 'Heartland', where the film sees the band on the banks of the Mississippi. For a record that was fed on choice snippets of America, it was inevitable that there should be a song set in the heart of the nation, the 'Heartland'. A piece that had been written for *The Joshua Tree*, it finally held down a place on *Rattle and Hum* as a companion to its predecessor 'In God's Country'. As a travelogue it was eloquently evocative, *'the cotton wool heat'* unmistakably the language of the South and the Mississippi delta, and it was in 'Heartland' that the America of dreams and the Amerika of nightmares clashed most piquantly. As a writer, Bono had wriggled free of his overt obsessions with America and Americana yet the country remained sufficiently fresh to sustain future visits, working neatly as a backdrop to the relationship songs that he was exploring. This time 'Heartland' was a song about America itself, 'a helicopter shot' as Adam termed it, musically something from Robbie Robertson's swamp courtesy of Lanois' production, his only credit on an album that was supervised by Jimmy Iovine who had worked on *Under A Blood Red Sky*. It watched the deserts, the valleys and the rivers flash past the tour bus but, as ever, Bono was quick to set up an opposing image, where in *'towers of steel belief goes on and on'*. That aside, 'Heartland' busied itself with a more hopeful vision of America, that new-found land that Bono had spoken of so often, where anything might just be possible after all, where people were open and willing to believe or give the benefit of the doubt, a very different facet of America to that exposed by 'Desire'.

The crashing power of the live music could also be seen in a number of the new songs that were included on the records, songs that were seemingly written on a diet of red meat, songs with throbbing temples and bulging veins that conveyed the emotions within the group. Elvis Presley had become a figure of fascination for the band, having come to represent the two sides of America that struggled side by side for supremacy – initially he embodied the American dream, a truck driver from nowhere, who suddenly became the King, not just of rock 'n' roll, but of America itself. Yet, in his success and his meteoric rise to fame there were sown the seeds of his eventual demise in the American nightmare, a star cocooned from the real world with only the material world for comfort. He was also a warning to U2 and others like them of the way in which success can turn on those on whom it has bestowed its greatest gifts, a reminder not to take their eye off the ball and to remember that it is the music that really counts, not the attendant publicity or the rewards.

Having become fans of Elvis's music, it was inevitable that while trekking across the States they should pitch up at Gracelands. Unfortunately, Spinal Tap had been there before them and, while U2 were aware of the obvious connotations and were striving to stare them down, they failed miserably. As Larry stood before Elvis's grave, expectations were raised for a capella version of 'Heartbreak Hotel' that never came, which was a shame since he had, moments earlier, provided one of the few genuinely moving moments of the film, talking about his reactions to Gracelands and his distaste for what it had become. If their version of 'Helter Skelter' and Bono's proclamation that preceded it had been deliberately tongue-in-cheek, their treatment of Gracelands was too deferential, though outtakes did apparently see Bono mentioning the 'Michael Jackson vibe' given off by the collection of stuffed monkeys.

To complete the Elvis double-header, the band went to Sun Studios in Memphis where he had begun his recording career, perhaps the most famous recording studio in the world outside Abbey Road. As they had become used to recording in modern facilities Sun was a radical departure, but the atmosphere of the place, the room where rock 'n' roll was born, was so inspirational they managed to record five songs in five hours, unheard of in today's climate where it takes five hours just to get a decent drum sound, The Edge revealing that they 'just set up and straightaway there was *that* sound.' Adam captured the mood, saying, 'You go through a reception and beyond that is the control room and in the control room is the toilet so it stinks of piss all the time. But it is where Elvis pissed, so it adds to the atmosphere!' The light-hearted nature of the sessions was accurately documented by Joanou's film, which portrayed the interplay between the members of the band who were clearly having the time of their lives. Bono got to sing through Elvis's old microphone ruefully admitting later, 'I only wish I could sing like him.' The atmosphere was completed by the addition of Cowboy Jack Clement, who had worked on all those early Sun classics that were worming their way into the U2 record collection.

The material they recorded in Sun was entirely right for the setting, comprising 'Angel Of Harlem', 'When Love Comes To Town', 'Love Rescue Me', 'She's A Mystery To Me', the song written for Roy Orbison, and Woody Guthrie's 'Jesus Christ'. Yet it was these songs, of which only the first three made it onto *Rattle and Hum*, that were broadly responsible for its underperformance in that they lacked the spark of originality that so characterized U2's finest work. 'Angel Of Harlem' was a fine pop song dedicated to the memory of Billie Holiday, perhaps identifying her as a kindred spirit. Adam later commented that 'everyone is broken in one way or another . . . this person had something even though her spirit was broken and people who do live on the extreme like that are still capable of making great music.' The lyric spoke of finding salvation in blues music, a redemptive quality in the 'devil's music', something which clearly struck a chord in the U2 camp. There may also be an autobiographical thread in a line which sees the Angel of Harlem losing her way down the side roads of celebrity life, just as U2 had lost the plot under the stresses of life in the spotlight, inflicting their own wounds by taking on extra responsibilities such as the film, the book, Mother Records, etc., etc., when their only real field of excellence was making great, original music. The music did suffer through the *Rattle and Hum* project and this was an admission of sorts.

And yet these songs and the music from which they grew were what got U2 through the tour. 'When Love Comes To Town' was proof of that, exuberance dripping from the grooves, the thrill of working with B. B. King tangible to the listeners. The song was the best of the three Sun recordings, again dealing with Bono's fascination with love as redemption, the close relationship between the sacred and the profane, the 'devil's music' again being a life-saver – '*as the music played I saw my life turn around.*' King's guitar playing was a brilliant shaft of light thrown onto what was otherwise a standard blues rocker, but Bono's lyrics again took it into other territory, delving into universal love, the promise of life after death, the perils of temptation, even giving himself the chance to play the villain piercing Christ's side at the crucifixion after all these years of being cast as Jesus. This was the most obvious physical exploration of their Christianity to date, still with their heads in the clouds perhaps but their feet firmly planted on the ground, a move away from its treatment as some kind of ethereal, fragile concept and an obvious extension from the songs on *The Joshua Tree*. The lyric was complex and yet clear, deep but a direct communication to the soul. On a musical level, however, King's presence made it all the more apparent that they were dealing with a form that already had masters of its own, a real blues guitarist and singer that had all the equipment to deal with the setting. Indeed, by the time a 12 inch version had been completed, featuring Little Richard extolling the virtues of love in best preacher shtick, the whole thing had degenerated into a Blues Brothers romp. It was also the site of one of the more potentially damaging scenes in the film, where Bono was giving B. B. King a reading of the lyrics and it is very hard to tell whether he's looking smug that he should have written such a powerful song or embarrassed that such a giant as B. B. King is actually consenting to play it. The former was generally selected by the critics, especially when the film was embellished with King explaining how great the songs were, an understandable desire to put the band at ease but something which again comes across as the band saying, 'Look how great we are, even B. B. King says so.'

Those two Sun recordings were enjoyable though uninspired, but 'Love Rescue Me' was a different situation altogether, an incoherent musical ramble that would have benefited from some sharp editing, though, written as it was in collaboration with Bob Dylan, maybe no one thought it could be anything other than perfect. It was, in fact, some way removed from that – a live version at the 'Smile Jamaica' benefit held at London's Dominion in October 1988 and which eventually crawled onto a single B-side was yet more ramshackle in execution – although once more it had a tale to tell about U2's transition, a tale which saw them looking for a simpler music that could be recorded more quickly and put onto record almost immediately in the mould of Lennon's 'Some Time In New York City' or, more interestingly, the style of the new rap music which was beginning to sweep the States through 1987 and 1988. Rap artists were able to take an emotion, sample a rhythm line, rap over the top and have a single ready and available in days, thereby maintaining the intensity of the initial feeling or motivation behind the song rather than living with it over the gestation period of an elephant, sometimes dissipating the original kernel of thought that made it initially so potent. While U2 were not becoming a rap act, their music going back to earlier inspirations, the attitude was not dissimilar and they were keen to react more quickly to their personal circumstances and those of the world around them. That kind of reaction time required a simpler musical approach and if *Rattle and Hum* did have one unifying musical element it was the cohesive force of the rhythm section, Larry and Adam both having slimmed down their playing to the nth degree so that they had a number of simple patterns that formed a bedrock for the songs. As a natural consequence, The Edge had had to simplify his own guitar work to the extent that at times he was barely recognizable as the man who had virtually redefined the sound of the guitar over the previous ten years. Now he was still a distinctive voice but one far more submerged within the pack than before, one of a dozen veteran soul bands.

Lyrically U2 continued to reveal themselves further in the company of Dylan, keen to show that while fans and critics might look to them as seers or sages, new prophets for the modern age, if anything they knew less than the rest of us. After all, superstars travelling and living in the heart of security, both physical and mental, are often divorced from the realities of real-life struggle, the diamonds in the dirt which can help provide the key to a higher conflict. 'I don't know either' was the only answer to those who would seek the meaning of life at the hem of Bono's garment. All that he had to offer was the idea of love as the final redemption, the last chance and a reminder that fame wasn't all it might be cracked up to be, an admission they seemed to fight shy of making too strongly within the context of an album release lest it be picked out and misinterpreted as spoilt rock stars complaining about their particular version of the Faustian pact. Nevertheless, on the 'Angel Of Harlem' B-side, 'A Room At the Heartbreak Hotel', they gave way to temptation and executed a full-blown 'Sunset Boulevard' epic on the back of a clanging guitar rant that cut to the hollow heart of celebrity without substance, of desire over morality.

Returning to 'Love Rescue Me', finally, after years of songwriting that fought death, there seemed to be an acceptance of the next world that would be entered through the gates of love, a connection further established in 'Hallelujah Here She Comes', the B-side to 'Desire', a gospel-tinged good-humoured look at the voyage into infinity, everyone dressed in black, Bono taking the hint *'guess I'm not coming back'* that suggests their excavation of that gospel seam has helped put their own music and their own searching into some perspective.

It's a shift that came in no small part from their dalliance with the New Voices of Freedom Choir based in Harlem. Again the record and film cleverly display two pieces of the same story, the film showing Bono peering through a hangover as all four members of U2 get caught up in the glorious sound that the choir can make, the way in which they were able to take a white rock song, albeit one with a gospel flavour, and turn it around, stretching it to the very limits of its construction to communicate more openly the subtle combination of spirituality and sexuality at which the song hints. Where the past had seen U2 criticized for their chasteness, their decision not to tackle the earthly, earthy passions, assertions that they were musically as pure as the driven snow in their refusal to tackle the tangled realities of sex and love, they now looked to attack head on the relationship between God, sex and music. Bono was later to say that it was only within sex and art that you could still catch glimpses of God, in that state of transcendence. That joyousness shone through 'I Still Haven't Found What I'm Looking For', making this the definitive reading of the song.

In the search for that transcendence, U2 did not forget the possible footfalls that would cross their path and it was in these new songs that the album came alive and showed a brief glimmer of a band that was finally kicking loose the last awkward remnants of a skin it had long outgrown. One such song came in the form of 'All I Want Is You', a tower of song that was lifted on to another plane at the end courtesy of a mesmeric and rather unsettling closing string arrangement from Van Dyke Parks that set off the tale of the unattainable quite poignantly. The obsessive root at the heart of so many songs through this period was but a precursor of what was to come later on *Achtung Baby*, but it's true to say that 'All I Want Is You' was effectively a refinement of 'With Or Without You' which was much better for the extra work. Another song in the same kind of category was one of the two savagely biting originals on the collection that gave those hoping for some new direction for U2 a germ of hope; 'Hawkmoon 269'. Again obsessive in tone, with a nod towards 'Luminous Times (Hold On To Love)', where the woman in question fills his mind throughout the day, not always benevolently, as a kind of addictive prison that won't let him go. When Bono needs her love like '*a needle needs a vein*', this is not a love housed neatly in a rose-covered cottage but an elemental love built on raw passion and desperate desire, a love that is as terrifying as it is exhilarating, as dangerous as it is a haven from the storm, as mentally twisted as it is spiritual in intensity. It's a love worth dying for and one with which it may be impossible to live, as the closing

minute of the song shows. This is one of the most frightening pieces
they've put on record, Bono's growling vocal giving way to sensual
backing vocals chanting over thudding drums and a wailing guitar
figure that ends in screeching feedback, one of Edge's major contributions to the album in pure playing terms. The whole piece is an
enormous, sprawling paean to need, lust, love and desire.

'Desire' was another hint at things to come, an incredible buzz
of energy that gave U2 their first number one single in the UK, yet
one so obviously based around Larry's hand-breaking Bo Diddley
rhythm that it was hardly any more original than any of the other
material that was around on *Rattle and Hum*. 'Desire' scored its
points by taking a well-worn musical phrase and then kicking it into
U2 shape with a U2 attitude on top, a clear progression from what
was slavish copying elsewhere on the album. The attitude was the
heart of the song since it was essentially the original demo of the
song that made it onto the record, all the later versions losing some
of the spark that had so vitalized the original. This was a piece of
U2 taking that rap attitude and putting it into practice, Bono saying
that the song was written in about five minutes, then recorded in
another five. The 12-inch mix of the song really did thrust it into
that context with lots of cut-up samples taken from a news broadcast, police sirens and gunshots that made a musical collage which
hinted at the frenetic speed of life and the decay in downtown Los
Angeles where they had spent so much time working on the film
project. The chaotic images that were flying in from all sides put the
listener underneath a barrage of aural missiles that were overwhelming in intensity, although it is a sound which has become more and
more commonplace in recent years as acts like Public Enemy have
gained greater access to mainstream radio. Nevertheless, for U2 to
release such a single in 1988 was a very encouraging sign that they
hadn't lost sight of their responsibilities towards mixing things up
on pop radio and that they were more than willing to abuse their
position by giving people something they didn't expect and which
might hit them on different levels.

For any observer of late twentieth-century culture and social
conditions, Los Angeles is a mind-blowing mix and match of
astonishing wealth in the Hollywood Hills and obscene poverty on
the downtown streets, where the people have to scrape any kind of
living they can and yet still try to live their own lives. 'Desire' caught
that all-consuming dream of ambition that consigns the losers to the
street corners and held it up to the light where it lost some of its

lustre. By extension, so too did U2, who were perfectly candid in exposing their own desire to be successful and to get off the streets and into the nice cars and the big houses and who were willing to go through many of the requisite hoops to get there, though, to their credit, the compromises they chose were restricted far more than those made by many before and since. That the band wanted to rid themselves of this earnest preachermen tag that was a noose around their neck could not have been more evident than in a song like 'Desire'; Bono, the avenger of all evils as he had been painted, wanted his real character and his real life back. The idea of Bono the pop idol was quite simply too ludicrous for words, leaving him to admit, 'I don't want to have anything to live up to.' The video that was made for the song vividly demonstrated the other side of the equation – where there was success on the one hand there had to be failure on the other, so in a dayglo Los Angeles that resembled nothing more than a set for some *Clockwork Orange*-style ultra-violence or the inner city on speed that Burroughs spoke of earlier, the consequences of 'failure' were displayed for all to see, calling to mind Bono's distillation of current-day Christianity: 'To me faith in Jesus Christ that is not aligned with social justice, that is not aligned with the poor – it's nothing.' The video for 'Desire' provided an impression of the mania that ensues in the mad scramble for material gain as people try to 'get on and do well', not worrying about stepping on anyone else in the process.

'God Part II' was a partner in that attitude, a song dripping with sarcasm, soaked in vitriol and anger. In its scattergun rage, it had the hallmarks of an end-of-term party where, having been wound up for months on the road, the band finally got the chance to vent their collective spleen with the most aggressive playing even this album had heard. In 'God Part II', U2 had pointed themselves in another and potentially more interesting musical direction for the future. One thing was absolutely certain – they were a noisy rock 'n' roll band again and they were going to trample over a whole different set of myths from those they'd tackled before. Although 'God Part II' lent its voice to the outcry of the rock 'n' roll community against Albert Goldman's book *The Lives of John Lennon*, there was much more to it than that; as Martin Luther King ushered in the 'hard metal dance mix' of the track, U2 were still determined to use 'the weapon of love' which, while it might sound like a Barry White song, had a real application across the spectrum of their sound and their attack. The hope must always be to build up rather than tear down, although the same mix began with Bono's vocal having been treated in the studio to come across with psychopathic restraint.

'God Part II' was a bundle of contradictions, including Bono's assertion that rock 'n' roll cannot save the world when his career to that point indicated a belief in the direct opposite, but now was the time to celebrate those contradictions rather than hide from them and pretend they didn't exist, of which more later. Suffice it to say that if a bridge did exist from *The Joshua Tree* to *Achtung Baby*, that bridge was 'God Part II', a song which contained so much it seemed likely to collapse beneath the weight. Part of its punch on *Rattle and Hum* lay in its following 'Heartland'. From a tribute to the potential of America, this driving metallic grind communicated the violent psychosis that lies beneath America's civilized veneer, constantly ready to explode. To that could be added the slap in the face it gave U2 themselves when, after a record that had built a case for deifying the legends of the past, Bono admonished himself with *'you glorify the past when the future dries up'*, although that was also aimed at a world fleeing from an unpalatable present into the arms of a past where everything was supposedly rosy. They added a spiritual or perhaps physical postscript that he always ends beside *'a presence I can feel'*, though whether this is some higher love or the woman who causes his wild thoughts to escape earlier in the song isn't clear. Most affecting of all for its very incongruity is the way in which, having completed each verse of confusion, Bono is able to make a clear and unequivocal declaration of his ultimate belief in the redemptive power of love.

Sonically and lyrically, 'God Part II' is a dense track rather than the dance track people might have wanted from U2 and one which would have nestled snugly next to 'Until The End Of The World' on *Achtung Baby*. It was a song that hinted at the transition phase that *Rattle and Hum* was supposed to revel in, enabling U2 to kick off the shackles and have fun with the new music they were uncovering, Bono gleefully admitting that it said, 'Look, they don't know where they're at but isn't that good?' And in a world of squeaky-clean supergroups, such naked doubt was indeed a healthy thing, yet it was undeniably clouded by reaction to Phil Joanou's film.

Joanou admirably met the conditions of his brief, the production of a film which was primarily about music, and it was to his credit that he captured some extremely strong performances on film and that his images were not overpowered by the music. The idea was to give the music the same weight that Scorsese had given to the boxing ring in *Raging Bull* and that epic quality tumbled down from the screen, yet it was incidents beyond pure music that were left in the public mind in the aftermath of *Rattle and Hum*, an experience which indicated that Hollywood might be an even more powerful industry than rock 'n' roll. The salient points that seemed to be picked out in review after review were Bono's passionate condemnation of the IRA in 'Sunday Bloody Sunday', the visit to Gracelands and the wisdom thereof, and Bono's onstage pronouncements about apartheid, TV evangelists and the recapturing of rock heritage from Charles Manson, and the rites of passage in the company of B. B. King and Sun Studios. While the humour in the 'Helter Skelter' piece was missed, largely because it was done with such tongue-in-cheek that it ceased to have meaning to an outside audience, the others were becoming something of a problem.

That Bono was entirely sincere in his condemnation of apartheid and the evangelists, that they saw themselves very much as apprentices in the court of B. B. King was not in too much doubt. The difficulty arose simply because it didn't look that way. Bono, blown up to cinema screen size, came across as a sleazy game show host. When to that was added the frantic hype that surrounded the film's opening across the world, it is perhaps less than surprising that accusations of putative megalomania were dusted down. The trick which U2 hadn't yet mastered was *looking* sincere and they paid for it. Had the new music been of the same quality as *The Joshua Tree* they might have got away with it all, but they had spent too much time on their other activities and had neglected their musical muse which then capriciously deserted them, further proof that they should concentrate on their musical activities before all else. A new persona might also be required for Bono, as the group's mouthpiece was being burdened by the baggage that being Bono carried with it. Brendan Kennelly, who crops up with great frequency in connection with the U2 of the 1990s, might have pointed the way with a piece from his *Book of Judas*, entitled 'Insincerity as a Detector of Human Worth':

> If on the other hand you experiment with lies
> Salted with what is deftly insincere
> You'll see their hearts as your words come and go.
> Let them take the bait. Assume a wise
> Look. Be hurt, if necessary. Say you're queer
> Or a Jesusfreak. Their eyes will tell you all you
> Need to know. What do you need to know?

These were ideas that took time to ferment properly into what was to become Zoo TV and at the time of *Rattle and Hum*, the very idea of U2 having a sense of humour seemed risible among many. In that regard, they were the agents of their own doom along with Joanou, since the film had been edited along very strict demarcation lines, omitting almost any behind the scenes footage that might have lightened the mood. The film as it stood was a powerful monument to a particular moment in U2's career, but it was only a part of that band's character. To show them as individuals away from the stage might have harmed the film but their refusal to include it – though Joanou was given final cut on the movie – left them looking rather stupid when they bemoaned people's refusal to credit them with an ability to laugh at themselves and the world. In that regard, they might have done better to make available a film made on the road in the early part of the tour by Barry Devlin, the producer of their original demo in Dublin a decade previously. Entitled *Outside it's America*, it was shown once in the UK on New Year's Eve, in Ireland and on American cable TV and it captured a far more buoyant spirit as they made their way across God's country.

When the *Rattle and Hum* experience drew to a close, there was little left except criticism and a band in some confusion as to what its next move should be. They were upset that the whole idea of *Rattle and Hum*, an off-the-cuff piece of simple music-making for its own sake, had been so widely misinterpreted as another huge artistic statement from the mighty U2. The 'bonus album' ethic of *Rattle and Hum* got lost in the hype, as did some of their initial motivations, with Adam left to talk of their narrowing options with the only real possibility open to them being to grow old gracefully. The future was opening up before them but it was clear that they would have to do something rather different from *Rattle and Hum* to shift some of the entrenched opinions in the media.

Ultimately, they took *Rattle and Hum* on the road through the Far East and Europe, including New Year shows at the end of the decade, in musical terms *their* decade, back in their home town, where Bono announced they were going away for a while to dream it all up again. The external pressures seemed to have got the better of them and they intelligently decided that the best thing for them to do was to drop out of sight for a while to take stock and to give an unfettered rein to their creativity once more away from all the business distractions that had made *Rattle and Hum* such an uneven album. Nevertheless, the Love Town tour, on which they were supported by B. B. King, proved useful in more ways than simply getting them out in front of an audience again for it gave some of the songs like 'Hawkmoon 269' and 'God Part II' the chance to further evolve to the point at which they became the fulcrum of the live show and provided sonic and lyrical possibilities for the future. The presentation was something that would be considered later, although there was no hint of what was to come as Bono continued to defend their search for some musical roots: 'When the 1970s were over the consensus of opinion was let's just enjoy rock 'n' roll for what it is. Let's enjoy rock 'n' roll with a sense of irony and trash. But I don't feel a part of that.'

chapter eleven

SIXTY-EIGHT AND I'LL OWE YOU ONE

Scene: A drab railway station filmed in black and white. A battered sign hangs in the breeze. It reads 'Zoo Station'. On one side of the platform we see a train in darkness. Looking through a window we see four men sitting around a table, upon which is a small cactus. The first is wearing a dark waistcoat and has a rough crucifix around his neck. His long hair is tied back and behind his seat is a white flag. Next to him sits an angular-looking man with a few days' growth of beard wearing a cowboy hat and a fringed jacket. Across from him sits a slightly older-looking chap with closely cropped hair and wire-rimmed spectacles – he has a bemused air about him as though he finds things a little ridiculous. Maybe he's slightly surprised to be on this particular train. The last of the four has on a leather jacket, a cut-off T-shirt with Harley Davidson written on the front and looks a little like James Dean.

The four are quiet. Around them sit lots of intense young people who wait to catch the pearls of wisdom that might drop from their lips. They are quiet too. The man in the hat heaves a sigh and looks quizzically at the other three, who return his gaze as if to say, 'What can we do?'

On the other side of the platform a new train arrives, this time in glorious technicolour. Again, in the middle of the compartment there is a table around which four men are sitting. The first is wearing a leather suit and huge bug-eye glasses. Next to him is an angular-looking man wearing a woollen hat and sporting a piratical beard. Across from him sits a slightly older-looking chap with a remarkable mohican-style hair cut and wire-rimmed spectacles. He isn't wearing any clothes. The last of the four has on a leather jacket and looks a little like James Dean.

The four are talking loudly, laughing and quaffing champagne. There is a cloth on the table which appears to have been made from a white flag. Behind them a dozen or more television sets are blaring away and the four are ringed by the rich and the famous who are having a similarly good time. In the corner of the carriage are a couple of dog-eared posters for Greenpeace and Amnesty International, between which stands a greying figure playing the saxophone with what can only be termed gusto. Someone walks over to the refrigerator to get another beer. When the door is opened, a small hunched figure is sitting at the back of it – he has long hair and a beard, a chain around his neck with the letter 'J' on it and is wearing a 'Kiss Me Quick' hat and he passes out the beer to the thirsty, awaiting his chance to strike. Back at the table, bug-eyes, whom we might call The Fly, is making a phone call while opening another bottle of champagne and spraying it everywhere in the grand style.

The camera pulls away from this carriage – as soon as we are outside the sound stops. Everything surrounding the train is back to black and white. We look into the first carriage again. The four men are looking at the other train. Eventually the man with the waistcoat turns to the angular-looking man. 'Edge,' he says, 'those bastards have stolen our train.' They get up and follow the chap who looks a little like James Dean and the man in the wire-rimmed spectacles, who is already half way across the platform, bounding towards the other train.

(With apologies to Woody Allen)

While such a Road to Damascus experience is probably overstating the dawning realization in the U2 camp that all was not perhaps as it should be, there is little question that by the end of the *Rattle and Hum* project, they were quite definitely on the wrong train in terms of their own music and enjoyment and other people's perception of them. The very success that they had looked for, the very audience that they had craved back in the Dandelion Market in Dublin was now creating all kinds of seemingly irreconcilable difficulties for them, as they had themselves already hinted on *Rattle and Hum*, especially in 'God Part II'. The huge success of their records and the extreme wealth which that created for them gave rise to an enormous contradiction – here were some of the loudest, most vociferous critics of the system, artists who were keen to expose social injustice and the appalling unfairness of modern life, in terms of the economic discrimination against so many sections of the population, and yet they were generating sums of money akin to the gross domestic product of many small African countries. U2, collectively and individually, were quite simply filthy rich and some of the most conspicuous beneficiaries of the system they were attacking, this being a state of affairs about which they were particularly sensitive since sections of the press suggested they were making money from the suffering of others.

Although such condemnation of the prevailing social conditions was highly welcome – better surely that they bite the hands that feed them than snuggle up to them in bed, as some of those taking corporate dollars were only too happy to do – the potential for hypocritical hogwash was not to be underestimated. Bono was to speak of success as a big bad wolf, giving them all these material advantages that they didn't know how to deal with as well as the inevitable guilt trip that is associated with the accumulation of great wealth when you've come from a less financially privileged background and when your contemporaries are still struggling to get by. While U2 might have been able to square their riches with their personal beliefs and the way in which they chose to redistribute some of the cash to charities, etc., the outside perception was rather different, something which acted as a creative straitjacket, leaving Bono in particular unsure of what his territory as a lyricist could be in the future. These were insecurities that were further magnified by the widely perceived view of him as an egomaniac who was solely interested in the sound of his own voice and who was busily telling ordinary people how to live their lives while hiding himself away in his mansion on the hill. Clearly, on their return to the fray Bono and his colleagues would need to look and behave rather differently from the earnest, seemingly eager-to-please men who had taken *The Joshua Tree* around the world.

A lengthy break was essential to kick-start the band again. Having struggled through a transitional phase on 'The Joshua Tree' tour and then seen that mutate into the beginnings of an intriguing new direction for the new decade on the Love Town tour, they had to take time out from the whole U2 whirl of activity in order to get fresh perspective and reorder their affairs. Having been the band that most sharply defined the 1980s, there must have been a real temptation to quit while they were ahead, especially in the wake of the *Rattle and Hum* débâcle, where the music had often found itself very low on the list of priorities. U2 had achieved, in commercial terms, everything they could ever have wanted but, in reaching that point, had they sacrificed their artistic integrity, were they left with anything more to say? The challenges for the future would have to be self-imposed. Since they'd had number one singles and albums across the globe, there were no targets left in that sense, so where was the motivation to come from?

Ultimately the reasoning behind making another U2 record would have to be artistic, Bono admitting to *Vogue* that 'you get your fancy homes and cars then you realize what you're strung out on is the idea of making a music that has never been heard before.' That being the case, U2 were in the best position of any rock 'n' roll band since the Beatles pre-*Revolver*.

With a back catalogue which stated that in today's world freedom of choice could only equate with the acquisition of wealth, U2 were now in the perfect position to use that freedom and would be able to release virtually anything they chose. They had secured the total and unquestionable freedom that all artists want and so to give that up would have been foolhardy. There were still things to say, but they realized only too well that they needed to find new ways of saying them. Their passions remained the same, but to maintain the soapbox proselytizing that had come across so badly on the *Rattle and Hum* film, with the notable exception of 'Sunday Bloody Sunday', would be a hideous mistake that would render them artistically redundant and irrelevant in a world that had moved on from there with bewildering rapidity. Bono as the earnest preacher was a well-recognized cartoon around the world, this even giving rise to its own jokes: a bass player dies and goes up to rock 'n' roll heaven where he's greeted by the Angel Gabriel. Just behind him he sees Jimi Hendrix, John Lennon, Elvis Presley, Janis Joplin and Keith Moon sitting around talking animatedly about music. In the middle giving instructions is a man with a cowboy hat and a leather waistcoat. The bass player says to the Angel Gabriel, 'Is that Bono? I didn't know he was dead.' The Angel replies, 'No, that's not Bono, it's Jesus Christ. He just thinks he's Bono.' Another creative straitjacket.

Having decided to continue with the band, Adam suggesting that Bono's speech in Dublin about the band going away to dream it up again had given them carte blanche to do whatever they wanted, they required inspiration. Much of the music that was to feed their imaginations was very new but there were also blasts from the past. *Rattle and Hum* had been based upon the roots of rock 'n' roll, while *Achtung Baby* and Zoo TV were to feed upon the roots of U2 as they began to look back into their own pasts to rediscover what it was that had excited them about the form when they were growing up – the way Jimi Hendrix would throw a spanner in the works and create something from the distortion, the exciting androgyny of Marc Bolan, the raw excitement of Slade, the endearing rock 'n' roll stupidity of Gary Glitter, in fact the surface of things as much as their substance. U2 became excited by rock 'n' roll because it was a blast. Their task as seasoned musicians at the top of the rock 'n' roll tree was to recapture that excitement.

From a musical standpoint, it was The Edge who, perhaps predictably, took the lead. A later convert to the blues than the others, he had become its most zealous follower by the time *Rattle and Hum* came around and so it was inevitable that his work on that record should have been the most traditional, archetypal-sounding rock guitar of his career. By the time the band were on the Love Town tour, however, he had absorbed this more fully and was moving off into other areas again, creating music that was again coming from left field as Television and Patti Smith had years previously. On the Love Town trek, Edge was busily listening to industrial and electronic music by the likes of Einstürzende Neubaten, KMFDM and the Young Gods, Bono later noting that the noises coming from his hotel room each night sounded like the end of the world.

These abrasive, confrontational sounds that forced the listeners to reassess their whole outlook on music summed up a period of Edge's own life when things were in a state of turmoil. Although just prior to the Love Town tour his wife Aislinn gave birth to their third child in November 1989, they were by then just eighteen months away from the end of their marriage and Edge was clearly going through a period of personal and professional reappraisal. In the programme notes for Zoo TV in Europe in 1992, Edge noted that he hadn't been happy with himself until coming to terms with his own personality over the previous couple of years. The uncompromising music that was his constant companion was a soundtrack to that personal development and change, which then found its way into the music he was writing, and when it was time to put the songs down on tape, Edge was seemingly given complete licence to do whatever he chose, ending up with a library of new guitar treatments, a harsh metallic quality that further advanced him in the vanguard of rock 'n' roll innovators.

The first new sounds from U2 came in February 1990, when Bono and Edge's score for the Royal Shakespeare Company's stage production of *A Clockwork Orange–2004* was unveiled at London's Barbican. The 'rap opera' was a novel departure for them, featuring rap rhythms, hip-hop samples as well as the requisite snatches of Beethoven, but it was an electronic soundtrack that didn't find favour with the book's author, Anthony Burgess, who described it as 'neo-wallpaper'. Nevertheless, there were elements to the score that were reminiscent of the feel of the 'Desire' remix and its evocation of the schizoid violence of inner cities and it was a hint that U2 had got their collective ear to the ground once more and were trying to pick up on the music that was around them.

That music was central to the new songs they were to write, just as the break they took from songwriting was crucial to the outcome of the upcoming album sessions. While U2 were away, the rock-music landscape underwent some very fundamental changes and new pretenders to the throne of the world's greatest rock band came along. The competitive instinct had long been one of the core components of U2's artistic rise. In the late 1970s they wanted to be the best in Dublin so they had to rise above the likes of the Virgin Prunes and the Radiators, then they were on to the European stage where they were spurred on by the sheer quality of music being produced by Echo & the Bunnymen, the Teardrop Explodes and then, later, the Smiths, before moving on to a world stage and taking on all comers. U2 had always wanted success, not just for its own sake but in order to achieve the kind of widespread communication they were looking for with large audiences. When those other bands were around, they kept U2 on the straight and narrow, forcing them to tread an artistically sound path simply so that they could make better records – if the Bunnymen released a record as great as *Porcupine* for instance, it pushed U2 into making an even better record like *The Unforgettable Fire*. By 1988, that competition had evaporated and U2 released *Rattle and Hum*. Had the Bunnymen still been around, it's unlikely that U2 would have reacted with such a sloppy album. *Rattle and Hum* was a record from a band that had already quashed all competition, the musical equivalent of a football team being ten points clear at the top of the league with one game to play and fielding its reserves instead of the first team.

A matter of weeks after *Rattle and Hum* hit the racks, however, the band who had recently seemed the most likely to threaten U2's position released the record that put them firmly at the top of the tree. The band was REM, the album *Green*, their first release on a major label after years with independents IRS who had struggled to promote and distribute the group's records on a global scale. With the Warner Brothers corporation behind them, REM delivered their best album to that date and began their reign at the top. The quality of *Green* and its successor, *Out of Time*, must have spurred U2 on to greater effort, just as the way in which REM dealt with their new success must have given them some kind of an object lesson. Rather than courting the press, as U2 had done, REM did the minimum number of interviews, closeting themselves behind an increasingly enigmatic image that was further enhanced by the occasionally impenetrable lyrics of front man Michael Stipe and their decision not to tour *Out of Time*. Despite record sales that certainly rivalled those of U2, REM kept their credibility intact with the simple refusal to disclose anything more about themselves than they chose, where U2 had always opened themselves up completely to the press when a restrained silence might have served them better.

REM's success was welcome – U2 had long been fans of Georgia's finest, giving them a support slot in Europe during 1985 – not only because their approach was broadly similar but because it acted as a legitimization of rock 'n' roll as 'ART'. Although U2 had been artistically motivated, and a record such as *The Unforgettable Fire* was as dramatic an artistic statement as any novel or film you might care to name, they had come through a period when it was tragically unhip to suggest that rock 'n' roll was anything more than simple entertainment, the soundtrack to a good night out. When, on a South Bank Show TV special on Irish music, Bono said, 'It isn't only rock 'n' roll to me,' implying a life or death importance to the music, he was well aware that he was stepping well out of line with the prevailing philosophy. However, the advent of REM and of other acts who fused art and rock 'n' roll, such as Jane's Addiction, had given some credence to that doctrine. Rock 'n' roll might well be considered a worthwhile artistic medium making important and intelligent comments about the world and its inhabitants.

This was, in part, a simple turning of the fashion circle to the point at which intellectualizing about rock 'n' roll was acceptable once more, but there was far more to it than that. The late 1980s and early 1990s saw the beginnings of a decline in rock music as a leading part in popular youth culture as young people began to spend their leisure time and money elsewhere, particularly on computer games and equipment, a product of the fast-food sixty-second attention span culture.

In an odd way, U2 actually benefited from this culture of diminishing interest in that over the intervening three years, when music had become culturally less important, the spotlight was not so sharply focused on them, nor indeed on any other band, which in itself was liberating – music was far less relevant than it had been a few years before, the proof being in the far fewer tabloid press inches devoted to the likes of Guns 'N' Roses and REM compared with that previously given to U2. Those who remained interested in rock music were therefore far more committed than they had been five or six years earlier since it was only those most intensely fascinated by the medium and its possibilities who were left to discuss it. But not only was the fight on to maintain its popularity and cultural importance, the battle was on to protect it from being overwhelmed by commerce. As advertisers chose to use more and more pop classics to sell their products, as more rock bands chose to take commercial sponsorship, as films were sold on the basis of the throwaway pop hit that went with them, rock 'n' roll was under threat from new angles, with the danger that the nostalgia boom and the safety first recording approach would strangle future creativity.

While money-making has always been a crucial part of the rock 'n' roll business, the financial investment had until recently been fairly low, thus providing a degree of artistic freedom since the costs needing to be recouped were comparatively small. As advertising budgets have increased, as the market for records has fallen and as the price of failure has risen sharply, record companies search more and more for commercial success at the expense of everything else. Elements of the musical community have fought back by infusing their music with a greater artistic integrity and it was in this new climate that U2 went about their work, allowing themselves the luxury of complete artistic freedom since that was what the market-place now required of them. In tandem with that new rock approach, rap had politicized music to a far greater extent than any other form in the past, taking it into a realm beyond pure entertainment. In essence, serious music fans who were really into the medium were listening with an intensity and maturity that had not been seen since the Vietnam-related scene of the late 1960s.

As they had been together for fourteen years, new stimulus was required to enable them to make any radical changes to their own sound. While the climate had changed and while they were listening to different kinds of music than over the previous writing phase, other inputs were required. The band wanted to work with Eno and

Lanois again, partly because the relationship was such a strong one and had resulted in two excellent albums and partly because, as a band, U2 were in the same iconoclastic frame of mind they had been in prior to recording *The Unforgettable Fire*. They wanted to tear up the rule books and approach U2 afresh and, as the producers had already proved, they were a reliable source of many fresh ideas and treatments for songs. With the same team in place, both in front of and behind the recording desk, there was a desire to introduce something new to the recording process. U2 had become too cosy in their Dublin surroundings and that had robbed them of some of the competitive instincts that had stood them in such good stead earlier in their career. John Waters noted the problems U2 had both in practice and in the way in which they were perceived in their home land, saying, 'The U2 experience provides an example at the moment of how society can impose an excessive burden of responsibility on its artistic voices. Because they are the biggest rock band in the world we (the Irish) have tended to see them as a statement of our own potential, but the much more interesting statement which U2 make is often lost in the celebration of their celebrity.' Therefore, it was decided to record some basic tracks in another city using that as a breath of fresh air and a source of new inspiration.

There was never any intention of recording in America, since their experiences in Los Angeles recording extra tracks for *Rattle and Hum* had not been entirely successful and the distractions that that city or somewhere like New York would provide might be too intrusive, preventing them giving the appropriate level of concentration to the job in hand. Additionally, after two records that were very American in approach and content, it was time to put that continent behind them and look elsewhere for inspiration. Since The Edge was particularly attracted to the industrial *Sturm und Drang* of Front 242 and Einstürzende Neubaten among others, Europe was the obvious place to record and, within Europe, Berlin began to stick out like a sore thumb. By the tail end of 1990, when U2 were readying themselves to record, the Berlin Wall was crumbling and reunification of East and West Germany was imminent. It made Berlin the most exciting city in Europe and also one that was well worth visiting in order to see it as it had been under Communism before things changed irrevocably under the new regime.

Berlin was vibrant as U2 arrived. They reached the city on the last flight into West Berlin and then celebrated Liberation and Reunification Day, 3 October, with the native Berliners, notwithstanding the fact that they initially found themselves in the wrong parade, marching with the hardline Communists who wanted to rebuild the wall! As a source of creative tension and inspiration, they could scarcely have found anywhere better in the world to record and over the course of a few months they began to lay the foundations for their next album. Work was particularly slow and difficult at first as Bono and The Edge were trying to push the music into areas they had already explored on the *Clockwork Orange* score, leaving Adam and Larry initially at sea, Daniel Lanois having similar problems. Lanois was in fact working alone as producer on the album since Eno found himself booked onto other projects and had to settle for arriving at regular intervals for a week to try to stir things up, a very valuable exercise since he had the requisite distance to see through to the heart of the songs, an objectivity which the group and Lanois necessarily lacked.

Berlin was a potent metaphor for much of what U2 themselves were going through; a city in confusion, a city where everything was suddenly up for grabs, where there were no rules, where the past was being thrown away in the hope of winning a new future and yet a city where a feeling of alienation and of unreality remained through all the celebration. It was also no coincidence that *Achtung Baby* was the first U2 record with a roof over its head, a record that moved to an urban pulse rather than to the sound of the great outdoors. To further intensify the atmosphere, U2 checked into Hansa 'By The Wall' studio, the site where Bowie had made *Low* and *Heroes*, David Byrne and Iggy Pop also having made albums there. The studio proved to be another source of inspiration to the band and, having overcome those early teething troubles, they were able to compile some music to take back to Dublin with them when they decided to complete the album in Elsinore, a large house in Dalkey just outside the city. This was the site for much of the completion of the album, where Bono in particular was required to choose a lyrical path and build upon the musical direction they had already begun to engineer. The harder, more aggressive music was generally thrashed out in Berlin, where that industrial hard-core sound seemed very appropriate, while Dublin saw a more baroque edge being applied to some of the music, particularly the ornamentation on 'So Cruel'. Part of that grew out of their surroundings, which they described as being 'Twin Peaks' in atmosphere with plastic chandeliers, flock wallpaper and fake log fire.

The two locations of Dalkey and Berlin might seem light years apart and yet there were strong, almost surreal links. Berlin was of course in the midst of its transition from one political system to another, with West Berliners colliding with their eastern counterparts who were totally at sea with their new freedom, unsure of how to cope and live within this new responsibility that they had been given to choose their own way of life. The 1990s Berlin of chaos, optimism and rebirth stood in opposition to the decadent Berlin of the 1930s – the last time part of the city had had any real freedom – with its cabaret, its darkness under the rule of the Nazis and the Dadaist stance of mocking the devil. Coming from that situation to the odd house in Dalkey was not the culture shock that it might have been and as a consequence the record is a surreal escapade in some respects, filled with odd lyrical and musical juxtapositions that somehow make sense.

Postmodern pranksters is the way in which U2 have come to be seen since Zoo TV and they have seized that position as contemporary satirists with relish, in part a reaction to the rediscovery of their European heritage and their Irishness. John Waters spoke with Bono for his radio series *Wide Awake In Ireland* on the subject of Ireland in the 1990s. Culturally, Bono noted the importance of Ireland maintaining its individuality, implicitly indicating his realization that they had perhaps immersed themselves too thoroughly in the music of another land, America. 'People are very glad to be Irish in the 1990s. They feel the freedom that they have in a way they never did before. This idea of being akin to the blacks but not having the sign of colour because we can blur and just disappear into Englishness or being American very easily. It's even more alluring to lose yourself in another culture but I don't think we should, I really think we have something very valuable.'

Anger with the past and the growing nostalgia market fuelled some of the artistic fire too. Bono was to rail against the retrogressive nature of the musical world as an artistic extension of the poverty of any rigorous intellectual argument in a social or political context. In the rock industry so many bands currently arrive to be lauded to the skies simply because they are reminiscent of another band that were truly great and original years previously. How many Beatles, Zeppelin, U2, Smiths, Bowie, Joy Division imitators have we heard in the last few years? The paucity of artistic talent at present is undeniably depressing – what will there be to revive when the time comes for the 1990s revival? By the same token, the voracious appetite for the past continues at such a pace that soon we'll be nostalgic for next week, all a function of our terror of the future. Eno summed up the position of the artist in relation to the future, telling *Vox*, 'I think perhaps the most important job the artist can do is to say, "Look, the world's going to be confusing from now on and you can either be frightened by it or you can celebrate it in some way."' A celebration of the future was very much on U2's agenda and they made their statement by throwing out all the remaining vestiges of the U2 sound and starting from scratch, while the opening song on the album, 'Zoo Station', was in part a letting go of the past and an abandonment of the spirit to whatever the future might offer. They also dispensed with their previously largely Luddite response to technology and embraced it in full on both *Achtung Baby* and the Zoo TV tour.

The music did express a new approach to their trade and, inevitably, it suggested lyrical areas for Bono to explore, although he had already compiled various threads that built upon themes he had previously written about on the preceding records. This time, however, the music was darker with a steamy sexuality that had never before been a part of the mix, a direct result of their dabbling in the blues. The rhythm was the sex in the music and now U2 had probably the finest rhythm section in rock 'n' roll. If Edge and Bono had been the catalysts in moving towards the more abrasive side of the U2 muse, Adam and Larry were the rock-solid foundation on which that new edifice was built. Larry, in particular, could quite legitimately claim to imbue the music with the same feeling of controlled power and infinite variety that John Bonham had given Led Zeppelin in their heyday, while he and Adam had clearly been maintaining an interest in contemporary music, listening to the output from the Madchester scene, since the shuffle beat so beloved of the Stone Roses and the Happy Mondays was very noticeable on a number of songs. Adam was strikingly inventive in underpinning much of the music, contributing an impressive melody to 'Ultra Violet (Light My Way)' and a rumbling line that was the propulsion behind the baggy sound of 'Mysterious Ways', perhaps the most popular of the songs on the record.

After listening to the album a few times, there's no sense of the struggle that went into its construction, the whole thing almost seamless in its flow from one extreme to another, and yet it was a record that began in complete uncertainty. While they were absolutely certain of what they did not want to do, there were fewer ideas as to where the record should actually go. The final direction was inward, a celebration of their own hypocrisy, their own uncertainties and their own inadequacies. Adam later spoke of having to 'redress the balance and that meant we had to expose the doubts, failings and weaknesses.' The album had to be a naked exposition of who and what U2 were, not simply in the physical sense that Mr Clayton chose, but in the mental sense, too. Edge was later to admit that perhaps U2 had never quite been able to compile a music that expressed all the facets of their collective and individual personalities accurately and that this time they wanted to inject some humour as well as making the doubts all the more obvious – *Rattle and Hum* had clearly failed in that regard. The widescreen production of *The Joshua Tree*, for instance, had put a surface sheen on the music that tended to cover over the mental cracks apparent in songs like 'I Still Haven't Found What I'm Looking For', which somehow could still sound affirmative rather than the admission of restless doubt that it was. By switching from the panoramic David Lean style picture to the claustrophobic introspection of a David Lynch movie, the underlying emotions were given more room to breathe and reach out to the listener. With the demise of the anthem, the songs were able to become more intimate and personal.

The contradictions that the band wanted to tackle were many and varied, some of the demons especially dark and intimate. Just being in a big band like U2 gave rise to so many of its own paradoxes, paradoxes they had tried to ignore or play down yet which had ultimately overwhelmed them. Even then, it was the creative friction that these contradictions created that made so much of their catalogue a highly combustible concoction and they were finally able to realize that attempts at resolution were futile and, indeed, dangerous. U2 were staunchly anti-image, anti-video and yet their ascetic image, while not an accurate reflection of the four men, was used to sell their records – for a better, brighter more righteous world, use new formula *Joshua Tree*. While they liked to pretend that all the hype and heavy marketing wasn't happening, it was going on all around them to the point at which it became almost as important as the music itself in winning the band a bigger audience. On the same tack, as people they were upset by the constant mention of the money they were making, but they did little to take the sting out of the marketing attack. They were a 'band with a conscience' that did more than they needed to for a number of causes and yet they benefited from Live Aid as much as anyone did, a painful truth, but a truth none the less. They had suffered from the argument that big meant bland, in part sympathizing with it despite the fact that it isn't always true, yet they had wanted success from the very start and had wanted the opportunities it gave. Their attitude to social justice was broadly in line with a socialist approach and yet their organization and their business dealings with Island had been ruthless to the point where they had won back all their own publishing rights and had shares in Island prior to its sale to Polygram, and were in fact a perfect example of how well a capitalist system can operate. They were idealists working with what was traditionally a nihilistic medium, making the most intimate music on the most enormous stage with the biggest sound system. They were followers of the punk ethic of 'no more heroes' and yet they were isolated from their audience to the extent that they had become totally unapproachable. Most worrying of all, as a band who preached the idea of love and of a certain level of morality, there were hints that their own performance in that field might not bear the closest scrutiny, that they too might have been unable to engage their higher side and remain faithful to their ideals.

In that context, 'Acrobat' is a pivotal song, touching as it does on the idea of betrayal dealing in moral ambiguities and also being, in a sense, autobiographical of U2 as a group. When Bono sings of talking one way and acting another, it's an admission of hypocrisy that strikes a nerve within many listeners who might put forward their own high-minded ideals whilst, far from the madding crowd, acting far less impressively. The contradiction of words and deeds *may* relate to Bono's own public image as the new rock Messiah with a private life that might be rather less than clean or it may well touch on the relationship that forms the heart of this canon of songs, but there is less ambiguity in lines that ask, in a barely audible mumble, what else is there to be said and where are the new ideas coming from. This is a scenario which conjures up visions of U2, in the early weeks at Hansa, attempting to get to grips with a new style of music and wondering if perhaps the well of inspiration had run dry. Having overcome those doubts, 'Acrobat' also censures those who had put U2 on a pedestal, asking them to have faith in themselves and their own abilities rather than placing the weight of the world on the shoulders of a pampered rock star, Edge's blood-curdling guitar scream indicating his distaste for the role. This idea had moved a stage further by the time of Zoo TV, when, during 'Desire', Bono would tell the audience, 'I believe in you! I believe for you!' as though U2 had taken over responsibility for holding the belief system of their audience together, enabling them to go away and enjoy themselves without having to worry about any questions of morality: 'What do you mean I'm in the wrong? I can't be, I'm a U2 fan, I believe in Bono!'

For all the mood of disenchantment in which the song wallows, with U2 fighting against those who would beat them down, indulging in some particularly vicious oral sex, finding themselves unable to believe in any kind of organized movement, 'Acrobat' does contain the only real shaft of optimism on the album. Having asked for new dreams on 'In God's Country', they are now asking that we should actually articulate our dreams in order to make them real, a favourite phrase of Bono's which he had earlier applied to Midnight Oil's front man Peter Garrett, a doughty supporter of environmental groups and a prospective politician in his native Australia. Accepting that with the granting of one's dreams, be they personal or pro- fessional, comes a share of responsibilities that while perhaps unwanted cannot be ignored, Bono seems to gain strength within himself, dedicating himself to love again as some strain of optimism suggests that things will get better once more.

'Acrobat' was the most comprehensive look at the paradox of rock 'n' roll stardom and all those contradictions formed a part of the new creative landscape and became integral parts of the live show, but generally it was personal relationships that were at the core of *Achtung Baby*. The roots of that new method had already been sent down as the band dealt with the intimate rather than the global – while it would be true to say that 'Bullet The Blue Sky' or 'Sunday Bloody Sunday' were songs that detailed the impact on individuals of certain political situations, they were essentially 'polit- ical' rather than 'personal' songs. As Bono, in particular, travelled further down the road of the twisted love song, they were able to write the most universally political songs of all without having to resort to the social specific – Bono noting, 'You can say a lot about what's going on in the world by writing about how two people tear at each other.' There were times on *Achtung Baby* when he sounded like a world-weary war correspondent reporting for CNN from battlefields where scenes of emotional carnage surrounded him. More than anything else, the themes that categorized *Achtung Baby* were betrayal, morality, spirituality, sexuality and confusion – optimism was largely conspicuous by its absence. The record struck at the very heart of modernity and the modern conundrums where, in these days of treachery, the refusal to betray your partner or friends had become the ultimate betrayal – we are now so attuned to being disappointed and disillusioned that we find sincerity and fidelity concepts that are too huge, too quixotic to deal with.

How much of this emotional turmoil was self-inflicted and how much the result of circumstances is open to conjecture. Edge's marriage had broken down, although Bono was quick to explain that the story of *Achtung Baby* was not simply the story of The Edge but the story of everyone around him, all of whom were going through similar emotional crises, leaving the implication that it was his own story too. 'In the 1990s, people are confused about sex and love. The idea of two people giving themselves to each other is one of the most mad ideas but it's a *grand* madness. As self-indulgent as we can be, a lot of us are going through that. A lot of us are trying to figure that out,' admitted Bono. Yet there remains the suspicion that too many artists are only too willing to destroy themselves, to push themselves out on to a limb or to place themselves in the firing line in order to gain raw material. If every artist actually is a cannibal, as 'The Fly' proposed, then the emotions of those around them are little more than fast food, giving the artist the chance to put his suffering into song and turn it into cash – another contradiction.

Whoever's story this was, U2 were to be commended for laying themselves so open. Much of the music was about betrayal, about temptation and falling prey to it and the impression created was of artists who actually were taking the big risks, not in the commercial sense but essentially in their own homes. While *Achtung Baby* is basically this year's model from U2 just as *Dracula* is this year's Coppola and there need be no greater autobiographical experience than that on the album, U2's track record suggests that they are commenting broadly from personal experience. The admissions of guilt that lie within these songs might well have left the band members open to accusations from those nearest to them. Bono was noncommittal in a long and slightly confused interview with *RCD*, saying, 'In every life, but especially in the life of an artist, there comes a moment when you can no longer allow yourself to be led by your feelings and you have to face up to the facts. Not just in what you do for a living, but also in your private life. Anyone who balances on the edge of an abyss and looks down sees a bottomless pit. Knowing that and daring to look it in the eye gives you courage. You know what the risks are. You can then turn your back on the abyss and try to find protection in your air-conditioned nightmare.'

Although the suggestion is that the infidelities and temptations detailed on the album came from his imagination – and let's remember that he is paid handsomely because of the quality of that imagination – rather than direct experience, it was nonetheless a very rickety limb to go out on in the face of the inevitable questions that would follow the release of a record of such dark sentiment. Never before had U2, especially Bono, so thoroughly stripped themselves of any emotional armour and allowed themselves to stand bare not only before their audience but before those closest to them. To expose their own hypocrisies, both personal and professional, they had been forced to make themselves vulnerable. In achieving that, they succeeded in no small measure in deconstructing the U2 myth and painting themselves as very human men once more, with all the inadequacies that implies.

Male inadequacy, especially within the changing face of culture and commerce, was one of the focal points of the album, most clearly articulated in the one chink of light 'Tryin' To Throw Your Arms Around The World', where the well-worn feminist line of a woman needing a man as desperately as a fish needs a bicycle is trotted out for hopefully its last outing. That line in the heart of a song that was going elsewhere betrayed one of the potential album titles, *Fear of Female*, something that was very much on their minds as they were writing the record. The truth in that joke is something that has sliced through so many relationships in recent years as the 'balance of power' between men and women moves towards a greater equilibrium, a development which many men, and perhaps almost as many women, find not a little bewildering.

Furthermore, sex, formerly the final consummation of a grand passion between two people, has now become another leaf in the book of Saatchi and Saatchi and the other advertising agencies as titillation has become their new major sales weapon – supermodels to sell ordinary new cars, bronzed hunks to sell jeans that have been a staple of everyone's wardrobe for decades anyway. Clearly everyone today keeps their purchasing power in their underwear and yet it is the adverts on TV or in magazines that say more about the world and are consequently more interesting than the features or programmes which they surround. The surface has overwhelmed the substance and it was within that climate that much of *Achtung Baby* was created.

Achtung Baby is that rarity in today's culture, a shiny, shiny surface that hides something far more interesting and absorbing below. It is a formidable monument to the modern age and modern thinking which has somehow been built against all odds on the shifting sands of early 1990s ephemera. A song like 'Even Better Than The Real Thing' says plenty about the relationship between the superficial and the supercharged with the first dubious puns (the whole album contains enough double entendres to keep the 'Carry On' team gainfully employed for another five years) and a lyric that is almost entirely couched in ad-speak, yet which still communicates impressions of the blurring of the lines between spiritual and sexual gratification, asking questions about which is more important, whether they can be mutually exclusive or inclusive.

The song again comes down to the final concept of love as the last chance for spiritual fulfilment. In the face of all the logical arguments that suggest that men and women should no longer attempt to live together in long-term relationships, for they are certainly doomed to failure, there is the acceptance that relationships begin with both parties acting completely irrationally as they fall in love. 'Love Is Blindness', the downbeat closer which leaves a bitter taste in the mouth returns to terrain mapped out on *The Joshua Tree*, love as an emotion that is self-defeating and which can tear you apart, blinding you to the potential threats in your lover as you are immersed within it. Love, and by implication marriage, is seen here as a lethal idea: love and relationships have been rendered unworkable by modern experience and yet isn't the passion of being in love sufficient to make it worth trying? There is a howling, anguished guitar figure in the song that suggests otherwise, the pain outweighing the pleasure and the potential rewards, the most desolate ending to any U2 record.

The woman who was the central figure on *The Joshua Tree* is also well-represented on *Achtung Baby*, but here the violence of love has been partially translated into the violence of sex, with 'Who's Gonna Ride Your Wild Horses' opening like an S & M dream/nightmare sequence, before treading yet darker emotional waters with the idea that we are often attracted to those who would inflict the most pain on us. Even at the end of a relationship that has gone sour, it's hard to cut loose, which reinforces the very fine distinction between love and hate as there's certainly no reason to hate something about which you're apathetic but plenty of motivation when you've been dumped. Hatred is best reserved as vengeance for love gone wrong, but to twist the knife there has to be further contact so maybe they can remain friends.

That parting is such sweet sorrow is borne out by 'So Cruel', a kind of Roy Orbison tribute that apparently came together in about fifteen minutes. It wallows in self-pity, returning us to 'Fear Of Female' territory once more as Bono tries to make some sense of the contrary nature of this woman to whom he gave everything she wanted, only to find that she didn't really want it anyway. There are elements of him mourning the passing of the 'kept woman' idea and struggling vainly to cope with her new lust for independence as his lust for her battles with his higher mind for supremacy. The nastiness of 'Wild Horses' is also a part of 'So Cruel' as he hangs on to watch her demise, but once again there's a suggestion at the end of the piece that he has so thoroughly lost himself within her, be it sexually or spiritually, that life without her is an impossibility, for though he admits that remaining with her would be foolish, even dangerous, what else is there to do? The idea of the fatal attraction to one who can bring nothing but harm isn't a new idea by any means, but it's given a new lease of life here simply because Bono is presenting the song in his new persona of the rock 'n' roll star, the man who traditionally has all the answers and every possibility for gratification open to him. The idea that that might not be enough is almost shocking in itself but that such a figurehead of modern day hedonism should be so trapped by a woman turns the whole theory of the rock lifestyle on its head.

Bono as rock star was a central part of the lyrical mix on *Achtung Baby*, an alter-ego that allowed him the freedom to go beyond his traditional lyrical boundaries into something far more sinister. 'The Fly' was the theme tune for this particular psychotic and never had U2 sounded so malevolent, laying to rest once and for all the choir-boy image that had dogged them for so long. As a list of aphorisms, it was an interesting artistic device that had been inspired by Jenny Holzer, an artist who put such maxims onto billboards. What stopped it becoming a simple indulgence was the manic performance of the song that Bono described as being like a phone call from hell, a place to which the Fly had grown rather accustomed. The industrial wail of the guitar, a degree of savagery that called to mind the Jesus and Mary Chain, allied to the flailing rhythm section created a claustrophobic, subterranean environment into which Bono's evil vocal was allowed to burn.

If there was any blatant admission of the Fly's inability to walk the marital straight and narrow in the face of temptation, this was it. Among his truisms was the painfully honest admission that having a conscience could be something of a pest in the face of the possible carnal free-for-all that might stretch out before him, though whether the fact that the call was made from hell was an attempt to point out the consequences of immoral actions is less than clear. Maybe for people who enjoy indulging themselves hell is the place to be, away from the angels playing their harps and singing dreary hymns all day. The Fly was all evil to all people, a cheat, a liar, ambitious to the point of psychosis, lustful, unable to remain faithful, in fact a guy pretty much like any other, which was the real triumph of Bono's creation – a living embodiment of the dark underbelly that lies within every man. 'The Fly' itself seemed to be a full-scale battle with a conscience, a fight between good and evil as indicated by the use of a double voice during the chorus, identified as a gospel voice and a 'low voice'. As elsewhere, the vicious guy seems to be having the most fun, but at the end of it there is generally a price to pay, a moralistic view which gives surprisingly little comfort.

Although 'The Fly' only hints at betrayal, a number of songs are very obvious in their treatment of that state. 'Until The End Of The World' leaves the conventional love song behind for a few moments to delve into the greatest betrayal in history, that of Judas towards Jesus in the Garden of Gethsemane. The whole piece is an uncomfortable mixture of joy and regret, which is the way in which the whole episode has to be viewed since, although Judas (who is played here by Bono, switching roles for a change!) perpetrated the most reviled act in the history of mankind, betraying the son of God, the son of Man to his executioners, by that very action he introduced the world to Grace and enabled Christ to complete his mission on earth. Without Judas's actions the crucifixion, the resurrection and the ascension, the very focal point of Christianity, would not have taken place in the way in which they did. The relationship between the two throws up so many conflicting ideas and theories. Why did Judas do it? Was he disillusioned with Christ? Was it for the money? Did he want to push him into taking up arms against those that would oppose him? Why did Christ choose Judas as a disciple? Did he know far in advance that he would be betrayed and by whom? Why was it allowed to happen? The story sets up a fascinating range of possibilities for any writer, but it is the betrayal itself that is addressed on this album that deals in the currency of treachery. The mixing of the spiritual and the profane on the album as a whole is the most subtly impressive yet on any U2 recording and it's fair to say that 'Until The End Of The World' could be treated as another malicious failed relationship song, particularly in the light of the final verse where there are several references to oral gratification that it would be hard to interpret in any other manner. Whether that final verse refers to a situation more personal than the subject matter of the rest of the song is impossible to say but it is still an impressive merging of the religious experience in faith and the religious experience that may arise through sexual abandonment.

British journalist Malcolm Muggeridge wrote that 'the orgasm has replaced the Cross as the focus of longing and the image of fulfilment.' U2's 'Mysterious Ways' equates women and the sexual experience with God and spirituality, since God and the object of the singer's desire both move in mysterious ways their wonders to perform. Where elsewhere the musical accompaniment was ferocious and caustic with a rhythm section of exaggerated power and fire backing lead guitar work that is startlingly expressive and original even by The Edge's lofty standards, 'Mysterious Ways' lollops in on a rumbling bass and a fat guitar lick that reminds everyone that Sly Stone was on the communal turntable just as regularly as T. Rex and My Bloody Valentine. Again Bono is on his knees, though whether in supplication to this incredible creature who fills his every waking hour or in the performance of some other act is open to debate. (Certainly on this album the references to sexual positions go by so thick and fast that at times it sounds like a Madonna record.) With 'Mysterious Ways', as the stage performance made clear, Bono is back once more in pursuit of the unattainable, the belly dancer who graces Zoo TV always just tantalizingly swaying away from his desperate clutches. It's the most simple straightforward expression of lust that Bono allows himself on *Achtung Baby*, but before he gets too carried away with his passions he is racked with doubts and his innate fear of women which is the central recurrent theme of the album. Now the conflict is not between lustful desires and the concept of fidelity but between his sex drive and his fear of commitment and rejection. Eventually the song lurches towards a celebration of his lover but, like every other song on the record, the peaks and troughs of an emotional rollercoaster are explored before there can be any solution. Transcendence is still his goal and there is within 'Mysterious Ways' much of that complete loss of control that characterized pieces like 'Spanish Eyes' and 'Desire', Bono finally confessing that the spirit is moved as powerfully as the flesh by the object of his desire in the kind of quasi-religious ecstasy that figured so boldly in Byrne and Eno's 'My Life In The Bush Of Ghosts'.

That kind of sublime experience gone horribly wrong was the subject matter in 'Ultra Violet (Light My Way)', which, with its melodramatic opening, intimated an almost suicidal depression as a once vibrant relationship had hit the skids. Where his partner had been the source of his strength and his will to live, where her love was the only thing that had given meaning to his life, she was now nothing but the source of his failures as they are stuck within a relationship where neither is content but from which neither is resolute enough to escape. When Bono sings of her love being like a well-travelled secret, his message is strikingly clear and yet, as so often on this album, he is too weak to walk out since his very existence is seemingly wrapped up in being around her. The most malevolent line on the record, and one which neatly encapsulates the whole mood, comes in discussing the cost of love. Reconciled to the pleasure in the pain, the song's subtitle, 'Light My Way', sums up his all-consuming need for her and for a sexual and spiritual passion for its own sake as a staging post on the road to final fulfilment.

As the record concerns itself with the side roads that offer temptation away from the straight and narrow, solutions are one of the things to which *Achtung Baby* does not address itself, the chill wind of irreconcilable difference permeating its every contour, but nowhere is there greater bitterness than on 'One', a song that has become something of a misappropriated anthem of unity which was used in the aftermath of the LA riots. Apparently written as a conversation between a man dying of AIDS and his father who has clearly disapproved of his lifestyle and cannot bring himself to forgive, it can again be treated as an acid love song. The verses drip with the language of reprisal, a vocabulary carefully selected to inflict the deepest wounds. Seen in that light, it's a depressingly accurate vision of the need to blame someone, the way in which we continually seek to hurt those closest to us as badly as we can in order to gain power over them by causing them to feel badly about themselves and their actions.

The album crests on the beautifully angry line about playing Jesus '*to the lepers in your head*', a lyric quite breathtaking in its brutality, one which is filled with bile and yet indicates a deeper love that abides in spite of itself, for a phrase like that could never be wasted on one for whom you feel only contempt. The son gets the opportunity to vent all his frustration and anger at his own plight, allowing years of suppressed grievances to come tumbling out in a venomous attack on his father, who, despite his own ingrained prejudices, is trying to make peace.

In the context of 'One', however, the position of the dying man is used as a metaphor for the wider problem of AIDS across the globe and the impotence of governments everywhere to commit resources to the search for a cure, to institute effective public education schemes and to provide satisfactory care for those who are suffering from the illness. On its release as a single, the proceeds from 'One' were donated to AIDS charities, the sleeve featuring striking photography by David Wojnarowicz, an American artist himself infected with the HIV virus. The picture was of the buffalo being hounded to their deaths by Indians who ran them off the edge of cliffs, a compelling allegory of the way in which gay people are being pushed back into emotional ghettos by the crisis which surrounds AIDS, where we are again reaching a point in time when to admit to homosexuality might become injurious to one's health at the hands of the mob, a return to the Dark Ages that might appeal to certain leaders for whom the blanket adoption of a code of pat moral fundamentalism precludes the need to come to a reasoned, balanced view on any issue.

The prime motivation behind 'One' was love as the highest, most sacred force but not in the drippy hippy sense of everyone being the same under the skin, which is clearly ridiculous. We all have highly idiosyncratic needs, desires, hopes and fears and until that is accepted as the basis for advancement rather than the unworkably simplistic hope that we will all be able to accept conditions that are identical to all the rest of mankind without wanting to improve our lot at the expense of others, progress towards a greater understanding of humanity is impossible. That we should experience as wide a range of emotions and conditions as we can was also a component of 'One', Bono regularly noting that it was not coincidental that Christ was born in the straw, in virtual poverty rather than the lap of luxury. As 'Zoo Station' noted, U2 were now on their hands and knees deep in filth, since within the trash and the grime can often be found true inspiration, while without going through personal trials materially and spiritually there can be no appreciation of the higher ground.

In all, *Achtung Baby* was, especially in the light of its very uncertain beginnings, a tremendous achievement that called for a complete reappraisal of U2 and their ideals. Unfortunately for a band of their vintage with such an enormous following behind them, such considered reappraisal is difficult to achieve in the midst of the ballyhoo that surrounds another 'momentous' release. U2 had already learned that simply changing their musical tune would not be enough to free themselves from the shackles of their past, although crucially they were now sufficiently relaxed as individuals, as a band, and with their achievements that they had far less interest in what others, particularly the press, might think of them anyway. Prior to working on *Achtung Baby*, U2 had recorded a version of Cole Porter's 'Night and Day' for the 'Red Hot & Blue' AIDS benefit project. The treatment was as far removed from the traditional U2 sound as anything to be found on the album, with its thumping rhythm and a sheet of glacial guitar from Edge that was deliberately removed from anything on *The Joshua Tree* or *Rattle and Hum*, yet it was barely noted as any kind of departure since the video that accompanied it was quintessential U2, Bono emoting passionately to the camera as the others stood by. Clearly, more than a musical overhaul was required and when the time came to release *Achtung Baby*, Paul McGuinness cleverly refused to allow the band to do any interviews to promote it, simply allowing the music to sell itself. Or at least sell itself in conjunction with a large-scale advertising campaign featuring the Trabant car that had become a symbol of the new U2.

That the Trabant should come to be the central image of the new U2 rather than the somewhat portentous symbolism of the past indicated just how far they were trying to distance themselves from the past in terms of vocabulary if not sentiment. The Trabant was the car of East Germany, a box-like affair that had engine power similar to that of a sewing machine. Adam laughingly termed it the Eastern bloc equivalent of the Cadillac, their rock 'n' roll car, but it was representative of the surreal nature of their stay in Berlin during liberation. Each morning on their way into Hansa, they'd find more and more Trabants abandoned by the side of the road. East Germans were making their way to Berlin as the nearest 'Western' city, but unfortunately the cars couldn't make it so they were left burnt out by the side of the road as their owners tried to buy Volkswagens instead. Photographer Anton Corbijn picked up on them as being a very playful sort of image, ideal for the new U2 ethic and reminiscent of their roots as a playful, mischievous band in their early days in Dublin. In addition, the Trabant was a reminder of the fall of the East and of the 'new world order' under which we supposedly lived. Later, when the Trabants were used as a light source during the Zoo

TV shows, they became a source of heavy irony as these antiquated vehicles played host to the latest up to the minute technology.

Although press interviews were frowned upon, Bono only occasionally breaking cover to talk to local radio for instance, there was no shortage of U2 activity, based around the virtual relaunching of the group into the 'alternative' sector of the market. The scatter-shot album sleeve was one move away from the classical designs of the past, but it was with video that the most obvious breakaway from previous imagery was made. U2 had spent the majority of their career making fairly unarresting video statements, blatantly viewing the form as simply a marketing tool in which they had no real interest, but *Achtung Baby* saw the visual medium take on almost as much importance as the music, if only to show how absurd rock 'n' roll actually was. Bono admitted that a sea change had taken place, saying, 'I'm not trying to make comparisons, but Dali and Warhol, if they had a chance to play with the technology that is now available, they'd go for it.' The first video, *The Fly*, featured the high-velocity buzzwords that were to characterize the live show and the new look U2 that traded heavily in glam-rock trash fashion allied to the first appearance of Bono's fly goggles. Subsequent promos included footage of buffalo chased across the plains to echo the sleeve concept used on 'One'; U2 appeared in drag, looking in some cases surprisingly at home; 'Even Better Than The Real Thing' featured state of the art video techniques to dizzying effect and 'Who's Gonna Ride Your Wild Horses' was an effective combination of the old and the new of U2, cutting between Bono putting everything into a studio performance and flashes from the live show. Video technology was all part of the new language U2 chose to use, but the final link in the chain came when they went back on the road with Zoo TV, an experience that changed the face of rock 'n' roll touring.

chapter twelve

EVERYTHING YOU KNOW IS WRONG

It was by no means certain that U2 would find themselves back on the road in support of *Achtung Baby*, in no small part an indication of just how much 'The Joshua Tree' tour had taken out of them as well as of their desire to move on and do new things. Tying themselves to what would inevitably be another two years of live work was not an obligation entered into lightly, but by the time they had completed work on the album and had been able to develop a new identity for themselves, they were ready to go again. The important thing was to maintain the spirit of the record in live performance, something easier said than done when dealing with music that was simultaneously darkly intense and mischievously playful. Sensibly, they had made no live commitments until the record was completed, avoiding the unsightly dash to complete the recording on time to meet other obligations that had caused artistic chaos on so many of their previous albums. Now having financial security for life, they no longer had to do anything they didn't want and were exercising that particular privilege for the first time. Eventually the decision was made to visit America in March with Europe to follow, doing a series of one-nighters in indoor arenas everywhere, a financially unrewarding move since the cost of transporting their show was enormous and ticket receipts insufficient to cover those costs. An outdoor version of the shows was tentatively scheduled for America in the latter part of the year, with Europe to follow in 1993, a venture that would more than recoup any losses.

Like U2 on record, Zoo TV was about the carnal rather than denial and so the stage set that had been so clean and uncluttered during 'The Joshua Tree' and Love Town tours now resembled the interior of a TV station. The stage was lit by Trabants flown above the stage with lights enclosed, there were TV screens around the stage that threw out subliminal aphorisms of the kind that had been used in 'The Fly' at a speed which made it impossible to take the whole thing in, leading to a kind of Chinese whisper where everyone in the auditorium had a different interpretation of what had been said, a visual equivalent of the cut-up approach to literature that William Burroughs had used so successfully. Presumably it's also a satirical poke at the Nintendo generation with its sixty-second attention span and a world where we now all do three things at once almost all the time.

The video screens were also used to blow the band's movements up to stadium size but, instead of using the staid, frankly rather dull video screens at the side of the stage, U2 made the screens part of the set, with Bono himself providing much of the footage, planting kisses on to one camera, using a camcorder to illustrate the healthy state of his dental work or the contours of his crotch. Additionally, Zoo TV had installed its own satellite allowing the band to steal pictures from whatever was in the air at the time, be it CNN, MTV, the Home Shopping Network, Sky TV or a sports channel, a kind of video-based human sampling that had its roots in the audio sampling that has become such a fundamental part of the current music scene. Last, but by no means least, from the TV screens were some specially shot sequences to highlight whichever song was being played – burning crosses making a powerful statement during 'Bullet The Blue Sky', for instance, or some 'digitally enhanced' footage of George Bush leading the crowd through Queen's 'We Will Rock You'. The whole thing was a mind-boggling concoction of leading-edge technology which dwarfed the four figures from Dublin who people had initially paid their money to go and see.

That reduction of the band to bit players in their own show may well have been a deliberate ploy to reinforce the oft-repeated complaint that the music is far more important than the musician. Here they were, virtually invisible for chunks of the concert, the show being kept afloat by the music and the video accompaniment. At other times Bono was egomania incarnate, simply deciding that if everyone already thought that U2 were puffed up with their own importance, they might as well enjoy it. On that level, Zoo TV was a hedonist's paradise, superficiality run riot and yet there have been few live shows, if any, that have been as intellectually provocative as this, a deliberate attempt by U2 to circumnavigate what can be a fairly hollow experience when at the back of an enormous football stadium. Where the inevitably ecstatic Pavlovian reaction to tiny figures on a stage in the far distance has been enough to prevent most rock bands investing any further thought in big-stadium staging than those video screens, U2 decided to challenge every last member of the audience from front to back, the logical conclusion of their desire to communicate that has fired the group almost from day one.

Zoo TV was an experience that grew out of a number of events, paramount among which was the Gulf War coverage on TV where the band found themselves joining the rest of the world watching people's lives being blown to pieces, death all around them and then, when it got a bit boring, switching to MTV or to watch the adverts – channel-hopping through the war, a voluble explanation of a world where the greatest disability that one could have is the loss of one's index finger, making it impossible to operate the remote control on one's TV set. The enormity of TV technology and its unparalleled global influence became the theme of much of Zoo TV, returning back to Lennon's line 'Gimme Some Truth'. How much of what we see on TV news is actually fact, how much of it fiction? In a world where politicians allegedly got a great deal of their information on the progress of the Gulf War from CNN, the director of those pictures – a TV director – becomes the most important and influential man in the world. Where is the real dividing line between truth and information in the environment of global data-overload? Marshall McLuhan's vision of a world where 'the medium is the message' appears more prophetic by the day.

That TV does create a 'global village', another of McLuhan's phrases, is echoed in the central cultural battle at present which seems to be between commerce and art, as the business wallet seems intent on buying up all the rock 'n' rollers, the painters, the writers to suck the venom out of them by rendering them impotent. U2 had decided to take that on with a live show that employed technology at its most extreme but under the control of people, indicating that you don't have to submit to those who would control you – as the video screens say, 'outsmart the ones without heart' or, as Brendan Kennelly put it in *The Book Of Judas*, 'The best way to serve the age is to betray it.' And do it 'Till someone senses things ain't as they should be.'

In that sense, U2 have thrown away their placards since everyone has become prepared for that assault and the powers that be are ready for them. By taking on wit and irony as weapons, nothing that they do seems serious, nothing seems to be a threat and that is where the real danger lies. If in the past people filed out of a U2 show with

Bono's condemnation of apartheid ringing in their ears, it may have been a thought that remained with them for a couple of hours, days, even weeks, but all it was was a repetition of a pat statement made by a rock star. In Zoo TV, Bono fought shy of any kind of 'political' speeches on stage – although Martin Luther King was allowed to speak for himself during 'Pride (In The Name Of Love)' – yet the whole show was far more politically inspired than anything U2 had ever done before since it forced people to think for themselves. Zoo TV provided the clues but it didn't give any answers as simple as 'join Amnesty.' The audience had to provide their own answers by racking their own brains to even work out what the questions initially were! Unlike pretty well any other rock show around, the current U2 live experience forces an intellectual response without sacrificing any of the mystery, lunacy, excitement and superficiality of great rock 'n' roll.

Perhaps the overwhelming image of Zoo TV is its vindictive exposure of the failures of the twentieth century, that the media, TV, satellites and all the rest that were supposed to supplant religion as the opium of the masses, that were supposed to fill the holes in your soul, have been a tragic failure which has left people empty and desperately searching for new answers. The media itself, especially the great god television, has become the ultimate betrayal, using the heavens above to beam real-time entertainment to us all feeding us with unwatchable, trite junk that we are hooked on. One of U2's support acts for their American tour were the Disposable Heroes of Hiphoprisy. Their single 'Television, The Drug Of The Nation', an intense diatribe that sticks a knife into the chest of the mindless white media, charges TV with controlling the population, hundreds of channels with nothing worth watching, a language of surface with no substance, a land where the experience is supposed to be even better than the real thing – telephone sex, adverts that give greater satisfaction than the products, flight simulators that are like the real thing (Gulf War pilots came back from bombing missions only to say that the experience was 'very realistic'), video games where you can blast the crap out of an infinite variety of enemies, a veritable pleasure dome of sensory excitement where you need never leave the comfort of your own home or invade the dormant space between your ears.

TV is a powerful medium and one which can have beneficial aspects. Who can deny that they have learned many things from TV shows over the years? The difficulty comes with indiscriminate viewing and the tendency to take everything at face value since t's so much easier than asking questions. The undercurrent to the show is that we take TV as gospel, indeed we use it to replace the Gospels, and that that is a very dangerous concept since it is tantamount to handing over your mind to those that control the TV stations and the newspapers. It's no coincidence over recent years, when the game of greed has become increasingly cut-throat, that the media has become the real battleground. In the UK, Rupert Murdoch owns a number of newspaper titles as well as a large chunk of British Sky Broadcasting, while in the US, Ted Turner owns CNN, probably the world's most powerful news network. These are men who know their way round a balance sheet and for whom the bottom line, the profit potential is all – firstly they must ensure they achieve high ratings or circulation by playing to the lowest common denominator, trivializing stories or ensuring that the most 'newsworthy' pictures are transmitted, even if they do not tell the full truth of any story. More threatening than that, however, is the simple fact that they are businessmen for whom capitalism is a way of life, a creed, a compulsion. It is little wonder that men as powerful as this give short shrift to any politician or leader who wishes to put forward any economic arguments against 'the market'. The case for socialism, whether one agrees with it or not, is something that should be argued in a democracy. That this debate can now only take place within TV studios, studios necessarily owned by capitalists, ensures that there is a very heavy bias against any dissenting view.

It probably had to be an Irish band that best illustrated the media danger since Ireland is a country less monopolized by TV and newspapers, indeed Ireland is one of the few countries in the West that is actually beginning to find its feet in the midst of this rapidly changing world. As Europe moves cumbersomely towards federalization, Ireland seems to have found itself within the possibilities of Europe, despite its own internal difficulties, since it has freed the people from the shadow of Britain next door. Ireland is now an important part of a great world power, not just a former colony. It's a nation which has revitalized its own electoral procedure, throwing off the yoke of the two-party state and the tired old arguments that brings and introducing fresh blood as the Labour Party under Dick Spring has doubled its representation in the Dáil, taking 33 seats in the November 1992 elections. Admittedly Ireland has a rich history of socialist activity to fall back on since socialism was a part of the nationalist dream prior to independence, socialism subsequently falling from favour as the nationalist aspiration has been tainted with the blood from the terrorist's bombs. The streak of mischievous independence that causes the nation to fly in the face of the perceived international wisdom is the source of its artistic achievement, its artists at present being among the most important voices of dissent within the world of popular culture. The modern Ireland is, as John Waters put it, 'Yeats and Sinead O'Connor.'

Irishmen and women come from a land that has not succumbed to industry and materialism as blindly or foolishly as much of the rest of Europe and a land that still retains a spiritual awareness even within a deeply flawed church and, as such they are outsiders, detached from so many Western cultures which have imperialistic histories and feel themselves to be in some way superior. Ireland never has been the top dog but it has been badly treated by the British and it has maintained a discreet observation of the foibles of the rest of the world. Consequently, it has seen the pollution that lies within the mainstream and has no wish to join that river. The future may see Ireland as a source of many of the most important ideas on how life should be lived rather than how profit can be maximized. Ireland, if it can overcome its own lack of self-confidence, may yet be one of the most important players in the next century. Eoin Harris, a force behind Mary Robinson's campaign for the Presidency, suggested that 'we should give up the experiment of trying to be an industrialized country ... Irish people are very prepared physically for a civilized society which has not broken out of the womb of the present mode of production. The world hasn't caught up with Irish people's readiness to live a good life.' Waters agrees, adding that what Ireland faces 'is not a dilemma, but an embarrasment of riches'.

In its own confusion about its past and its future, Ireland can be seen as a breeding ground for the ideas at work on Zoo TV. Bono admits, 'U2 really is mixed up and in a way that's where Ireland is. I think that's probably the most interesting aspect of U2 sociologically speaking, it's kind of the way it is, that there is no pure Irishness any more and there shouldn't be. It has to be allowed to mutate and crossbreed and what you get is a new kind of Irishness that comes out of it. The old idea of Ireland is that we're an aberration in it, we don't really make sense but in the new Ireland we make perfect sense.' That sense of chaos and of development towards a goal which no one can quite locate is another aspect of the live show, though the condemnation of the indiscriminate TV-watching fast-food society is very clear in Zoo TV, even if the band are forcing themselves to reject the cheap thrills which are undeniably appealing for a short space of time. The live experience is very much of the next century in its technology but, more importantly, in its intellectual experimentation, the attempt to work out the conflicting impulses that we are subject to within modern life. At the end of the century, Ireland is the crucible of modernity in that it comprises both the First and Third Worlds, Waters noting: 'that tension is an enduring theme of the music of U2.' Ireland has a folk memory which dates back to the potato famine of the last century and which ties it inextricably to the disasters of Somalia and Ethiopia and yet it is also an extraordinarily literate society with more than its fair share of great artists and thinkers. U2 have taken elements of both – the frailty and humanity of the Third World, people who still understand the value of the spirit, of faith and of the unknown – and allied it to their own talent and to the glorious imaginations of those who they work with to create an enormous culture clash, contradictions which, in the friction they create, point a way forward.

John Waters has noted that 'U2 are Irish by birth but also by their essence. They pinpoint a way of connecting Ireland with the wider world which they have conquered,' a perceptive analysis which may allow those who form Irish opinion to get things right, although it's a responsibility that U2 would probably be slow to accept. Even so, Bono has strong thoughts on the matter: 'I'm really wary of people putting too much importance on the past. You go to America and you get these really awful Irish people and they use all the old terms and they talk to you in such clichés about an Ireland that just doesn't exist, it's an Ireland of the imagination that's way out of date. And we're not quite sure what the new Ireland is, but there's certain things we don't want in it.' One thing that they don't want is a church that outlaws contraception and therefore prevents its people using condoms in the midst of the AIDS epidemic – U2 sold *Achtung Baby* condoms at their shows with all proceeds going to AIDS research. In a sense, the way in which U2 conduct themselves at present is one huge, vituperative two-fingered gesture towards the Catholic Church and the sexual uptightness that it promotes so strongly in Irish life with its negative attitude towards human sexuality.

Hackneyed stereotypes and backward-looking thinkers are in-gredients best left out, as is the overdependence on the media that disfigures much of the rest of the world. Our respect for the media has reached extreme and extremely frightening proportions to the point where we are willing to place a childlike trust in what we see dished up on our TV screens. Zoo TV was an attempt to illustrate the enormity of our respect for the media, to show how much we rely on it and believe in it and then to strip away and expose it as a potentially dangerous tool. That particular trick is turned to devastating effect on 'Satellite Of Love', a highly apposite cover of the Lou Reed classic. Opened by the band, the video screens suddenly reveal rock's greatest writer singing along with the band, leaving the audience in a state of disbelief – is Lou in the stadium, is he in a TV studio somewhere? Of course, he's actually on video tape and so this powerful live moment isn't live at all, underlining the whole point of the show. Quite apart from its contextual significance, it's a show stopper, coming across like some nightmar-ish Warholian interpretation of the saccharin-sweet *Unforgettable* video pieced together to show Natalie Cole and her late father singing together.

In revealing the myth of television, U2 were, by extension, doing a similar job on themselves: don't trust TV and don't trust media stars. U2 had already been burned by the media and its desire for disposable heroes. U2 had been frightened of the bullshit that surrounds rock 'n' roll and stardom, terrified that they would be overcome by it, causing them to hold on to the music and their image far too tightly, which then led to the problems which did overwhelm them under the auspices of the *Rattle and Hum* project. The old U2 bubble needed to be burst and during 'Where The Streets Have No Name' the screens displayed some speeded-up footage of the band in the photo-shoot for *The Joshua Tree*, Bono shouting, 'Hey, I remember you!' U2 seem to be indicating that the time has come to start using some discrimination in viewing choices but, most importantly, to have faith in your own ability and your own qualities. The most interesting point is that this is what they've been saying all along but it has taken the reduction of themselves to minor TV celebs, even if it is their station, to make the point that they don't really know anything either. In the enormity of their stage set, U2 finally become individuals who are dwarfed by the inconsistencies and stupidities of ordinary life just like the rest of us.

When U2 returned for the encore of 'Desire', Bono had taken on another alter-ego, turning himself into a heart-stealing preacher in a mirrorball suit, a cross between a sleazy TV evangelist and a money-grabbing media mogul, a man for whom everything is legal as long as it pays, a man for whom money is the new religion, the only religion, a man for whom there is only one commandment, the eleventh (don't get caught), a man for whom there is no unknown, no spirit, no God, only ratings, a man who looks at his reflection and says, 'You're fuckin' beautiful!' At the end of the song Bono would regularly hold forth with a psychopathic rant: 'I believe in love, love and money, poetry, electricity, James Brown's hairdo, the smell of a new sedan. I have a vision, now and forever, peak time, prime time, all the time. I have a vision! Television!' It's a diatribe that says a lot about American culture and the encroaching threat to European culture of the global TV network which reduces us all to one huge homogeneous consumer of everything. Because after all, that's the other role of TV: advertising. It's also a reaction to an America where you sometimes wonder if there is any life beyond TV. We get to see *Oprah* or *Donahue*, where earnest Americans conduct their personal lives in the glare of TV lights before an audience of millions. Do those people who are watching actually exist since they themselves aren't on TV? Since U2 are dealing with the blank generation, a generation browbeaten by television into willing zombie-like submission, Zoo TV is a move towards waking them up and pointing to a life beyond television. That they are still able to come out to what is a truly subversive rock 'n' roll show is encouraging and force-feeding them crap TV set against the power of the music makes the point: were they not at a U2 show, they might be sitting at home channel-hopping and watching the very programmes they were laughing at when Bono called them up on screen.

'The Mirrorball Man' is perhaps even more interesting than 'The Fly' since it contains a reference to Vegas kitsch and the King of Rock 'n' Roll, Elvis Presley, and the glitz of his cabaret years. Phil Ochs was a protest singer back in the 1960s when that kind of thing was considered a real threat, to the extent that he attracted a 410-page FBI file. According to Robin Denselow in *When The Music's Over*, the album *Phil Ochs In Concert* 'proves why Ochs was such a danger. He was an entertainer who could be both angry and very, very funny.' Ochs deplored American foreign policy in Central America during the 1960s, though his sister Sonny said of him, 'He really believed in the US and in the political system, but he saw all the evils – and he cared about the Blacks, the miners, and that the war in Vietnam was insane and so he wrote about all that.' He spent time with Senator Robert Kennedy the year before he was set to run for Presidential office and then became a founding member of the Yippies, who believed in the theatre of the absurd. By the early 1970s he had gone for a change in image, as Denselow again describes: 'He ordered a gold lamé suit with silver trim, identical to that once worn by Elvis Presley . . . Ochs explained the politics of the Elvis suit to his audience at New York's Carnegie Hall in April 1970. "If there is any hope for a revolution in America," he told his hostile followers, "it lies in getting Elvis Presley to become Che Guevara. . . ."' Eight months later, Elvis Presley received a Bureau of Narcotics badge from President Nixon. Allegedly, when watching TV, if he didn't like the show, Elvis would shoot the TV set . . .

The other aspect of Zoo TV is U2's love affair with rock 'n' roll, something they had tried to keep under wraps in the past but which was now a central part of their career. In some ways they were trying to reinvent the idea of rock 'n' roll as a rebellious force by making it new, dabbling with the old clichés and proving how ridiculous they were. When Elvis arrived on the scene his sexuality actually was shocking but, since sex is now the property of Coca Cola and General Motors under a complex licensing agreement with the human race, what could be shocking about sex? There are still the boringly predictable bands who go through the whole sex & drugs thing, trashing hotel rooms, getting arrested and winning cheap publicity but in 1993 that's sad, not subversive. Subversion comes from kicking against the system in ways more subtle but more effective – betray the age, show the prophet TV to be false, ask why we are fed inanity to cause insanity, rebel against those with the power and the influence by making them feel uncomfortable, be smarter than they are. By becoming rock 'n' roll stars, U2, the one band that always refused to become rock 'n' roll stars, have shown the stupidity of the star system and have shown the elevation of ordinary musicians to heroic status to be bogus. When musical or sporting heroes are reduced to the level of the man in the street, maybe their endorsement of products will be less effective, perhaps it's one of the foundation blocks of our material world that's been chipped away. By showing the mysterious sensuality of the sexual experience in the performance of 'Mysterious Ways' with a belly dancer and then juxtaposing it with the porn shots used in 'Desire', perhaps it makes a few people reject the shoddy selling of corporate sex. It's an undeniably fine line – even if Bono is taking the rise out of himself and playing at rock 'n' roll stars, he still *is* a rock 'n' roll star enjoying the fruits of that position, the fast limos, the great hotel rooms, the private aeroplanes, the champagne and cigars. Irony is a commodity that went out of fashion some time ago and his performance may be lost on many, but there's a sense that he and the band are playing up to this position in a bid to maintain their own sanity and to protect themselves from the possible dangers of rock 'n' roll excess.

Even in that light, however, the lines between reality and parody have become increasingly blurred as Bono has draped himself over supermodel Christy Turlington for a *Vogue* fashion spread – 'one of God's great jokes' as he has termed it – while Adam has become engaged to supermodel Naomi Campbell, a relationship which apparently blossomed on a transatlantic flight. He proposed to her over the 'phone when she was in New York and she then flew to Dublin to accept. That's *real* rock star behaviour but then Adam always was the true rock 'n' roller in the band. Having said in the Zoo TV programme that Naomi Campbell was the one thing that he hadn't got that he would most like to have, it's nice to know that he at least has found what he was looking for.

One saying which Bono has regularly noted of late is 'mock the devil and he will flee from thee' and as proverbs go, it's pretty accurate. When you hate a style of behaviour with a fierce intensity it can be very difficult to prevent yourself slipping into that role; so many people finally become what they hate, hippies into yuppies for example. If, however, you take that thing which you hate and reduce it to the point of ridicule, you are insulated from its dangers since no one likes to be thought of as being ludicrous and will therefore avoid that trap. In becoming the tackiest, trashiest, stupidest rock star, Bono has ensured that he won't become a real rock star. In dumping the position of spokesman by effectively saying, 'Don't believe a word,' Bono and the rest of the band are now free to develop their own agenda for the future without being hemmed in by his previous position as the Pope of rock and to develop artistically. Rock has always suffered from a kind of inverted snobbery where it refuses to consider itself as an art form because, hey, art's not cool, it's pretentious. Since Bono's always been pretentious, he's never hidden the fact that U2 are interested in rock 'n' roll as a vital force within popular culture, popular culture being an art form in itself.

U2 have essentially inverted the typical career of a band in popular music, most groups starting out by talking about sex, getting drunk and generally playing up to the part of the rock idiot before they 'get their shit together, man' and return as non-smoking, non-drinking, non-drugging friends of the environment, preferably with some religious guru in tow. U2 are almost the exact opposite in terms of appearance, the real difference being that they are playing with the star trip rather than believing in it, even if they are getting to be a little too attached to it, while their spiritual values are still intact even if no easier to reconcile with their lifestyle than previously. In rock terms, Zoo TV somehow manages to be the most spiritually enlivening show around at present. Even though there are no overt references to their higher beliefs, the concerts have soul, mocking the TV creed that if you can't see it, it doesn't exist and putting heavy subliminal emphasis on the spiritual dimension.

That mechanics have not won out over humanity is illustrated by a brief acoustic set that the band play on the satellite stage which is placed in the middle of the auditorium where, with the gimmickry turned down, U2 just get to play some music in an antidote to the high-tech activity that surrounds it. The point is well made for, though they're suddenly naked, the level of intensity doesn't flag for a moment during songs like 'Angel Of Harlem' and 'When Love Comes To Town', Larry even getting to exercise his lungs on 'Whiskey In The Jar' and 'Dirty Old Town' in what seems like a Pogues piss-take. Whether that's the case or not, it's hard to escape that conclusion when Larry's spot is often followed by 'Tryin' To Throw Your Arms Around The World', where Bono takes the opportunity to play the bar-room philosopher that he's always wanted to be, the drunk in the corner putting the world to rights without any real knowledge or any real responsibility. The contact with the audience reaches its peak as Bono exercises his penchant for bringing attractive young ladies onto the stage before drowning them in a phallic shower of champagne.

Freedom was all now for U2, which allowed them to race around like some latter-day version of Ken Kesey's merry pranksters, wisecracking at press conferences and generally making fun of the whole show business equation. Sample comment: 'Bono, have you ever been to Israel?' 'Yeah, about 2000 years ago.' No longer prepared to put up with hero status, U2 were having a great time largely because no one quite knew what to make of them any more and they were back in total control of both music and image, a position with which they seem happiest. At the end of it all, U2 are currently best summed up by the Zoo TV experience. What is that exactly? The Edge: ' "Everything You Know Is Wrong." A perfect description of Zoo TV. Mocking it and milking it.'

chapter thirteen

IT'S A MUSICAL JOURNEY

To hysterical laughter from the rest of the group, when asked what exactly was the subject matter for U2's movie *Rattle and Hum*, Larry Mullen Junior, the man who started the whole thing off more than a decade earlier, explained, 'It's a musical journey.' And that's a fair assessment of the career of one of rock's few enduring bands, a band who, after something of a wobble at the tail end of the 1980s, have reasserted themselves as probably the finest rock 'n' roll band in the world today.

Many of the reasons behind U2's appeal and success lie in their Irish roots, roots that didn't really begin to mean anything to them until they had already begun to carve out a career for themselves on the broader world stage. It's a heritage that has had impacts both positive and negative, a geographical location that initially rendered it virtually impossible for them to reach out to the rest of the world, which made them all the more determined, but a location to which they could return once they were successful in Europe and America and where they were given the cold-shower treatment if they ever got above themselves. It's a land that nurtured their artistic dreams, since writing was one of the fields in which Ireland had consistently led the world over the years – poets and writers effectively pieced together the constitution according to Bono – and it's a land where ideas of artistry, of saying something in a creative field are not derided. It's a country where music can aspire to being far more than a simple piece in the light entertainment jigsaw, where it can be a force that tells stories, contains ideas, can inspire and seduce without running from accusations of overbearing, overreaching, overambition.

Dublin, as a city that is away from the media centres, is a place that gives necessary perspective to those who have spent three months in American hotel rooms eating junk food while watching junk TV or listening to junk radio. The environs of the city can give the artist the necessary natural inspiration, while the inner city has more than enough problems of its own to prevent the mind wandering too far away from the real issues of the day. It is the ideal base for a band that aspires to producing more than wallpaper muzak, a band that hopes to make some kind of difference, to have touched the world by the time of its passing in the way that some of the great artists of the past have done. U2 have used that setting intelligently to achieve success that renders the term success almost redundant. Materially they are set for life, an irony in that such riches seem to have been far less of a motivation in their story than in that of many others; naturally money was important, but U2 have always been on a search far greater than that. Unlike acts such as the Stones and the Beatles in the 1960s, religious conversion had taken place within U2 well before wealth rendered avarice irrelevant and made lives empty. They have continually struck out towards bigger answers, larger truths, yet have never been afraid to expose their own doubts and failings, the inconsistencies that their position has thrust upon them.

The career of U2 has received column inches because they have spoken out against the IRA, in favour of Greenpeace, Amnesty International, against the insidious influence of TV, more often than for the music they make. Yet without that quite extraordinary sound that they produce those issues would never have been commented on. There is no chicken and egg situation with U2; the music quite definitely came first and they were then concerned and committed enough to share their platform with issues that should trouble any decent thinking person. The noise that came out of a car park in Dublin was undeniably raw but it was original. The bass player wasn't able to lay down typical underpinning bass parts through lack of experience and instead played like a lead guitarist. The drummer had to provide the foundation alone and arrived at an aggressive style that leapt out of the speakers once it was put onto record. The guitar player had to compete with the bassist and so restricted himself to certain frequencies which he then employed with startling economy and originality to the point where his playing said more about the song's mood than the lyrics did. And the singer had a rough voice, total lack of restraint, no approximation of anything which would be called 'cool' in rock 'n' roll circles, but he had a fire within, a desire to talk to people, and a burning curiosity to find out about them, about his bandmates and about himself. Then they had a manager who knew a bit about the industry but was more than capable of filling the gaps in his knowledge with exemplary speed. Eventually, with the power that the quality of the group invested in him, he proved himself to be a skilled and highly successful negotiator. The five of them now sit at the head of a very profitable organization and have continued to build up a crew of highly capable and enthusiastic people who have ensured that everything runs smoothly. They are a collection of people of quiet efficiency who take their lead from the four men who make the music. It's the music that has made them the best in their field; not the hype, not the good causes, but the music.

The most valuable attribute which U2 have is an uncanny ability to capture the moment. There are times when they bluster, they swagger and they appear to be at sea when suddenly they achieve a performance of 'Sunday Bloody Sunday' like that on *Rattle and Hum*, they write a song like 'I Still Haven't Found What I'm Looking For' or they invent Zoo TV, moments that capture what they are about, what we the audience are about and what the world is about. In the midst of the confusion that we all live in, U2 can, for a brief moment, cut through and suddenly, fleetingly it all makes some kind of sense, suddenly they have created a community of like minds and they have justified everything that could ever be written about them. Their true genius, and if any band in the last decade justifies the term genius it is U2, is in turning the broad generalization into the specific and deeply personal. 'Twilight', 'Bad', 'Silver And Gold', 'Gloria' or 'So Cruel' are all songs that have a direct line to the listener's subconscious, direct one-to-one communications that give a new slant on wider issues or ideas that are common to us all by turning them into human stories rather than social slogans. Perhaps their greatest achievement is in rescuing tired old concepts like peace and love and making them real again, portraying them as they truly are in the real world – heroic, almost impossible ideas that struggle for survival against the rising tide of cynicism and a world that is not interested in them, that positively conspires against them for financial reasons.

The tasks that face them in the future are ones they must construct for themselves. Commercial success must be irrelevant, artistic achievement can be the only criteria, 'this music that's always just a light in the distance' as Bono once described it. In a time when popular music seems to be in terminal decline, bereft of ideas or inspiration, it falls to U2 and their ilk to revitalize the music, to generate the excitement that was once such an integral part of the experience, to instigate new and relevant means of expression and rebellion. Zoo TV was a commendable start in that regard but there are stiffer challenges ahead.

Rock 'n' roll suffered at the hands of its supposed golden age in the 1960s. While that era was perhaps little different in its overall mix of the good, the bad and the ugly in general terms, it was a period when rock 'n' roll was comprehensively reinvented and reconditioned for a new decade by the Beatles, the Stones, the Beach Boys, the Byrds, the Band, the Velvet Underground and many other artists. Now, in 1993, surely we don't need to hear the Beatles any more and yet they remain rock's finest band and are maybe more relevant than around 95 per cent of the current acts in circulation. To be rejuvenated, rock needs to be made contemporary again, someone has to come along and wipe away the references to that golden canon of albums that stretched from *Rubber Soul* through to *Abbey Road*, to compile a series of records that can compete with them and make them irrelevant except in a purely historical context.

U2 have the musical armoury to do it for they can write songs that aspire and inspire, that dream and act, music that bleeds, kicks, cries, spits, laughs, wails and caresses. Their songs offer solace and a sense of community, while for the members of their own generation they have provided a soundtrack to our own quests, our own experiments, our lives and loves and have sometimes helped us understand ourselves better just as we, the audience, have helped them make sense of themselves. More than anything else, and certainly more than anyone else, they have that quality which is the true test of timeless music that resonates against human emotions – they are a soul band. That doesn't mean a career doing James Brown covers or learning sharp dance routines, but a quality that ignites the music from within, that stamps a rare and sincere passion on the songs and which marks a band out as truly special. Having made much of the finest music of the 1980s, U2 have entered the 1990s with a bang, releasing *Achtung Baby*, which may yet prove to be the first of a really golden period for them, far above and beyond their previous work, though to dismiss that so lightly would be to heap a grave injustice on some of the most exciting rock 'n' roll of the 1980s. However, in twenty years the musical references may be back to what U2 did in the mid-1990s, a fond hope for it is music of that quality which will resurrect rock 'n' roll and enrich our lives as a consequence.

In making *Achtung Baby*, U2 have already proved themselves to be virtually unique, a rock band that is not trapped within a decade.

By this late in their career almost every other band you might care to name were running on empty, relics from the past performing to those who came to relive their youth. Solo artists have managed to stay vital and challenging, perhaps because of the opportunity they have to interact with fresh blood on each new project should they so choose, but self-contained bands have to create new ideas from within. It is to their credit and is indicative of the breadth of their vision that U2 are still more than capable of challenging and testing themselves, their very Irish enthusiasm pushing the group and their perception of it into new situations, new corners, new lights in order to draw more inspiration.

U2's greatness is the indefinable chemistry that somehow exists between the four of them. U2 was never a group of virtuosos, not musicians of instinctive genius or songwriting ability, but it was a band of inspiration. Admittedly, even when they started it didn't take long to realize that Edge brought a rare intellect to the playing of his instrument which enabled him to paint in colours that were all his own, but even that rare ability was given confidence and strength from the solidity of the group as a social entity. From that base, they have been able to craft songs and statements which, since they are drawn from highly personalized sources, are all the more valuable when shared. The songwriting process can be slow and laboured simply because it's a form that they have never mastered fully, but that very lack of assurance has been highly valuable since they've never underestimated the power of the muse or neglected it.

The problem which faces U2 is a simple one, that of age. The time has come where U2 really do have to produce work on a more regular basis while the fire is still with them, for so many artists, once they pass their mid-thirties, seem to have lost touch with their initial inspiration, perhaps because music is no longer the most important factor in their lives. With someone like David Bowie, a man who clearly has a very comfortable lifestyle courtesy of the music he made in the 1970s and early 1980s, one has to ask if these distractions have been the root cause of the series of dreadful solo records that followed *Let's Dance*. While U2 have proved themselves up to the task of creating fresh challenges for themselves, diminished interest may be harder to fight off in the face of family responsibilities, etc. In that light, the answer may be to forgo the road for a period of time in the same way that REM have, thereby creating far more time for themselves in which they can write and record new music, though this might in itself be a problem since U2 do genuinely seem to enjoy the concert experience and seem to gain a creative buzz from it. The recent flurry of recording activity which gave birth to the *Zooropa* album is testament to that. At the last show on the Zoo TV tour in 1992, Bono told the crowd, 'For a performer sometimes going home is harder than being on a stage,' before conceding, 'In truth I don't know if we'll ever be back to play like this again,' and going on to thank the entire U2 entourage. Perhaps the time has come for U2 to let go of touring and make more records – their output has scarcely been prolific – for it is records that will stand as their achievement long after the concerts are but a memory. Their records have never quite matched up to the quality of their live performance and that is perhaps the ultimate challenge for the 1990s.

U2 have been the human face of rock 'n' roll for many years now, their charm being that they can be just as bad or as stupid as they are so often thrillingly brilliant, a humanity that the choreographed, computerized chart-fodder can never allow themselves. For that very reason, the fact that U2 are exceptionally successful is very, very important as it says much about what a large section of the rock audience is crying out for: the human touch. Contrary to popular opinion, however, U2's importance does not lie in their success since they are so much more than lists of sales statistics, platinum records, Grammy awards or whatever. In a society that seems terminally confused, U2 are a beacon of encouragement, an admission that a blank cheque doesn't always provide all the answers. U2 truly inspire a conspiracy of hope.

U2 discography

SINGLES

U2—3 Out of Control; Stories For Boys; Boy/Girl
CBS Records Ireland Only September 1979

ANOTHER DAY Twilight
CBS Records Ireland Only February 1980

11 O'CLOCK TICK TOCK Touch
Island Records May 1980

A DAY WITHOUT ME Things To Make & Do
Island Records August 1980

I WILL FOLLOW Boy/Girl (live)
Island Records October 1980

FIRE J. Swallo; Cry (live); The Electric Co. (live); 11 O'Clock Tick Tock (live);
The Ocean (live)
Island Records July 1981
Chart Position: 35

GLORIA I Will Follow (live)
Island Records October 1981
Chart Position: 55

A CELEBRATION Trash, Trampoline And The Party Girl
Island Records March 1982
Chart Position: 47

NEW YEAR'S DAY Treasure (Whatever Happened To Pete The Chop);
Fire (live); I Threw A Brick Through A Window (live); A Day Without Me (live)
Island Records January 1983
Chart Position: 10

TWO HEARTS BEAT AS ONE Endless Deep; New Year's Day (US Remix); Two Hearts Beat As One (US Remix)
Island Records March 1983
Chart Position: 18

PRIDE (IN THE NAME OF LOVE) Boomerang; Boomerang II; 4th Of July; 11 O'Clock Tick Tock; Touch; A Celebration
Island Records September 1984
Chart Position: 3

THE UNFORGETTABLE FIRE A Sort Of Homecoming (live); The Three Sunrises; Love Comes Tumbling; 60 Seconds In Kingdom Come; Bass Trap
Island Records April 1985
Chart Position: 6

WITH OR WITHOUT YOU Luminous Times (Hold On To Love); Walk To The Water
Island Records March 1987
Chart Position: 4

I STILL HAVEN'T FOUND WHAT I'M LOOKING FOR Spanish Eyes; Deep In The Heart
Island Records May 1987
Chart Position: 6

WHERE THE STREETS HAVE NO NAME Race Against Time; Silver And Gold; Sweetest Thing
Island Records September 1987
Chart Position: 4

IN GOD'S COUNTRY Bullet The Blue Sky; Running To Stand Still
Island Records December 1987
Chart Position: 48
NB: This was not an official UK release but sufficient import copies were sold for it reach the charts.

DESIRE Hallelujah Here She Comes; Desire (Hollywood Remix)
Island Records September 1988
Chart Position: 1

ANGEL OF HARLEM A Room At The Heartbreak Hotel; Love Rescue Me (live)
Island Records December 1988
Chart Position: 9

WHEN LOVE COMES TO TOWN Dancing Barefoot; When Love Comes To Town (Live From The Kingdom Mix); God Part II (The Hard Metal Dance Mix)
Island Records April 1989
Chart Position: 6

ALL I WANT IS YOU Unchained Melody; Everlasting Love; All I Want Is You (Edit)
Island Records June 1989
Chart Position: 4

THE FLY Alex Descends Into Hell For A Bottle Of Milk/Korova 1; The Lounge Fly Mix
Island Records October 1991
Chart Position: 1

MYSTERIOUS WAYS Mysterious Ways (Solar Plexus Extended Club Mix); Mysterious Ways (Apollo 440 Magic Hour Remix); Mysterious Ways (Tabla Motown Remix); Mysterious Ways (Solar Plexus Club Mix); Mysterious Ways (Perfecto Mix); Mysterious Ways (Ultimatum Mix)
Island Records December 1991
Chart position: 13

ONE Lady With The Spinning Head (UVI); Satellite Of Love; Night And Day (Steel String Remix)
Island Records February 1992
Chart Position: 7

EVEN BETTER THAN THE REAL THING Salome; Where Did It All Go Wrong; Lady With The Spinning Head (Extended Dance Mix)
Island Records June 1992
Chart Position: 12

EVEN BETTER THAN THE REAL THING (REMIXES) Even Better Than The Real Thing (The Perfecto Mix); Even Better Than The Real Thing (Sexy Dub Mix); Even Better Than The Real Thing (Apollo 440 Stealth

Sonic Remix); Even Better Than The Real Thing (V16 Exit Wound Remix); Even Better Than The Real Thing (A440 Vs U2 Instrumental Remix)
Island Records July 1992
Chart Position: 8

WHO'S GONNA RIDE YOUR WILD HORSES (TEMPLE BAR EDIT)
Paint It Black; Fortunate Son; Who's Gonna Ride Your Wild Horses (Temple Bar Remix); Salome (Zooromancer Remix); Can't Help Falling In Love (Triple Peaks Remix)
Island Records November 1992
Chart Position: 14

ALBUMS

BOY I Will Follow; Twilight; An Cat Dubh; Into The Heart; Out Of Control; Stories For Boys; The Ocean; A Day Without Me; Another Time. Another Place; The Electric Co.; Shadows And Tall Trees.
Island Records October 1980
Chart Position: 52

OCTOBER Gloria; I Fall Down; I Threw A Brick Through A Window; Rejoice; Fire; Tomorrow; October; With A Shout (Jerusalem); Stranger In A Strange Land; Scarlet; Is That All?.
Island Records October 1981
Chart Position: 11

WAR Sunday Bloody Sunday; Seconds; New Year's Day; Like A Song . . .; Drowning Man; The Refugee; Two Hearts Beat As One; Red Light; Surrender; '40'.
Island Records March 1983
Chart Position: 1

UNDER A BLOOD RED SKY Gloria; 11 O'Clock Tick Tock; I Will Follow; Party Girl; Sunday Bloody Sunday; The Electric Co.; New Year's Day; '40'.
Island Records November 1983
Chart Position: 2

ALBUMS

THE UNFORGETTABLE FIRE A Sort Of Homecoming; Pride (In The Name Of Love); Wire; The Unforgettable Fire; Promenade; 4th Of July; Bad; Indian Summer Sky; Elvis Presley And America; MLK.
Island Records October 1984
Chart Position: 1

WIDE AWAKE IN AMERICA Bad (Live); A Sort Of Homecoming (Live); The Three Sunrises; Love Comes Tumbling.
Island Records May 1985
Chart Position: 11
NB: This was not originally an official UK release, but the quantity of imported copies prompted Island to release it as such.

THE JOSHUA TREE Where The Streets Have No Name; I Still Haven't Found What I'm Looking For; With Or Without You; Bullet The Blue Sky; Running To Stand Still; Red Hill Mining Town; In God's Country; Trip Through Your Wires; One Tree Hill; Exit; Mothers Of The Disappeared.
Island Records March 1987
Chart Position: 1

RATTLE AND HUM Helter Skelter; Van Diemen's Land; Desire; Hawkmoon 269; All Along The Watchtower; I Still Haven't Found What I'm Looking For; Freedom For My People; Silver And Gold; Pride (In The Name Of Love); Angel Of Harlem; Love Rescue Me; When Love Comes To Town; Heartland; God Part II; The Star Spangled Banner; Bullet The Blue Sky; All I Want Is You.
Island Records October 1988
Chart Position: 1

ACHTUNG BABY Zoo Station; Even Better Than The Real Thing; One; Until The End Of The World; Who's Gonna Ride Your Wild Horses; So Cruel; The Fly; Mysterious Ways; Tryin' To Throw Your Arms Around The World; Ultra Violet (Light My Way); Acrobat; Love Is Blindness.
Island Records November 1991
Chart Position: 2

SOURCES

The following publications, radio or TV shows have all been of immeasurable help in researching this book. Not all of them have been directly quoted from, not all of them have any obvious direct relevance, but all have provided a glimmer of additional light or inspiration somewhere along the line – in a sense this provides a kind of U2 bibliography, not in any authoritative or complete way, but it might be a useful starting point for any future student of U2's music. It also enables reviewers to raise the charge of pretension and pomposity, and us to namecheck lots of people who we think do a great job. For those from whom we have quoted, we give our grateful thanks for your gracious permission. Those we didn't ask, we didn't use, so no lawsuits please!

BOOKS

Alan, Carter, *U2 Wide Awake in America*, Boxtree, 1992.

Allen, Woody, *Hannah & Her Sisters*, Faber & Faber, 1988.

Beckett, Samuel, *The Beckett Trilogy*, Picador, 1959.

Benn, Tony, *The End of an Era: Diaries 1980–1990*, Hutchinson, 1992.

Clayton-Lea & Taylor, *Irish Rock*, Sidgwick & Jackson, 1992.

Denselow, Robin, *When the Music's Over*, Faber & Faber, 1989.

Dunphy, Eamon, *Unforgettable Fire*, Viking, 1987.

Fletcher, Tony, *Never Stop*, Omnibus Press, 1987.

Gans, David, *Talking Heads – The Band and Their Music*, Omnibus Press, 1985.

Golding, William, *Lord of the Flies*, Faber & Faber, 1954.

Graham, Bill, *U2 – Another Time, Another Place*, Mandarin, 1989.

Henke, James, *Human Rights Now*, Bloomsbury, 1988.

Kennelly, Brendan, *The Book of Judas*, Bloodaxe, 1991.

Morgan, Ted, *The Literary Outlaw*, Bodley Head, 1991.

Parker, Tony, *Red Hill – A Mining Community*, William Heinemann, 1986.

Parkyn, Geoff, *U2 – Touch the Flame*, Omnibus Press, 1987.

SOURCES

Stokes, Niall, *The U2 File*, Omnibus Press, 1985.

—— *U2 – Three Chords and the Truth*, Harmony, 1989.

Thompson & Christie, *Scorsese On Scorsese*, Faber & Faber, 1989.

Upshall, Michael, *The Hutchinson Encyclopedia*, new 10th edition, Helicon, 1992.

Williams & Turner, *U2 – Rattle and Hum*, Pyramid, 1988.

Wills, Garry, *Reagan's America – Innocents At Home*, William Heinemann, 1988.

MAGAZINES

INSIGHT   'The Story of Rattle and Hum', Steve Turner, October 1988.

JAMMING   'The Pride Of Lions', Tony Fletcher, October 1984.

PREMIÈRE   'Band of Gold', David Rensin, November 1988.

PROPAGANDA   The Official U2 magazine. Details from P. O. Box 18, Wellingborough, NN8 3YY.

Q   'Restless', Paul Du Noyer, April 1987.
'Another Day Another Dollar', Steve Turner, July 1987.
'Bringing It All Back Home', Paul Du Noyer, November 1988.
'Pennies From Heaven', Dermott Hayes, April 1989.
'Heroic', Mat Snow, December 1991.
'All Shook Up', Paul Du Noyer, July 1992.
'Eyebrow Entertainment', Paul Du Noyer, November 1992.
'Let's Hear It For . . . Us!', Paul Du Noyer, January 1993.

RADIO TIMES   'Death Of A Dream', Charles Wheeler, 3 April 1993.

RCD   'The Zoo 2', Bert Van De Kamp, Issue 2.

ROCK WORLD   'Who Made Zoo TV?', Christian Eckert, February 1993.

ROLLING STONE   'The Band that Beat the Boss', James Henke, 10 March 1988.

SOURCES

'U2 On Location', Steve Pond, 11 February 1988.
'Now What?' Steve Pond, 9 March 1989.
'Bringing Up Baby', Brian Eno, 28 November 1991.
'U2 Finds What It's Looking For', David Fricke, 1 October 1992.
'Behind The Fly', Alan Light, 4 March 1993.

SELECT 'To The New World', Dermott Hayes, November 1991.
'Planet Narcissus, Man!', William Shaw, April 1992.
'Everything You Know Is Wrong', Dermott Hayes, May 1992.

SKY 'Penthouse & Pavement', Steve Turner, November 1988.

SPIN 'Animal Farm', Jim Greer, July 1992.

SUNDAY EXPRESS 'The Rock of the Irish', Steve Turner, 16 October 1988.

TIME OUT 'Bono Contentions', Bruce Dessau, 25 November 1992.

VOGUE 'I Feel Good!' Georgina Howell, December 1992.

VOX 'Five Men And Achtung Baby', Max Bell, December 1991.
'From Revolution To Revelation', Gavin Martin, December 1991.
'When U2 Comes to Town', April 1992.
'Zoo Gold Dream', Parke Puterbaugh, May 1992.
'A Head Of The Pack', David Quantick, December 1992.

YOU 'Meet Minimal Mr Eno', Pete Silverton, 21 October 1984.

NEWSPAPERS

BOSTON GLOBE 'U2 'n' TV', Steve Morse, March 1992.

DAILY MIRROR 'This Protest Was For All Our Kids And That Means U2', Mary Riddell, 18 June 1992.
'Beach Invasion', Jan Disley, 22 June 1992.

SOURCES

GUARDIAN 'Judge Bans U2 Demo At Sellafield', David Pallister, 17 June 1992.

HOT PRESS 'Yep! It's U2', Bill Graham, 28 April 1978.
'U2 Could Be A Headline', Bill Graham, 8 March 1979.
'U2 Treats U', Declan Lynch, 31 August 1979.
'Boys in Control', Niall Stokes, 26 October 1979.
'Close to the Edge', Peter Owens, 20 June 1980.
'The Battle of Britain', Bill Graham, 19 July 1980.
'The Boy Can't Help It', Declan Lynch, 10 October 1980.
'Growing Up In Public', Neil McCormick, 17 December 1980.
'U2 Could Be In L.A.', Charlie McNally, 17 April 1981.
'U2 Versus The U.S.' Bill Graham, 1 May 1981.
'Autumn Fire', Neil McCormick, 16 October 1981.
'The Kids Are Alright', Neil McCormick, 8 January 1982.
'U2 – Poll Winners Speak Out', Niall Stokes, 19 February 1982.
'The Odd Couple', Bill Graham, 3 December 1982.
'Blood on the Tracks', Liam Mackey, 18 February 1983.
'The People's Choice', Bill Graham, 18 March 1983.
'The Greatest Show On Earth', Cecil Hollwey, 24 June 1983.
'Articulate Speech of the Heart', Liam Mackey, 5 August 1983.
'It's a Celebration', Bill Graham, 25 November 1983.
'Light A Big Fire', Liam Mackey, 19 October 1984.
'Quest For Fire', Bill Graham, 30 November 1984.
'This is the Edge', Bill Graham, 15 November 1984.
'The Unforgettable Fire', Niall Stokes, 26 April 1985.
'Stories of Boys', Jackie Hayden, 20 June 1985.
'The Homecoming', Liam Mackey, 5 July 1985.
'All Ireland Champions', Niall and Dermot Stokes, 18 July 1985.
'The Great Leap of Faith', Neil McCormick, July 1985.
'Outside It's Donegal', Bill Graham, February 1986.
'Wide Awake in America', Pat Singer, July 1986.
'The Drummer's Disability', Niall Stokes, September 1986.
'Out on his Own', Bill Graham, October 1986.
'Emotional Rescue', Bill Graham, February 1987.
'The World About Us', Niall Stokes & Bill Graham, March 1987.
'Rockin' All Over The States', Liam Mackey, June 1987.
'All Ireland Was There', Bill Graham, June 1987.
'The Unbelievable Book', Neil McCormick, December 1987.
'Band on the Run', Bill Graham, December 1987.
'Shake, Rattle and Hum', Bill Graham, October 1988.

SOURCES

'A Mighty Long Way Down Rock 'n' roll', Niall Stokes, October 1988.
'Hum's The Word', Graham Linehan, November 1988.
'I Still Haven't Found What I'm Looking For', Liam Mackey, December 1988.
'With and Without U2', Dermot Stokes, August 1989.
'The Verdict', Liam Fay, September 1989.

INDEPENDENT 'Injunction Forces Greenpeace to Cancel U2 Protest', David Nicholson-Lord, 17 June 1992.

INDEPENDENT ON SUDAY 'Greenpeace Pro-Bono, Anti-Nuclear', Caroline Beck, 21 June 1992.

MAIL ON SUNDAY 'U2 Defy Court Over Sellafield Protest', Kim Willsher, 21 June 1992.

MELODY MAKER 'Clarendon Hotel, London', Paulo Hewitt, 19 July 1980.
'Getting Into U2', Paulo Hewitt, 13 September 1980.
'U2 Take Us Over The Top', Lynden Barber, 4 October 1980.
'The Art of Survival', Adam Sweeting, 10 October 1981.
'Songs of Praise', Lynden Barber, 6 February 1982.
'The Life of Brian', Helen Fitzgerald, 29 September 1984.
'The Only Flame in Town', Adam Sweeting, 5 January 1985.
'Bringing It All Back Home', Colin Irwin, 14 March 1987.
'Under Foreign Skies', Ted Mico, 6 June 1987.
'Awe or Nothing', Simon Reynolds, 13 June 1987.
'Helter Skelter', Ted Mico, 22 October 1988.
'The Bono God Hoo-Haa Band', Jon Wiederhorn, 21 March 1992.
'Achtung Stations!', Andrew Mueller, 30 May 1992.
'U2 Defy Ban On Nuke Demo', 20 June 1992.
'Nuke Ids On The Block', Dave Bennun, 27 June 1992.
'U2 Outwit Nuke Demo Ban', 27 June 1992.
'Power Without Glory', Everett True, 19 September 1992.
'Rock'n'roll Is An Act Of Revenge', Andrew Mueller, 5 December 1992.
'U2 Nuke Call', 2 January 1993.

NEW MUSICAL EXPRESS 'Moonlight Club', Paul Morley, 12 January 1980.
'U2 Can Make It In The Rock Business', Paul Morley, 22 March 1980.
'Acklam Hall', Paul Rambali, 29 March 1980.
'11 O'Clock Tick Tock', Paul Morley, 9 August 1980.

SOURCES

'Boy's Own Weepies', Paul Morley, 25 October 1980.

'Marquee Club', Gavin Martin, 6 December 1980.

'Lyceum Theatre', Paul Du Noyer, 7 February 1981.

'Kings of the Celtic Fringe', Gavin Martin, 14 February 1981.

'Portrait of the Artist as a Consumer', Bono, 13 June 1981.

'U Turns', Barney Hoskyns, 10 October 1981.

'A Dreamboat Named Desire', Richard Cook, 27 February 1982.

'Gateshead Stadium', David Durrell, 7 August 1982.

'U2 Run Aground On Rock', Gavin Martin, 26 February 1983.

'War & Peace', Adrian Thrills, 26 February 1983.

'Post War', Paul Du Noyer, 26 March 1983.

'Goria!' Barney Hoskyns, 26 November 1983.

'Call Us Unforgettable', Gavin Martin, 27 October 1984.

'Out of Little Acorns', John McCready, 14 March 1987.

'Cactus World Views', Adrian Thrills, 14 March 1987.

'The Band of Holy Joy', Sean O'Hagan, 6 June 1987.

'You Don't Actually Believe Sinead, Do You?', Jack Barron, 29 October 1988.

'The Cutting Edge', Eugene Masterson, 27 January 1990.

'Burgess: I Am Furious Orange', Eugene Masterson, 17 February 1990.

'Adam & the Trabants', Andrew Collins, 23 November 1991.

'On the Dog and Bono', Eugene Masterson, 30 November 1991.

'Lights! Camera! Achtung!', Stuart Bailie, 14 March 1992.

'Zoological Warfare', Stuart Bailie, 21 March 1992.

'Rock and Roll Should Be This Big', Stuart Bailie, 13 June 1992.

'Fight the Power Station!' Stuart Maconie, 27 June 1992.

'Zoo TV – Drug of the Nation', Ian McCann, 26 September 1992.

'Zoo World Order', David Quantick, 28 November 1992.

NEW YORK TIMES 'Bono & Mates Change With The Times', Larry Rohter, March 1992.

SOUNDS 'Bonoheads', Mr Spencer, 6 October 1984.

'Giants of Rock with Human Faces', Richard Cook, 14 March 1987.

'In God's Country', Richard Cook, 21 and 28 March 1987.

'Conquistador', Ann Scanlon, 1 August 1987.

'Reach for the Sky', Peter Kane, 15 October 1988.

'The Million Dollar Quartet', Neil Perry, 22 October 1988.

'Rockin' the Not So Free World', Gavin Martin, 16 and 23 December 1989.

THE TIMES 'Taking A Predictable Path', Steve Turner, 15 December 1989.

SOURCES

USA Today 'A Flashy New Shoot to the Global Village', Edna Gundersen, March 1992.

RADIO

Bono interview, Radio Forth, 1981.
David Jensen Show, BBC Radio 1, January 1983.
Rise and Rise of U2, BBC Radio 1, December 1987.
U2 On Radio 1, BBC Radio 1, 30 October 1988.
Classic Albums – The Joshua Tree, BBC Radio 1, 8 July 1989.
U2 interview, Sydney Radio MMM, 27 October 1989.
Rockline with Dave Herman, 28 August 1992.
Zoo Radio, BBC Radio 1, 1 January 1993.
Wide Awake In Ireland With John Waters, BBC Radio 4, 1993.

TELEVISION

Old Grey Whistle Test, BBC2, 1981.
Countdown, Dutch TV, 1981.
The Tube, Tyne Tees, 18 March 1983.
Old Grey Whistle Test, BBC2, December 1984.
Live Aid, BBC1, 13 July 1985.
Self Aid, RTE, 17 May 1986.
Meadowlands, MTV, June 1986.
The Tube, Tyne Tees, 6 March 1987.
Old Grey Whistle Test, BBC2, 11 March 1987.
Island 25, Channel 4, 4 July 1987.
World In Action, Granada, 27 July 1987.
Rock of Europe, Music Box, December 1987.
Outside It's America, Dreamchaser Productions, 1987.
Visual Eyes, RTE, 1987.
Rockline, Belgian TV, 1987.
Smile Jamaica, Channel 4, October 1988.

SOURCES

Film 88, BBC1, November 1988.

Breakfast Time, BBC1, 1988.

Dublin Point Depot, RTE, 31 December 1989.

Lovetown, Dreamchaser Productions, 1989.

All I Want Is You, Dreamchaser Productions, 1989.

South Bank Show: Clear Cool Crystal Streams, LWT, 1990.

Bringing It All Back Home, BBC, 1991.

120 Minutes, MTV, 24 May 1992.

Rockumentary, Dreamchaser/MTV, May 1992.

The Trabant Land, Dreamchaser/MTV, May 1992.

C4 Daily Box Office, Channel 4, 1 June 1992.

Zoo TV, Channel 4, 28 November 1992.

Assorted MTV News clips, 1990–93.

INDEX

A & M, 42
'A Celebration', 108
abortion, 102, 103
Achtung Baby, 238; new territory, 135;
    production, 266; promotion, 280–82;
    relationships, 210, 211; shift in
    expression, 122–3; songs, 268,
    270–80; struggle for love, 23
'Acrobat', 84, 270–71
AIDS, 278–9; ireland and, 289–90; Irish
    dilemma, 103
alcoholism, 103
'All Along the Watchtower', 242, 243
'All I Want Is You', 249
'All You Need Is Love', 1
Allen, Woody, 217
Amnesty International, 190, 197–204,
    232; Conspiracy of Hope tour, 202–4
'An Cat Dubh', 60
'Angel of Harlem', 246, 294
'Another Day', 45
apartheid, 196–7, 200, 229–30
Artists Against Apartheid, 196–7, 197
Australia, 179
Averill, Steve, 25, 30, 40

'Bad', 172, 178, 203; Live Aid
    performance, 184
B.A.D. II, 190
Baez, Joan, 202
Ballymun, 172
Band Aid, 182–3
Bangs, Lester, 2
Barber, Lynda, 89
Barsalona, Frank, 64
Bay City Rollers, 9, 20
Beatles, 242, 300; influence, 20; a real
    group, 9; religion, 71; social
    importance, 1
Beckett, Samuel, 61, 85

Behan, Brendan, 135
Benn, Tony, 155–6
Bhraonain, Maire Ni, 194
Blackwell, Chris, 47–8, 64
Blondie, 32
Bloody Sundays, 114
blues, 196–7, 234; Edge absorbs, 261;
    Rattle and Hum, 246
Bolan, Marc, 261
Boland, Tony, 101
Bonnie, Joe, 14
Bono (Paul Hewson): abrasive side, 268;
    admits aggressive streak, 86; audience
    contact, 182; background, 12–13, 18,
    27; B. B. King and, 247; chastisement,
    60; confidence, 47; Dublin politics,
    98–9; early musical ability, 18;
    Ethiopian visit, 195–6; enthusiasm,
    240; on evolving music, 236–7; film
    presence, 253; on Geldof, 183; on
    greed, 90; honesty and passion, 121,
    123; identifying self, 7; injuries, 242;
    on Irish identity, 267; Irish past, 289;
    on Jesus, 91–2; joshua trees, 211–12;
    leadership, 24; Live Aid performance,
    184–5; on London, 49; loosening up,
    178; lyric notes stolen, 85, 95; lyrical
    ideas, 32–3; marries Alison, 139;
    method of lyric writing, 195, 197;
    mother's death, 13, 15–16, 91, 92;
    music not the musicians, ix; musical
    education, 196–7; musicianship at
    first recording, 29–30; origin of name,
    17; on origins of band, 18–19; on
    people and group, 5; perceived as
    egomaniac, 259; on politics, 224–5;
    postman role, 210; press relations, 67;
    pursues belly dancer, 277–8; *Rattle
    and Hum* reviews, 253; religion, 16,
    33, 34, 59; rock star playing, 293–5;

INDEX

INDEX